THE HANGMAN'S DIARY

A Calendar of Judicial Hangings

THE HANGMAN'S DIARY

A Calendar of Judicial Hangings

Rocky Stockman

HEADLINE

First published in 1993
by HEADLINE BOOK PUBLISHING PLC

10 9 8 7 6 5 4 3 2 1

British Library Cataloguing in Publication Data

Stockman, Rocky
Hangman's Diary
I. Title
364.6

ISBN 0–7472–0683–X

Typeset by
Letterpart, Reigate, Surrey

Printed and bound in Great Britain by
Clays Ltd, St Ives PLC

HEADLINE BOOK PUBLISHING PLC
Headline House
79 Great Titchfield Street
London W1P 7FN

Contents

Introduction
by Colin Wilson

What could be more dramatic than the following story? On 11 April 1919, a domestic servant named Amelie Lacoste was walking down the rue de Rivoli in Paris when she saw a short, bearded man in front of her with a pretty girl on his arm. She immediately recognised him as a certain M. Fremyet, to whom her sister Celestine had become engaged, and with whom she had gone to live in the small village of Gambais. Since then, Mlle Lacoste had not heard a word from Celestine. So now she hurried after the couple as they entered a jeweller's shop, and stood behind them as they ordered some china. The bearded man handed the shop assistant his card so it could be delivered. Amelie Lacoste followed the pair until they boarded a bus – she was in such a hurry she bumped into the man at one point, and thought he recognised her. Then she hurried to the nearest telephone and rang the Sûreté. Only that morning, she had told her story to a detective named Belin, and his last words to her had been 'If you should see him, telephone me immediately.'

Belin rushed to the shop; it was now closed, but the watchman gave him the address of the manager. The manager in turn took him to see the salesman who had served the couple. They returned to the shop and found the receipt and the visiting card. For a moment, Belin thought he had the wrong man; the card said: 'M. Guillet, 76 rue Rochechouart'. Yet Mlle Lacoste was sure this was her sister's fiancé.

Belin hurried to the address, which was in Montmartre. His heart sank when the concierge told him that M. Guillet and his wife had left for the country that evening. Had Guillet recognised Amelie Lacoste and fled Paris? For days, Belin hung around the building in Montmartre. Then, one evening, just as he had almost given up hope, the concierge hurried into the cafe where he was sipping a *fine* and whispered, 'He's back.'

In France, it was against the law to enter domestic premises after dark; Belin and a colleague waited all night. Soon after daylight, Belin knocked on the door of the flat. A man's voice asked who it was. 'I've come about the car you advertised,' said Belin. 'Come back later.' 'I can't – I have to catch a train.' The door opened, and a small, red-bearded man in a nightshirt peered out. Belin pushed open the door. 'M. Guillet, we are policemen. You are under arrest.'

The little man's manner was so indignant that for a moment Belin wondered if he had made a bad mistake. Then they heard a faint scream and a crash from the bedroom. Belin pushed open the door; a beautiful girl lay naked on the floor. She had fainted – hardly the reaction of a normal housewife when her husband is approached by the police. Hoping that Guillet did not notice that the warrant was made out in the name of Fremyet, Belin told him to get dressed.

While his colleague escorted the little man back to the Sûreté, Belin searched the flat. In a cupboard he found an envelope addressed to 'Henri Landru'. 'Who is this Landru?' he asked the pretty girl, whose name was Fernande Segret. 'I don't know.' She was obviously telling the truth.

In the car on the way to the Sûreté, Guillet, alias Landru, was fumbling in his pocket. The policeman noticed and caught his wrist as he was about to throw something out of the window. It was a small notebook, and it proved to contain the names of women – dozens of them.

That notebook was to be the downfall of Henri Desire Landru, the Bluebeard who had lured ten women and a teenage boy to his rented villa and murdered them. The bodies had vanished, burnt in his kitchen stove; not a trace remained. Landru, who advertised for brides in a newspaper, swore he had no idea of what had happened to the women or the boy (the son of Jeanne Cuchet, another of Landru's victims), and there was not an atom of proof that he was lying. But their names were in the notebook, their money had gone into Landru's bank account, and their clothes and other possessions were in Landru's garage. The jury decided he was guilty, and he died on the guillotine.

For more than four centuries the reading public has been fascinated by cases like this, and – to the delight of publishers and pamphleteers – has been willing to pay good money to satisfy their interest. Our Elizabethan ancestors were just as morbid, and loved nothing so much as attending a hanging and buying a pamphlet about the condemned's life and crimes while they watched him or her strangle to death. In the 1770s an enterprising publisher brought out *The Newgate Calendar*, the lives of all the criminals who had been hanged at Newgate, and it has seldom been out of print. Even the respectable Victorians loved a public execution, although English gentlemen preferred France's methods because the sight of a head falling into a basket was more dramatic than that of a man dangling on the end of a rope.

And now, in the last two decades of the twentieth century, this appetite seems to be developing into a passion. Why this sudden intense interest? Does it indicate an increase in morbidity? I doubt it.

Is it a sign of morbidity to be fascinated by the story of Landru? Surely not. It is a remarkable drama, and it grips us for the same reason that a great novel or play grips us. We put ourselves into Landru's shoes – and then thank God that we can step back into our own.

The difference between real-life murders and those that take place on the stage or in novels is that academics devote theses and encyclopedias to the latter, while they regard the real thing as the domain of the mere crime reporter. This attitude always struck me as absurd; after all many great novelists, including Balzac, Stendhal and Dostoevsky, have been fascinated by true crimes. What made it doubly irritating was that nearly all books on crime were aimed at the popular market, and did not even contain an index. By the late 1950s I had dozens of books with titles like *Guilty or Not Guilty?* and *Strange Crimes of Passion*, but if I wanted to look up a particular case I had to do my best to recall which book it had appeared in. And, as my crime library grew, this became increasingly difficult.

Which is why in 1960, after writing several books about existentialist philosophy, I decided to produce the first encyclopedia of murder. I compiled it in association with Pat Pitman, another *aficionado* of crime, and it appeared in 1961. The book became a standard reference work for criminologists and crime writers, but when I suggested updating it some ten years later, the publisher turned down the idea, explaining that not enough people were interested in crime. Ten more years went by and I tried again; this time *An Encyclopedia of Modern Murder* was immediately accepted by the same publisher. In fact, by that time, my friend Joe Gaute (a director of Harraps publishers), had collaborated with Robin Odell on *The Murderers' Who's Who* and asked me to write an introduction. The book was by no means an updated rehash of my own *Encyclopedia* for it contained a unique feature: a comprehensive list of all the books in which each murder case appears. It was virtually an index to my own crime library. Finally, the American crime writer Jay Robert Nash produced the book we had all been waiting for: the massive six-volume *Encyclopedia of World Crime*. It is a unique achievement whose occasional inaccuracies are more than counterbalanced by its immense range.

By the time *An Encyclopedia of Modern Murder* appeared in print, books on crime had caught up with the rise in the crime rate. In America books on recent murder cases began to appear at the rate of about one a week, which by the end of the decade had escalated to about a dozen a week. Even in England a widely publicised case, like that of the Black Panther or Yorkshire Ripper, was followed within weeks of the trial by at least two paperbacks, often more. In May 1992 alone I bought two encyclopedias of serial killers. Every major city has bookshops devoted to 'true crime'. In America, schoolchildren have even been collecting cigarette cards with pictures of serial killers.

I must admit that what did surprise me was to learn, in a crime bookshop in Melbourne, that the majority of its customers were schoolgirls. I brooded about that for a long time until the likeliest solution struck me. All young people use art, in the guise of music, literature, the cinema, etc., to come to terms with life. We are all tormented by a need to grow up. (I expected it to disappear as I got older, but it is still as urgent at sixty.) And since life in the modern world is unprecedentedly violent, teenagers try to come to terms with the violence by reading or watching videos, or even listening to music, about it. And since girls are more often the victims of violence than males, they have a stronger need to come to terms with it. I was taken to the Melbourne bookshop by a pretty young blonde, the daughter of a friend, who has an encyclopedic knowledge of serial killers.

The flood of books on murder has become so great that publishers are obviously beginning to find it difficult to think of a subject that has not already been covered in depth. This is why my eyes lit up when Rocky Stockman wrote to tell me about his own *Hangman's Diary* and to ask whether I could loan him a copy of *The Hangman's Record*, a list of all British hangings since 1600. I immediately realised that his book would fill an important gap. The only similar work I know of is James Bland's *True Crime Diary* which covers crimes that took place on about half the days of the year. Regrettably, it is of no use to the serious student of crime because it lacks an index.

On the other hand, Rocky Stockman's *Hangman's Diary*, with its hundreds of cases and 2,400-odd entries in his Index of the Hanged, is the most comprehensive work of its kind apart from Nash's *Encyclopedia of World Crime*. It is the kind of book that I could not afford to write, for the amount of labour that has gone into it must have taken years. And, because it covers all the important murder cases since Elizabethan times, it is also the nearest thing to a complete history of modern murder that has been written.

So I feel that between us, Rocky Stockman, Jay Robert Nash, Joe Gaute, Robin Odell and I have brought to fruition the project I dreamed about in 1959. Rocky has produced a work that can be used as a reference book, or simply read for pleasure. (When the typescript arrived, I spent most of a day just browsing through it.) There can be no doubt that it will become a classic of its kind, and I feel privileged to be allowed to introduce it to the British reading public.

Foreword

**'The past is a foreign country:
they do things differently there.'**

from the Prologue to *The Go-Between*
by L. P. Hartley (1895–1972)

In this book I have told the stories or recorded the details of some
2,400 judicial hangings, covering every day of the year except Christmas Day and encompassing executions through the centuries, in many
different countries and for all manner of crimes. It is a collection of
fascinating stories which all end in the violence of sudden death at
the end of the rope. It is also a reference book for all true
crime enthusiasts, criminologists, authors and journalists, for whom
the Index of the Hanged at the end of the book will be an invaluable
aid.

In addition to the headlined stories, each day has a list of those
people who were also hanged on that day: giving the brief details of
who, what, where, when and why. (Occasionally, I have been unable
to trace the exact location of the hanging, especially for the World War
Two years when paper shortages forced the press to report only brief
details. In all such cases I am confident that the dates/names and other
details are accurate.)

The account of 2,400 personal tragedies in one book? It is even
worse than that when you multiply the 2,400 culprits by the even larger
number of victims – it is too easy to forget the victims, and those left
behind, yet they were the first to suffer in these tragedies.

The 2,400 condemned in this book suffered their ignominious
deaths for a wide range of crimes: for foul murders and evil treasons
through the scale of offences from mutiny, rape, violent robbery,
forgery, sheep-stealing, burglary and shop-lifting, to a nine-year-old
boy who was publicly hanged in 1833 for stealing a pennyworth of
printer's ink.

PLACES OF EXECUTION

The earliest known regular execution sites in London, dating from Norman times, were at 'The Elms at Tyburn' (near today's Marble Arch) and at 'The Elms at Smooth Field' (now Smithfield, London EC1). Many execution sites were called 'The Elms' because the Normans considered the elm to be the tree of justice; indeed the gallows were usually made from elm.

Through the following centuries, in different towns in Britain as well as in other countries, public executions were held wherever the local authorities ordered: sometimes at the scene of the crime but more usually at regular execution sites, in local market squares or in other open spaces.

Tyburn Tree was London's most used site for 700 years and it is estimated that 50,000 men, women and children perished there. ('Tyburn' was used as the name for some execution sites in other towns and even abroad; there were other Newgate Prisons too. Throughout this book where Tyburn, Newgate Prison, Horsemonger Lane Gaol, Pentonville Prison, Wandsworth Prison, and Holloway Prison are named they refer to the ones in London unless another location is specified.)

From 1783 most of London's hangings were at Old Bailey, in the street outside the gate to the Press Yard of Newgate Prison. Horsemonger Lane Gaol was another regular hanging place, sometimes on the roof of the gaol and at other times outside in the street (it was then in Surrey but is now in London SE1). Hangings at Execution Dock, Wapping, were for capital crimes committed on the high seas. The authorities continued to order executions elsewhere in London if they deemed it necessary to 'encourage' the public to behave themselves.

Public executions in Britain ended in 1868 and thereafter 'private executions', as they were called, were carried out within the prison walls. Newgate Prison* and Horsemonger Lane Gaol* continued as London's main hanging centres, later succeeded by Pentonville Prison, Wandsworth Prison, and Holloway Prison.

IN OLDEN TIMES

Life was more basic in days of yore. From Norman times until even as recently as the 1850s there were no complicated systems of centralised or local government, and public amenities were scarce and basic. Law

* *Originally the term 'gaol' ('jail' in the USA) was often used for a local or temporary lock-up, whereas 'prison' usually meant a longer-term establishment: today the terms are interchangeable, although some are traditionally referred to as 'gaols' (Durham Gaol, Chelmsford Gaol etc.) while for others the nomenclature of 'prison' is standard (Pentonville Prison, Maidstone Prison etc.).*

breakers had to be dealt with, but in that simpler society the main concern was with day-to-day survival. There was no concept, or public purse, to cope with long-term offenders. Punishments for criminals were as basic as the times: fine them, whip them, or hang them.

Even from our vantage point in the 1990s we can perhaps understand why, in those days, capital punishments were meted out for the crimes of high treason, murder, mutiny on the high seas and rape. But why should a man be hanged for sheep-stealing?

We were a mainly agricultural society then, communities were smaller and separated from each other, and they eked out a precarious living at the mercy of the elements or a sudden outbreak of disease. If a band of thieves raided a village's sheep, whether or not they made away with the whole flock, it could represent a large enough margin of loss to cause ruin and starvation for the villagers. The law made it necessary only to prove the theft of a single sheep or lamb to exact the highest penalty, hanging, in retribution for this crime against the very survival of the community.

THE ADVENT OF CIVILISATION

It is too easy to explain our forefathers' readiness to hang criminals for such a wide range of offences as simply because 'life was cheap then', although this was partly true. The towns were over-supplied with some elements of society and criminals were definitely surplus to requirement. There were other reasons too.

During the Industrial Revolution (roughly 1760–1830), as people swelled the populations of towns, some crimes took on a more serious interpretation by the authorities. For example: theft from a dwelling house in those dangerous times was a violation of the sanctity of a home; theft of goods from a shop or warehouse threatened the trade upon which the growing towns depended; forgery could bring about a loss of confidence in commercial credit, a relatively new concept upon which the growing importance of the City of London was based, and as a consequence forgers were hardly ever reprieved.

Therefore it was the advancement of civilisation that brought about the need for greater severity in dealing with criminals, and hence the creation of more than two hundred capital crimes in the early 1800s.

JUVENILES

The savagery of the wholesale infliction of hanging became especially horrifying, to my 1990s viewpoint, when I discovered the following:

1517 13 boys 'some not in their teens' were hanged at Leadenhall, Newgate, and Aldgate in London.

May 1772 A boy named Peter McCloud was hanged at Tyburn Tree for attempted house-breaking. *Hangman: Edward Dennis*

June 1777   Joseph Harris (15) was hanged for theft (see 27 June).

1782   A girl (14) hanged 'for being found in company of Gypsies'.

1801   A boy (13) was hanged for the theft of a spoon from a dwelling house.

July 1807   Richard Faulkner (15) was hanged at Wisbech, Cambridgeshire, for murder (see 13 July).

1808   Two sisters (11) and (8) were hanged at Lynn, Norfolk.

1816   Four boys aged between 9 and 13 were hanged in the City of London for begging and stealing. (Reverend Dr Cotton told a Parliamentary Select Committee on the Police that between them the four boys had been in custody more than 70 times. The youngest had been abandoned when he was 6 years old and for the past three years had supported himself and his girl by begging and stealing. The Select Committee chairman, Henry Grey Bennet, said that there were 'above six thousand boys and girls living solely on the town by thieving'. Most child thieves were aged from 6 to 10 and were sent out by Fagin-like criminals, or relatives, and flogged if they returned without anything worthwhile.)

1816   Joseph Wood (14) and Thomas Underwood (12) were hanged at Tyburn Tree for highway robbery.

1820   Charles Elliott (9) sentenced to death at the Old Bailey Sessions (with no recommendation for mercy) for stealing six handkerchiefs, valued at £1, from an Oxford Street haberdashery.

1831   A boy (9) was hanged by William Calcraft at Chelmsford, Essex, for setting fire to a house. Later that year Calcraft hanged John Any Bird Bell (14) at Maidstone (see 1 August for the story that caused me the greatest sadness).

1833   A boy (9) was hanged for stealing a pennyworth of paint from a shop by poking a stick through a starred crack in the window until the hole was large enough to get his small hand through. The 'paint' may have been printer's colour.

There were no children's homes, social workers or state benefits to cope with the hordes of abandoned children in the early 1800s. To survive from day to day they had to fend for themselves and this inevitably led to thievery: first, perhaps, of food from a market stall; then from picking pockets as part of an organised gang. A burglar might make use of a tiny child by shoving him or her through a small window or down a chimney. As the children got bigger and stronger they might take to mugging in dark streets or alleys. It would be just a matter of time before they took the cart ride to Tyburn Tree. Charles Dickens did not invent Fagin and his thieves' kitchen of juvenile criminals; he was reflecting reality.

THE END OF HANGING IN BRITAIN

Capital offences were reduced in number until, by 1861, only four remained: treason, piracy, mutiny and murder.

It was not until this century, 1908, that we stopped hanging the under-16s. In 1933 this immunity was extended to anyone under the age of 18.

Peter Anthony Allen and Gwynne Owen Evans were the last murderers to be hanged in Britain, on 13 August 1964.

MORE ENLIGHTENED TIMES?

We live in an enlightened age in the 1990s, at least in Britain, where most convicted murderers are released from 'imprisonment for life' after serving only seven to ten years. In many European countries they are set free even sooner. There are hundreds of condemned men and women in those states of the USA where the death penalty for murder is still in force, but it is rarely carried out and then only after years of delays in the legal process.

It is nearly 30 years since the last judicial hangings in Britain and yet, every time a public opinion survey is taken asking whether capital punishment should be brought back for murder, there is a huge majority 'yes' vote. In spite of this public demand, and the rising tide of serial-killings, gun-murders, sickening sex-murders of children, bomb-killings and other terrorist murders, our MPs have consistently voted to deny the will of the pro-hanging lobby.

I would not want to see the return of hanging for all murders. Most murders occur in the heat of a furious domestic upset and many such murderers find themselves on the wrong side of the law for the first time in their lives. There are others who take a life in circumstances where killing had not been premeditated. They must be punished of course, but the death sentence is not appropriate.

There are other types of murderers who, by the wickedness and ghastly manner of their crimes, I sincerely believe to be suitable candidates for capital punishment: sadistic child killers who do it for the sexual charge it gives them; armed robbers who deliberately shoot the people they are robbing or any innocent passer-by who gets in the way; terrorists who detonate a bomb in a public place to achieve the greatest toll of random killings; killers of the police officers who protect the rest of us.

Clearly, there are degrees of murder. There should be degrees of punishment too.

FORWARD – INTO THE PAST!

As you read through the stories in this book you will be horrified by some of the ghastly punishments, sometimes for seemingly trivial crimes. You will read about shocking miscarriages of justice, and of sad cases where the hanged prisoner was as much a victim as any that he or she offended against. But you will also read about the villains who met their ends on the gallows and whose deaths seemed to confirm that justice had been done.

It is all in the past, when the times were quite different to those we know today. When reading the stories always look at the date and try to see things as our forefathers had to see them, when their way of life was much less favourable than ours – and remember the words of L. P. Hartley in the Prologue to his novel *The Go-Between*: 'The past is a foreign country: they do things differently there.'

ROCKY STOCKMAN
Wingham, Kent

Acknowledgements

Colin Wilson gave me a tremendous boost by his interest and encouragement while I was writing *The Hangman's Diary*, although we have different opinions about the role of capital punishment in modern times. I could scarcely believe my good fortune when, unasked, he later offered to write the Introduction: if I had been given unlimited power to choose from the world's authors, he is the one I would have wanted to contribute it.

Brian Lane, another prolific true crime author, kindly allowed me to use two prints to illustrate 'The Saddest Story in This Book' (see 1 August).

David Birch, a retired prison officer, read through some of my stories to check the accuracy. Mike Petty of the Cambridgeshire Collection at Cambridge Central Library gave me the details of the interesting tale of the Caxton Gibbet. Steve Fielding generously helped me locate some of the Manchester and Liverpool prisons where some of the executions took place.

Elsewhere in this book you will find the British Hanging Chronology. I purloined the idea from the distinguished criminologist and author, Jonathan Goodman, in his introduction to the 1972 reprint of *My Experiences As an Executioner* by James Berry. I have expanded upon and updated his theme where it applies to judicial hanging, with his kind permission.

The quotation at the beginning of the Foreword is from *The Go-Between* by L. P. Hartley (Hamish Hamilton, 1953) and is reproduced by permission of Hamish Hamilton Ltd.

JANUARY

1 January

1857 MURDER ON THE WHITE CLIFFS OF DOVER
Serbian-born Dedea Redanies (25) publicly hanged at Maidstone for the murder of teenage sisters, Caroline (18) and Maria Ann Back, on the White Cliffs at Steddy Hole near Folkestone.
Hangman: William Calcraft

Private Dedea Redanies, although born in Serbia, was a soldier in the British Swiss Brigade which was based at Shorncliff Barracks in Folkestone. He had befriended John Back in Dover and was a visitor to his house, where he met Mrs Back and their two teenage daughters. Mrs Back did the laundry for Redanies' unit and he volunteered for the duty of taking it to her on a regular basis.

Either in fact or only in his romantic imagination, he and the elder daughter, Caroline, became lovers. He later claimed that she had told him that she was pregnant, and he wanted to marry her.

He arrived at the house at 8 p.m. on the night of Saturday 2 August 1856. He stayed for about an hour and a half and during this time, so he said later, Caroline had given him back his picture, which he interpreted as a rejection. He left to join some friends in Dover for drinks.

His drinking companions led him to believe that Caroline was not pregnant at all, and that, even worse, she would shortly be going to Woolwich to marry another soldier. Inflamed by the drink or jealousy, or both, he bought a dagger and returned to the Backs' house at about 3 a.m.

Concealing his emotion he was welcomed in and given breakfast with the family. He suggested that as the weather was fine Caroline should walk with him along the White Cliffs to Shorncliff Barracks, a distance of about eight miles. This was agreed, but only if Maria Ann went too.

The girls' bodies were discovered on the cliffs at 8 a.m. on that Sunday morning, about 15 yards from each other, at Steddy Hole near Capel-Le-Ferne on the outskirts of Folkestone. They had both been stabbed repeatedly in the chest and were drenched with blood.

The next day Redanies sent a letter to 'Mother Back' from the post office at Lower Hardres, near Canterbury. Written in German, it was an amazing letter expressing mainly Redanies' own self-pity for the situation in which he found himself and the reason why he had killed them:

'. . . rather that Caroline should die by my hands than to allow Caroline's love being bestowed upon others. However, I did not also intend to murder Mary Ann, her sister, but, not having other

3

opportunity, and as she was in my way, I could not do otherwise – I must stab her too.'

He even described how he killed them: persuading them to sit apart with their backs to him, he stabbed Maria Ann first and then Caroline.

He was caught on a road near Canterbury by a constable who recognised him. When Redanies saw the constable, and another man, running towards him he stabbed himself in the chest three times. He was taken to Dover, given medical treatment and recovered.

He was tried at Maidstone, confessing to the stabbing of Caroline, but denying that he had killed Maria Ann. However, in his letter to Mrs Back he had admitted the stabbing of Maria Ann and more evidence was found on him when arrested, including articles belonging to both girls. His counsel tried to have him certified as insane; the jury was not convinced and found him guilty.

He was hanged outside Maidstone Prison on New Year's Day, facing death with resigned fortitude. Unlike a number of Calcraft's executions, this one produced instant death with no tortured writhing at the rope's end. One report suggested that '. . . the faces of few murderers have borne so peaceful an expression after suffering death by hanging'.

Also hanged this day:

1889 at Maidstone Prison: William Gower (18) and Charles Joseph Dobell (19) for the gun-murder of Bensley Cyrus Lawrence, a timekeeper at a sawmill in Tunbridge Wells. Without remorse, they were cold and defiant to the end. *Hangman: James Berry*

1894 at Warwick Gaol: William Harris a.k.a. Haynes for the murder of Florence Clifford.

1907 at Warwick Gaol: John Davis, for murder. This was the first occasion on which John Ellis was the hangman; he had been an assistant since 1901 and would hang 203 men and women by the time he retired in 1923.

1952 at Winsom Green Prison, Birmingham: Horace Carter (30) for the sex-murder of Sheila Attwood (11). *Hangman: Albert Pierrepoint. Assistant: Syd Dernley*

2 January

1827 FIGHTING ALL THE WAY!
Charles Thomas White, a book seller, hanged at Old Bailey for
burning down his house in Holborn for the insurance money.
Hangman: James Foxon

Charles White owned a prosperous bookshop in Holborn so it is a
mystery why he set fire to it to obtain the insurance money. He must,
too, have known what the consequences would be because arson was a
crime that struck horror into the authorities' hearts. There were still
more than two hundred capital offences in 1827, but the death penalty
was applied for only about one tenth of them: arson was one of these.

While awaiting execution in Newgate, White's behaviour was violent: screaming that he was innocent, cursing the judges, and struggling with the turnkeys.

In expectation of more trouble from the prisoner at the execution,
Foxon was given two assistants. They were needed. White fought and
yelled all the way to the gallows outside the prison. Even after being
pinioned while on the scaffold, he managed to free himself and get
away from the trap door to the firmer floor of the platform. Another
fight ensued and he was forced back on to the drop and secured again.

As the trap was released White managed to jump and lodged his feet
on the edge of the opening, getting his hands free again and clawing at
the rope. The spectators watched the ghastly struggle of White,
hanging over the gaping hole with his tongue sticking out and his face
horribly contorted, who now seemed to be trying to climb up the rope
to the gallows beam.

Hangman Foxon kicked White's legs away and the desperate man at
last plunged and hung by his neck with his full weight. His face was in
clear view of the crowd and his agony obvious, as his body convulsed
and shuddered. Foxon ran down below and had to hang on to White's
legs until the death-twitches stopped.

Also hanged this day:

1673 at Tyburn Tree: Mary Moders (30) for returning from banish-
ment. An actress, she was also a notorious harlot, bigamist, swindler
and thief who posed as an aristocrat and bilked men of their fortunes.

1827 at Old Bailey: Amelia Roberts and William Davis for robbing
their employer. Robert Young for highway robbery.

1877 at Horsemonger Lane Gaol: Isaac Marks for murdering Frederick Barnard.

1883 at Maidstone Prison: Louisa Jane Taylor (37) for the poison-murder of Mrs Tregillis at Plumstead.

1914   at Folsom Prison, California, USA: night club entertainer and female impersonator Samuel Raber (late 20s) for the murder of Sacramento madam Cherry de St Maurice.

1953   at Wandsworth Prison: John James Alcott (22) for the murder of booking clerk Geoffrey Charles 'Dixie' Dean (27) at Ash Vale railway station near Aldershot. Alcott had previously been sentenced to death in 1949; he was court-martialled while serving in the Grenadier Guards in Germany for the murder of a German civilian, Peter Helm, but the sentence was quashed on a technicality (because his mother in Eltham in south-east London, who was his official next of kin, had not been informed that he was on trial for his life).

3 January

1946 THE END OF LORD HAW-HAW
William Joyce (40), dubbed 'Lord Haw-Haw', hanged at Wandsworth Prison for treason.
Hangman: Albert Pierrepoint

Before the war William Joyce had been a fascist rabble-rouser and street fighter. He left England between 29 August and 18 September 1939, using his British passport. War was declared against Germany on 3 September.

From 18 September to the end of the war he broadcast from Germany to the British people, trying to undermine their war effort by urging them to give up the struggle and surrender, taunting and sneering at them.

A radio critic on a national newspaper, Jonah Barrington, called him 'Lord Haw-Haw'. The description became his famous nickname, probably because of his ridiculous attempts to assume what he imagined to be an upper-class accent. His propaganda broadcasts began with 'Jairmany calling, Jairmany calling. . .'. Being called Lord Haw-Haw devalued his effect, making him something of a joke.

Joke or not, he certainly unsettled and dismayed many of his listeners during their times of hardship, fear, and grief. An old man joined the small group outside Wandsworth Prison on the morning of the execution and told authoress Rebecca West of the night he had seen the bodies of his grandchildren at the mortuary, victims of a V-1 bombing. When he got home he turned on the radio and heard Haw-Haw's voice. 'There he was, mocking me' recalled the old man.

Joyce's treachery was undoubted by the people he had sneered at and gloated over during the dark days of 1940, yet his trial for treason, at the Old Bailey in the autumn of 1945, ran into legal difficulties and went on appeal to the House of Lords.

Joyce had been born of British parents in America after his parents had taken US citizenship. It was argued by his defence that he was an American citizen until he was granted German citizenship in September 1940, and thereby owed no allegiance to the king and therefore could not have committed treason against the Crown.

But the Joyce family had returned to England when William Joyce was a baby. Their American citizenship was revoked and the family reverted to being British. It was the British passport that Joyce had used to flee Britain in 1939, and which he had used since 1933, that was his undoing.

The passport gives protection to the individual as a British subject in foreign countries, and that protection requires allegiance in return: the legal maxim is *protectio trahit subjectionem et subjectio protectionem* (protection draws allegiance and allegiance draws protection). His guilt and sentence of death was confirmed at the House of Lords, to the relief and satisfaction of ordinary Britons.

Also hanged this day:

1786 at Chester, Pennsylvania, USA: Elizabeth Wilson for the murder of her twin children (ten weeks old). Reprieve arrived 23 minutes too late to save her. Now a Pennsylvanian folk-tale.

1812 at Manhattan, New York, USA: George Hart for the clubbing-murder of his mistress Mary Van Housen.

1822 at Amherst, New Hampshire, USA: Daniel Davis Farmer for the murder of Mrs Anna Ayer.

1845 at Luneberg, Massachusetts, USA: Thomas Barrett for the rape-murder of Mrs Houghton (70).

1862 at McAlisterville, Pennsylvania, USA: John E. Lovering for the axe-murder of elderly shop keeper Henry Auker during a robbery.

1889 at Armley Gaol, Leeds: Charles Bulmer of Huddersfield for wife-murder (almost cut off her head). At Stafford Gaol: Thomas Clewes for the murder of Mary Jane Bovell.

1893 at Walton Gaol, Liverpool: Cross Duckworth for the murder of little Alice Barnes.

1899 at Newgate Prison: Johann Schneider for the murder of Conrad Berndt, a baker, afterwards disposing of the body in a bakehouse oven. Schneider's effigy was displayed in Madame Tussaud's Chamber of Horrors until after World War Two.

4 January

1946 FATE OF WAR-TIME SPIES
Herr Schurch hanged at Pentonville Prison for treason.
Hangman: Albert Pierrepoint

Albert Pierrepoint did not have far to travel, only from Wandsworth where he had hanged Lord Haw-Haw the previous day. Little is known of Schurch except that he had been spying for Germany. He is believed to have been a British subject.

Other spies captured in Britain during World War Two were interrogated and assessed at Latchmere House, near Ham Common in Richmond, Surrey. It was here that the 'Hanging Committee' decided whether to send them for trial or to turn them, that is use them to send misleading information to Germany under strict British control.

A total of 17 were sent for trial: one was acquitted (or reprieved), 15 were hanged* by Albert Pierrepoint, sometimes as assistant to Tom Pierrepoint, at Pentonville and Wandsworth Prisons, including Jose Waldberg and Carl Meier at Pentonville on 10 December 1940. They had landed with a third spy, Van Den Kieboom (see below), each equipped with a portable wireless transmitter and plenty of British money. They were expected to send to Germany all the information they could gather but were arrested soon after landing. They were tried at the Old Bailey and sentenced to death.

Charles Albert Van Den Kieboom (26), a Dutchman born in Japan, was hanged at Pentonville seven days after Waldberg and Meier. His execution was delayed because he entered notice of appeal. He believed that he could convince the judges that he had been forced to spy by threats of reprisals on his relative. He later withdrew the appeal. After landing Van Den Kieboom was taken prisoner at bayonet-point by troops.

Karel Richard Richter and Johannes Maximum Dronkers were hanged at Wandsworth Prison on 31 December 1942. Both parachuted into Britain and were captured within hours. Richter came with the special task of assassinating the President of the Czechoslovakian Government in Exile in Britain, while Dronkers had been briefed to infiltrate the BBC and broadcast coded information back to Germany.

* Only one spy was shot at the Tower of London during World War Two: Josef Jakobs, a special case, held military rank so was tried by court martial and executed under military authority. During World War One, however, 12 German spies were shot at the Tower; another committed suicide.

Also hanged this day:

1814 at Edinburgh: Christian Sinclair.

1859 at Taunton: W. Burgess for the murder of his daughter.

1864 at Bannock, Montana, USA: Erastus 'Red' Yager who turned informer on Sheriff Plummer and the 'Innocents', but this did not save him. (See also 10 January.)

1875 at Newgate Prison: James Cranwell (59) for the murder of Emma Bellamy. At Kirkdale Prison, Liverpool: John M'Crave and Michael Mullen for the murder by the kicking to death of Richard Morgan, and William Worthington for wife-murder.

5 January

1969 BAGHDAD 'SPIES'
Fourteen alleged spies publicly hanged in Baghdad.

The alleged Zionist 'spy ring' (including 11 Jews) were given a short trial by the Ba'ath Party regime and then publicly hanged in Liberation Square, Baghdad. Their bodies were left hanging to be viewed by (according to a government report) 'hundreds of thousands of people'.

Also hanged this day:

1819 Near St Giles', Edinburgh: Robert Johnson for robbery. *Hangman: John Simpson.* Ghastly scenes when Johnson's feet were touching the floor after the drop and he was slowly strangled into unconsciousness. The angry mob pelted officials and rescued Johnson, but he was carried back after soldiers restored order. At the second hanging his trousers fell down and he got a hand free and tried to loosen the rope until Hangman Simpson grabbed the hand away and Johnson slowly strangled and twitched for many minutes before dying. John Simpson was sacked as hangman.

1858 at New Jersey, USA: Dr James P. Donnelly for the murder of Albert S. Moses with a scalpel. He had lost $55 gambling with Moses and was discovered while trying to steal back the money.

1874 at Kirkdale Prison, Liverpool: Thomas Corrigan for the murder of his mother.

1880 at Newgate Prison: Charles Surety for the murder of an infant.

1892 at Armley Gaol, Leeds: James Stockwell for the murder of Catherine Dennis.

1897   at Wandsworth Prison: Henry Brown for wife-murder.

1934   at Dublin: John Fleming (34) for the hammer-murder of his wife Ellen (39).

6 January

1950 KILLING THE IN-LAWS
Daniel Raven (23) hanged at Pentonville Prison for the murders of his parents-in-law, Leopold (49) and Esther Goodman (47).

Leopold Goodman was a wealthy businessman, possibly shady, who kept large amounts of cash and valuables in the house. It had recently been burgled and, according to Raven, Mr Goodman had black-market enemies and feared another burglary. Daniel Raven was a successful advertising agent with no money problems.

The Goodmans and Raven left Muswell Hill Maternity Home at 9 p.m., after visiting Mrs Raven who had given birth to a son four days before. Raven drove the Goodmans to their home at Edgware and, he claimed, had offered to stay overnight but this was refused and he went to his own house (bought for the couple by Leopold Goodman) a mere five hundred yards away.

Another relative called on the Goodmans at 10 p.m. and, failing to get a response at the door, climbed in through an open window. He discovered their bodies in the dining room with blood splattered everywhere. They had both been bludgeoned to death with a series of violent blows to the head and the murder weapon, a television aerial base, was found in the kitchen. There were no signs of a break-in or robbery, the piles of £1 notes around the house were untouched.

Raven was called to the Goodmans' house by the police and arrived immaculately dressed in a light grey suit and a fresh white shirt. He sat on the stairs sobbing 'Why did they tell me to go? Why didn't they let me stop?' The officer in charge of the case, Detective Inspector Diller, was immediately suspicious. He took Raven to the Edgware Police Station.

Learning from other relatives that Raven had worn a dark blue suit earlier that evening, Diller went to Raven's house. The heat caused Diller to investigate the boiler from which he retrieved parts of a dark blue suit. The suit was blood stained. In the garage he discovered a pair of recently washed shoes, and that the upholstery of Raven's car was still damp from washing. Blood traces, found on all of these objects, were later matched with the Goodmans' blood group.

Raven could not, at the time, explain the blood stains. In a later story he said he had gone back to the Goodmans and found them already dead and his suit must have got blood on it when he knelt down by the bodies. Afterwards he fled in panic.

At his trial at the Old Bailey he maintained that he was innocent. His wife supported him but admitted that her husband and her parents were not always on good terms. No clear motive was established for Raven to kill his parents-in-law, just the likelihood of a family row.

He was found guilty but appealed, claiming insanity with a history of mental blackouts. His attempts to destroy the blood-stained evidence indicated that he knew what he was doing and was trying to escape the consequences. His appeal failed and he was hanged.

Also hanged this day:

1721 at Grassmarket, Edinburgh: Nicol Muschet for wife-murder. He had killed his wife by cutting her throat one night on a path known as Duke's Walk in the King's Park near Holyrood House. A pile of stones, known as Nicol Muschet's Cairn, marked the murder spot until it was removed in 1789. The cairn was restored in 1823 and remains to this day, although the actual murder spot was slightly west of the present cairn.

1798 at Reading, Pennsylvania, USA: Benjamin Bailey for murdering and robbing a pedlar, Jost Follhaber.

1862 at Washington DC, USA: Private Michael Lanahan for the gun-murder of Sergeant Brennan an hour after reporting late for guard duty and being slapped in the face by the sergeant. He was hanged in front of hundreds of spectators and six regiments of infantry. His last words were 'Goodbye soldiers, goodbye!'

1909 at Pentonville Prison: John Esmond Murphy a.k.a. McDonald for the murder of foreign banker G. W. M. J. Schlette.

1920 at Armley Gaol, Leeds: Louis Massey a.k.a. Hind, for wife-murder. At Strangeways Prison, Manchester: Hyman Perdovitch for murdering his foreman, and David Caplan for the murder of his wife and two children.

7 January

1898 THE 'DEMON OF THE BELFRY'
William Henry Theodore Durrant (24) hanged at San Quentin Prison, USA, for the sex-murders of Blanche Lamont (21) and Marion Williams (21).

Theodore Durrant was a young man of respectable standing in the community. He was a medical student as well as being a Sunday school teacher, librarian, and organist at the Emmanuel Baptist Church in San Francisco.

The repressive Victorian attitudes and the prudish hypocrisy of those times applied in the United States as well as throughout the British Empire and, besides, all was not what it seemed with young Theodore Durrant.

Taking Blanche Lamont for a walk in the park one afternoon he greatly offended her sense of decency. What act of his caused this outrage is not known, but she refused to speak to him for weeks after.

Another girl, Anne Whelming, was with him in the church library when he disappeared for a while and then jumped out in front of her, stark naked. Anne screamed and ran away, but nice young girls didn't talk about such things and she kept her silence.

By 3 April 1895 Durrant and Blanche Lamont were on speaking terms again. They spent the afternoon together and were seen entering the church at 4.15 p.m., Durrant unlocking the door with his own key. He took her to the library and excused himself for a few minutes. When he came back he was naked and he sprang on her and raped her, although no screams were heard. He then dragged her by the hair, probably unconscious, up the steps to the belfry tower. There he stripped her of all her clothes, strangled her and raped her again.

At 5 p.m. another organist arrived and commented on Durrant's appearance which was explained away by saying that he had accidentally inhaled gas.

The disappearance of Blanche was suspected to be the work of white-slavers.

Durrant's next guest in the church library was Minnie Williams. When the naked Durrant suddenly presented himself she screamed, but he overpowered her and choked her with her own skirt. He tore off some of her clothes and raped her. Then he indulged in a frenzy of stabbing, wounding her in the chest, face, and wrists. The walls were splashed with Minnie's blood, as Durrant must have been, but he didn't stop until the knife broke leaving the blade still in her ribs, when he raped her again. He spent the rest of the evening at a church service.

The next day Pastor George Gibson reported that the door of the church had been broken open. A cleaner later discovered Minnie's bloody and mutilated body in the library. Foolishly, Gibson tried to prevent a scandal by having undertakers remove the body before he called the police. Blanche Lamont was found in the belfry the next day by policemen searching the church.

Durrant was soon arrested and many witnesses established that he was the last person to be seen with both victims. Anne Whelming at last came forward with her story. If she had reported it at the time, the murders might never have happened.

The lurid sex-murders became a newspaper sensation on both sides of the Atlantic, with readers clammering for more details of the 'Demon of the Belfry' as the case was called.

The trial lasted from July to November and was followed by two years of appeals and four stays of execution, to the delight of American and European newspaper editors.

Durrant is said to have screamed as he fell through the trap door at his execution. His mother and father were present at the hanging in San Quentin Prison. Afterwards they ate a meal in their son's cell, provided by the prison's kitchen, with the open-topped coffin nearby with their son's strangled blue face and protruding tongue in view. They ate heartily and left nothing!

Durrant's death did not stop the stream of newspaper speculations about the Demon of the Belfry. Every false confession, and there were plenty, was given sensational treatment. Stories accusing Pastor Gibson of the murders were aired, to which his attempted cover-up gave colour. Even the other organist was suspected at one stage.

Also hanged this day:

1754 at Execution Dock, Wapping: Captain John Laney for ship-burning.

1806 at Old Bailey: S. Wild Mitchell for murdering his child.

1817 at Execution Dock, Wapping: John Norbury, James Parry, David Bruce, and William Hastings, for piracy. They were afterwards hung in chains on the Isle of Dogs.

1890 at Warwick Gaol: Charles Lister Higginbottom for the murder of an old woman named Phillips.

1903 at Kilkenny County Gaol, Ireland: Joseph Taylor for the murder of John Daly. Mary Daly was hanged two days later.

1919 at Armley Gaol, Leeds: Ben Benson for the throat-cutting murder of his mistress, Annie Mayne. *Hangman: Tom Pierrepoint. Assistant: Robert Baxter*

1948 at Armley Gaol, Leeds: George Whelpton (31) for the murder and mutilation in Doncaster of Mrs Alison Parkin, Joyce Parkin (23), and Maurice Parkin (15). The killings were probably committed during a fit.

8 January

1848 MURDER BY THUNDERCLAP!
Patrick Reid (25) publicly hanged at midday at York Castle, for the
Water Royd House murders.
Hangman: Nathaniel Howard

Irish hawker Patrick Reid murdered the three occupants of Water
Royd House as thunder roared from the sky at midday on the hot and
muggy 12 May 1847. While he awaited execution in the condemned
cell at York Castle he said, 'I thought when I heard it that it was God
Almighty speaking to me, and I never have that impression out of my
mind.'

The news of the horrific murders at Water Royd House in Mirfield,
near Huddersfield in Yorkshire, spread across northern England and
attracted thousands to watch the killer being hanged. The railway ran
extra 'execution specials'.

Reid was known at Water Royd House. Six weeks before the
murders took place he had been ordered by the master, James Wraith
(77), to 'never come near this place again' after Reid had falsely
accused the servant-girl of stealing a tea caddy from his basket. Reid
vowed revenge.

He returned on 12 May intent on robbery. He entered the kitchen,
spoke to the 21-year-old servant-girl, Caroline Ellis, and hit her on the
head with his heavy soldering iron. She screamed and staggered to the
door and he hit her again. James Wraith came out of the cellar and
Reid struck him down with the soldering iron. Mrs Ann Wraith (67)
arrived to see what was causing the noise and was also hit on the head.
Reid collected an iron poker from the kitchen and repeatedly hit all
three about the head.

Then there was a knock at the door. Reid opened it to see another
Irish hawker, Michael McCabe*, who asked Reid whether he wanted
to buy anything. Reid told him he didn't, and slammed the door
shut.

Reid went through the house, taking jewellery and about £40 in
cash. He also found a razor inscribed with Mr Wraith's name, which he
used to slit the throats of his victims.

The bodies were discovered at 1.30 p.m. by Wraith's great-nephew
Joshua Green, and what an awful sight met his 12-year-old eyes! The
three bloody corpses, each had multiple skull fractures, battered faces,
and their throats had been slit from ear to ear.

Curious crowds flocked to the house, walking through the rooms to
stare ghoulishly at the bodies and the ransacked interior. The police
investigation, and the trials that followed it, were similarly confused
and incompetent. Reid was acquitted at the first trial, for the murder

of old James Wraith, but convicted and sentenced at the second for the other murders.

Reid made a full written confession, but this was not revealed by his defending counsel (Mr Digby Seymour) until the judge had completed sentencing him to death.

He was hanged outside York Castle before an immense crowd, and it was not an easy death. Hangman Nathaniel Howard had fixed the rope too loosely about the neck and it was a matter of some minutes before Reid's 'severe expiring convulsions' were over.

Michael McCabe (35) had been the first suspect because he had been seen in the vicinity at the time, and because of his evasive answers. He was tried with Reid at both trials, and sentenced to death. Mr Digby Seymour, acting for Reid, had tried throughout the trials to place the blame on McCabe. At the same time he was carrying in his pocket Reid's confession, which specifically exonerated McCabe. After this, McCabe had to remain in the condemned cell with Reid for a week. Then his sentence was commuted to transportation for life. He was allowed to return to Huddersfield years later, where he lived until nearly 70 years old.

Also hanged this day:

1751 at Edinburgh: Norman Ross for the murder of a lady by whom he was employed as a footman.

1889 at Warwick Gaol: George Nicholson, a baker, for wife-murder.

1899 at Kilkenny County Gaol, Ireland: Patrick Holmes for the murder of a woman at Paulstown.

1919 at Armley Gaol, Leeds: George Cardwell and Percy Barrett for the 'Pontefract Murder'. *Hangman: Tom Pierrepoint. Assistant: Robert Baxter*

9 January

1900 A TALE OF THREE RAILWAY STATIONS
Louisa Josephine Masset (33) hanged in Newgate Prison for murdering her son, Manfred Louis Masset (4), and dumping his naked body in the ladies' lavatory at Dalston Junction railway station, London.
Hangman: James Billington

Mlle Louisa Josephine Masset, of mixed French and English parentage, had left France some years earlier because of the scandal caused when she gave birth to her illegitimate son Manfred.

She settled at 29 Bethune Road, Stoke Newington, London, and placed the baby with foster-mother Miss Helen Gentle in Tottenham. The arrangement worked satisfactorily and the monthly fee of 37 shillings (£1.85) was always paid promptly. Louisa worked as a day-governess and earned extra money as a piano teacher. She became the mistress of Eudore Lucas (19), son of a prosperous French merchant, who lived next door.

Feeling that the presence of young Manfred was a hindrance to her relationship with Eudore, Louisa cold-bloodedly decided to get rid of him. She wrote to Miss Gentle on 13 October 1899 telling the foster-mother that Manfred's father wanted the boy back in France. She arranged to collect him from a public house on Friday 27 October.

She set out from 29 Bethune Road, having equipped herself with a clinker brick from the rockery border in the front garden. She met Miss Gentle for the tearful farewell from little Manfred, also taking the parcel of clothes packed by Miss Gentle. Manfred was dressed in a blue serge frock trimmed with white braid and topped with a red sailor's hat marked HMS *Raven*.

Louisa took him to London Bridge station, where she was seen with him in the first-class waiting room at 1.45 p.m. She left at 3 p.m. with the child, saying she was going to buy him a piece of cake. She returned alone three hours later.

At 6 p.m. a woman went into the lavatory of the ladies' waiting room on number three platform at Dalston Junction railway station and discovered the still warm body of Manfred Masset. He was naked except for a black shawl; his face and head were battered, and a piece of broken clinker brick lay on each side of the body.

Meanwhile at London Bridge, Louisa caught the Brighton train. She left the brown-paper parcel of clothes in a waiting room at Brighton station and checked in to an hotel. She was joined on Saturday by Eudore Lucas and they enjoyed a lovers' weekend.

Back in London the unknown boy's murder was a sensation. Doctors reported that he had been first stunned and then suffocated. The horror at the discovery of the naked and bloody corpse in the lavatory of a ladies' waiting room at a railway station, excited the Victorian reading public. Newspapers reported every detail.

Miss Gentle received a letter from Louisa on Monday saying that Manfred missed her, had cried all the way to London Bridge, been sick on the boat to France, but was now well and sent his love.

Miss Gentle was not fooled; she had seen the newspaper stories and the description of the victim alarmed her. She identified his little body at the mortuary, and later the parcel of clothes abandoned at Brighton railway station. A Stoke Newington draper's assistant identified the black shawl as the one sold to Mlle Masset on 24 October.

Louisa Masset was arrested. It was not until her trial at the Old Bailey that she produced a story: that at London Bridge station she had handed the boy over to two women named Browning, who were to care for him at £12 a year. But it was too late. She could produce neither a receipt nor an address for the Brownings, and the latter could not be traced.

Her sentence to hanging was met with approval by the public and newspapers. What with public hostility, the evidence of cold premeditation, and the brutal nature of the crime, there could be no reprieve. The illicit weekend in Brighton, coming as it did after the murder of her young son, was an outrage to Victorian concepts of morality and motherhood.

Also hanged this day:

1824 in front of Hertford Gaol: John Thurtell for the brutal murder of fellow gambler William Weare.

1832 at Old Bailey: Eliza Ross (38) (a.k.a. Cook, a.k.a. Reardon) for the murder of Catherine (or Caroline) Walsh (84).

1903 at Tulamore Gaol, Ireland: Mary Daly for the murder of her husband John Daly. Her accomplice, Joseph Taylor, was hanged two days earlier.

1923 at Pentonville Prison: Frederick Edward Francis Bywaters (20) for the murder of Percy Thompson (32), his lover's husband. *Hangman: William Willis. Assistants: Seth Mills and Tom Pierrepoint.* At Holloway Prison: Edith Jessie Thompson (28) for her part in the murder of her husband by Bywaters. When hanged, Mrs Thompson's underwear became drenched with blood and it was suggested that she had, unknowingly, been pregnant and had miscarried. Thereafter all women hanged in British prisons had to wear canvas knickers at their executions. *Hangman: John Ellis. Assistants: Robert Baxter and Thomas Phillips*

1945 Horace Beresford Gordon for the murder of Mrs D. M. Hillman.

1953 at Quebec Prison, Canada: Marguerite Pitre, mistress of 'Love Bomb' murderer Joseph Albert Guay, for her part in the aircraft bomb murder of Guay's wife and 22 others. (See 12 January.)

10 January

1864 'YOU WOULDN'T HANG YOUR SHERIFF, WOULD YOU BOYS?'
Sheriff Henry Plummer and 28 accomplices hanged at Bannock, Idaho, USA, on the gallows he had had built as part of his law and order campaign.

Henry Plummer had a string of murders and robberies on his record when he arrived at the boom town of Bannock, Idaho, where he anticipated rich pickings. He was right.

He became a prominent citizen and, amazingly, had himself appointed Sheriff. He was behind most of the crime. He had a gang of about two hundred desperadoes, ironically called 'The Innocents', and they controlled the town. He even had the nerve to launch a fake campaign against the robbers, and tried to win more power for his bogus law and order activities. A permanent town gallows was one of his innovations, from which he strung up non-Innocent crooks.

Before he and his gang could bleed the town completely of its wealth, a band of vigilantes emerged. A number of Innocents were rounded up and they soon opened their mouths and ratted on their leader. The rest of the gang was hunted and captured. Plummer and 28 Innocents were convicted and sentenced to hang from the gallows they had conveniently provided for the town.

Henry Plummer and four of his leading accomplices stood side-by-side on the scaffold, with the other 24 waiting their turn. Plummer's nerve and persuasive charm deserted him at the last and he begged for his life wailing, 'You wouldn't hang your Sheriff, would you boys?' They would, and did!

Also hanged this day:

1867 at Maidstone Prison: James Fletcher (20) for the murder of Warder James Boyle with a stone-hammer in the Convict Prison at Chatham; Ann Lawrence (29) for the axe-murder of her infant son Jeremiah and the attempted murder of her adulterous lover Walter Highams at Tunbridge Wells. *Hangman: William Calcraft*

1879 at Limerick County Gaol, Ireland: Thomas Cunceen for murdering his mistress Johanna Hogan and their bastard child.

1888 at Cork County Gaol, Ireland: Dr Philip Henry Eustace Cross, former army surgeon, for wife-murder. He told warders 'I do not fear death for I have met it face to face more than once on the battlefield.' He died resolute. *Hangman: James Berry*

1893 at Northampton Prison: Andrew M'Rae for the murder of Annie Pritchard at Althorpe.

1899 at Armagh County Gaol, Ireland: Thomas Kelly for murdering his father.

1946 at Oakalla Prison, Vancouver, Canada: American Private Bruce Potter (47) for the murder of Mrs Edna Ina Rogers. Given too long a drop, he was decapitated.

11 January

1866 THE DOUBLE FAMILY MAN – HE KILLED THEM BOTH!
Stephen Forward, a.k.a. Ernest Walter Southey (35), hanged outside Maidstone Prison, Kent, for the murders of his wife and daughter in Ramsgate. He also admitted to the murders of the sons of his mistress (aged 6, 8, and 10) in London.
Hangman: William Calcraft

Stephen Forward spent his youth in Ramsgate where he was apprenticed to a baker. He married a local girl, Mary, and her family set him up in his own bakery. After little more than a year the bakery went broke and Forward ran off to London, leaving Mary behind with their daughter, Emily. He drifted from job to job and, after a ruinous attempt at setting himself up in the rope trade, fled London to evade imprisonment for debts of £1,800. He moved from the West Country, to the North, from Scotland to Ireland; but his lack of success continued. At some time he took on the name of Ernest Walter Southey, and it was under this name that he arrived in Brighton.

There he met Mrs White, a woman with four children, who was as unsettled, and as unstable, as he was. Yet it was here, in 1863, that he enjoyed a spectacular success. In one night of gambling he won £1,172 from the Honourable Dudley Ward. However, the Honourable Dudley did not honour the debt.

Ernest Southey appealed for payment to Ward's brother, the Earl of Dudley, who had settled his younger brother's debts in the past. Unfortunately, the Earl had reached his financial limit rescuing his wayward brother, and refused to pay. Southey began a crazed and obsessive campaign in pursuit of the Hon. Dudley, of the Earl, the Bishop of London, and even the Prime Minister, Lord Palmerston.

Mrs White decided to leave Southey and take her family to Australia and, while making the arrangements, she left her three boys with their father, William White, in Holborn. Southey returned from France (where he had been badgering the Hon. Dudley Ward, unsuccessfully, for his money). Upon learning that Mrs White was

19

leaving him he collected the children from Mr White, telling the father that he was accompanying the family to Australia.

He took the children only as far as The Star, a coffee-house with boarding rooms in Holborn. Then he set off on his own for Ramsgate. He briefly met his wife, Mary, and arranged to meet her the next morning at her lodgings. It was there that he shot both Mary and his daughter, Emily, and then quietly surrendered his gun and himself to the landlord.

He caused a sensation when he appeared before Ramsgate Magistrates that afternoon and admitted that he had also murdered the three White children at The Star in Holborn, by poisoning them with prussic acid.

No good motive for the murders was established at his trial in Maidstone, except that the killer was exhausted by his troubles and was probably tired of life. Southey, as he insisted on being called, was sentenced to death and seemed relieved that all his troubles would soon be at an end.

Although the hanging was in public it did not attract as big a crowd as hangings had in earlier years. Hangman Calcraft apparently did a reasonable job and caused no adverse comment in the press. The *Maidstone Journal* concerned itself mainly with a description of the gallows:

> 'The scaffold was hung round with black cloth to such a height that when the drop fell only just the top of the convict's head was visible to the crowd.'

Also hanged this day:

1901   at Belfast, Ireland: William Woods for the murder of a woman. At Cork County Gaol, Ireland: Timothy Cadogan for the murder of a gentleman.

1933   at Nairobi, Kenya: Charles William Ross (19) for the murders of Margaret Keppie and Winifred Stevenson (20).

12 January

1951 THE LOVE BOMB MURDER
Joseph Albert Guay (32) hanged at Quebec, Canada, for the time-bomb murder of his wife, Rita Guay, and 22 others on board a Canadian Pacific Airways' Dakota.

Guay, a French-Canadian jewellery salesman, determined to murder his wife so that he would be free to remarry. He had Genereux Ruest, the crippled brother of his mistress, make a time bomb from an alarm clock and dynamite. The time bomb was parcelled up marked as containing a religious statuette, and addressed to a fictitious person.

Guay had his mistress, Marguerite Pitre, deliver the parcel to Quebec Airport for shipment on the flight to Seven Islands on 7 September 1949. The bomb was timed so that it would explode when the Dakota was flying over the sea.

Mrs Rita Guay was a passenger on the flight. Take off was delayed and the explosion occurred only 40 miles from the airport, over land. All 19 passengers and the crew of four were killed.

Guay had left a string of clues, and investigations led to his arrest. It is not clear whether he had intended marrying Pitre or another mistress, 19-year-old Marie-Ange Robitaille. Newspapers called the case 'The Love Bomb Murder'.

Guay confessed after conviction, disclosing the roles played by Pitre and Ruest, and they were later tried and also hanged.

Also hanged this day:

1813 at York: Hangman John Curry hanged 12 Luddites for riot and other offences. The first six were hanged at 11 a.m.: John Hill, Joseph Crowther, Nathaniel Hoyle, John Dean, John Ogden, and Thomas Brooke. The others at 1.30 p.m.: John Walker, John Swallow, William Hartley, James Haigh, James Hay and Joseph Hay. (See 14 January.)

1819 at Old Bailey: Andrew Crisp for cattle-stealing and Stephen Morris for burglary.

1853 at Taunton: John William Beale for the murder of his sweetheart Charlotte Pugsley.

1874 at Gloucester Prison: Edward Butt, Edwin Bailey and Ann Barry for child-murder.

1886 at Mullingar Gaol, Ireland: John Cronin for the murder of his father.

1949 at Strangeways Prison, Manchester: Margaret Allen (42) for the murder of Nancy Ellen Chadwick (68). *Hangman: Albert Pierrepoint*

13 January

1928 THE 'GORILLA' MURDERS
Mass murderer 'Gorilla' Earle Leonard Nelson (30) a.k.a. Roger Wilson a.k.a. Virgil Wilson (and other aliases) hanged at Winnipeg Prison, Canada, for the murder of Mrs Emily Paterson.

The man who became known as the Gorilla Murderer looked like something that you only see in nightmares. He was short with a round ape-like face, protruding lips, receding forehead, dark complexion, bright and piercing blue eyes, and huge fists.

His life had been the stuff of nightmares too. He never knew his parents and was an orphan before he was a year old; his mother died from syphilis which she had caught from his father. He was brought up by an aunt and, a quiet and withdrawn boy, he became fascinated by religion and the bible.

At ten he suffered ghastly head injuries when he was hit by a tram while playing in a Philadelphia street. The tram dragged him for 50 feet and he was unconscious for almost a week afterwards with a hole in the side of his head. For the rest of his life he suffered from dizzy spells and had severe head pains, sometimes so intense that he rolled around in agony.

His religious interest became obsessive and he had violent outbursts which included sexually motivated offences which resulted in him being committed to mental homes, from which he often escaped. He married in 1919 during one of these escapes, when he remained free for two and a half years, but the marriage broke down after six months because of his abnormal behaviour.

His raping and murdering rampage across America and Canada apparently began in 1926. Nearly all the offences were perpetrated on landladies in boarding houses. There may have been earlier rape-murders committed by Nelson, but 22 have been positively traced to him:

1926
24 February San Francisco, California. Miss Clara Newman (63) found naked in attic lavatory, strangled and raped.

2 March 30 miles south east at San Jose, California. Mrs Laura E. Beale (60) found naked in a lavatory, strangled and raped.

10 June 30 miles north west at San Francisco. Mrs Lilian St Mary (63) found naked under a bed after being strangled and raped.

24 June 28 miles south east at Santa Barbara, California. Mrs George Russell found naked, strangled and raped.

August 30 miles north west at Oakland, California. Mrs Mary Nesbit strangled and raped.

19 October 570 miles north at Portland, Oregon. Mrs Beata Withers (35) found in trunk (the Portland police suspected suicide!).

20 October Portland. Mrs Virginia Grant (59) found strangled behind the cellar furnace, some jewellery and a coat missing (police suspected death by natural causes!).

21 October Portland. Mrs Mable Fluke found strangled in an attic with the ligature still round her neck.

18 November 570 miles south at San Francisco. Mrs William Edmunds (56) strangled and raped.

24 November 700 miles north at Seattle, Washington. Mrs Florence Monks found naked, strangled and raped. Jewellery stolen.

November 160 miles south at Oregon City, Oregon. Mrs Blanche Myers (48) strangled and found under a bed.

23 December 1,350 miles south east at Council Bluffs, Iowa. Mrs John E. Beard (49) strangled and raped.

December 170 miles south at Kansas City, Kansas. Mrs Bonnie Pace (23) strangled and raped.

27 December Kansas City. Mrs Germania Harpin (28) strangled and raped and her 8-month-old baby suffocated with a rag.

1927

27 April 1,000 miles east at Philadelphia, Pennsylvania. Mrs Mary McConnell (60) strangled.

30 May 260 miles north west at Buffalo, New York. Mrs Jenny Randolph (35) strangled and raped.

1 June 230 miles west at Detroit, Michigan. Mrs Minnie May (53) (landlady) and Mrs Atorthy (tenant) strangled.

3 June 230 miles south west at Chicago, Illinois. Mrs Mary Sietsema (27) strangled and raped.

8 June 750 miles north west at Smith Street, Winnipeg, Manitoba, Canada. Lola Cowan (14), daughter of fellow tenants, killed and mutilated: found under her bed in vacated room four days later.

9 June At Riverside Avenue, Winnipeg. Mrs Emily Paterson found under her bed naked, after being raped and hammered to death. $7 and some clothing stolen.

11 June 350 miles west at Regina, Saskatchewan, Canada. Assaulted a young girl but was interrupted and he fled.

12 June 250 miles south east at Killarney, Manitoba. The Gorilla is arrested as he flees south, only a few miles from the border with North Dakota, USA.

His trial for the murder of Emily Paterson began at Winnipeg on 1 November 1927 and lasted four days. Despite his medical and mental history, his defence of insanity failed. This may have been because his use of aliases, changing his appearance, and his fleeing the scenes of his crimes to distant locations, convinced the jury that he was in a state of mind where he knew what he was doing and knew that what he had been doing was wrong. He was found guilty and sentenced to death.

He insisted that he was innocent 'before God and man' and at another time shouted 'I have never committed murder: never, never, never!'

He showed no remorse until the end: according to one report he broke down when actually on the gallows, begging for the forgiveness of his victims and 'for my own sinful self'.

Also hanged this day:

1885   at Wandsworth Prison: Horace Robert Jay for the murder of Florence Julia Kemp.

1899   at Armagh County Gaol, Ireland: Philip King for the murder of his wife and mother-in-law.

14 January

1813 MORE LUDDITES HANGED
John Swallow, John Bailey, Joseph Fletcher, and John Lamb, hanged at York for burglary connected with the Luddite riots.
Hangman: John 'Mutton' Curry

Two days earlier 12 Luddites had been hanged for riot and mayhem at Cartwright's Mill at Rawfolds, the destruction of which was later to be recounted in Charlotte Brontë's novel *Shirley*. The four men hanged today had taken advantage of the disorder to carry out some thieving.

The Luddites were well organised gangs of wreckers who raided mills and factories to destroy the machinery that had replaced textile workers. The unemployment brought about by the introduction of the machines had added to the economic hardships that followed the Napoleonic Wars. The Luddite movement began in Nottinghamshire in 1811 and rapidly spread to other industrial areas and so alarmed the Government that the destruction of machinery was made a capital offence. Luddite riots continued until 1816. Another three men were hanged on 16 January for murders committed at the same riot.

Hangman John Curry was an unsavoury character himself. He had been appointed hangman for Yorkshire in 1802, while serving a life sentence in York Castle after having twice been sentenced to death and escaping the gallows when the sentences were commuted. He had been condemned in 1793 and 1800 for sheep-stealing and the mob derisively nicknamed him Mutton Curry.

Also hanged this day:

1811   at Old Bailey: Antonio Cardoza.

1853   at Paisley, Scotland: John Thompson a.k.a. P. Walker for the poisoning-murder of Agnes Montgomery.

1889   Arthur McKeown, a cab driver, for the murder of Mary Jane Phillips.

15 January

Hanged this day:

1812   at Old Bailey: Thomas Flanagan, Neal Daley, and George Smith.

1815   at Old Bailey: H. Horler for wife-murder. At York: James Barbour for murder.

1879   at Mauch Chunk, Pennsylvania, USA: James McDonnell and Charles Sharpe for the 'Molly Maguire' murder of George K. Smith (see 21 June). *Hangman: Sheriff Raudenbush*

1883   at Galway County Gaol, Ireland: Patrick Higgins (70) for the gun-murder of two bailiffs, Joseph and John Huddy, at Lough Mask (see 17 January). *Hangman: William Marwood*

1918   at State Prison, Concord, New Hampshire, USA: Frederick Small for the strangling- and arson-murder of his wife to gain $20,000 life insurance.

16 January

1978 'I THINK I SHOULD BECOME A HOMOSEXUAL MURDERER . . .'
Ronald Frank Cooper (26) hanged at Johannesburg, South Africa, for the strangling-murder of Mark John Garnet (12).

Ronald Cooper had been a problem child who had attempted to strangle a girl when he was 11 years old. By the time he was 26 he was an unemployed labourer living a lonely life in the St Kilda Hotel in Berea, Johannesburg.

His thoughts were dominated by sexual fantasies in which he would kill 30 boys and six females. He wrote in his diary for 17 March 1976:

'I have decided that I think I should become a homosexual murderer and shall get hold of young boys and bring them here where I am staying and I shall rape them and then kill them.'

and:

'I shall only take boys between the ages of 7 years old and about 16 years of age. The first few victims shall each be killed in a different way. . .' (the list of his intended methods followed).

and:

(After killing 30 boys) 'I must kill at least 6 girls and women between about 8 and 50 years . . . Age won't count as long as they look attractive. I can either rape them or not.'

To develop his fantasies into action, a few days later, he made two separate attempts on 10-year-old boys, but in each case the boy screamed and Cooper fled. On 16 May it was different. He followed Mark John Garnet (12) into the lift of an apartment building and grabbed him, squeezing his throat until he was unconscious and then tying a rope round the neck. He removed the boy's trousers and unsuccessfully attempted sodomy. Relenting, he loosened the rope and departed, but Mark Garnet was already dead.

Back at the St Kilda Hotel, and shaken by the difference between fantasy and reality, he recorded his remorse in his diaries: 'I never want to do such a thing again. To strangle an innocent boy is not a good thing to do.' And 'I really am a monster.'

He never did do such a thing again because an earlier victim had been on his trail. In February, a month before composing his killing strategy in his diary, Cooper had abducted Tresslin Pohl (10) and taken him at gun-point to a nearby park. The young lad was in luck because Cooper suddenly told him he could go and he ran home.

The boy had accompanied police touring the streets, but his attacker was not spotted. Then, three weeks later, Tresslin Pohl saw Cooper at a children's Saturday morning cinema show and followed him home. He did not report this until after his school friend Mark Garnet had been murdered. He then led policemen to the St Kilda Hotel and identified Cooper when he appeared. He was arrested after a brief chase. The diaries were found in his room, and it was all over for the misfit who had planned to become a mass murderer.

Also hanged this day:

1716 at Tyburn Tree: John Springett for robbery.

1813 at York: George Mellor, William Thorp, and Thomas Smith,

26

for murder of Mr Attersfall during the Luddite riots.

1826 at Old Bailey: Mary Crane for murder.

1875 in the Canary Islands: three Spaniards for murdering a servant-girl as she tried to protect her master's house which they were robbing.

1879 at Pottsville, Pennsylvania, USA: Martin Bergen for the 'Molly Maguire' murder of Patrick Burns. (See 21 June.)

1880 at Galway County Gaol, Ireland: Martin M'Hugo for the murder of Michael Brehaney.

1884 at Kilmainham Prison, Ireland: Peter Wade for the murder of a man named Quinn.

1885 at Galway County Gaol, Ireland: Michael Downey for the murder of a man named Maylan.

1890 at Fort Smith, Oklahoma, USA: John Billee for murder.

17 January

1776 THE PERREAU TWINS
Daniel and Robert Perreau (twins) and five others hanged at Tyburn Tree.
Hangman: Edward Dennis. Assistant: William Brunskill

They were dissimilar twins, physically and morally. Daniel was a wastrel living by his wits with a mistress, Mrs Margaret Rudd, while Robert was a successful and respected surgeon with a wife and three children living in Golden Square, London.

Daniel duped his brother into taking a fake £7,500 bond, probably forged by Mrs Rudd, for cashing at a bank: its validity was questioned and the brothers and Mrs Rudd were arrested. Mrs Rudd was acquitted but the Perreau twins were convicted and condemned. Forgery was a capital crime which threatened the structure upon which the City of London financial institutions were based, and forgers rarely escaped the gallows. Even so, many people thought that Robert, having been tricked by his dissolute brother, should be reprieved and 78 bankers signed a petition with this hope in view, but King George III refused to show mercy.

Others were to die with the Perreau twins on this day: two men for coining, a highwayman, and two Jews for house-breaking. Watched by a crowd of thirty thousand, the Jews were hanged from one beam of the famous Tyburn Triple Tree while the five Christians were hanged side-by-side from another.

Also hanged this day:

1883 at Galway County Gaol, Ireland: Thomas Higgins (30) and Michael Flynn (26) for the murder of Lord Ardilann's bailiffs, Joseph and John Huddy (see 15 January). *Hangman: William Marwood*

18 January

1749 MURDEROUS SMUGGLERS
Smugglers Benjamin Tapner, John Cobby, John Hammond, William Carter, Richard Mills senior and Richard Mills junior hanged at Chichester for the murders of HM Customs Officer William Galley and informer Daniel Chater.

The notion that eighteenth century smugglers were jolly, lovable rogues belongs only in books of romantic fiction. They were among the most vicious and depraved of all criminals.

In September 1747 a small smuggling ship carrying a cargo of tea and brandy, under the command of Captain Richard Perrin, was intercepted by a government cutter close to the Sussex shore. Perrin and his cut-throats abandoned ship and escaped in a rowing boat. Their ship was towed to Poole harbour and its cargo was locked up in the Customs House. The contraband had belonged to the most feared of all smuggling gangs – that led by the ferocious Thomas Kingsmill. Furious at the loss, Kingsmill decided to raid the Customs House. The following night the 30-strong gang led by Kingsmill and his two subordinates, Captain Perrin and the brutal John Farrell* attacked the Customs House, smashing down the doors with axes, and got away with their loot on 50 pack horses. They fled through the night and stopped at dawn to share out the tea and brandy into 30 equal lots. Although such a large convoy must have been seen by many, fear of the ruthless brutality of the Kingsmill gang stilled all tongues.

The Poole Customs House outrage caused a national sensation, but many months passed before the authorities had a lead. Daniel Chater, a shoemaker, had seen the gang immediately after the raid and was willing to talk. He was sent with Customs Officer William Galley to make a deposition to Major Battine, the Justice of the Peace at Stanstead in Sussex.

Chater and Galley were intercepted by members of the gang near Havant, on the road to Stanstead. They were attacked at an inn, but saved by the landlord after which, amazingly, the gang apologised and then plied them with rum until the pair were insensible. Galley was searched and the gang found the letter he was carrying to Major Battine, which confirmed that Chater would be giving evidence. This

28

so enraged one of the brutes, William Jackson, that he put on spurs and jumped upon the sleeping pair and stamped the spurs into their foreheads and flailed at them with a horsewhip. They were taken outside and tied on to a horse and the raging William Jackson forced the rest of the gang to whip the wretched pair.

The gang set off across country, each member taking turns to whip their tied captives. Galley died and was quickly buried, near Scardefield. Chater was to suffer further beatings and was slashed across the eyes with a knife. Eventually he was taken to a dry well at Harris's Wood near Leigh and, with a noose round his neck, pushed off the edge. He hung there for 15 minutes without dying. They untied him and threw him headfirst down the 30-foot shaft. Even then he still lived, moaning horribly. To complete the nightmarish scene, the killers stood over the well and hurled down everything at hand: gateposts, railings, and huge stones which they could barely carry. When the ghastly moans stopped they departed.

The bodies were discovered with the aid of bloodhounds after an intensive search. William Jackson and his blood-thirsty comrades were rounded up and taken to Chichester where they were tried and found guilty. Jackson collapsed in prison and died that night, the others were hanged the next day. There was nothing 'jolly and lovable' in any of them.

* *Thomas Kingsmill, John Farrell and Captain Richard Perrin were caught later and hanged at Tyburn Tree on 26 April 1749.*

Also hanged this day:

1803 at Old Bailey: George Foster for drowning his wife and child in Paddington Canal. A weird 'galvanic' experiment was carried out on the body by a surgeon after execution. This caused muscle flutters and grimaces that so shocked Mr Pass, the Beadle of the Surgeons' Company, that he dropped dead with fright when he arrived home!

1878 at Bloomsburg, Pennsylvania, USA: at 10.27 a.m., 'Black Jack' Kehoe, the 'King of the Molly Maguires', in front of 150 spectators (see 21 June). *Hangman: Sheriff John W. Hoffman*

19 January

1866 'I LOVED TO SEE DEATH . . .'
Martha Grinder (51) hanged at Pittsburgh, Pennsylvania, USA for poisoning her neighbour, Mrs Carothers, for the joy of it.

Mrs Carothers was ill and Martha did the neighbourly thing and lovingly took care of her, at least, that is what the other neighbours were supposed to think. Sadistically, Martha mixed arsenic into her patient's food and watched her slowly die in agony – to her own joy and sense of accomplishment. Her sick enthusiasm astonished jurors as she told them:

> 'I loved to see death in all its forms and phases, and left no opportunity unimproved to gratify my tastes for such sights. Could I have had my own way, probably I should have done more.'

The hangman's rope prevented any further opportunities.

20 January

1813 THE MAD AXEMAN
John Schild hanged at Berks City, Pennsylvania, USA, for the deranged axe-murders of his parents.

Many killers have been described as 'the mad axeman', but there can have been few who suddenly went as berserk as John Schild. It was a hot summer day down on the family farm at Berks City on 12 August 1812 when something snapped in Schild's brain. He suddenly jumped up and accused his wife of poisoning his tea. Rushing out into the yard, he grabbed an axe and chased around after the chickens, wildly swinging in all directions and failing to hit any of them.

Roaring back into the house, he smashed the axe into his father's head and followed this by decapitating his mother. By now his wife had fled in terror so he attacked the furniture, chopping it all to bits, and set fire to the house. Axemen don't come any madder than that.

Also hanged this day:

1885   at Galway County Gaol, Ireland: Thomas Parry for the murder of Miss Burns, his sweetheart.

1886   at Cork County Gaol, Ireland: William Sheehan for the murder of Catherine Hannah Sheehan and Thomas Sheehan.

1905   at Charlottesville, Kentucky, USA: J. Samuel McCue for the clubbing- and shooting-murder of his wife, Fannie, at their 30-room mansion.

21 January

1670 'THE REMBRANDT OF HIGHWAYMEN'
Claude Duvall (27), legendary and chivalrous highwayman, hanged at Tyburn Tree.
Hangman: Jack Ketch

Claude Duvall was born and raised at Domfront in Normandy, France. The village of Domfront had a dubious reputation at that time: it was said that there were many baptisms in the local church but few burials, because its natives usually died on the gallows at Rouen! It was also a hotbed of Royalist exiles from the English Civil War.

When the English monarchy was restored in 1660 Claude Duvall moved to England as a page of the Duke of Richmond, but he did not stay in service for long. He took to the road and, for ten years, became the most famous highwayman of his day, described as 'The Rembrandt or Raphael of the profession'.

His gallant and chivalrous manners charmed the ladies, even those he robbed: his dancing of the *coranto* (a lively dance with a running, gliding step) with a pretty passenger during a robbery on Hounslow Heath added to his legend. He lived at a riotous pace, spending his ill-gotten funds lavishly. It was said of him at the time, 'Maids, widows, and wives, the rich, the poor, the noble, the vulgar, all submitted to the powerful Duvall.' He was arrested during a drunken party at The Hole In The Wall Inn in Chandos Street, less than a mile from Tyburn Tree, in 1670. His trial followed with its inevitable sentence.

His body was claimed by friends after the hanging and it was laid in state in a room draped in black at The Tangier Tavern in St Giles. The mourners included people of high social rank. The funeral service was conducted at St Paul's in Covent Garden and his epitaph read:

Old Tyburn's glory,
England's illustrious thief,
Duvall the Ladies' Joy,
Duvall the Ladies' Grief.

Also hanged this day:

1713 at Kingston, Surrey: Richard Noble for the murder of J. Sayer.

1829 at Old Bailey: Thomas Wheeler for highway robbery.

22 January

Hanged this day:

1802 at Old Bailey: Henry Cock for forgery.

23 January

1819 TEARS ON THE GALLOWS
James Munks publicly hanged at Bellefonte, Pennsylvania, USA, for the gun-murder of Reuben Guild.

No one knew why, but James Munks had a secret hatred of Reuben Guild. Munks was walking along Howard Township Road on a normal day in the small, peaceful town of Bellefonte when he saw Reuben Guild coming towards him. They had passed each other when, suddenly, Munks spun around with a pistol in his hand, took aim and shot Guild dead. He was arrested, tried, and condemned. Munks broke down in tears on the gallows, and was hanged while still weeping.

Also hanged this day:

1822 at Old Bailey: William Reeves and John Tye for issuing forged notes, Richard Jago for burglary, and Henry Thompson for forgery.

1824 at Old Bailey: Charles Johnson for murder.

1883 at Tralee County Gaol, Ireland: Sylvester Pof and James Barrett for the murder of Thomas Brown.

24 January

1767 AN IRISH HANGING
Patrick Redmond publicly hanged in Cork, Ireland, for street robbery.

After hanging for 28 minutes Redmond was cut down and the mob carried off his body to a surgeon who, by prior arrangement, was waiting to conduct an experiment in tracheotomy. An incision was made into the windpipe and he was brought back to life – one report says that it took place five or six hours after the hanging, highly unlikely. The same report claims that 'the man had the hardihood to go to the theatre the same evening'. He was subsequently pardoned.

Also hanged this day:

1814   at Execution Dock, Wapping: Martin Hogan.

1846   at Fulton Jail, New York, USA; Mrs Elizabeth Van Valkenburgh (47) for the arsenic-murders of her two husbands to stop their heavy drinking.

25 January

1825 THE 'TAME MOB'
Two Australian aborigines, Musquito a.k.a. the 'Black Napoleon', and Black Jack, hanged at Hobart, Van Diemen's Land (now Tasmania), for murder and bushranging.

Musquito was transported from Australia, to the penal colony in Van Diemen's Land after murdering his first wife. He was successfully used to track the famous bushranger 'Black Mike' Howe in 1818, but the promised reward of repatriation was unfulfilled and Musquito became bitter.

He was suspected of killing an overseer and later another wife, Black Hannah. He gathered a gang of other black outcasts and made himself leader and Black Jack second in command. They called themselves the 'Tame Mob' but were the very opposite, spreading terror across Van Diemen's Land with their rustling and raiding. By 1823 Musquito had killed yet another wife, Gooseberry, and was the leader of a 60-strong gang of murderous native outlaws. His leadership earned him the title of the 'Black Napoleon'.

Musquito, who had once famously tracked a notorious outlaw leader for the authorities, found himself and the Tame Mob being hunted by another aborigine convict tracker. Tegg was appointed by the new Governor of the Colony and he, too, succeeded in finding his man. Musquito and Black Jack stood on the gallows together and the Black Napoleon opined 'Hanging no good for black fellow. All right for white fellow, they used to it.'

Also hanged this day:

1738   at Execution Dock, Wapping: John Richardson and Richard Coyle for murder and piracy.

1797   at Glasgow: James M'Kean for murder. At Old Bailey: Maria Theresa Phipoe for cruelty resulting in the death of a servant.

26 January

1942 SPY'S SHORT CAREER
Franciscus Johannes Winter (40) hanged at Wandsworth Prison for war-time espionage*.
Hangman: Albert Pierrepoint

Winter was a former ship's steward from Antwerp who was captured as he landed in Britain, posing as a refugee, to spy on convoy movements.

* For the fate of other German spies see 4 January.

Also hanged this day:

1864   at Bannock, Montana, USA: Cy Skinner, saloon-keeper, robber and outlaw, an important member of Sheriff Plummer's 'Innocents' gang (see 10 January).

27 January

1928 'PROTECTOR' KNIFED BY OTHER 'PROTECTORS'
Cardiff gang-killing: Edward Rowlands (40) and Daniel Driscoll (34) hanged at Cardiff Gaol for the murder of Dai Lewis in a street fight.

Violent gangs plagued the race meetings of the 1920s, demanding protection money from bookmakers and small traders alike. The violence could spill out after meetings as well when personal grudges were settled among the underworld crooks.

Former professional welterweight boxer Dai Lewis was a small-time crook by September 1927, well known in the tough Tiger Bay area of Cardiff in South Wales. He acted alone when he demanded protection money from bookmakers at Monmouth Races, and thus invaded the territory of the vicious Rowlands brothers' gang.

Lewis was stabbed in a street fight when he was set upon by the Rowlands gang after closing time outside the Blue Anchor pub in St Mary's Street. Lewis died later in hospital, refusing to identify his attackers even though the Magistrate and his clerk, with the accused,

34

were at his bedside to take down his dying deposition.

Four men were tried for the murder: John Rowlands (30), Edward Rowlands (40), Joseph Price (42), and Daniel Driscoll (34). Price was acquitted and the others sentenced to death. John Rowlands, who may have been the one who actually struck the deathblow, was certified as insane and reprieved. The campaign for mercy was carried to the floor of the House of Commons and eight members of the 12-man trial jury signed a letter begging for the men to be reprieved, all without success.

Huge crowds waited outside Cardiff Gaol on the morning of the execution. Rowlands was shaking when the hangman arrived, but Driscoll was calm, even remarking with a grin that 'They've given us a nice day for it!' Rowlands had to be assisted to the scaffold, but Driscoll, calmly leading the way, looked up at the two nooses and asked 'Which is mine?'

Both men had protested their innocence to the end. They may have been innocent of the actual stabbing, but they were accomplices in the murderous gang-assault on a lone man in Cardiff's main street and knew that knives had been used. Driscoll maintained his composure to the end and his final words, with the rope round his neck, were 'Well, I'm going down for something I never done, but you don't have to pay twice.'

Also hanged this day:

1833 at Old Bailey: William Johnson for a murder at Enfield.

1854 at the Tombs Prison, New York, USA: James L. Hoare for the murder of Susan McAnnany by shooting her in the neck while kissing her.

1866 at Malden, Massachusetts, USA: Edward W. Green for the murder of bank employee Frank E. Converse during a $5,000 robbery – believed to be the USA's first bank-robbery.

1943 at Wandsworth Prison: Harry Dobkin (49) for the murder of his estranged wife, Rachel.

28 January

1953 'LET HIM HAVE IT, CHRIS!'
Derek Bentley (19) hanged at Wandsworth Prison for the murder of PC Sidney George Miles (42) who had been shot by Christopher Craig (16).
Hangman: Albert Pierrepoint

Chistopher Craig (16) and the mentally retarded Derek Bentley (19), and possibly a third youth*, attempted a break-in at a confectionery warehouse in Tamworth Road, Croydon, on the night of 2 November 1952. Christopher Craig, whose brother Niven Craig (26) had been sentenced to 12 years for armed robbery three days before, was armed with a revolver and a knife. Derek Bentley already had a criminal record and was carrying a knife and a brass knuckle-duster: although older than Craig he was illiterate and was said to have a mental age of 11.

The police were alerted and Craig and Bentley were chased across the flat roof, resulting in Bentley being grabbed by Detective Constable Frederick Fairfax. Craig produced his revolver and Bentley broke away from Fairfax and yelled 'Let him have it, Chris!' – a remark which may have cost him his life and which he later denied having made. Craig then shot Fairfax in the shoulder at close range, knocking him down. Fairfax rose and chased after Bentley, recapturing and disarming him. Bentley told Fairfax 'He's got a Colt .45 and plenty of bloody ammunition too.' Craig fired more shots, one of them hitting PC Sidney Miles between the eyes and killing him.

Craig's hatred of the police was at fever-point: 'Come on you brave coppers! Think of your wives!' he yelled. The unarmed policemen continued after him, throwing anything they could find: a truncheon, a milk bottle, a lump of wood. 'I'm Craig! You've just got my brother 12 years. Come on you coppers, I'm only 16!'

More policemen arrived, some of them armed. When they started closing in on Craig, and he realised that his gun was empty, he jumped from the roof and broke his spine as he hit the ground 30 feet below. 'I hope I've killed the fucking lot' he muttered before losing consciousness.

Craig and Bentley both pleaded not guilty at their trial at the Old Bailey just over a month later. Craig's defence was incredible, that he had not intended to kill any policemen but only frighten them. Bentley had a partly more plausible case, claiming that he was under arrest at the time of the killing, and that he did not know that Craig was armed (unlikely, in view of how they were both equipped and of what he had told Fairfax).

Bentley's exhortation to 'Let him have it, Chris!' could be interpreted two ways. The defence suggested it meant for Craig to hand the gun over to the police, the prosecution claimed it was an incitement to shoot. Bentley had just broken away from Fairfax' grip at the time, and Craig had replied by shooting the detective. Bentley then tried to escape with Craig, but was forcibly recaptured by the courageous Fairfax, and PC Miles was murdered while Bentley was being held on the roof.

The jury found them both guilty of the murder of PC Miles. They were accomplices and had both gone to the warehouse armed with offensive weapons, and their actions on the roof showed that they intended to resist arrest. They were equally guilty in law for a criminal act in which they were partners. Craig, the actual killer, was too young to be sentenced to death and was instead 'detained at Her Majesty's pleasure'. He was released on licence after ten years. Bentley was sentenced to death. A massive campaign was launched to save Bentley from the rope. Emotional arguments were used, and myths started, in the effort. Two hundred MPs joined in the campaign for a reprieve, but the Home Secretary refused to recommend it.

It was the fact that the guiltier Craig was to live, and the half-truth that Bentley was to be hanged 'for a crime he did not commit', that offended the public's sense of justice. Had both the young men been hanged for their shared crime it is unlikely that there would have been such a public furore, then or in the following decades.

An estimated five thousand people stood outside Wandsworth Prison while Bentley was hanged, some of them singing the hymn 'Abide With Me'. Bentley is said to have been crying when led to the scaffold, although this was later denied by Hangman Pierrepoint.

The campaign for a posthumous pardon has been carried on ever since by Bentley's family, and been taken up by the anti-hanging lobby. In 1991 a dramatically powerful film of the case *Let Him Have It* was released. On 16 August 1991, after MPs had seen a special screening of the film, the Home Secretary ordered Scotland Yard to reopen the case. The following month Christopher Craig appeared in a television programme claiming that there had been a police conspiracy at the trial and that Bentley had never said 'Let him have it, Chris!'

On 1 October 1992 Home Secretary Kenneth Clarke published the findings of his review. While agreeing that he would have recommended a reprieve he refused a posthumous royal pardon because 'I have concluded that nothing has emerged from my review of this case which establishes Derek Bentley's innocence'.

* *Barrister John Parris, who represented Craig at the trial, later revealed in his book* Most of My Murders *that a third youth was claiming that he had been at the warehouse with Craig and Bentley, but had got away. If true he could still be charged with murder, or for acting as an accessory, for which there is no statute of limitations.*

Also hanged this day:

1802 at Old Bailey: Governor Joseph Wall (65), 20 years after the flogging-murder of a soldier. *Hangman: William Brunskill*

1828 at Edinburgh: body snatcher William Burke publicly hanged before a huge crowd for murder. *Hangman: (possibly) Williams*

29 January

1913 THE CRUST OF BREAD
George Mackay a.k.a. John Williams (29) hanged at Lewes Prison, Sussex for the murder of Inspector Arthur Walls.
Hangman: John Ellis. Assistant: William Willis

George Mackay was the son of a Scottish clergyman who had been brought up in a decent home and given a good education, but who opted for a life of petty crime and had a criminal record.

His beautiful mistress, Florence Seymour, was expecting his child and he took her with him to Eastbourne early in October 1912. (He was then using the name John Williams.) They went along the beach on the evening of 9 October and Mackay left her there while he 'went for a walk'. When he returned it was without his felt hat, which he told her he had lost.

During the time that Mackay was supposedly enjoying a walk, a man had been seen crouching on the portico above the door of Countess Sztaray's house in South Cliffe Avenue. When her coachman told her of this, the Countess returned to the house and telephoned the police. Inspector Arthur Walls, who had been in the area, arrived a few minutes later. He saw the man still crouching in the shadows above the door and ordered him to come down: the man replied with two pistol shots, one of which hit Inspector Walls who died a short time afterwards. The gunman got away, but left his felt hat on the portico.

When the hatless Mackay returned to Florence on the beach he buried his gun there. Mackay borrowed some money from a man named Edgar Power and returned alone to London to go into hiding. Mackay wrote to his brother asking for more money and the brother allowed Edgar Power to see the letter. Power wanted Florence for himself and betrayed Mackay to the police as a way of getting rid of his rival.

Power tricked Florence into showing him where the revolver was hidden on the beach and passed the information on to the police: when Power and Florence arrived the police were waiting for them. Florence, terrified at being discovered by the police, confessed what had happened.

Edgar Power, still posing as a friend, was able to lure Mackay into a police trap at Moorgate underground station in London, where Mackay was arrested. Refusing to give his real name, he was charged under the name of John Williams with the murder of Inspector Walls.

Mackay, or Williams, was defended by Sir Patrick Hastings. There was little direct evidence against Williams to link him with the murder. The felt hat was of a common type which could have belonged to anyone and the revolver hidden on the beach was of the same type and calibre as the one that killed the inspector, but could not be identified as the one that fired the fatal shot. It was probably his proximity at the time of the crime, and his actions after it, that convinced the jury of his guilt – but a man should not be hanged on such circumstantial evidence. Modern forensic techniques could positively establish the facts from both the gun and the felt hat, and conclusively prove Mackay's guilt – or innocence.

Sir Patrick Hastings told of a touching scene in the condemned cell on the day before Mackay's execution. He was visited by Florence with their baby and Mackay put a piece of prison bread in the boy's hand and said 'Now no one can say your father never gave you anything.'

Also hanged this day:

1812 at Old Bailey: F. Phillips, J. Frazier, W. Haberfield, P. Whitehead, E. Hall, and W. Higgins.

30 January

1606 THE GUNPOWDER PLOT
The first of the Gunpowder Plot conspirators executed: Sir Everard Digby (28), Grant, Thomas Bates, and Robert Winter hanged, drawn, and quartered in St Paul's Churchyard, London.
Hangman: (probably) Derrick. Assistant: (probably) Gregory Brandon

King James I's continued persecution of the Catholics drove Robert Catesby and others to plot to blow up the king, his family, and his government at the ceremony of the Opening of Parliament on 5 November 1605. It was a desperate attempt to bring about an uprising that would restore the Catholic religion. The plot was discovered when a mysterious letter reached Lord Monteagle warning him not to attend the ceremony. Learning of the letter, the king ordered a search of Parliament: Guy Fawkes was discovered hidden in the cellar with 36 barrels of gunpowder which were ready to be fired.

Guy Fawkes was tortured into revealing the names of the conspirators: some, including Catesby, were killed when Holbeach House was raided, while others were captured and tortured on the rack. They were tried at Westminster Hall and condemned to be hanged, drawn and quartered.

Sir Everard Digby is reported to have displayed remarkable fortitude.

After being hanged until almost dead he was cut down and the grisly next phase was begun. Tearing out the heart, Hangman Derrick cried out the traditional 'Behold the heart of a traitor': an eye-witness claimed that Digby cried back 'Thou liest!'

Also hanged this day:

1852 at Pittsburgh, Pennsylvania, USA: Pamela Lee Worms for the arsenic-murders of her husband and daughter.

1942 A. Peach for the murder of Kitty Lyon at Walsall.

31 January

1606 'REMEMBER, REMEMBER! THE 5TH OF NOVEMBER. GUNPOWDER, TREASON AND PLOT!'*
Guy Fawkes (36), Ambrose Rookwood, Thomas Winter, and Robert Keyes, the remaining conspirators in the Gunpowder Plot, hanged, drawn and quartered in Old Palace Yard in front of the Houses of Parliament.
Hangman: (probably) Derrick. Assistant: (probably) Gregory Brandon

After his dramatic capture with the barrels of gunpowder under Parliament, Guy Fawkes first gave his name as Johnson. He was questioned throughout the night and one of his interrogators was the king himself, who ordered torture.

Guy Fawkes suffered a cruel series of tortures in the dungeons of the Tower of London, including the rack. He was also enclosed in a tiny cell where it was impossible to sit or to stand upright. In his agony he revealed his own identity and those of the conspirators. With a weak, trembling hand he signed the confession that can still be seen in the Public Records Office.

On the day of their execution Fawkes, Ambrose Rookwood, Thomas Winter, and Robert Keyes, were dragged over the cobble-stones on hurdles, with their heads to the rear, the lowest end, to Old Palace Yard. There they were hanged until half dead; then cut down, laid on a trestle, stripped naked, and butchered.

After execution their heads were placed on poles on London Bridge and the quartered bodies hung at the gates to London.

* *The British still remember the 5th of November and Guy Fawkes is burned in effigy at the top of bonfires across the land. This has led to the mistaken belief that Fawkes was burned at the stake; what we are remembering and re-enacting*

is his attempt to blow up Parliament with fire and gunpowder.

Also hanged this day:

1816   at Execution Dock, Wapping: John Gillman and John Brookman for murder on the high seas.

1821   at Old Bailey: Joseph Martin, John Davis, George Johnson, and John Reeves for highway robbery, and Henry Torbin for extortion.

1882   at Devizes Prison: Charles Gerrish for the murder of fellow pauper Stephen Coleman.

FEBRUARY

1 February

1827 HANGED PIRATES GALVANISED
Sylvester Colson (real name Winslow Curtis) hanged at Boston, Massachusetts, USA, for piracy and the murders of Captain Edward Selfridge (23) and the mate Thomas Paine Jenkins on the schooner _Fairy_.

Sylvester Colson and Charles Marchant were a pair of evil rogues. Colson's real name was Winslow Curtis. He was an American with a violent criminal record. Marchant was also using an alias, to hide his true background as a British sailor turned pirate named John Duncan White. This rough pair signed on as crewmen on the _Fairy_, under Captain Edward Selfridge who desperately needed extra hands before setting sail. The _Fairy_ sailed out of Boston on 20 August 1826 bound for Gottenburg, Germany, with a cargo of coffee, fustic timber, rice, sugar, and tobacco. Thomas Paine Jenkins was mate and the remainder of the crew were John Hughes and John Murray.

Colson and Marchant were surly and idle from the start and had to be closely supervised by the captain and the mate while on watch. During the early hours of 25 August Captain Selfridge and Jenkins were killed and thrown overboard. Colson was the probable killer of the captain while Marchant killed Jenkins. Hughes and Murray were spared, probably because they were needed until land was reached. When Hughes asked why they had killed the officers Marchant muttered 'No cause at all' and then, as an afterthought 'I am sorry now that I did it.' An infuriated Colson snarled 'Sorry! For killing them two fellows? I would kill them two rascals as I would a dog!' Hughes and Murray went in fear of their lives.

By the night of 29 August they were in sight of Louisburg, Nova Scotia, when the killers decided to scuttle the _Fairy_ and make for the shore in the lifeboat. First they plundered the ship for valuables, which they packed in wooden chests and loaded into the boat thereby completing the act of piracy.

Remarkably, for such a callous pair, they did not kill Hughes and Murray, but allowed them to come ashore in the boat: it was a mistake which cost them their lives. Murray got away and joined another schooner, the _Sally_, and immediately reported what had happened to his new captain. Colson and Marchant were captured by the Canadian police and handed over to the authorities in Boston. They were found guilty in December and both sentenced to death. Marchant's first reaction was to burst into tears and scream that he was innocent. Colson raged at everyone in the court with foul and angry curses. The guards had to man-handle the violently struggling killers from the courtroom, with Colson yelling 'Damn you, damn all of you!' Marchant hanged himself in his cell the day before the execution, using knotted strips from his blanket. Colson died on the gallows as arranged, telling the small crowd 'God forgive me, we did it.'

Dr John White Webster (then 33) performed bizarre medical experiments on the dead bodies of Colson and Marchant at Harvard Medical School in front of goggle-eyed students. He inserted pins and wires all over the bodies and, for an hour, carried out galvanic experiments touching different pins with positive and negative leads from a primary battery. The direct-current contacts induced muscular reactions from the bodies, to the horrified astonishment of the watchers. The *Columbian Centinel* (3 February 1827) described the reactions to Colson's body:

'The first experiment was made by introducing a negative wire into the mouth, and a postive wire into the urethra, and convulsive motions ensued. Applied to the eye the organ opened, and rolled wildly and the face distorted. . .' (The report continued with examples of more galvanic responses: arm-raising, fist-clenching, the mouth snapping open and shut, kicking, chest-heaving, toe movements, etc.)

Dr Webster was himself hanged, in 1850, for the murder of financier Dr George Parkman, to whom he owed money. (See 30 August.)

Also hanged this day:

1693   at Porters Block, Smithfield Market, London: James Whitney for highway robbery.

1725   at Tyburn Tree: Thomas Parker and Joshua Picken for highway robbery.

1820   at Old Bailey: John Pater for the murder of his brother.

1885   at Derby Gaol: George Horton, a coal miner, for poisoning his young daughter at Swanwick for the £7 life insurance.

1886   at Devizes Prison: John Horton for the murders of his father and his lover.

1887   in the USA: Hugh Brooker for the murder of Mr Maxwell, a friend.

1929   at Louisiana, USA: Dr Tom Dreher (52) and his mistress, Ada Le Boeuf, for the murder of her husband Jim Le Boeuf.

1935   at Parish Prison, New Orleans, USA: Kenneth Neu (25) for murdering and robbing two men during homosexual encounters. Neu's neck snapped with the drop, but his heart continued beating for a reported 20 minutes. *Hangman: Henry Meyer*

2 February

1785 20 HANGED AT OLD BAILEY
The hangings began at 8.50 a.m. in front of an immense crowd. The eldest convict was aged under 30.
Hangman: Edward Dennis. Assistant: William Brunskill

The condemned men and their crimes were as follows: John Evans, stealing printed books from a dwelling house. James Dunn, publishing a forged will. James Hamilton, stealing from a dwelling house. William Attel, stealing leathers/sealskin from a warehouse. William Stewart, stealing silver and a pair of pistols from a dwelling house. William Abbott, forgery. Thomas Tabbs, John Moody, George Harris, Thomas Buttledore, John Shaw, and Allen Williams, highway assault and robbery. Richard Hobson, John Jones, George Goldsmith, Lawrence Hall, William Finder, John Kelsey, Melvyn Simmonds, and Edward Johnson, burglary.

This was the greatest number hanged at one time since 1740 when Jenny Diver and 20 others were executed at Tyburn Tree.

3 February

1903 HOLLOWAY'S FIRST HANGINGS
'Baby farmers' Annie Walters and Amelia Sach became the first to be hanged at Holloway Prison, London.
Hangman: William Billington. Assistant: Henry Pierrepoint

'Baby farmers' were a common feature of Victorian times and the early part of this century. Unscrupulous women were paid a fee to take away 'unwanted' babies – usually those born to servant-girls and other unmarried women who were unable to look after them themselves – promising to place them in good homes. The worst of these women would take the money and, afterwards, kill the children (see 10 June).

Amelia Sach was the younger of this pair and it was she who negotiated with the unfortunate mothers and then passed the children to Walters who killed and disposed of them.

Holloway had only recently become exclusively a prison for women, and Walters and Sach were the first to be executed there. One of them had to be more or less carried to the scaffold, such was her state of near collapse, and held upright on the trap door by Pierrepoint.

Also hanged this day:

1724   at Tyburn Tree: Stephen Gardner, for house-breaking.

1832   at New York, USA: Guy C. Clark for wife-murder. Because Clark was dawdling on the way to the gallows the Sheriff told him to hurry up; Clark replied 'Nothing will happen until I get there!'

1860   at New York, USA: James Stephens for wife-murder.

1948   at Cardiff Gaol, Wales: Hadyn Evan Evans (22) hanged at Cardiff for the murder by kicking of washerwoman Rachel Allan (76).

1991   in Jordan: two Royal Jordanian Air Force officers for high treason during the Gulf War.

4 February

1921 THE CRUMBLES MURDER
Jack Alfred Field (19) and William Thomas Gray (29) hanged at Wandsworth Prison, for the brutal murder of Irene Munro (17) at the Crumbles near Eastbourne.
Hangman: Tom Pierrepoint

The Crumbles is a desolate two-mile stretch of shingle beach between Eastbourne and Pevensey Bay, almost a mile wide in places. It is a melancholy place, with an evil reputation locally, which prompted Sir Edward Marshall Hall to ask a witness if the Crumbles was not a place where unpleasant things were expected to happen?

The brutal murder of holiday-maker Irene Munro (17) on Thursday 19 August 1920 caused the whole nation to shudder at the mention of the Crumbles. Nearly four years later it was the scene of an even more sensational and ghastly murder (see 9 September).

Irene Munro was a Scot, working as a typist in London, who had come on her own for a holiday in Eastbourne. Jack Field and Bill Gray, both ex-servicemen, were unemployed and living off the dole and petty crime. At midday on Thursday 19 August they were in the Albemarle pub, broke and asking for drinks on the slate. By the evening they were back there, spending freely and 'fairly throwing it about' according to the barmaid.

During the hours in-between they had met Irene Munro and

arranged to take her on an afternoon walk. The walk was on to the Crumbles.

Her body was discovered the following morning when a small boy saw the toe of her shoe sticking up from the shingle; she had been buried hastily, in a shallow grave. The boy ran off screaming and the police were called.

Irene Munro had been battered to death with a walking stick and then with a large rock dropped on to the left side of her head as she lay on the shingle. She was fully clothed and the only item missing was her handbag containing a fortnight's holiday money.

Witnesses came forward who had seen the young girl in her bright green coat accompanied by two men on the afternoon of her death. The men were soon identified as Field and Gray.

They were tried at Lewes and Gray was represented by the great defender, Sir Edward Marshall Hall. However, the mass of evidence against the pair was overwhelming and the case for the defence was hopeless. It became more hopeless after Gray tried to persuade a fellow prisoner to give him a false alibi, and even worse when another prisoner revealed that Gray had described how the girl had died when the rock was dropped on her head. Gray and Field were found guilty and sentenced to death.

The hearing of the Court of Appeal was fought on evidence that had not been heard at the Lewes trial: Jack Field and Bill Gray each accused the other of carrying out the murder. The judges were not convinced by either of the callous killers. Even Marshall Hall, who usually believed passionately in the innocence of his clients, privately remarked to a friend that he hoped they would both hang. They did.

Also hanged this day:

1816 at Philadelphia, Pennsylvania, USA: Lieutenant Richard Smith, US army, for the murder of Captain John Carson, 'his wife Ann's real husband'. Ann failed in an attempt to kidnap the State Governor, Simon Snyder, to demand Smith's release. Ann later led a gang of counterfeiters until they were caught and given long prison sentences in 1823.

1878 at Strangeways Prison, Manchester: George Piggott, for the murder of Frances Gallaway.

1879 at Maidstone Prison: Stephen Gambrill (28), for the murder of a young farmer, Arthur Gillow, who caught him breaking steam machines. *Hangman: William Marwood*

1896 at Wandsworth Prison: William James Morgan, for wife-murder.

1937 at Strangeways Prison, Manchester: Max Mayer Haslam (23) for the murder of Ruth Clarkson (74) during a robbery. It was known as the Crippled-Dwarf Case (Haslam was only four-foot-seven-inches tall.)

5 February

1889 THE JOHN LEE THEY *COULD* HANG!
John Lee hanged at Alexandria, Minnesota, USA, for the gun-murder of Charles Cheline.

John Lee yearned for local girl Sophie Mathieson, but he had a rival: Charles Cheline. Lee had spent the evening of 19 July 1888 drinking with his friend Martin Moe in a saloon in Brandon and, as they emerged into the fresh air, who should they see walking by but Charles Cheline. At the enthusiastic suggestion of Martin Moe, Lee took out a pistol and shot Cheline through the head.

Lee and Moe were arrested and charged with murder. They were both found guilty and sentenced to be publicly hanged on 5 February 1889. As they started their final walk from the jail to the gallows, Martin Moe was told that he had been reprieved.

John Lee continued his walk to the scaffold and, unlike his famous namesake in England four years earlier (see 23 February), they could – and did – hang him.

Also hanged this day:

1842   at Dublin: J. Delahunt for the murder of T. Maguire.

6 February

1952 PC's DEATHBED EVIDENCE
Alfred Moore (36) hanged at Armley Gaol, Leeds, for the murders of Detective Inspector Duncan Fraser and PC Arthur Jagger.

In the darkness before midnight on 14 July 1951, policemen surrounded the house at Whinney Close Farm, Kirkheaton, near Huddersfield in Yorkshire. They had long suspected that the poultry farmer, Alfred Moore, supplemented his low income by burglary and had reason to believe he was out 'on a job'. The trap to catch him in possession of stolen goods was set. Midnight passed and the silent policemen stayed hidden, watching and waiting.

At 2 a.m. five pistol shots shattered the silence. Alfred Moore had been returning home and was surprised by PC Arthur Jagger, who attempted to arrest him, but Moore dived through a hedge. The farmer-burglar then pulled a gun from his coat and shot the constable, who fell to the ground unable to move. As Detective Inspector Duncan Fraser approached him, Moore fired three shots into him. Jagger and Fraser were rushed to hospital but Fraser died on the way.

Moore had escaped into the house. When armed police reinforcements arrived he gave himself up and claimed that he had been in bed since midnight. In the search of the house and farmyard a pair of wet shoes was found, as well as ammunition, sets of burglar's keys, stolen gold and silver items, and partly burnt stamps and dollars lay in the fireplace.

PC Jagger was in hospital, badly injured and not expected to survive, but he wasn't dead yet! He was conscious and able to make a statement describing the shootings and who was responsible. An identity parade was held at his hospital bedside later in the day, and he picked out Moore as the man who had shot him and the Inspector. Next, a special magistrate's court was convened and PC Jagger gave evidence from his deathbed. This courageous constable died the following day. Moore was charged with both murders at Leeds Assizes at the end of 1951 and the jury took less than an hour to pronounce him guilty.

Also hanged this day:

1934   at Armley Gaol, Leeds: Ernest Brown (35) for the shotgun murder of his employer, cattle dealer Frederick Morton. *Hangman: Tom Pierrepoint*

1948   at Perth Prison, Scotland: Stanislaw Miszka (23) for the murder of Catherine McIntyre (47).

7 February

1894 WILL PURVIS WAS INNOCENT
Bungled hanging of Will Purvis (21) at Columbia in Marion County, Mississippi, USA, for the Ku Klux Klan murder of his negro neighbour, Will Buckley, at Devil's Bend.
Hangman: Sheriff Irving Otho Magee. Assistants: three Deputies

Will Purvis was charged with being a member of a branch of the Ku Klux Klan called the White Caps and of murdering his negro neighbour Will Buckley. The murder had been carried out the previous year after brothers Will and Jim Buckley and their hired farm hand Sam Waller had given information to the authorities about the White Caps. Purvis claimed that he *had* been a White Caps member, but had taken no part in the crime. He also said that he had left because he was disgusted by the murder. Nonetheless he was found guilty and sentenced to hang, with the full approval of State Governor John Stone.

From the gallows he again declared his innocence, adding that there were some in the crowd who knew it. His arms and legs were bound and a black hood placed over his face. The Reverend J. Sibley, a family friend, led the praying. The sheriff operated the trap door by using an axe to cut the rope that held it in place. As Will Purvis fell the noose-knot came undone and slipped from his neck; he crashed to the ground and was stunned. Still bound, he was made to hop up the steps back to the gallows. While Dr Ford was looking at the rope-end under the scaffold, the sheriff asked him to 'Toss the rope up here, will you Doc?' Dr Ford refused: 'I won't do any such damn thing, that boy's been hung once too many times already!'

Reverend J. Sibley climbed on to the scaffold and addressed the silent crowd: 'All who want to see this boy hanged a second time hold up their hands.' None did, and Will Purvis was returned to his cell. But the surprises did not end there.

Sheriff Magee joined others who doubted Purvis' guilt and pleaded for his release. Governor Stone refused to let him go and ordered a new execution. There were a number of unsuccessful appeals and a new execution was eventually fixed for 12 December 1895, but his friends helped him escape from jail and he remained free for over a year.

After a new state governor took over Purvis gave himself up, in February 1897, and his sentence was changed to life imprisonment. After a popular campaign, he was pardoned by the end of 1898. He went back to farming, married and had 11 children. Then in 1917, 24 years after the crime, a 60-year-old farmer named Joe Beard made a death-bed confession admitting that he and a man named Louis Thornhill had killed Buckley. Will Purvis was voted $5,000 compensation by the State. He lived until 1938 to die a natural death at the age of 66 – still with the rope burn marks on his neck.

Also hanged this day:

1940 at Winsom Green Prison, Birmingham: Peter Barnes (32) and James Richards (29) for the IRA time-bomb murder of Elsie Ansell (21).

8 February

1886 NETHERBY HALL KILLERS MET HANGMAN – TWICE
Antony Benjamin Rudge, John Martin and James Baker hanged at
Carlisle Prison, Cumberland, for the murder of PC Byrnes.
Hangman: James Berry. Assistant: 'Charles Maldon'

Rudge, Martin, and Baker were three common criminals. After a
robbery at Netherby Hall, ten miles north of Carlisle and near the
border with Scotland, they shot four policemen, three of whom died.
The gang was charged with only one of the murders but, because
killers of policemen were hardly ever reprieved, it was enough to
ensure that all three of them met the Hangman. They each walked
firmly to the gallows and, arriving there, greeted each other with
handshakes and exchanges of 'Good bye, old pal, good bye.' They
died side-by-side without fear: Baker on the left, Martin in the centre,
and Rudge on the right. It was not the first time that this trio of
ruffians had met Hangman Berry.

By a remarkable turn of fate Berry had shared a train compartment
with Rudge, Martin and Baker in 1884. They had suspected that he
was the public Hangman, but Berry remained reticent about who he
was. The three men joked about which of them would be the first to
face him officially. It has not been recorded whether they made any
jokes the second time!

The assistant hangman Charles Maldon was later discovered to be
Sir Claude de Crespigny, Bart., of Maldon in Essex. He was a
magistrate who expected to be county sheriff one day. He had
suggested to Hangman Berry that he should go through the experience
of hanging a man before nominating others to do it; he also offered
Berry £10. Questions were asked in Parliament, to which the Home
Secretary replied that a baronet was as entitled as anyone else to be a
hangman's assistant provided he carried out his duties properly (which
Sir Claude evidently had).

Also hanged this day:

1720 at Tyburn Tree: William Spiggot and Thomas Phillips for
highway robbery, after suffering *peine forte et dure* (pressing with
weights) at Newgate.

1804 at Greenville, Mississippi, USA: Wiley 'Little' Harpe (34) and
Sam Mays for multiple murders and robberies; their heads were
displayed on poles as a warning to other highwaymen. Little Harpe
was the brother of William 'Big' Harpe, leader of the so-called
Terrible Harpes gang.

1808 at Carlisle, Pennsylvania, USA: Edward Donnelly for the murder, dismemberment and burning of his wife Catherine.

1858 at Old Bailey: Christian Sattler, a German, for the murder of Inspector Thain.

9 February

1961 IS THE REAL KILLER STILL IN SHREWSBURY?
George Riley (21) hanged at Shrewsbury Prison for the murder of
Adeline Mary Smith (62).
Hangman: Harry Allen

George Riley, butcher's assistant and son of a local schoolteacher, lived in Westland Road in Shrewsbury. He was a big, strong lad, but local people considered him to be the sort who used his strength to be a peacemaker rather than a troublemaker.

After 62-year-old widow Adeline Mary Smith, also of Westland Road, was savagely battered to death in her bedroom, the police questioned young Riley. Smith's bedroom had been splattered with blood, but no trace of any of it was found on Riley's person or clothing; however, he confessed under questioning. His confession, which he later retracted, was the only evidence against him at his trial at Stafford Assizes. He pleaded not guilty and was asked whether he had thought he had committed the murder when he had made the confession. Riley made the astonishing reply: 'I could not be sure myself, but the police seemed sure I had and I believed them at the time.'

He was found guilty and despite an appeal, a two thousand-signature petition, and questions to the Home Secretary in Parliament, there was to be no reprieve. The case against him relied solely on his own retracted confession. He protested his innocence to the end. His case is still talked about in Shrewsbury pubs, some claiming that they know who did it, but aren't saying.

Also hanged this day:

1830 at Old Bailey: James Butler for burglary.

1897 at Maidstone Prison: Robert Hayman for the murder of Esther Allchin.

1946 at Barlinnie Prison, Glasgow: John Lyon (21) for the bayonet-murder of John Smyth in a gang fight. Three others sentenced to death with him were reprieved. *Hangman: Albert Pierrepoint*

10 February

1750   at Tyburn Tree: Richard Butler for forgery.

1879   at Worcester Prison: Enoch Whiston for the murder of Alfred Meredith.

1886   at Norwich Castle: John Thurston for the murder of Henry Springall during a robbery.

1943   Ronald Roberts for the murder of Mrs Nellie Pearson.

1956   at Quebec City Prison, Canada: Wilbert Coffin (43) for the murder of three Americans on a hunting trip in 1953: Eugene Lindsay, his son Richard, and Frederick Klaar.

1959   Ernest R. Jones (39) for the murder of a storekeeper during robbery, £75 in this case, making it a capital crime under the 1957 Homicide Act.

11 February

1869   CANADA'S FIRST ASSASSINATION – AND LAST PUBLIC HANGING
James Whelan publicly hanged in Ottawa, Canada, for the assassination of the Hon. Thomas D'Arcy McGee MP (43).

There is a plaque in Sparks Street, Ottawa, which records the murder nearby of D'Arcy McGee MP. The killing was a Canadian sensation at the time as it was the first murder since Canada achieved Dominion status and became self-governing, and its first murder victim was one of the founding Members of Parliament.

McGee, born in Ireland, had been a fierce advocate of the Fenian Brotherhood who sought an Irish revolutionary uprising. He had to flee his homeland in 1857 and settled in Canada, where he was elected to the Legislative Assembly the following year. By this time he had broken his ties with the Fenians, considering them too violent for the good of their own cause, and became their opponent. Fenians called him a traitor.

James Whelan, an Irish tailor in Montreal, visited D'Arcy McGee's home and warned him that the Fenians were plotting to set fire to the house. The police were informed and the house was watched, but no attempt was made and it was later considered to be a hoax.

Whelan moved to Ottowa in 1867 and carried on his trade there. In the early hours of 7 April 1868 he was in the public seats at a late night sitting of the Canadian House of Commons, listening to McGee making a speech. He left before McGee and hid by the gateway to the Toronto House at 71 Sparks Street, where McGee boarded.

D'Arcy McGee left the House of Commons at a short time after 2 a.m., walked home, passed the hidden Whelan by the gate and reached the front door. There was a third man in Sparks Street, only 15 yards away, a man named Jean Baptiste Lacroix who was on his way home. In the moonlight Lacroix saw McGee stooping to put the key in the door when another man crept up behind him and fired a single shot into his neck. D'Arcy McGee fell to the ground and died instantly. Lacroix stepped into the shadows and kept quiet. The gunman walked quickly away, passing close to the spot where Lacroix was standing and from where Lacroix saw the killer clearly enough to identify him later as James Whelan.

He was tried in September amid massive newspaper coverage. The Prime Minister attended as a spectator throughout the seven-day trial. Canada's most famous lawyer, John Hillyard Cameron, vigorously defended Whelan, but the evidence against his client was too much even for him: the murder weapon was found in Whelan's pocket when arrested; witnesses testified to having heard him threaten to kill McGee, and there was an eye-witness to the crime – Lacroix. Whelan's dying words on the gallows were 'God save Ireland and God save my soul.' It was to be Canada's last public execution.

Also hanged this day:

1750   at Tyburn Tree: William Parsons, Esq., Old Etonian and son of a baronet, for highway robbery and returning from transportation. *Hangman: John Thrift*

1853   at the Tombs Prison, New York, USA: Joseph Clark for beating to death George T. Gillespie because he would not lend him $1.

1878   at Winchester Prison: James Caffyn for the murder of Maria Barber.

1879   at Lancaster Castle: William M'Guiness for wife-murder.

1887   Thomas Bloxham for wife-murder.

1941   at Strangeways Prison, Manchester: Clifford Holmes for wife-murder.

12 February

1942 SKETCH-PLAN FOR MURDER
RCAF airman William Newell (27) hanged at Don Jail, Toronto, Canada, for the murder of his second wife.

William Newell was a good-looking and muscular airman in the Royal Canadian Air Force. Because he had matrimonial problems he was posted to St Thomas, Ontario, from where he could get home to Toronto more easily.

He had married Winnifred when he was 20 and they had a daughter, but they later divorced. His second wife was Aune, a Finnish-Canadian who had presented him with a son even before his first divorce was finalised. It was not long before he and Aune separated and he went to live with another Finnish-Canadian, Elna Lehto.

The big problem was who was to receive the generous RCAF dependents' allowances? Winnifred and her daughter were entitled to support as was his legal wife, Aune, and her son. His current common-law wife, Elna Lehto, would be entitled only if Aune signed away her rights or agreed to a divorce, but Aune would not agree to this.

Newell was in the habit of using YMCA envoloves with the RCAF crest and, in a letter inside one of them, he had mentioned to Elna Lehto that if Aune were murdered it would solve all their problems.

In September 1940 as the Battle of Britain was being fought in the skies over the mother country, things were more quiet in Canada and William Newell was able to go on leave to Toronto. He spent most of the leave with Aune before luring her to a lonely and overgrown spot near St Andrew's Cut, a lagoon on Centre Island, and there he strangled her with a piece of rope he had brought with him. Then a couple came by in a canoe. Newell saw them before they noticed him. He balanced Aune in a sitting position and the canoeing couple saw Newell in his uniform apparently fishing, but thought it odd that the woman with him should be sitting in so rigid a position and taking no notice of anything.

The body was discovered a week later and William Newell was soon in police custody. His letters to Aune in which he tried to persuade her to give up her rights to his allowances, and the letter to Elna Lehto suggesting murder, provided strong evidence of motive. The rope found at the scene of the strangling was matched with some found at the home he shared with Elna Lehto. Witnesses came forward who had seen him with Aune on the day she died, including the couple in the canoe. All this was not enough for the juries at his first two trials and they failed to agree on a verdict.

The third trial was different, with a scrap of new evidence that sent him to the gallows. A torn envelope had been found at the murder spot: a YMCA envelope with the RCAF crest. Roughly drawn on it was a sketch map of that isolated part of Centre Island, with written notes that were proved to be in William Newell's handwriting. On the last morning of his life he ate a substantial fried breakfast, refused a drug to dull his senses, and walked firmly to the scaffold.

Also hanged this day:

1878   at Kirkdale Prison, Liverpool: James Trickett for wife-murder.

1883   at Strangeways Prison, Manchester: Thomas Abraham for the murder of Christina Leigh.

13 February

1814 THE HUMAN YO-YO
Madman John Ashton hanged at Old Bailey for highway robbery –
twice.

One of five to be hanged, he ran up the ladder and jumped up and down chanting 'I'm Lord Wellington! Look at me, I'm Lord Wellington!'

After the trap fell Ashton bounced back on to the platform: unhurt, he started dancing again and yelling 'What do you think of me now? Am I not Lord Wellington now?' After a struggle he was hanged again, and died.

He may have been the one who, according to gallows' folklore, asked the hangman 'What do you think I am, a yo-yo?'

Also hanged this day:

1818   at Woodstock Green, Vermont, USA: Sammel E. Godfrey for the murder of Warden Thomas Hewlet at Vermont State Prison.

1821   at Old Bailey: Henry Bullock, James Wootton, and Thomas Elliott for highway robbery.

1832   at Old Bailey: John Barratt for letter-stealing.

1844   at Darlinghurst Hill, Sydney, Australia: John Knatchbull (55) for the tomahawk-murder of Ellen Jamieson. The Knatchbulls were (and still are) a distinguished Kentish family and John was a younger son of Sir Edward Knatchbull, Eighth Baronet. He served in the Royal Navy and reached captain's rank, but was discharged because of debts.

He was convicted for picking pockets and was transported to Australia in 1824 and degenerated further until his bloody murder of a widow. Ten thousand watched his execution.

1878   at Nottingham: John Brooks for the murder of Caroline Woodhead.

1882   at Strangeways Prison, Manchester: Robert Templeton for the murder of Betty Scott.

1894   at Carmarthen Prison, Wales: George Thomas for the murder of Mary Jane Jones.

1906   at St Paul, Minnesota, USA: homosexual drifter William A. Williams (27) for the gun-murders of Mrs John Keller and her son Johnny (16) after Mrs Keller had tried to break up his relationship with her son. He was the last man to be executed in Minnesota.

14 February

1845 NO LICENCE FOR THE IRISH BROTHERS
Irish immigrant John Gordon publicly hanged at Providence, Rhode Island, USA, for the murder of Amasa Sprague.

John Gordon and his brother William had left Ireland to start a new life in America and eventually arrived in Providence. They had planned to open a saloon and applied for a licence, but their bid was blocked by Amasa Sprague.

Sprague was a prominent citizen and a man of influence in Rhode Island affairs, for which his brother was a US Senator. This example of high-handed rejection was not what the Gordon brothers had expected in the land of opportunity, and their Irish blood was inflamed. They waylaid Sprague on a lonely road and set upon him, beating him to death.

This was not the kind of opportunity that America was offering, and the brothers were both charged with the murder and found guilty, although only John faced the hangman.

Also hanged this day:

1732   at Tyburn Tree: Robert Hallam for murder.

15 February

1919 THE DEADLY FEAR OF 'AMMUNITION' EDDIE
'Ammunition' Eddie Wheed, a gangster who had a life-long fear of
dying on the gallows, hanged at Chicago, Illinois, USA, for murder.

Ammunition Eddie Wheed was the tough and ruthless boss of a gang
of armed robbers in Chicago in the days before its gangsters became
world famous in the Prohibition era.

During a robbery he would allow no one to get in his way and, in his
criminal career, shot and killed a total of six men, injuring many more.
He was apparently fearless, but he had one life-long dread: that he
would die on the gallows. The mere mention of hanging would cause
his face to pale, and he would abruptly change the subject. He would
kneel in prayer before a crucifix and pray to God not to let him die by
hanging. Then he would take his gang out on a payroll robbery, armed
with sawn-off shotguns and revolvers.

It was in 1917 that he became known as Ammunition. The police
learned that a gang had a hide-out somewhere on the West Side of
Chicago, which had been fitted out as a stronghold with a massive
arsenal of guns and ammunition. They did not know the identity of the
gang leader, but called him Ammunition.

The gang's last robbery was on a payroll delivery from a Brinks
Express van to a warehouse on West Harrison Street. They got away
with $8,722, but had killed two Brinks' guards with shotgun blasts. The
haul was shared out and they separated, deciding to lie low for a while.

Ammunition Eddie Wheed took refuge at his mother's house,
where he had filled a small room with rifles, shotguns, pistols and an
enormous hoard of bullets and cartridges. He was there on his own
when the police arrived, and he started shooting right away.

The siege led to a furious exchange. There were 250 armed
policemen outside from every station in Chicago, led by the Chief of
Police himself; inside was Ammunition Eddie, firing from front and
back windows.

An excited crowd of up to five thousand people had gathered to watch,
and some of the police were diverted to control them from a safe
distance. It was estimated that more than five hundred rounds were fired
into the house by the police, and Wheed was firing back all the time.
Amazingly, no one was killed although four policemen were injured.

The siege ended when police threatened to throw in dynamite, and
then only after a lengthy negotiation during which Ammunition Eddie
demanded assurances that he would be sent to prison and not be
hanged. A sergeant pretended to be the Assistant State Attorney and
promised Eddie that he would not be hanged and, after the (real)
Deputy Chief of Police gave a similar guarantee, Ammunition Eddie

60

Wheed came out quietly and surrendered.

Of course the police had no authority to make deals like that, it was for the courts to decide the sentence. The rest of the gang was rounded up and given prison terms, but Ammunition Eddie met the fate he had feared all his life – to be hanged to death on the gallows.

Also hanged this day:

1819   at Old Bailey: John Corderoy and John Fellows for burglary.

1878   at Madison, Indiana, USA: a man named Beavers.

1887   at Strangeways Prison, Manchester: Thomas Leatherbarrow for the murder of Kate Quinn.

1910   at Carnarvon Prison, Wales: William Murphy for the murder of his girlfriend.

16 February

1884 LIFE INSURANCE KILLINGS
Mrs Catherine Flannigan and Mrs Margaret Higgins hanged at Liverpool for the murder of Thomas Higgins, having insured his life.

This seedy pair took out a life insurance policy on Mrs Higgins' husband, and then poisoned him to claim the money. Their guilt was without doubt and, after the trial, it was discovered that they had committed other murders for the same motive.

Also hanged this day:

1880   at Strangeways Prison, Manchester: William Cassidy for wife-murder.

1886   at Ipswich Gaol: George Saunders for wife-murder on Christmas Eve.

17 February

1926 THE MURDEROUS POLICEMAN
PC Herbert Burrows (22), hanged at Gloucester Prison for the murders of publican Ernest George Elton Laight (31), Mrs Doris Sabrina Laight (30) and their baby son, Robert.
Hangman: Tom Pierrepoint

PC Burrows, a probationary constable in the Worcester City Police Force, was due to have some leave. He needed money and realised that, with the end of the month near, there would be a large sum waiting to be banked in the cash box at the Garibaldi Inn opposite his lodgings in Wylds Lane, Worcester.

He went into the Garibaldi Inn at about 10 p.m. on 26 November 1925 ostensibly for a few drinks, but he had gone there equipped with a loaded revolver and rubber gloves. He stayed after closing time with the publican and his wife, his friends, 'Ern' and Dolly Laight. Just before 1 a.m. on the 27th he was in the cellar with Ern when he drew his revolver and shot his friend in the back. Mrs Laight rushed into the cellar and asked what had happened; her husband replied 'He's shot me.' Mrs Laight started to scream and Burrows shot her in the chest.

He ransacked the house, wearing the rubber gloves, collecting all the money he could find. In the bedroom the Laights' baby son Robert woke up and started to cry. Burrows struck him on the head, fracturing his skull. Leaving the silent six-year-old Joan Laight upstairs, he went back to the cellar and scattered paper on the floor. He set light to it, probably hoping to destroy any incriminating evidence. He then went across the road to his lodgings and had a good night's sleep. However Burrows' attempt at arson failed and the bodies were discovered in the morning, while he was out on his beat elsewhere. He attracted suspicion to himself by some remarks he made to another constable when he called in for breakfast at the police station.

He was questioned and his room at 92 Wylds Lane was searched: the murder gun, ammunition, £34 in £1 notes, £13 in ten shilling notes, and £22.8.0 in silver coins were found. Police also found a mounted gold sovereign later identified as belonging to Mrs Laight. Burrows wrote the following statement:

'I, Herbert Burrows, voluntarily and freely admit that I killed, at 12.50 a.m. on the 27th, Mr and Mrs Laight and Robert Laight. The cause will remain unknown. I apologise to the officers and men of the Worcester City Police Force for the disgrace thus incurred.'

At his trial in January 1926 he pleaded not guilty and medical witnesses were called to try to prove that he suffered from insanity brought on from congenital syphilis. The jury was not fooled, it was a clear case of coldly premeditated murder for robbery: they returned a verdict of guilty after 30 minutes.

Burrows retained his callous attitude, expressing no remorse except for baby Robert. Visited by his stepfather after being sentenced to death, and later by his mother, he admitted to them both that he had killed purely for the robbery and remained unmoved by what he had done.

He spent his time in the condemned cell singing or playing patience. He ate a good breakfast on the morning of his execution and faced the hangman with indifference at 8 a.m. The 150 onlookers gathered outside the prison gates saw the official notice of execution displayed and, at 8.05 a.m., they saw a waiter hand over Hangman Tom Pierrepoint's breakfast, which had been sent from a Gloucester hotel.

Also hanged this day:

1829 at Old Bailey: Thomas Dunlop 'for scabrously shooting'; Joseph Burnham for burglary and Joseph Smith for robbery.

1887 at Gloucester Prison: Edward Pritchard for the murder of Henry Allen (14) at Stroud, and robbing him of the £200 factory wages he was carrying. Pritchard showed great remorse and wrote to the boy's father begging forgiveness. He went to the gallows submissively, but when he saw his ready-dug grave, in the corner of the prison yard, he shuddered and moaned.

1903 at Ruthin Prison, Wales: William Hughes for wife-murder.

18 February

Hanged this day:

1818 at Old Bailey: Mary Ann Jones for forgery; Charlotte Newman; John Attel for burglary; and William Hatchman.

19 February

1951 'BADGER GAME' KILLERS
Jean Lee (33) and her accomplices, Robert David Clayton and Norman Andrews, hanged at Pentridge Jail, New South Wales, Australia, for the 'badger game' murder of bookmaker William George Kent (73).

The so-called badger game is a form of blackmail which involves a prostitute luring a man into a compromising situation, at which point her 'husband' suddenly arrives and catches them at it. The husband feigns betrayal, or rage, with or without the threat of violence. In all cases divorce or other means of public exposure is threatened to force the frightened and embarrassed victim into paying generous 'compensation'.

The pretty red-haired Jean Lee became a prostitute in war-time

Australia when there were great numbers of foreign servicemen stationed there. Robert Clayton was her pimp and lover. After the war, they more or less specialised in the badger game and in ordinary thieving from Lee's clients. They were joined by Norman Andrews in 1949, who was to provide extra muscle when violence was needed.

On 7 November 1949 the three shared drinks with wealthy William Kent in the bar of an hotel in Carlton, New South Wales. Jean Lee and Kent retired to his room where Lee tried to make Kent incapably drunk so that she could rob him, but the old man held on to his money. Eventually she stunned him by hitting him on the head with a bottle. She was joined by Clayton and Andrews, and the room was ransacked without success. They tortured the old man by tightly tying his thumbs together with one of his shoelaces, thrusting a broken bottle into him and kicking him. They left him unconscious and got away with a roll of notes from his pocket.

When the battered body was found, hotel staff were able to give a good description of the killer trio, from which the police were able to identify them and Lee, Clayton and Andrews were arrested in Sydney. They were found guilty at their trial, but a second trial was ordered because of a procedural problem. They were found guilty a second time and none of them escaped their appointment with the hangman.

Also hanged this day:

1812 at Old Bailey: Cloytan and Jenkins.

1883 at Lincoln Prison: James Anderson for wife-murder.

1901 at Newgate Prison: Sampson Silas Salmon for the murder of a young female cousin.

20 February

1587 HANGED MAN SURVIVES THREE DAYS
An unnamed man publicly hanged at St Thomas Wateringes (near the present London Bridge railway station) 'for felonie'.
Hangman: Bulle

The man was left hanging until pronounced dead and then handed over to the Chirurgions for anatomy classes. The following extract from Hangman Bulle's account survives to explain what happened next:

'. . . cut down, stripped of his apparell, laide naked in a chest, throwne into a carte, and so brought from the place of execution through the Borough of Southwarke over the bridge, and through the Citie of London to the Chirurgions Hall nere unto Cripelgate. The chest being there opened, and the weather extreeme cold hee was found to be alive, and lived till three and twentie of Februarie, and then died.'

Also hanged this day:

1733   in Lincolnshire: brothers Isaac Hallam (at the place where they murdered Thomas Gardner) and Thomas Hallam (at Faldingworth Gate where they murdered William Wright) for murder and 63 highway robberies.

1874   at Montgomery, Alabama, USA: Thomas Sankey, a negro, for the murder of a Mr Graham.

1890   at Bellefonte, Pennsylvania, USA: William Seeley Hopkins for the gun-murders of his unfaithful wife and nagging mother-in-law.

21 February

1679 TITUS OATES AND THE 'POPISH PLOT'
Green, Berry and Hill hanged at Tyburn Tree for the murder of Sir Edmundbury Godfrey – on Greenberry Hill!
Hangman: Jack Ketch

Robert Green, Henry Berry, and Lawrence Hill were convicted on perjured evidence given by Popish Plot informer Titus Oates and others. During the previous summer Titus Oates, perjurer and unfrocked priest, produced a list of spurious allegations: the so-called 43 Articles. These claimed that there was an evil Popish Plot for a Catholic rising to slaughter Protestants, burn London, and to kill King Charles II so that his Catholic brother, the Duke of York (later James II), could become king and outlaw the Protestant religion.

Sir Edmundbury Hill, magistrate and coal-merchant of London, was commanded to investigate. The depositions were sworn before him and resulted in a furore of anti-Catholic panic and Titus Oates became a hero.

Sir Edmundbury left his lodgings on the morning of 12 October 1678 and was never seen alive again. His battered body was found strangled, with his own sword thrust into his chest after death, in a ditch alongside Barrow Hill (in sight of the north-western boundary of today's Regent's Park in St John's Wood). The identity of the murderer has never been established.

Robert Green, Henry Berry, and Lawrence Hill were respectable servants of Queen Catherine, a Catholic, at Somerset House. Green and Hill were also Catholics, while Berry was a Protestant. Amidst a fever of anti-Catholic feeling, and attracted by the lure of a reward of £500, informers were not hard to find: Captain William Bedloe and another perjurer named Miles Praunce, as well as Titus Oates, offered information against Green, Berry, and Hill.

False evidence at their trial alleged that they had murdered Sir Edmundbury in the yard of Somerset House, kept the body there for four days and then removed it to Barrow Hill during the night. The informers' stories were contradictory on most points, and Green and Berry produced witnesses who could vouch for their being elsewhere on the night of the crime.

The judge was the bullying Lord Chief Justice Scroggs and he was assisted on the bench by Sir George Jeffreys (later to become the infamous Judge Jeffreys of the 'Bloody Assizes' after the Monmouth rebellion of 1685). At the end of a trial that was a disgrace to justice, Titus Oates and the other perjurers were triumphant and the luckless defendants were found guilty and sentenced to death.

Green and Hill were hanged at Tyburn on 21 February 1679. Berry's execution was delayed because he was a Protestant, in the hope that he would 'cleanse his soul' by confessing his guilt. Still protesting his innocence, he was hanged at Tyburn a week later. Most of the ignorant and superstitious public were convinced of the trio's guilt, despite the travesty of the trial, because of the eery former name of Barrow Hill: Greenberry Hill.

Awful retribution caught up with Titus Oates, but not until 1685. He was found guilty of being responsible for 35 judicial murders because of his perjuries. He was sentenced by Judge Jeffreys to be: pilloried in Palace Yard; led around Westminster Hall with a notice above his head declaring his infamy; pilloried in front of the Royal Exchange; whipped at the tail of a cart from Aldgate Pump to Newgate Prison and, after an interval of two days, to be whipped from Newgate to Tyburn; then imprisoned for life and annually brought from his dungeon and pilloried in different parts of London. The sentence was carried out, but he was freed after the revolution of 1688, and lived until 1705.

Also hanged this day:

1803 on the roof of Horsemonger Lane Gaol: Colonel Edward Marcus Despard (52), John Francis, John Wood, James Broughton, James Sedgewick, Arthur G. Wrutton and John MacNamara, hanged and beheaded for high treason. *Hangman: William Brunskill*

1826 at Old Bailey: Edward Cockerill for forgery and John Tombs for burglary.

1862 at the Tombs Prison, New York, USA: Captain Nathaniel Gordon for piracy and slave-trading. Probably the first execution for piracy in USA for 40 years, and the first man to be condemned for slave trading under US Federal laws.

1881 at Chester Castle: William Stanway for the murder of Ann Mellor.

1887 at Lincoln Prison: Richard Insole for wife-murder.

22 February

1864 *FLOWERY LAND* **MUTINEERS**
Spaniards John Lyons (a.k.a. Leon), Blanco, Lopez, Duranno and the Turk, Vartos, hanged at Old Bailey for mutiny and murders on board the vessel Flowery Land bound for Singapore from London.
Hangman: William Calcraft

The *Flowery Land* set sail from London with a cargo of wine and other goods, bound for Singapore. The officers were Captain John Smith, First Mate Karswell and Second Mate Tiffin. The rest of the crew were a mixed bag of ruffians of different nationalities, and they were troublesome from the start.

Eight of the vicious crew became mutineers and murderers in the middle of the night of 10 September 1863. Half of them attacked First Mate Karswell on deck, battering him about the head with handspikes and capstan bars until all his features were pulped, and yet the poor man was still alive when thrown overboard. The other mutineers set upon Captain Smith as he came on deck to investigate the uproar, stabbing him to death with their daggers. They also killed the captain's brother, who had been a passenger.

The mutineers ransacked the ship of cash and valuables and broke open crates of champagne from the cargo. The Chinamen in the crew were bullied and disfigured with knife-cuts, but not killed that night. The life of second Mate Tiffin was spared because he was the only one left capable of navigating. He was ordered to take the ship to within ten miles of the Brazilian coast, which was reached on 2 October. The *Flowery Land* was scuttled and the mutineers allowed Tiffin to leave with them in a boat. One of the Chinamen was battered and thrown into the sea and the other two were left on board the sinking ship: they were last seen clinging to the tops as the water engulfed them.

Landing near the entrance to the River Plate, Tiffin got away and reported the crime. The mutineers were arrested and taken to England for trial at the Old Bailey, where the awful tale of wickedness on the high seas horrified the nation. One man, Carlos, was acquitted and the remaining seven were sentenced to death, of whom two were later reprieved to life imprisonment. Carlos was tried a second time, for scuttling the *Flowery Land*, and sentenced to ten years' imprisonment.

On the morning of the execution the five to die were brought on to the scaffold one at a time. As the first man out would have to wait for the others, Duranno was chosen because he was thought to be the bravest. In fact, he almost fainted when he saw the gallows and the huge crowd, and had to be sat in a chair while the others were brought out. They died with one drop. Their wax effigies were displayed at Madame Tussaud's Chamber of Horrors for about ten years. They were an evil-looking bunch, and their villainous appearance caused horrified shudders to the visitors.

Also hanged this day:

1825   at Old Bailey: Cornelius Wood for rape, Henry Denham for burglary, and Edward 'Kiddy' Harris for assault with intent to murder Sarah Drew to prevent her giving evidence against him in a robbery.

1881   at Stafford Gaol: James Williams for the murder of Elizabeth Bagnall.

1886   at Knutsford Gaol: Owen M'Gill (39), for wife-murder. *Hangman: James Berry*

1887   at Nottingham Prison: Benjamin Terry for wife-murder.

1898   at Strangeways Prison, Manchester: George W. Howe (33) for the murder of Joseph K. Pickup.

23 February

1885 THE 'MAN THEY COULD NOT HANG'
John Lee (19) was the 'Man They Could Not Hang' at Exeter Gaol. He had been sentenced for the murder of his employer Emma Keyse (68).
Hangman: James Berry

John Lee was an ex-convict employed as a footman at the home of Emma Keyse in Babbacombe, Devon. Miss Keyse, a moneyed spinster who had once been a maid to Queen Victoria, was dissatisfied with his work and docked his weekly pay from half-a-crown to a florin

(12½p and 10p respectively). He battered the old woman about the head with an axe and cut her throat so savagely that there were knife-marks on the vertebrae. Then he set fire to the house. There is no doubt about the guilt of John Lee. The speculation is why it was that he survived three attempts to hang him that Monday morning at Exeter Gaol, so that he was known forever after as the Man They Could Not Hang.

Hangman James Berry arrived at the gaol at midday on Saturday 21 February. He inspected the coach house, where the execution was to be performed. It had a flag-stoned floor with two wooden trap doors which were six feet long by four-and-a-half feet across covering a pit which was 11 feet deep. He tested the operation of the lever twice and the traps opened satisfactorily each time. He was not entirely happy about the thickness of the wood or the condition of the ironwork, both of which he considered too frail for the purpose.

It rained heavily on the Saturday and Sunday nights. Berry inspected the gallows again at 7.30 a.m. on Monday, but did not carry out another test as they appeared to be just as he had left them. He fixed the rope and left.

At 8 a.m. John Lee was pinioned and taken from his cell to the coach house and stood on the trap. He waited calmly as the chaplain, the Reverend John Pitkin, stood in front of him saying prayers while Hangman Berry pinioned his legs, pulled down the white cap and adjusted the rope around his neck. Berry stepped aside and pulled the lever – and nothing happened! The leg-strap was loosened and Lee was removed to an adjoining room. He was quite calm. Berry pulled the lever and the trap doors opened easily. They were pulled back into position and Berry pulled the lever a second time: they opened easily again. Lee and the chaplain were brought back and they resumed their positions; Berry adjusted the white cap and the noose.

Berry stepped to the lever and pulled, but again the trap doors failed to open, the condemned man standing there silent and motionless. John Lee was removed again and Berry got to work with warders. Wood was trimmed from the edges and, when tested again, the doors fell open. Within a few minutes Lee was placed on the trap for the third time, and the shaken chaplain again took his position in front of him. Berry operated the lever for the third attempt to hang John Lee, and the trap doors stayed closed yet again. Berry jerked the lever again and agitated it so vigorously that it was strained, and stamped on the trap doors: they remained firmly shut.

Amazingly, John Lee had not uttered a sound during this fearsome succession of events and had calmly complied with whatever was asked of him. Not so the poor chaplain, whose nerves had been badly shaken: he refused point-blank to take any further part. The execution was postponed and John Lee, apparently the calmest man present, was taken back to his cell. Within hours he had been reprieved and his sentence commuted to life imprisonment.

He served 22 years and was released on 17 December 1907. He sold his story to newspapers and published a book, inevitably titled *The Man They Could Not Hang*. He married and settled in America, dying there in 1933.

What *did* happen? There seem to be as many theories as there are years that have passed since 1885. Among the more prominent are:
1. That the weekend rain had warped the wood of the trap doors so that Lee's weight forced the two doors against each other and prevented them opening.
2. When the tests were made, neither Lee nor the chaplain were in position. Their combined weight bearing down on the warped woodwork flattened it and caused the doors to jam.
3. That the iron bands under the doors were bent and, when Lee was stood on the trap, the bands were straightened so that they extended on to the top of the pit walls and prevented the doors dropping.
4. A convict-carpenter is dubiously reported to have inserted a wedge in the doors when preparing the gallows and removed it each time a test was made, replacing it before Lee was brought back.
5. Hangman Berry himself offered this explanation: 'I am of the opinion that the iron-work catches of the trap doors were not strong enough for the purpose, that the woodwork of the doors should have been about three or four times as heavy, and with the ironwork to correspond, so that when a man of Lee's weight was placed upon the doors the iron catches would not have become locked, as I feel sure they did on this occasion. . .'

A different murderer, also named John Lee, was hanged in America four years later, but his partner escaped death at the last minute. (See 5 February.)

Also hanged this day:

1719 at Tyburn Tree: Lieutenant Edward Bird for murder.

1723 at Tyburn Tree: Robert Oakey, John Levy and Matthew Flood for robbery.

1807 at Old Bailey: John Holloway and Owen Haggerty for the murder of Mr Steele, a lavender merchant. *Hangman: William Brunskill.* (More than forty thousand onlookers crammed into the Old Bailey. As Holloway and Haggerty appeared on the scaffold the crowd surged for a better view. A cart collapsed tumbling those on it to the ground, including women and babies, where they were trampled underfoot. Panic seized the mob, some scrambling to escape, others pressing forward to see what was happening. Thirty-two were crushed or suffocated to death with more than a hundred badly injured. Estimates of the number of victims vary – some reports claim hundreds were killed.)

1818   at Old Bailey: David Evans for the murder of his child.

1822   at Old Bailey: William Ablett for murder. Edward Cockin and John Waylor for burglary.

1906   at Chicago Prison, Illinois, USA: Johann Otto Hoch (46) 'The Stockyard Bluebeard' who married 24 times and killed at least a dozen wives, usually with poison.

24 February

1953 AN UPPER-CLASS WASTER
Miles William Giffard (27) hanged at Horfield Gaol, Bristol, for the murder of both parents.

The Giffards were descended from a de Giffard who came to England with William the Conqueror in 1066. They were still a distinguished family when the wayward Miles Giffard slaughtered his parents on the night of 7 November 1952 at their home overlooking St Austell Bay in Cornwall.

His uncle, Sir George Giffard, was a general. His father was Charles Giffard (53), senior partner of a prominent firm of solicitors in St Austell, clerk to the local Justices, and Under Sheriff of Cornwall. His mother, Elizabeth Giffard, was vice-chairman of the St Austell Conservative Association and president of the Conservative Women's Association.

Miles Giffard failed to live up to family expectations. He lacked the concentration and self-discipline to make anything of himself, despite the opportunities that had been available to him. He had been sent to Rugby School, but had been obliged to leave, if not actually expelled, after only four terms. At his subsequent public school, Blundell's, he at least did well in sports and later played cricket for Cornwall. He enlisted in the Royal Navy and stayed three years as a lower-deck sailor. After that he studied law, then estate agency, but did not apply himself to either. He became an upper-class waster without the funds to live in that style, beyond a four-month spell during which he squandered a £750 legacy. He sponged off others, especially his disappointed parents to whom he returned at the beginning of November 1952.

He had met and fallen in love with Gabrielle Vallance (19) and wanted more than anything to be back with her in London. This fixation was thwarted when his father forbade his return to London, and the use of his car. On Tuesday 4 November Gabrielle received a letter from Miles explaining the restrictions imposed by his father. Part of the letter read, 'Short of doing him in I see no future in the world at all. He has stopped my allowance anyway, and is giving me a pint of beer and 20 cigarettes a day and said: "No pubs".'

On Friday 7 November he phoned Gabrielle while his parents were out, at 5.30 p.m., and told her that he might be coming to London for the weekend in his father's car but would phone later confirming it, which he did at some time after 8 p.m. At 7.30 p.m. his parents had returned home. Miles had gone into the garage and battered his father over the head at least five times with an iron pipe. He went into the house and found his mother in the kitchen and attacked her from behind with the pipe, beating her about the face and head, crushing her skull and fracturing both her wrists and an arm. He phoned Gabrielle and went to the garage to get the car only to find his father recovering, so he hit him several times again. Going into the kitchen he found his mother regaining consciousness, and bludgeoned her some more.

He put his mother in a wheelbarrow while she was still living, carried her out of the garden to the edge of the cliff and tipped her over so that she fell on to the rocks 120 feet below: that killed her. His father was similarly wheeled out and thrown over the cliff, sending the wheelbarrow tumbling after him. Then Giffard drove to London to see Gabrielle.

The bodies were found on Saturday morning and it was noted that the car, and the wastrel Miles, were missing. He was arrested as he returned with Gabrielle to her flat in Chelsea after a pub-crawl on Saturday night. He had confessed to Gabrielle during the evening that he had murdered his parents, as she was to testify at his trial. A defence of insanity was offered, but the jury rejected this and took a mere 35 minutes to find him guilty. There was no chance of a reprieve.

Also hanged this day:

1688   at the Cross of Edinburgh: Philip Stanfield for the murder of his father, Sir James Stanfield, by strangling and drowning in the River Tyne to avert being disinherited. He was the last man in Scotland to be convicted by the Ordeal of Touch, whereby it was believed that if the corpse was touched by the murderer it would bleed. As it happened there was plenty of other evidence.

1817   at Old Bailey: Martha Parry for murdering her child.

1823   at Old Bailey: William Nutt 'for an abominable offence', John Harris for robbery and John Waite for forgery.

25 February

1879 THE LAST MINUTES OF CHARLIE PEACE
Charles Peace (47) hanged at Armley Gaol, Leeds, for the murder of
Mrs Katherine Dyson. He confessed to a further killing, of PC
Nicholas Cock, while awaiting execution.
*Hangman: William Marwood**

Charlie Peace, burglar and double-murderer, was the archetypal
Victorian criminal, and he looked it. The sight of his ferocious face
must have struck terror into anyone meeting him on a dark night.
Adults would invoke him to scare children into obedience (as I
remember from my own childhood in the 1930s and 1940s): 'Charlie
Peace will come and get you!'

He was troublesome to the end. While eating his last breakfast of
eggs and a huge amount of bacon, he complained 'This is bloody poor
bacon!' (He considered that it was too salty.) He tried to drag out
every last moment before being hanged, taking so much time in the
lavatory that a warder knocked on the door. Peace snarled 'You're in a
hell of a hurry. Who's going to be hanged this morning, you or me?'
Even on the scaffold he made delays, with prayers and the delivery of
a sanctimonious sermon. To prolong matters further he used the salty
bacon as an excuse to request a drink of water while actually standing
on the trap door, but this was ignored.

As Marwood fixed the white hood and the noose on him, Peace
complained again 'the rope fits very tight'. Just before the drop he
muttered 'Goodbye and God bless. . .'

* *William Marwood's fame was such that his name was on the lips of London
street-urchins in the riddle 'If Pa killed Ma, who would hang Pa?' – answer
Marwood!*

Also hanged this day:

1746   at Oxford Street, London: Matthew Henderson for murder.

1818   at Old Bailey: William and John Rawlinson for robbery on the
River Thames. Another member of the family, also named John
Rawlinson, had been hanged for a similar crime on 2 December 1816.

1884   at Taunton Prison: Charles Kite for the murder of Albert Miles.

1896   at Newgate Prison: Alfred Chipperfield for wife-murder.

26 February

1914 LIVERPOOL SACK MURDER
George Ball (22) hanged at Walton Gaol, Liverpool, for the callous 'Liverpool Sack Murder' of Christina Bradfield (40).
Hangman: John Ellis

George Ball (22) and Samuel Angeles Elltoft (18) both worked for Bradfield's, tarpaulin makers of Liverpool. On the evening of 10 December 1913 they attacked and robbed their employer, Miss Christina Bradfield (40), in her shop in Old Hall Street. Ball rained down blow after blow with a blunt instrument upon the poor woman and then, with Elltoft's help, sewed her body and some iron bars into a sack.

By the unlikiest of chances, the shutter on the shop window fell away and came down on the head of a man standing outside. He was a ship's steward, Walter Eaves, waiting for his girlfriend to arrive: happily for him, the shutter fell in such a way that his bowler hat prevented him from being hurt. Elltoft came outside to replace the shutter and Eaves complained about his damaged hat. Elltoft went back into the shop and told Ball and Ball came out and apologised to Eaves and gave him two shillings (10p) by way of compensation. Eaves would not forget the pair. When Ball and Elltoft emerged again, pushing a tarpaulin covered handcart, Walter Eaves was still waiting for his girl. Little did he realise that he was watching a murder victim's body being carted away for disposal!

The weighted sack was thrown into the Leeds and Liverpool Canal, but was discovered next day fouling a lock gate. Miss Bradfield's battered body was soon identified from a medallion. The news of the crime spread rapidly through Liverpool and Walter Eaves told the police what he had seen at Bradfield's shop. Elltoft was arrested almost at once.

Ball had fled and the ten-day hunt for him was intense, as the people of Liverpool were appalled by the savagery of the murder. His photograph was shown on all Liverpool cinema screens and this led to his capture at a lodging house. When arrested he was found in possession of Miss Bradfield's watch, and some of his clothing was blood stained.

Ball and Elltoft were tried at Liverpool Assizes in February 1914. Elltoft was found not guilty of murder, but given four years as an accessory after the fact. George Ball was found guilty and sentenced to death; he confessed while in the condemned cell. He was hanged a little more than two-and-a-half months after committing the crime that had horrified and disgusted the whole of Liverpool.

27 February

1948 'GREAT ESCAPE' VICTIMS AVENGED
Thirteen Gestapo gunmen hanged at Hameln Prison, West Germany, for the murder of 50 Allied air-force officer prisoners-of-war after the Great Escape.
Hangman: Albert Pierrepoint. Assistant: Regimental Sergeant Major O'Neil

Seventy-nine Allied air-force officers escaped from Stalag Luft III in Sagan, Silesia, in Germany, on the night of 24–25 March 1944. It became known as the Great Escape.

When Hitler was informed of the escape by Himmler, at the morning conference in Berchtesgaden, he flew into a rage and ordered that the officers were to remain with the SD (the Security Service of the SS) after recapture and not be returned to the Luftwaffe.

After this conference Field Marshal Von Keitel (who was hanged at Nuremberg; see 16 October) summoned General Von Gravenitz, who was in charge of prisoners of war, to his office and told him that Goering had reprimanded him in front of Hitler about the escape. He told Von Gravenitz, 'These escapes must stop. We shall take very severe measures. The men who have escaped will be shot. . .' Von Gravenitz protested that this was contrary to the Geneva Convention, but his protest was ignored.

Of the escaped officers, three eventually reached Britain, but the other 76 were recaptured and 50 were shot. The murders were carried out by the Gestapo, usually in small groups in secluded wooded areas. In all cases it was claimed that they were shot 'while trying to escape', which was of course untrue.

After the war the RAF Special Investigation Branch carried out a dedicated hunt for the killers. Seventy-two were accused: 21 were hanged, 17 were imprisoned, 11 committed suicide, 7 were untraced (4 of whom are presumed dead), 6 were killed in the war, 5 were arrested but not charged for political reasons, 3 were acquitted or had their sentences quashed, 1 was used as a prosecution witness and not charged, 1 found refuge in East Germany. The following were hanged at Hameln on 27 February 1948: Kriminalsekretar Eduard Geith, Oberregierungsrat Josef Gmeiner, Kriminalkommissar Walter Herberg, Kriminalassistant Walter Jacobs, Polizei Inspektor Hans Kahler, Sturmbannfuhrer Johannes Post, Kriminalsekretar Otto Preiss, Regierungsrat Dr Alfred Schimmel, Kriminalobersekretar Oskar Schmidt, Kriminalassistant Johan Schneider, Kriminalsekretar Emil Schulz, Kriminalsekretar Emil Weil, Erich Zacharias.

Also hanged this day:

1811 at Old Bailey: W. Trueman, J. Cove and J. Fruin.

1833 at Old Bailey: Thomas Atterell for extortion.

1852 at New York, USA: Otto Grunsig for the arsenic-murder of his wife Victorine.

1906 at Strangeways Prison, Manchester: Jack Griffiths (19) for the murder of Kate Garrity (17). *Hangman: Henry Pierrepoint*

1947 at Strangeways Prison, Manchester: Walter Graham Rowland (39) for the murder of prostitute Olive Balchin after another man had confessed to the crime. *Hangman: Albert Pierrepoint.* Rowland had occupied the same condemned cell in 1934 for the murder of his daughter, but had been reprieved and released in 1940.

1974 at Pretoria, South Africa: Robert Victor Morton (23) for the frenzied killing of Sharon Ashford (14).

28 February

1749 SOVEREIGN TREASON
Usher Gahagan and Terence Conner hanged at Tyburn Tree for treason.
Hangman: John Thrift

The treason in this case was of clipping sovereigns for the spare gold. 'Clippers' could make huge profits and the resulting under-weight coins in circulation threatened to undermine trade. So seriously was this crime considered that the defacing of coins of the realm, which bore the king's likeness, was defined as treason and the punishment was death. Rarely did a 'clipper' obtain a reprieve, and then only for informing on others so engaged.

Also hanged this day:

1883 at Zagazig, Egypt: five Arabs for the murders of three Britons, Professor Palmer, Captain Gill and Lieutenant Carrington. After further anti-British actions and anarchy throughout Egypt, Britain took over the government of the country. This was to safeguard the Suez Canal. (See 9 June.)

MARCH

1 March

1877 KILLER OF 'WILD BILL' HICKOCK
'Black Jack' McCall (26) hanged at Yankton, South Dakota, USA, for the assassination of James Butler Hickock (39), better known as 'Wild Bill' Hickock.

Wild Bill Hickock was one of the legendary lawmen of the old Wild West. He had been a scout for the Union army, marshal at Fort Riley, Hays City, and Abilene. On 2 August 1876 he was playing poker* in the No 10 saloon in Deadwood City when he was shot in the head from behind by 'Black Jack' McCall, a cross-eyed drunkard and saddle-tramp.

McCall's motive had been to gain notoriety by shooting the famous lawman and gunslinger, although he said that it was to avenge Hickock's killing of his brother, which was untrue as he had no brother. Asked why he shot Hickock from behind instead of facing him, he replied 'I didn't want to commit suicide.' He was later arrested by a US marshal, taken to Yankton for trial and found guilty of murder.

Hickock's hand was two pairs, aces and eights: from that day on it was known as the 'dead man's hand' in card-playing terminology.

Also hanged this day:

1861 at Albert Lea, Minnesota, USA: Henry Kriegler for the gun-murder of his neighbour Nelson Boughton. Kriegler was an unpleasant brute of a man who beat his wife as an almost daily occurrence. In 1859 Mrs Kriegler ran in terror to Boughton's home to escape from her husband's latest beating. Kriegler went after her and shot Boughton to death.

1867 at New York, USA: George Wagner for the axe-murder of his wife.

1892 at Newgate Prison: James Muir for the murder of Abigail Sullivan.

1910 at Pentonville Prison: George Henry Perry for the murder of his sweetheart.

2 March

1918 VOISIN THE BUTCHER
**Louis Marie Joseph Voison (42) hanged at Pentonville Prison for the
murder and butchery of Madame Emilienne Gerard (32), dumping
parts of her in Regent Square, Bloomsbury, London.**
Hangman: John Ellis

After 11 p.m. on the night of 31 October 1917, German Zeppelins
carried out one of their most fearful air raids in World War One upon
the unprotected citizens of London. Mme Emilienne Gerard (32), wife
of a West End hotel chef away serving his country in the French army,
fled from her flat at 50 Munster Square near Regent's Park. Her rent
was paid by her lover, a powerfully muscled French butcher named
Louis Voisin, and she went to find comfort from her terror at his
nearby basement flat in a tenement building at 101 Charlotte Street.
An even greater, and more immediate, terror awaited her there.

Mme Gerard arrived and found her lover, Voisin, in bed with
another woman: Berthe Roche. What happened next was recon-
structed by Crown Prosecuter Sir Richard Muir and the pathologist
Bernard Spilsbury:
1. The women had never met before and flew at each other in a
   jealous rage. From the splattered blood stains, it was clear that the
   fight had taken place in an open doorway leading to the yard.
2. Although Mme Gerard sustained dozens of blows to the head with
   a blunt instrument, and stab wounds, none had been delivered with
   great force and her skull had not been fractured. It was very
   unlikely, therefore, that they were struck by Voisin, who could
   have felled her with one blow.
3. A blood-stained towel, in which one of Mme Gerard's earrings was
   found, seems to have been wrapped around her head to smother
   her screams and to suffocate her partially.

Voisin, therefore, probably held her in his strong grip while Berthe
Roche plied her rival for his affections with a series of head-blows and
knife-thrusts.

Voisin then got to work in his Charlotte Street kitchen to use his
butcher's skills to render the body unidentifiable. He neatly severed
her legs at the knee joints, the hands from the wrists, and her head
from the trunk. He visited her Munster Square flat at some time and,
among other items, removed a sheet from her bed, leaving blood
stains on the counterpane and elsewhere.

Voisin and Roche now had to dispose of the body. The head and
hands were sealed in a cask and hidden in a room in the cellar at
Charlotte Street. The torso and arms were wrapped in the sheet and

stuffed into a meat sack (marked 'Argentina La Plata Cold Storage'). To add a bit of international confusion for the police, Voisin scrawled 'Blodie Belgiam' on a piece of brown paper and put it in the sack. More brown paper was used to wrap the legs. The two parcels were loaded into Voisin's cart, taken nearly a mile away and dumped in the central garden of Regent Square.

The grim remains were discovered on the morning of 2 November, by a street cleaner colourfully known as 'Jack The Sweeper', and the police took over. The sheet wrapping the torso had a laundry mark 'II H' embroidered with red cotton in one corner, it was traced to Mme Gerard and the police went to her Munster Square flat. Apart from the blood stains, they found a framed picture of Voisin and an IOU for £50 signed by him. He was next on their list.

When the police arrived at 101 Charlotte Street one look at the blood-splattered kitchen, and the sullen responses from Voisin and Roche, caused the pair to be taken to Bow Street police station for further questioning. Voisin flatly denied everything and Roche shrieked abuse. At one stage Voisin was asked to write 'bloody Belgium': five times he slowly scrawled 'Blodie Belgiam'. The last version was identical to the note found with the torso. His attempt to lay a false trail as good as convicted him. When the head and hands were found in the cellar at 101 Charlotte Street his case was hopeless. Voisin and Roche charged with murder.

By the time of the trial Voisin had declared that Berthe Roche was completely innocent and, even though she probably struck the death-blows, the judge ruled that she should be remanded until later and charged only with being an accessory after the fact. Voisin, of course, was found guilty and sentenced to death. Berthe Roche was sentenced to seven years' imprisonment on the day before Voisin went firmly and stoically to his death on the gallows. She went mad in prison and died at a hospital for the insane on 22 March the following year.

Also hanged this day:

1814   at Newgate Gaol, Dublin: a man named Tuite.

1880   at Kirkdale Prison, Liverpool: Patrick Kearns and Hugh Burns for the murder of Patrick Tracy.

1886   at Cardiff Prison: David Roberts for the murder of David Thomas.

1926   at Shepton Mallet Military Prison, Somerset: Bombardier John Lincoln for the murder of Edward Charles Ingram Richards.

3 March

1903 THE LEYTON MURDERS
**Edgar Owen a.k.a. Edgar Edwards (44) hanged at Wandsworth
Prison for murdering the Darby family.**
Hangman: William Billington. Assistant: Henry Pierrepoint

This tragedy earned temporary fame as the 'Leyton Murders', even
though the murders were committed six miles away and on the other
side of the River Thames, at 22 Wyndham Road, Camberwell. The
crime took its title from the place where the bodies were found: buried
in the back garden of a villa at 89 Church Road, Leyton.

Edgar Owen, using the name Edgar Edwards, answered an advertisement for the sale of a grocery shop on 29 November 1902 but,
ominously, he took with him an 8lb lead weight from a sash-window
hidden in newspapers. The discussion of the sale appeared to go well
with John William Darby and his wife Beatrice in their busy shop.
When Edwards asked to see the accounts books John Darby stayed in
the shop while Mrs Darby, with 10-week-old baby Ethel Beatrice in
her arms, led Edwards to the upstairs front living room.

When they were alone he savagely brought the sash-weight down on
the back of Mrs Darby's head and then strangled the crying baby. John
Darby was similarly bludgeoned to death in the same room. Blood was
splashed on the floor, wall, furniture, windows and on the floor of the
balcony outside.

Using the money from the shop's cash box, Edwards rented the villa
in respectable Church Road, Leyton. For the next few days he
stripped the shop of its stock which he sold to dealers and pawned
some of the Darbys' belongings. The bulk of the furniture he kept for
himself, and had it removed to the villa in Leyton. Included in the
move were three packing cases later proved to have contained the
crudely dismembered bodies of John and Beatrice Darby. He buried
the cut-up bodies of Mr and Mrs Darby in six sacks, and the intact
remains of baby Ethel tied in a bundle, in a deep pit in the back
garden.

Edgar Edwards appeared to have got away with murder, but it
was when he tried to repeat the successful formula that he came
unstuck. On 23 December he invited John Garland to 89 Church
Road to discuss the sale of Garland's shop and Edwards, wielding
another lead sash-weight, suddenly launched himself upon Garland.
Garland resisted and got away, going to the police immediately and
reporting the assault. Edwards was arrested and searched. The
police were puzzled that he should have a number of visiting cards
and printed bill-heads belonging to John Darby, whose missing
family had already been reported by Mrs Darby's sister. Then they

found *two* blood-stained lead sash-weights.

Further police inquiries established that the furniture at 89 Church Road had belonged to the Darbys. Neighbours reported having seen Edwards digging a pit in the garden and this led to the sensational discovery of the mutilated bodies at the end of December.

At his trial at the Old Bailey in February 1903 there could be no denying that he had committed the awful killings. His lawyers attempted a defence of insanity, citing the mental records of some of his relatives, and Edwards played along by occasionally bursting into laughter and seemingly treating the trial as a joke. The jury was not convinced and when he was found guilty, his reaction was to burst into even greater roars of laughter. His crazy antics were not manifested until he was caught. Until then he had shown cool and ruthless determination to carry out premeditated plans to murder for gain, and had done so with horrifying results.

When Hangman William Billington came for him in the condemned cell, Edwards jumped up and instructed him: 'Now get on with it as quick as you can.' It is also claimed that he told the chaplain, on the scaffold, 'I've been looking forward to this!'

4 March

1763 HERCULEAN HANNAH!
Hannah Dagoe (33) hanged at Tyburn Tree for theft from a dwelling place.
Hangman: Thomas Turlis

Hannah Dagoe, described in the *Newgate Calendar* as a 'herculean Irishwoman', was by occupation a porter in Covent Garden. She supplemented her wages for years by thieving in the Covent Garden district and was finally sentenced to death for robbing the house of a poor widow, stealing from a dwelling place then being a capital crime.

This tough and ferocious woman was a terror. While at Newgate prior to execution, other prisoners feared her violent temper: while she was there she stabbed the man who had given evidence against her. She was at her most furious under the gallows' beam at Tyburn Tree. When the cart came to a stop under the triangular Tree she loosened her hands from her bonds, grabbed Hangman Turlis and struggled with him, daring him to hang her! Screaming abuse, she gave him a mighty thump in the chest, almost flooring him, and tore off her hat and clothes and threw them into the crowd: stripping herself to deny the hangman his usual perks of hanged criminals' clothing. Turlis grappled with her and after much effort got the rope around her neck, but she broke away from him again. She threw herself from the cart with such force that her neck was broken and she died instantly.

5 March

Hanged this day:

1817 at Old Bailey: William Kelley and Eliza Fricker for burglary; Thomas Cann, Benjamin and Andrew Savage (twins) for issuing forged notes; and James Baker and George Gates for highway robbery.

6 March

1868 AN UNLOVED BRUTE
Andreas Roesch hanged at St Peter, Minnesota, USA, for the gun-murder of Joseph Saurer (16).

Andreas Roesch was as nasty a piece of humanity as you could wish to avoid knowing. Described as dull-witted, he was a sullen and violent man. Out hunting in the woods one day with his son they encountered Joseph Saurer (16). Roesch took Saurer's gun away, turned it on him and wordlessly shot the boy to death. The son lost no time in reporting his murderous father who was tried and sentenced to death. The community had to bury him after the hanging because his wife refused to claim the body.

Also hanged this day:

1853 at Bethlehem, New York, USA: John Hendrickson for the murder of his wife, Maria, with aconite poison – perhaps the first aconite-murder in the USA.

1889 at Wandsworth Prison: Ebenezer Samuel Jenkins for the murder of his sweetheart at Guildford.

7 March

1733 TRIPLE MURDER IN FLEET STREET
Sarah Malcolm (22) hanged in Fleet Street, close to the scene of the murders of her mistress and two other servants.
Hangman: John 'Laughing Jack' Hooper

This was one execution where Laughing Jack Hooper carried out his task with sadness, either thinking that his victim was innocent or sympathetic to her pitiful story as told in the broadsheets. Sarah is reported to have begun life in comfortable circumstances as the daughter of a merchant who later lost his fortune. Reduced to penury, she worked as a laundress around Fleet Street and the Temple.

One of her employers was a wealthy widow, Mrs Duncombe (80), who was strangled in her home in Fleet Street, between Mitre Court and Fetter Lane, in early February 1733. An elderly servant, Elizabeth Harrison, was found strangled in another room while her young servant-girl, Ann Price, lay disarrayed in her bed with her throat cut. Mrs Duncombe's strong box had been broken open and emptied, and some pieces of silver plate were missing.

Sarah Malcolm was an early suspect as she had regular access to Mrs Duncombe's rooms. When caught she was found with a blood-stained silver tankard belonging to Mrs Duncombe, also a number of gold and silver coins (some hidden in a bag under her hair). She tried to put the blame on some local men, the Alexander brothers, who immediately reported to the authorities, and were cleared. She also accused a woman named Mary Tracy, but she was able to prove her innocence.

Malcolm was visited in her cell at Newgate by William Hogarth who made two portraits of her, afterwards remarking that her face showed that she was capable of any wickedness. Like the authorities, he had come to a different conclusion about her than Laughing Jack the hangman.

Also hanged this day:

1808   at Hertford: Thomas 'Man of Blood' Simmons for murder.

1811   at Old Bailey: Hepburn and White.

1813   at Old Bailey: James Johnson for forgery and John Smith for robbery.

1837   at Old Bailey: John Pegsworth for murder.

1890   at Charlestown, West Virginia, USA: Felix Kampf for the knife-murders of his son (19) and daughter (20) for being late with his dinner.

1901   at Mountjoy Gaol, Belfast, Ireland: John Toole for the murder of a woman.

1941   Henry L. White for the murder of Miss Emily Wardle.

8 March

1945 'CLEFT CHIN MURDER'
Private Karl Gustav Hulten (23), US army, hanged at Pentonville
Prison for the murder of taxi driver George Edward Heath (34). It
was known as the 'Cleft Chin Murder'.
Hangman: Albert Pierrepoint

'Lieutenant Ricky Hulten' met 'actress Georgina Grayson' on 3 October 1944: they were not what they claimed to be. He was really Private Karl Gustav Hulten, a Swedish-American deserter from a US parachute regiment; she was a strip-tease dancer whose real name was Elizabeth Maud Jones.

He pretended that he was a Chicago gangster and she was excited by the idea of being a gangster's moll. They used an army truck to commit small-time robberies upon pedestrians and cyclists. One of their victims, a woman, was almost killed after being hit with an iron bar, partly strangled, and thrown into the Thames.

They were more than likely just two silly immature people living out fantasies developed from watching Hollywood films. The impetus was probably the excitement rather than the puny amounts of cash and valuables they took. But on 6 October they became real-life killers. They hired George Heath, a taxi driver with a cleft chin, to drive them to King Street, Hammersmith, but when they got there Hulten ordered him to drive on to the beginning of the Great West Road. When the cab stopped Hulten shot Heath in the back and ordered Betty Jones to empty his pockets: their haul from the murder was 19 shillings (95p), a silver pencil and a cigarette case. Hulten drove to Staines where they dumped the body in a ditch and then drove back to Hammersmith.

The body was discovered the next morning and details of Heath's taxi were circulated. With remarkable stupidity, Hulten kept on using the car. It was seen parked in Fulham Palace Road on 10 October and he was arrested when he tried to get in it. The murder gun was found in his pocket with some ammunition.

Betty Jones was questioned and then released as the police did not think that she had been involved in the killing. Later that day an acquaintance remarked that she looked pale and she stupidly told him, 'If you had seen someone do what I have seen done you wouldn't be able to sleep at night': he was a Special Constable and he reported the conversation. Jones and Hulten were charged with murder. Their six-day trial began at the Old Bailey on 16 January 1945 and they were found guilty and sentenced to death, the jury adding a recommendation for mercy in the case of Betty Jones.

Jones was reprieved 48 hours before she was due to hang (she was released on licence from her life sentence in 1954), but Hulten had to meet the hangman. It is usual practice for the condemned to change from their prison garb into their own clothes a few hours before execution; Karl Hulten opted not to wear his uniform at his final ignominy.

Also hanged this day:

1784 at Gallows Hill, near Winchester: John Quinn for the murder of Cornelius Bailey, the husband of Quinn's mistress. Mary Bailey was strangled and burnt at the stake for the murder and petty treason. (See British Hanging Chronology.)

1819 at Gallows Hill, near Winchester: Sarah Huntingford (61) for the murder of her husband, Thomas Huntingford (71).

1884 at Deming, New Mexico, USA: Daniel Kelley for his part in the Bisbee Massacre in Arizona when four bystanders were killed after a robbery. He was arrested in Deming while having a shave: the barber held a razor to his throat and sent for the lawmen.

1900 at Newgate Prison: Ada Chard Williams for drowning a child whom she had 'adopted' for a few pounds, believed to have been one of many to have suffered the same fate at her hands.

1915 at Terrace Jail, Wellington, New Zealand: Arthur Rottman (21), an interned German sailor, for the Ruahine Farm axe-murders of Joseph and Lucy McCann and their baby son.

1950 J. F. Rivett for the murder of C. R. Cuddon.

9 March

1950 WAS THE WRONG MAN HANGED?
Timothy John Evans (25) hanged at Pentonville Prison, for the murder of his 14-month-old daughter Geraldine, and suspected of murdering his wife Beryl (19).
Hangman: Albert Pierrepoint. Assistant: Syd Dernley

Timothy Evans lived with his wife and baby as sub-tenants at the infamous 10 Rillington Place, Notting Hill, where John Reginald Halliday Christie was also in residence.

Evans confessed to killing his wife and daughter, but later retracted this and accused Christie instead. Christie was a prosecution witness and his word was believed. Evans was found guilty and hardly anyone, at the time, considered that any other verdict was possible. It was different three years later when bodies were found hidden in different parts of the house and garden at 10 Rillington Place. Christie admitted to killing seven women (he was hanged on 15 July 1953) including Mrs Evans, but not baby Geraldine. All had died by strangulation with a ligature.

Was it Evans who killed his wife, or baby daughter, or both, by strangulation with a ligature inside 10 Rillington Place? This is the question that has occupied the minds of top criminologists ever since the discovery of the Christie murders in 1953. It is most unlikely that Evans would have been convicted if it had been known at his trial that he shared the house with a strangler who used a ligature. It *is* possible that he was an accessory to the murders of his wife and child, and therefore shared the guilt with Christie. The truth will never be known now.

At the time of Timothy Evans' execution there was no serious doubt about his guilt. He made no last-minute protestation of innocence, no struggle, and uttered not a single word when the hangmen came for him. He was petrified when Pierrepoint and Dernley entered the cell, remaining frozen and seated for a few seconds. He did not resist and was then quickly walked into the execution chamber. Being a slightly-built man, he was given an eight foot drop and he died at the end of the rope 15 seconds after the hangmen had entered the condemned cell. This was a long time by Pierrepoint's speedy and humane standards, caused by Evans' numbed immobility at the arrival of the hangmen.

In 1966 Evans was posthumously granted a free pardon.

Also hanged this day:

1883   at New York, USA: Pasquale Majone for the gun-murder of his mother-in-law Mrs Maria Velindino Selta as she ran into the kitchen after he had shot and wounded his wife.

1904   at Cheltenham Prison: Sidney George Smith (23) for the murder of his sweetheart.

1926   at Maidstone Prison: Harry Thompson for the murder of Rose Smith at Chatham.

10 March

1820 THE WICKED SQUIRE
John Scanlan (26), Squire of Ballycahane Castle, hanged on Gallows Green, Limerick, Ireland, for the murder of his wife Ellie Hanley (15).

Lieutenant John Scanlan, Squire of Ballycahane Castle, had fought against Napoleon in the British army and was retired on half pay in

1819. His batman, Stephen Sullivan (32), also left the army and accompanied Scanlan back to Ireland as his valet and servant. They spent their time drinking, gambling, and whoring.

Squire Scanlan took a strong fancy to a pretty young girl in Ballycahane named Ellie Hanley (15), the niece of rope maker Connery. Scanlan wanted to bed her, but she resisted and said she would only give herself to him if they were married. The Squire duped Ellie into eloping with her uncle's life savings of £100 in banknotes and 12 guineas in gold coins, and hired a defrocked priest to perform a secret wedding ceremony in June 1819. He took her to Glin, a village on the bank of the River Shannon, for the honeymoon. Sullivan went with them. Within three weeks the Squire had not only 'had his wicked way with her', he had had more than enough of her. It was then that he discovered that, although the wedding was performed by a defrocked priest, it was legally binding by Irish law. This did not suit Scanlan at all, especially as his sister, who had married into the nobility, was arranging his marriage to a wealthy heiress. Ellie had to go.

Sullivan did not need much persuading to do the dirty deed; Ellie had been getting in his way as well. He took her for a pleasure ride in a rowing boat on the Shannon. When they arrived at a lonely spot he beat her to death with his gun, inflicting terrible damage: her skull was shattered in many places, her teeth beaten out, her eyes dislodged from their sockets, an arm and a shoulder were broken, and multiple fractures were caused to one leg. He stripped her body, except for the bodice which he could not unlace, doubled her up with her knees to the neck and tied them together. Then he tipped the body into the river weighed down with a large stone.

Scanlan and Sullivan fled the district. Two months later, on 6 September, the decomposed remains of a woman were washed up on the river bank near Glin: it was Ellie. The evil master and servant had been seen with her by the boat and Sullivan had sold some of her silk clothes. The jury at the inquest named them as her killers.

The search was hampered by Scanlan's influential family who prevented details of the killing, and descriptions of the wanted men, from being published in the newspapers. To prevent more interference, soldiers from the neighbouring county were used to surround Ballycahane Castle (a cluster of farm buildings) after Scanlan had been seen there. He was later discovered hiding in a pile of straw by a soldier who had thrust his bayonet into it.

Squire Scanlan was tried and quickly found guilty for his part in the awful murder. The judge, Baron Smith, ordered his immediate execution in case Scanlan's family tried to exert their influence to prevent justice being done. He was taken at once to Gallows Green and hanged, allowing no time for a messenger to ride to Dublin. Scanlan's family was still able to suppress the reporting of the crime outside the district. The full details at last became public knowledge when Stephen Sullivan was caught and hanged, his final confession being widely published (see 27 July).

Also hanged this day:

1720 at Tyburn Tree: Thomas Butler Esq. for robbery.

1821 at Northampton: Philip Haynes and Mary Clarke, after two years of adultery, for the murder of her cuckolded husband John Clarke.

1884 at Kirkdale Prison, Liverpool: Michael McLean (17) for the murder of a Spanish sailor.

1903 at Lincoln Prison: Samuel H. Smith for the murder of Lucy M. Lingard.

1930 at Bedford Gaol: Alfred Arthur Rouse (37) for the murder of an unknown man in a blazing car on Guy Fawkes night 1929. *Hangman: Tom Pierrepoint*

1932 at Oxford Castle: Private G. T. Pople for the murder of cyclist Mrs Mabel Mathews.

11 March

1735 JOHN THRIFT TAKES OVER
Thirteen hanged at Tyburn Tree by new hangman.
Hangman: John Thrift

John Thrift had been sworn in as hangman only a few hours earlier, succeeding 'Laughing Jack' Hooper. Required to hang 13 people with one drop, he panicked. In his confusion he not only bungled the execution, he also forgot to draw the hoods down over their faces. The ghastly grimacing as they struggled in their death-agonies angered the crowd who soundly booed the new hangman. Thrift never became an efficient hangman, and was often in trouble with the law himself, yet he retained the job until 1752.

Also hanged this day:

1686 at Romsey, Hampshire: John Noyse for the murder of publican William Ives who was the cuckolded husband of Noyse's mistress. Esther Ives was convicted of murder and petty treason* and therefore strangled and burnt at the stake at the same place that day. (* See British Hanging Chronology.)

90

1812 at York: Edith Murray and John Dallas for the murder of Mr Murray, Edith's husband and Dallas' master.

1889 at Carlton Prison, Edinburgh: Jessie King for the murder of her two children.

1890 at Worcester Prison: brothers Joseph (27) and Samuel (39) Boswell for the murder of gamekeeper Frank Stephens. Condemned with them was Alfred Hill, who was the actual killer and the worst of the trio. Inexplicably, Hill was reprieved. *Hangman: James Berry*

1942 at Wandsworth Prison: Harold Dorian Trevor (62), a professional criminal who had spent only 48 weeks outside prisons in the previous 42 years, for the murder of Theodora Jessie Greenhill (65) to rob her of £5.

12 March

1817 THE SPAFIELDS RIOTS
John Cashman hanged at Skinner Street in the City of London, opposite Beckwith's gun shop which he had plundered with others during the Spafields riots.
Hangman: John Langley

Following the war with France (1793–1815), there was great hardship throughout Britain due to failed harvests, the devasting effect of the Corn Laws on the poor, Luddite fears, and mass unemployment: the common people were starving.

The resulting unrest produced riots and one of the worst was in London on 2 December 1816 when between ten and twenty thousand people massed at Spafields. They were harangued by inflamatory speakers who did not confine themselves to the crowd's real and legitimate grievances, but incited against persons in authority up to and including the Prince Regent himself. Someone had organised gangs of ruffians (who arrived by the cart-load) to start a riot. Soon the inflamed mob swarmed into the City, smashing shop windows, looting, and intimidating anyone in their path.

Beckwith's gun shop in Skinner Street was entered and a Mr Platt, a customer, was shot in the hip and groin though not fatally injured. Guns and ammunition were stolen and the mob surged along Cheapside, with guns being fired into the air, towards the Royal Exchange. Peace was eventually restored by the arrival of regiments of soldiery.

Five men were charged for offences during the riot: none of them were ringleaders. To the astonishment of the judge, the jury declared four of the accused not guilty. John Cashman, a sailor, was the only one sentenced to death. He had not even attended the mass meeting at Spafields, but had delivered a message to the Admiralty and joined the riots while drunk on his way home. He may well have been one of those who stormed Beckwith's gun shop.

At 5 a.m. on the day of execution, the gallows' platform was drawn from Newgate Prison to Skinner Street: the authorities had decided to hang the culprit at the scene of the crime as an example to others. Cashman remained composed and quite without fear. He dressed in a new shirt, a pair of sailor's white trousers and a blue jacket, with a black silk handkerchief around his neck. The crowd groaned for him as he arrived in the cart, sitting between Hangman Langley and his assistant.

When on the platform he joined in the crowd's anti-government chantings and when Langley tried to put the hood over his face he said 'For God's sake let me see to the last, I want no cap.' This was allowed. Cashman turned and faced Beckwith's house and yelled 'I'll be with you there!', probably threatening to haunt the place after his death.

While Langley was under the platform and about to release the bolts, Cashman addressed that part of the crowd closest to him: 'Now give me three cheers when I trip. Hurrah! . . .' He was in the act of cheering when the trap fell and he died after only a slight struggle. The real culprits escaped punishment.

Also hanged this day:

1877 at Reading Gaol: Henry Tidbury and George Francis for the murder of two policemen while poaching.

13 March

1935 'VD ELSIE' APPEARS!
Charles Lake a.k.a. George Harvey hanged at Pentonville Prison for the murder of a bookmaker.

The crime was an unsensational murder of a bookmaker by a disgruntled punter after an argument over money. However, the execution marked the beginning of the career of Mrs Violet Van Der Elst as a campaigner for the abolition of the death penalty. She would appear outside a prison before an execution, dressed in black, and exhorted her supporters to follow her in prayer as the execution took place.

She attracted a great deal of newspaper publicity and frequently appeared before the magistrates for disrupting traffic and bothering passers-by, for the next 20 years or so. Most people regarded her as just another eccentric, derisively calling her VD Elsie!

Also hanged this day:

1808 at York: John Cotton for robbery.

1817 at Boston, Massachusetts, USA: Henry Phillips for the drunken murder of Gaspard Denegri.

1945 at Norwich Gaol: Leading Aircraftman Arthur Heys (37) for the rape-murder of Winifred Mary Evans (27), a WAAF radio operator.

14 March

1887 JAMES BERRY HANGS MRS BERRY
Mrs Elizabeth Berry hanged at Kirkdale Prison, Liverpool, for murder.
Hangman: James Berry

Mrs Berry poisoned her 11-year-old daughter for the £10 life insurance for which she had paid a premium of one penny a week. She wrongly believed that a new policy had been completed mutually insuring her own and her child's life whereby another £100 would be paid to the survivor.

Also hanged this day:

1722 at Tyburn Tree: James Appleton (27) for the theft of three wigs.

1738 at Tyburn Tree: John Uddal for robbery.

1739 at Tyburn Tree: Henry Johnson for stealing roof-lead.

1808 at Baltimore Jail, USA: convicts Caleb and Daniel Dougherty, William Morris, and William Robinson for the murder of George Walker during a gaolbreak. At Philadelphia, USA, John Joyce (a.k.a. John Davis) and Peter Mathias (a.k.a. Peter Mathews) for strangling shopkeeper Sarah Cross with her own clothes line during a robbery.

1817 at Old Bailey: Andrew Barton, John Frampton, and Patrick Brown for highway robbery.

1845 at Old Bailey: J. Tapping for the murder of Emma Whitier.

1898   at Carlton Prison, Edinburgh: John Herdman for the murder of Jane Calder.

15 March

1684 NEVISON AND THE 'RIDE TO YORK'
John Nevison (45), highwayman and protection racketeer, hanged at the aptly-named Knavesmire in Yorkshire.

It was John Nevison, not Dick Turpin, who made the famous ride to York to establish an alibi. Fearing that his victim would recognise him after a hold-up at Gad's Hill, on the London to Rochester road in Kent, he set off on horseback on the 225-mile journey to his home town of York. He arrived there that same evening, an amazing achievement for those days, in time to be seen at a bowling match by a number of respectable witnesses who knew him, including the Mayor. When brought to face the charge for the Gad's Hill robbery he was able to 'prove' that he had been in York when the crime was being committed. In those days it was considered impossible to be in Kent and York on the same day. When King Charles II heard of this exploit he asked to meet Nevison. The king was amused at the audacity of it all, called him 'Swift Nicks' and granted him a Royal Pardon.

As well as practising highway robbery, Nevison accumulated a fortune from operating what we would call a protection racket among the drovers on the roads near Pontefract. They willingly paid him a regular fee not to rob them and to keep others from robbing them. After a longer career than most highwaymen enjoyed, his downfall was the number of rewards offered for his capture. In 1684 he was pursued by two thief-takers, the brothers Fletcher, one of whom he shot dead during the chase. The clamour for his capture increased and he was arrested for murder at an inn near Wakefield. He was publicly hanged at a place called Knavesmire, near York.

Also hanged this day:

1723   at Tyburn Tree: George Sayer Esq. for treason.

1862   at Carlisle: William Charlton (engine driver) for the murder of Jane Emmerson to rob her of money she had saved for her funeral.

1932   at L'Original Jail, Ontario, Canada: William J. Larocque and Emmanuel Lavictoire for the murder of Leo Bergeron in an insurance fraud.

16 March

1990 BAGHDAD HANGING OUTRAGE
Farzad Bazoft, correspondent of the *Observer* London office, hanged in Baghdad, Iraq, for spying.

Farzad Bazoft was an Iranian journalist working for the *Observer*, the British Sunday paper. He was arrested in September 1989 with a British nurse, Mrs Daphne Parish, while on a reporting assignment at the rocket-testing establishment at Qaba, south of Baghdad. Mrs Parish had taken him there in her car. They had visited Qaba once before, without incident.

Bazoft had heard a rumour of a massive explosion that had killed hundreds of people at the Qaba site and he went there to gather information, hoping for a scoop. As a part of his investigation he had collected soil samples in sterile glass phials, obtained for him by Mrs Parish from the hospital in which she worked.

He was charged with spying at a revolutionary court on 11 March and Mrs Parish was accused of helping him. The evidence against them was the soil samples, some photographs taken by Bazoft at Qaba, and an unlikely confession extracted from Bazoft by Iraqi security investigators who routinely used torture and other forms of 'persuasion'. Bazoft was sentenced to death and Mrs Parish was jailed for 15 years*. The sentences caused international outrage and much diplomatic activity followed. The British Government and the *Observer* protested the innocence of the pair.

Five days after the trial a diplomat from the British Embassy was summoned to the prison just before dawn on the morning of the execution. It was only when the diplomat was ushered into the cell that Bazoft realised that he was to be hanged that day, and within a few minutes.

* Mrs Parish was released on 16 July 1990.

Also hanged this day:

1812   at Horsemonger Lane Gaol: William Cundell and John Smith hanged and beheaded for treason.

1831   at Lancaster: William (38) and Ashton Worrall (25) for the rape-murder of Sarah McCrinn (64).

1841   at Page River Valley, New South Wales, Australia: Edward 'The Jewboy' Davis and five of his gang for murder and robbery.

1893   at Gloucester Prison: Albert Manning for the murder of Jane Flew.

1934 in USA: seven blacks hanged in three southern states for murder or assault including Isaac Howard, Ernest McGhee and Johnny Jones publicly hanged at Hernando, Missouri.

17 March

1718 'FOR KILLING A SERVANT!'
The Marquis de Paleotti hanged at Tyburn Tree for killing his servant, John Niccolo, who had refused to borrow money for him.
Hangman: Bailiff Banks

An Italian nobleman with expensive tastes, the Marquis de Paleotti came to England to visit a sister who had married the wealthy Duke of Shrewsbury. He had soon spent all of whatever funds he had brought with him. This did not stop his wildly extravagant way of life and he amassed debts from which his sister, the duchess, rescued him time and again until even she refused to help anymore.

He was committed to Newgate as a debtor. His sister secretly arranged for his release in February 1718, probably by paying off the most pressing creditors. Although he had his freedom, he had no money. Disdaining to obtain cash himself he sent his servant, John Niccolo, to perform the distasteful task of obtaining loans or credit. The marquis was furious when Niccolo returned empty-handed and ordered him to go out and try again. The *Newgate Calendar* reported '. . . the servant, having met with frequent denials, declined going, at which the Marquis drew his sword and killed him on the spot'.

De Paleotti fled to the house of the Bishop of Salisbury and caused a rumpus, imagining that he could demand sanctuary in the house. He was disarmed, his sword still stained with Niccolo's blood, and removed to Newgate. His trial was uncomplicated and, much to his astonishment, he was sentenced to hang: 'It is disgraceful' he raged, 'to put a nobleman to death like a common malefactor for killing a servant!'

Also hanged this day:

1717 at Stamford Hill: Joseph Still for murder.

1800 at Aylesbury: Richard 'Galloping Dick' Ferguson for highway robbery.

1830 at Libberton's Wynd, Edinburgh: Robert Edmund (34) for the murders of widow Catherine Munro (40s) and her daughter Madelina (15) at Haddington in East Lothian. Mrs Munro's mutilated body was found dumped in a pigsty.

1885 at Winsom Green Prison, Birmingham: Henry Kimberley for the murder of Mrs Palmer.

1892 at Oxford Castle: Frederick Eggleton and Charles Rayner, poachers, for the murder of Joseph Crawley and William Puddlephot, gamekeepers.

1896 at Fort Smith, Oklahoma, USA: Crawford Goldsby (20) for murder and robbery. He had shot and killed 13 men including lawmen. 'Hanging Judge' Isaac Parker offered a $1,300 reward, which led to his arrest.

18 March

1789 LAST HANGING AND BURNING
Mrs Christian Murphy hanged and burned at the stake after her husband and seven others had been hanged, at Old Bailey, for high treason – in this case coining.
Hangman: William Brunskill

The counterfeiting of coins of the realm was not only a capital offence, it was deemed to be high treason. Condemned male coiners were sentenced to be hanged until nearly dead, then cut down while barely alive, stripped naked, castrated, drawn and quartered. Female traitors, 'for the sake of public decency', would be hanged and then burned.

Mr Murphy and the other seven men were taken out and hanged on the gallows, the rest of their grisly sentence being omitted. Mrs Murphy was not shown similar mercy. After the eight men had been executed, and were still hanging on the main gallows, she was led out to another scaffold and there hanged. After 30 minutes cart loads of faggots were unloaded and piled up over her head so that she was completely covered, and set afire. This was the last such burning as the penalty was abolished the following year.

Also hanged this day:

1740 at Tyburn Tree: Mary Young, known as the 'Female Mackheath', for robbery.

1741 at Tyburn Tree: Robert Legrose, ex-sailor, for stealing clothes.

1772 at Tyburn Tree: James Bollard for forgery.

1812 at Old Bailey: George Skene.

1830 at Ennis, County Clare, Ireland: Mr Comyn for arson.

1898 at Minneapolis, Minnesota, USA: John Moshik for the gun-murder of John Lemke at Minneapolis Union Station to rob him of $14. He scolded the hangman 'You haven't got the rope tight enough about my neck!'

1902 at Shrewsbury Prison: Richard Wigley for the murder of a barmaid, Mary E. Bowen. At Maidstone Prison: Harold Amos Apted (20) for the sex-murder of Frances Eliza O'Rourke (7) near Tonbridge, Kent. *Hangmen: William and John Billington*

1932 at West Virginia, USA: 'America's Worst Bluebeard' Herman Drenth for the gassing-murders of five women (there may have been 50) in his concrete blockhouse, fitted with a plate-glass partition so that he could obtain sexual excitement watching their death-throes.

1947 at Wandsworth Prison: Harold 'Basher' Hagger a.k.a. Sydney Sinclair (45) for the murder of Dagmar Peters (47) on the A20 road in Kent.

19 March

1921 WANDERER'S RETURN
Carl Otto Wanderer (34) hanged at Chicago Prison, Illinois, USA, for shooting his wife (21) and a hired 'attacker' Al Watson.

Wanderer had returned to Chicago from active service in World War One a hero, and had plenty of medals to prove it. He married and his wife was expecting their baby in 1920 when the couple were attacked and Mrs Wanderer was shot to death in the hold-up. Ever the hero, Wanderer overpowered the gunman and killed him with his own gun.

Police became suspicious when Wanderer was seen happily strolling down the street, whistling, soon after the funeral. Investigations proved that Wanderer was a covert homosexual who could not accept the thought of becoming a father. He had hired Watson, a penniless tramp, for $5 to stage a hold-up then double-crossed him, killing Watson and then his wife. He was sentenced to death by hanging.

Wanderer had befriended a couple of young reporters who later became famous playwrights, Ben Hecht and Charles MacArthur. They wrote his 'dying speech' which he was to read on the gallows, and they took the opportunity to include some unflattering words about their editors. The speech was hidden, fixed to his ribs with sticky-tape. They had all forgotten that his arms would be tied before he mounted the scaffold and the solemn occasion became a farce. Wondering what to say, all that Wanderer could think of were the words of the song, 'Dear Old Pal Of Mine'. Afterwards a thwarted Charles MacArthur grunted, 'That son-of-a-bitch should have been a song-plugger!'

Also hanged this day:

1819 at Schoharie, New York, USA: John Van Alstine for the clubbing-murder of Sheriff William Huddleston.

1824 at Angelica, New York, USA: David D. How for the gun-murder of Othello Church.

1875 at San Jose, California, USA: Tiburcio Vasquez (40) for multiple murders and robberies. He was betrayed by a fellow gang member who caught Vasquez making love to his wife.

1901 at Wandsworth Prison: George Henry Parker for the shooting-murder of Mr Pearson in a railway carriage near Surbiton, to rob him of money for his mistress.

1912 at Knutsford Gaol: John Williams (38) for wife-murder: the last man to be hanged in Cheshire. *Hangman: John Ellis. Assistant: Lumb*

20 March

1809 THE YORKSHIRE WITCH
Mary Bateman (41) the 'Yorkshire Witch' publicly hanged at Leeds, her skin stripped into fragments and sold as charms, for the murder by poisoning of Mrs Rebecca Perigo, one of her dupes.
Hangman: (probably) John 'Mutton' Curry

Mary Bateman began her criminal career thieving as a small child. She developed into a petty fraudster, duping people who were miserably poor already and seeming to take pleasure in cruelly reducing them to even greater wretchedness. Her favourite game was to use fortune telling, for which she had acquired a reputation. She would warn her victims of awful things that were about to overtake them, from which she could save them by appealing to a fictitious 'Miss Blythe' who had magical powers. The letters from Miss Blythe always suggested payments, in cash or in goods, to Mary Bateman.

Her most gullible customers, Mr and Mrs Perigo of Bramley near Leeds, were also the cause of her undoing. This superstitious couple believed all of Mary's forecasts, and her incredible series of remedies to offset them. From December 1806 to April 1807 they handed over a total of £70 in varying amounts of cash and a long list of foods, clothing and household goods. Bateman decided to poison them in May 1807, but it is a mystery why she embarked upon killing a pair of 'gooses' who were laying so many golden eggs for her.

She prophesied that they would suffer an awful illness: 'You will escape the chambers of the grave; though you seem to be dead yet you will live.' She gave them powder (arsenic, of course) to put into puddings that were to be eaten for six days starting on 11 May. All went well until the sixth day when Mr Perigo tried one mouthful and felt so ill that he refused any more. Rebecca Perigo ate four mouthfuls. Perigo suffered violent pains, his wife even worse. Rebecca died on 24 May; Mr Perigo recovered although he was severely weakened. Even after this, it was months before Perigo called in the authorities. The Yorkshire Witch was tried at the Lent Assizes at York, amid great public excitement, and sentenced to death. Even in the condemned cell she swindled other prisoners.

After the hanging, her body with its hideously stretched and rope-burned neck was put on public display at Leeds Infirmary. Some 2,400 visitors were charged three pennies each admission and this alone raised £30 (there were 240 pennies to the pound in those days). This was not the Infirmary's only enterprise in fund-raising: her body was skinned and fragments were sold as charms to satisfy a local superstition about the benefits to be had from the skin of a witch.

Also hanged this day:

1776 At York: Thomas Aikney for the knife-murder of smuggler John Broadingham at the suggestion of his mistress, Elizabeth Broadingham. Elizabeth was also charged and was strangled before being burned for petty treason (see British Hanging Chronology).

1820 at Old Bailey: Edward Voss and Daniel Keston for issuing forged notes; John and George Bird for burglary; William Frith and William Kennett for theft from a dwelling house.

1868 at Williston, Vermont, USA: John Ward for the murder of Mrs Griswold at her home.

1888 at Hereford Prison: Alfred Scandrett (21) and James Jones for the murder of Philip Ballard who disturbed them while they were robbing his house. Scandrett struck the deathblows. *Hangman: James Berry*

21 March

1901 STRANGLED WITH A BOOTLACE
Herbert John Bennett (22) hanged at Norwich Gaol for the murder of his wife Mary Jane Bennett (24).
Hangman: James Billington. Assistant: Thomas Billington

On Sunday 23 September 1900 a young woman's body was found on South Beach at Yarmouth; she had been strangled with a bootlace and her disarranged clothes suggested rape. A Yarmouth landlady, Mrs Rudram, identified the body as being 'Mrs Hood' who had been staying with her since 15 September and was now missing. Mrs Hood had the laundry mark '599' on her clothes and this was traced to Mrs Mary Bennett from South London. Her estranged husband, Herbert John Bennett, was arrested at Woolwich on 6 November and he told the police that he had never been to Yarmouth and had not seen his wife since January. The evidence against him was damning:

1. A gold chain with a silver watch was found among his possessions. It was positively identified by Mrs Rudram as the chain and watch worn by Mrs Hood when she went out on the Saturday night. She had also been wearing it when snapped by a beach photographer a few days before she was killed.
2. Bennett was seen with his wife in a bar in Yarmouth on the Saturday night she was murdered.
3. He was identified as the man who stayed the night at the Crown and Anchor hotel in Yarmouth on the Saturday night.
4. He was identified by a railway booking clerk as having caught the 7.20 a.m. train from Yarmouth on the Sunday morning.

Bennett was vigorously defended by Marshall Hall who believed that he was innocent of the murder, even though Bennett was a worthless scoundrel. Marshall Hall's sharp cross-examination of witnesses did cast some doubts and slightly devalued their evidence. He also produced two surprise defence witnesses.

The first was a fancy-goods manufacturer named Sholto Douglas who claimed to have had a casual meeting with Bennett at Lee Green, South London, on the Saturday evening. This respectable man truly believed that it had been Bennett. Bennett, it seemed, did not recall the meeting, but agreed that Marshall Hall should call Sholto Douglas.

Then there was Mr O'Driscoll, a newsagent from Lowestoft, ten miles along the coast south of Yarmouth. He and his assistant had been in the shop four days after the murder when a customer came in and asked for the best account of the Yarmouth murder. The man had a dark moustache, his face was scratched, and one of his shoes was without a bootlace. He muttered and groaned in great excitement as he read the paper until he noticed that O'Driscoll and his assistant were staring at him, when he rushed away.

However, the weight of the more substantial prosecution evidence was too much and the jury took a scant 35 minutes to find Bennett guilty. Nonetheless Marshall Hall continued to believe in his client's innocence. He wrote to a friend on the Sunday after the verdict: 'I am convinced that he did *not* murder his wife. He is much too clever a criminal to have done such a deed in such an appallingly bungling way . . . I am confident that the murder was done by some erotic maniac. . .'

Bennett was hanged without incident at Norwich Gaol, but there was a sensation for the members of the public watching outside. As the black flag was being hoisted the flagpole snapped and it and the black flag crashed to the ground, causing the superstitious to believe that an innocent man had been hanged.

Was the real murderer still at large in Yarmouth? There was an eery postscript 11 years later. On Sunday 14 July 1912 a young woman's body was found on South Beach at Yarmouth; she had been strangled with a bootlace and her clothes were disarranged, suggesting rape. Her name was Dora Gray (18) and her murder has remained unsolved.

Also hanged this day:

1706   at Gallows Hill, Maumbury Rings, Dorset: a man for murder and another for house-breaking; also Mary Channing (19) strangled and burnt at the stake for petty treason* in murdering her husband Thomas Channing. (* See British Hanging Chronology.)

1873   at the Tombs Prison, New York, USA: William Foster for the murder of fellow passenger Avery Putnam after a pointless drunken argument on a Broadway tramcar.

22 March

1889 THE BOYS FROM 'THE HUB OF HELL'
Peter and Timothy Barrett hanged at Minneapolis, Minnesota, USA, for the gun-murder of a tramcar conductor.

Their parents owned an ill-famed saloon called The Hub of Hell in Minneapolis. On 27 July 1887 the three brothers, Henry, Peter and Timothy Barrett held up a horse-drawn tramcar at gun-point. They shot the conductor, grabbed their haul, $20, and made their getaway. To save his own neck, Henry informed on his brothers and they were convicted. Peter and Timothy were hanged side-by-side.

Also hanged this day:

1722   at Tyburn Tree: William Burridge (33) for horse-stealing.

1880   at Newgate Prison: John Wingfield for wife-murder.

1892   at Carlisle Prison: Joseph Wilson for the murder of Marion Greaves Crossman.

1898   at Durham Gaol: Charles Smith (33) for wife-murder.

23 March

1926 LIVERPOOL'S CHINATOWN TRAGEDY
Lock Ah Tam (54) hanged at Walton Gaol, Liverpool, for the shooting to death of his wife and two daughters.

Lock Ah Tam came to England in 1895 as a humble ship's steward. He settled in Liverpool and became a wealthy man. Before long he was the most respected Chinaman in England: president of the largest Chinese republican organisation, European representative of a Chinese dockers' federation, superintendent of Chinese sailors for three British shipping lines, and founder of a seamen's club in Liverpool. He was considered a wise man by fellow Chinese, and consulted as such to settle disputes.

In 1918 he was hit on the head by a drunken Russian sailor with a billiard cue in the club he had founded. From then on his personality changed: he became morose, irrational, and took to drinking heavily and when drunk he would turn into a terrifying madman. In 1924 he lost his money and was declared bankrupt.

He held a party in honour of his son's birthday on 1 December 1925 and was kindly and charming all evening. After the guests had gone, at about 1 a.m. on 2 December, he flew into one of his uncontrollable rages: screaming at his wife and stamping his feet on the floor. While his son fled to bring a policeman, Lock Ah Tam shot his Welsh-born wife Catherine and daughters Doris (20) and Cecilia (18). They all died shortly afterwards. Before the son returned with a policeman Tam had phoned the police station: 'Send you folks, please, I have killed my wife and children.'

Funds for his defence poured in from Chinese people all over England. Sir Edward Marshall Hall defended him at his trial, pleading insanity at the time of the offence. Unhappily, the jury rejected this plea and found him guilty after 12 minutes of consideration. Lock Ah Tam retained his dignity and stoicism throughout the trial, in the condemned cell, and on to the scaffold.

Also hanged this day:

1824 at Old Bailey: John Wagstaff, a broker, and William Hill, a former police officer, for issuing forged notes; John Easterly for burglary and John Smith for robbery.

1860 at St Paul, Minnesota, USA: Ann Bilansky for the poison-murder of her rich husband. She is the only woman to have been executed in Minnesota.

24 March

1829 QUADRUPLE HANGING AT OLD BAILEY
Joseph Redguard (23), William Kelly (21), and Thomas Birmingham (21) hanged for highway robbery. Charles Goodlad (22) hanged for robbing his master of goods to the value of £170.
Hangman: James Foxon

A few minutes before 8 a.m., as the bell of St Sepulchre's tolled the death-knell, the condemned men were led out to the gallows. Birmingham's arrival on the platform was greeted with cries of 'Good-bye Tom!' and 'God bless you, my trump!' from a large group of dissolute women. There was a mishap in the dispatch of Birmingham, caused by him jumping just before the trap opened which dislodged the noose from under his chin. He dangled for five minutes making agonised gasping noises before the angry shouts of the mob forced Hangman Foxon to hang on the poor man's legs until he expired.

Also hanged this day:

1819 at Old Bailey: Edward Dent and John Adams for issuing forged notes and John Willett for sheep-stealing.

1873 at Durham Gaol: Mary Ann Cotton (40) for the arsenic-poisoning of her stepson Charles Edward Cotton (7). She was a mass poisoner with 14 to 21 fatal victims. She suffered a slow death, hanging for three minutes before losing consciousness. *Hangman: William Calcraft or Thomas Askern*

1875 at Sligo County Gaol, Ireland: M'Daid for the murder of Ferguson.

1879 at Newgate Prison: James Simms for the murder of Lucy Graham.

1905 at Parish Prison, New Orleans, Louisiana, USA: Lewis W.

Lyons (55) for the gun-murder of District Attorney J. Ward Gurley. Still smarting from a grudge for being wrongly arrested in 1895, Lyons had walked into Gurley's office and challenged him to a duel, which was refused. He shot Gurley three times then picked him up and shot him again. Encouraged to be brave on execution day, Lyons replied 'There's no dunghill in me, I'll walk to the gallows as easily as I'll walk through that door.'

1908   at Durham Gaol: Joseph William Noble for the murder of a man named Patterson.

1922   at Exeter Gaol: Edward Ernest Black (36) for the murder of his wife Annie Black (50).

25 March

1723 CHAPLAIN NEARLY HANGED!
William Summers and a man named Tipping (and almost the chaplain) publicly hanged at Hertford.
Hangman: (drunk)

The unknown hangman was an intoxicated ruffian. He was able to put the rope around the necks of Summers and Tipping successfully, but he had it firmly fixed in his drunken mind that he was to hang three men. The sensation occurred when he tried to put the third noose on the local parson. As the determined hangman and the terrified chaplain fought each other on the tail of the cart the waiting Summers and Tipping were getting bumped about in the struggle. After they were pulled apart order was restored and Summers and Tipping were dispatched to the next world, hopefully with the fervent prayers of the spared chaplain.

Also hanged this day:

1762   at Execution Dock, Wapping: Captain James Lowry (40) for the flogging to death of one of his crew, Kenith Hossack. *Hangman: Thomas Turlis*

1805   at Penenden Heath, Kent: Elizabeth Barber a.k.a. Mrs Dalby (53) for the stabbing-murder of John Dalby, a pensioner at Greenwich.

1878   at Bloomsburg, Pennsylvania, USA: Pat Hester, Pat Tully, and Pete McHugh, for the 'Molly Maguire' murder of Alexander Rea (see also 21 June). *Hangman: John W. Hoffman (who was drunk)*

26 March

1810 MURDER ON A THAMES PRISON HULK
William Coleman (20) hanged on Penenden Heath*, near Maidstone, Kent, for the murder of another convict, Thomas Jones, on a prison hulk moored at Woolwich.

Old ships were moored on the Thames at Woolwich and used as prisons to hold convicts sentenced to transportation. The hulks were mostly rotting and vermin infested. They held the most desperate prisoners in the land and the convicts were employed at hard labour on the Thames or in the Royal Arsenal.

William Coleman suspected that Tom Jones, another convict, had informed on him after a brick had been thrown at a prison officer and, inflamed, swore that he would have his revenge. On the night of the 29 August 1809 Coleman faked a reconciliation with Jones, shook his hand and spent the evening with him.

When Coleman thought everyone was asleep he got out of bed and crept to the place where he knew a knife was hidden. From there he went to the sleeping Tom Jones and stabbed him in the throat and chest, killing him instantly and silently. Unfortunately for him, Coleman had been seen as he went for the knife by two other prisoners. Their evidence sealed his fate at the next Kent Assizes and he was hanged three days after his short trial.

* Penenden Heath was the normal place for public hangings in Kent until a new scaffold and drop was located at Maidstone. Public executions were performed outside the prison gates at Maidstone from 1831 until 'private' hangings were begun within prisons in 1868.

Also hanged this day:

1789 at Exeter: William Weyburn and William Snow for housebreaking and robbery.

1794 at Bury St Edmunds: John and Nathan Nichols, father and son, for the murder of John's daughter, Sarah Nichols, having beaten and strangled her and dumped her body in a ditch.

1803 at Horsemonger Lane Gaol: Stephen Stilwell for murder.

1812 at Ipswich: E. Trower, John Smith, and Elizabeth Smith.

1827 at York: Martin Slack for murder.

1877 at Lincoln Prison: William Clarke for the murder of Henry Walker.

106

1890 at Newgate Prison: bricklayer Thomas Neal (69) for wife-murder.

1895 at Nottingham Prison: Edmund Kesteven for the murder of Sarah Ann Oldham.

1913 at Agra, India: Dr Henry Lovell William Clark (42) for the 'Agra Double-murder' of his wife and the husband of his mistress.

27 March

1710 POOR GRACE
Grace Tripp (19) hanged at Tyburn Tree for murder, condemned by the evidence of the killer.

Grace Tripp was a servant at the London house of Lord Torrington. She had fallen for a rogue named Peters who had plans to burgle his lordship's home: the plan required Grace to let him into the house after dark. The foolish girl agreed, after Peters promised to marry her when the deed was done.

On the night of the burglary the house was empty except for Grace and the housekeeper. Thinking that the housekeeper was fast asleep, Grace kept her appointment and smuggled Peters indoors. It was the silverware that he was after and he must have made a noise while loading it into his sack. The couple were surprised when the door opened and they were confronted by the housekeeper. Peters immediately grabbed her and slit her throat before she could raise an alarm. Grace stood there, holding the candle to light the room, while the murder of her mistress took place. The two of them searched the dead woman and discovered some 30 guineas, after which they fled the house. They were caught a few days later.

That Grace Tripp was guilty of capital offences, as an accomplice to murder and to burglary, there is no doubt. The injustice occurred when the active murderer and burglar, Peters, was given immunity for turning Queen's Evidence. Tripp was convicted and sentenced to death by the words of her treacherous lover. Poor, foolish, Grace Tripp.

Also hanged this day:

1718 at Tyburn Tree: James Sheppard for treason.

1771 at Tyburn Tree: five unnamed criminals. *Hangman: Thomas Turlis.* Mainly notable as it was the last executions by Turlis at Tyburn; he died on the road five days later while returning from a hanging at Kingston, Surrey.

1821   at Old Bailey: James Kitsell and James Pilcher for robbing their employers.

1877   at Strangeways Prison, Manchester: John M'Kenna for wife-murder.

1888   at Winchester Prison: George Clarke for the murder of his stepdaughter, nearly cutting off her head.

1894   at Nottingham Prison: Walter Smith for the murder of nurse Catharine Cross.

1940   Ernest E. Hammerton for the murder of Miss E. M. Ellington.

28 March

1950 THE LIVERPOOL TOUGH GUY
George Kelly (27) hanged at Walton Gaol, Liverpool, for murder during a cinema robbery.
Hangman: Albert Pierrepoint

George Kelly was a small-time Liverpool tough guy. On 19 March 1949 he entered the Cameo Cinema in Webster Road, Liverpool, while Charles Connally (26) remained outside as look-out. The Cameo's manager, Leonard Thomas, was in his office counting the night's takings with his assistant, John Bernard Catterall, when Kelly burst in with a gun. The box-office cashier heard six shots fired in quick succession and she and the doorman, showing great courage, rushed towards the office. The masked George Kelly emerged and ordered them out of the way, waving the gun at them, and escaped. Mr Thomas and Mr Catterall had been shot and both died later.

The police investigation got nowhere until six months later when an informer contacted the police. As a result, Kelly and Connally were both charged with the murder of Mr Thomas, but the jury failed to agree at the first trial. At the next assizes, in February 1950, they were tried separately. This time Kelly was convicted and sentenced to death. Connally was convicted on lesser charges at his trial, and given two concurrent two-year sentences.

George Kelly's tough image in the Liverpool underworld did not survive very long when it was learned, via the grapevine from the prison, that he had lost control of his bowels on the way from the condemned cell to the gallows next door.

Also hanged this day:

1752 at Epping Forest: Eliza Jefferies and John Swan for murder.

1767 at Hertford: William Harrow, described as 'a desperate fellow', for robbery.

1811 at Gloucester: William Townley.

1839 at Maidstone: Samuel Seager (40) for the murder of baby-sitter Hannah Giles. *Hangman: William Calcraft*

1845 at Market Square, Aylesbury: John Tawell for the murder of Sarah Hart. *Hangman: William Calcraft*

1876 at Morpeth Prison: George Hunter for the murder of William Wood.

1878 at Mauch Chunk, Pennsylvania, USA: Tom Fisher for the 'Molly Maguire' murder of Morgan Powell. Fisher may have been innocent and convicted on the perjured testimony of the town drunk. He had to be dragged, weeping and still protesting his innocence, to the gallows (see also 21 June). *Hangman: Sheriff Raudenbush*

1899 at Newgate Prison: George Robertson for the murder of a young girl.

29 March

1949 THE 'HOLLYBUSH MURDERER'
James Farrell (19) hanged at Winsom Green Prison, Birmingham, for the strangling rape-murder of Joan Mary Marney (14).
Hangman: Albert Pierrepoint. Assistant: Harry Kirk

This was the common-place sex murder of a 14-year-old schoolgirl. The rapist-killer, James Farrell, was dubbed the 'Hollybush Murderer' by newspapers because he had dumped the girl's body among holly bushes near the Banner Gate entrance to Sutton Park, a Birmingham beauty spot, on 22 November 1948. They had both lived at Kingstanding, the killer in Bevis Grove and his victim in Sidcup Road, within walking distance of the scene of the strangling.

This was the first execution attended by Syd Dernley, who was there as an observer prior to becoming an assistant hangman. In his book *The Hangman's Tale* he recalled that Farrell was a blond-haired youth who had spent his 19th birthday in the condemned cell and, as he entered the execution chamber, he had the most terrified eyes that Dernley had ever seen. It was a quick hanging: from the instant that Pierrepoint and Kirk entered the condemned cell at 9 a.m., Farrell had exactly eight seconds of life to live before dying with a sudden jerk at the end of the rope. In his state of terror, it must have seemed an eternity.

Also hanged this day:

1849 at Maidstone: George Millen (17) for the murder of Mr Law (82) during a burglary. *Hangman: William Calcraft*

1875 at Chelmsford Gaol: Richard Coates for the murder of a young girl.

1892 John Noble for the murder of a woman.

1905 at Nottingham Prison: John Hutchinson (29) for the murder of Albert Mathews (5), the son of the house where he lodged.

1939 at Wandsworth Prison: William Butler (29) for the murder of jeweller Ernest Percival Key (64).

1950 at Winsom Green Prison, Birmingham: Piotr Maksimowski (33), a Polish refugee, for the murder of his mistress Dilys Campbell (30) which may have been a bungled suicide pact. *Hangmen: Albert Pierrepoint and Syd Dernley*

30 March

1991 HANGINGS IN IRAN
Six Iranians hanged at Zahedan, south eastern Iran, 'for distributing narcotics, homicide, armed robbery, terrorising people, blackmailing, illegal possession of arms, gambling and other corrupt activities'.

The hangings were reported by the Iranian national news agency, IRNA. The six men were not named, but were the members of a criminal gang convicted by an Islamic court. During the previous 27 months, to the end of March 1991, two thousand people were reported to have been hanged in Iran.

Also hanged this day:

1807 at Stafford: George Allen for the murder of his wife and three children.

1812 at Winchester: J. Dubois and G. Beury.

1825 at Old Bailey: James Lintott and John Ferguson for burglary.

110

1852 at Newark, New Jersey, USA: German immigrant John Erpenstein for wife-murder.

1860 at New York, USA: bar-owner John Crummins for the murder of Dennis McHenry with a series of sword-thrusts in response to drunken insults.

1875 at Maidstone Prison: Bandsman John Morgan (19) for the throat-cutting murder of Bandsman Joe Foulstone at Shorncliffe Barracks. *Hangman: William Marwood.* At Stafford Gaol: John Stanton for the stabbing-murder of his uncle, Thomas Neald.

1950 at Armley Gaol, Leeds: Walter Sharpe for the murder of A. H. Levine.

31 March

1856 CARRIED ON TO THE SCAFFOLD
William Bousfield hanged at Old Bailey, sitting in a chair, for the murders of his wife and three children.
Hangman: William Calcraft

Bousfield had attempted suicide by throwing himself on to the fire in the condemned cell at Newgate Prison and came to his execution in a very weak condition. He was carried out of the prison by four warders supporting his arms and legs and strapped into a chair on the trap door. Calcraft was in a hurry to get the execution over with; he had received a letter threatening that he would be shot when he appeared on the scaffold. He quickly released the bolt, and disappeared out of sight.

Bousfield found the strength to raise himself up and jump to the edge of the drop as the trap opened. A turnkey pushed him off, but he struggled back again. Calcraft returned and forced Bousfield down through the trap, and then hung on to his legs until the poor man stopped struggling.

Also hanged this day:

1836 at Maidstone: James Joy (19) for setting a barn on fire at Sturry; Thomas Pryor (18) for highway robbery and attempted murder at Wingham. *Hangman: William Calcraft*

1860 at Bedford: J. Castle for wife-murder.

1874 at Northampton Prison: Thomas Chamberlain for the murder of John Cox Newet.

1884 at Carlton Prison, Edinburgh: William Innes and Robert Flockart Vickers for the murders of John Fortune and John Diarmid, gamekeepers who caught them poaching. *Hangman: James Berry (his first execution). Assistant: Richard Chester*

1925 at Horfield Gaol, Bristol: William Francis A. Bressington for the murder of a boy at Staple Hill.

APRIL

1 April

Hanged this day:

1716 at Tyburn Tree: John Thompson and William Smith for robbery.

1847 at Derby: John Platts for the murder of Collis.

1878 at Oxford Prison: Henry Rowles for the murder of Miss Allington.

2 April

1868 LAST PUBLIC HANGING OF A WOMAN
Mrs Frances Kidder (25) hanged outside Maidstone Prison for the drowning of Louisa Kidder-Staple (12).
Hangman: William Calcraft

Frances was married to William Kidder, a vegetable dealer of New Hythe, Kent. Her stepdaughter, Louisa Kidder-Staple, was the offspring of a woman with whom William had previously cohabited. It was clear that Frances disliked the child; she ill-treated her and threatened to poison her.

On 24 August 1867 Frances had gone to visit her parents at New Romney, taking Louisa and a child of her own with her. Her mother went out for a while and Frances drowned Louisa in a ditch, holding her under where the water was 14 inches deep. When her mother returned she claimed that two horses had frightened them both into the ditch, a hopeless story to which she adhered at her trial.

She was hysterical during her days in the condemned cell at Maidstone. William Kidder visited her there and she accused him of being intimate with her sister, extracting a promise from him to desist. When he departed after the second, and last, visit she began screaming. William ran down the passageway to escape the awful noise of his wife's shrieking, but was stopped by the chaplain, who delivered a sermon warning him to alter 'his wicked course of life'.

Kidder's hysteria continued to the last morning of her life and she had to be supported on her way to the scaffold outside the prison gates. A warder stood on each side of her on the trap as she prayed intently with her eyes tightly closed. After the drop she struggled painfully for some time. A minor riot occurred outside William Kidder's house later that day when a crowd assembled, hooting, burning an effigy, and breaking his windows until the police arrived to disperse them.

Also hanged this day:

1778 at Warwick: J. Donelan Esq. for the murder by poisoning of Sir Theodosius Broughton, Bart.

1814 at Old Bailey: William Sturman for arson. At Horsemonger Lane Gaol: Charles Calaghan for the murder of Mr Berry.

1824 at New York City centre, USA: John Johnson publicly hanged in front of fifty thousand spectators for the axe-murder of his room-mate James Murray.

1877 at Chester Castle: James Bannister for wife-murder.

1894 at Kirkdale Prison, Liverpool: Margaret Walber for the murder of her husband.

1901 at Stafford Gaol: Joseph Shufflebotham for wife-murder.

1946 Marion Grondkowski (33) and Henryk Malinowski (25) for the gun-murder of black-marketeer Ruben 'Russian Robert' Martirosoff.

3 April

1755 IN THE BUREAU DRAWER
'Mail-robber' Davis hanged at Gerrard's Cross, Buckinghamshire, the scene of his crime of robbing the Cirencester mailcoach.

'Mail-robber' Davis had apparently evaded justice after his successful haul from holding up and robbing the Cirencester Mail two years before. If he had been able to pay for his rent he might have got away with it for ever.

His legal occupation was as a tallow chandler in London's Carnaby Market where he was considered to be a respectable trader. In the spring of 1755 he was short of funds and could not pay his rent so his landlord obtained authority to take possession of his tenant's goods. While the landlord was inventorying them, a bureau drawer revealed a pistol, parts of banknotes and some bills of exchange, all of which led to Davis being committed to Newgate Prison for the Cirencester Mail robbery. He was taken to Aylesbury for trial where he pleaded not guilty but was convicted after a five-hour hearing. He was sentenced to be hanged at Gerrard's Cross, the scene of the crime, and was afterwards gibbeted in chains at the same spot.

Also hanged this day:

1739 at Tyburn Tree: James Roberts for treason.

1841 at Shrewsbury: J. Misters for wounding a man named Mackreth.

1877 at Armley Gaol, Leeds: John Henry Johnson for the murder of Amos Waite.

1894 at Armley Gaol, Leeds: Philip Garner for wife-murder.

4 April

1979 EX-PREMIER HANGED
Ali Zulfikar Bhutto (51), former Prime Minister of Pakistan, hanged at Rawalpindi Gaol for ordering the assassination of a political opponent.

Bhutto was Prime Minister of Pakistan between 1973 and 1977 after many years as a cabinet minister. He was a man of culture, intelligence and charm with a flair for international affairs.

His party won the election in 1977, but there were accusations that the result had been rigged and internal unrest was followed by an army coup d'état. Bhutto was charged with ordering the murder of an opponent. Other charges were added later, of financial corruption and government malpractice. He was convicted in March 1978 and sentenced to death.

He was forced to spend his final months in appalling squalor in his cell as he awaited execution, not allowed even the most basic of sanitary facilities and his own bodily refuse littering the floor of his cell. His gaolers permitted him to bathe before he faced the hangman.

Also hanged this day:

1761 at Panton Street, near the scene of his crime in Leicester Square, London: Swiss artist Theodore Gardelle for the murder of Mrs King. His body was hung in chains on Hounslow Heath. *Hangman: Thomas Turlis*

1868 outside New Bailey Prison, Manchester: Miles Wetherill for the murder of the Reverend Mr Plow and his maid at Todmorden vicarage, and Timothy Flaherty for the murder of Mary Hanmer. Last public hanging in Lancashire. *Hangman: William Calcraft*

1876 at Maidstone Prison: Thomas Fordred (48), a labourer, for the murder of Mary Ann Bridger 'by knocking her about and kicking her' at Thanet. *Hangman: William Marwood*

1893 at Armley Gaol, Leeds: Edward Hemmings for wife-murder.

1894 at Winsom Green Prison, Birmingham: Frederick W. Fenton for the murder of Florence Elborough.

1962 at Bedford Gaol: James Hanratty (25) for the murder of Michael Gregsten at Deadman's Hill on the A6 road.

5 April

1722 HANGED FOR NOSE-SLITTING
Arundel Coke (or Cook), Esq., and John Woodbourne (or Woodman) hanged at Bury St Edmunds for the attack on Coke's brother-in-law Edward Crispe.

These were the first executions ever carried out under the Coventry Act (see British Hanging Chronology), whereby it was a capital offence to lie in wait with intent to disfigure by putting out an eye, disabling the tongue or slitting the nose.
  Arundel Coke, a lawyer of Bury St Edmunds, hired Woodbourne to murder Edward Crispe: the motive was that Coke's wife would inherit upon the death of her brother. Coke lured his brother-in-law out of the house and returned alone. Woodbourne attacked Crispe with a billhook but failed to murder him. Crispe escaped, his face a bloody mess. Coke admitted his complicity, with the result that he and Woodbourne were put on trial. Because Crispe's facial injuries included his nose being slit open, the Coventry Act was invoked.

Also hanged this day:

1898 at Clonmel County Gaol, County Tipperary, Ireland: Private Kenny for the murder of Private Goodwin in barracks.

1904 at Winsom Green Prison, Birmingham: Charles Samuel Dyer for the murder of Martha Eliza Simpson

1926 at Connecticut, USA: Gerald Chapman (36) for shooting a policeman while robbing a department store in New Britain, Connecticut. With the noose round his neck and the hood over his head, his last words were: 'Death itself isn't dreadful, but hanging seems an awkward way of entering the adventure.'

6 April

1946 GORBALS HARDMAN
Patrick Carraher (40) hanged at Barlinnie Prison, Glasgow, for the murder of an innocent bystander in a street fight.
Hangman: Albert Pierrepoint

Patrick Carraher came from a decent working-class family in Glasgow, but he grew up to be an alcoholic Gorbals hardman and delighted in being known as 'Killer' Carraher. Standing only five feet six inches when fully grown he achieved his hardman ambition by his ruthless desire to fight without limits: he used fists, boots, head, knives, razors – anything. He received his first prison sentence when aged 17 and he was destined to spend more than half his adult life in prison, including the last morning of his life.

He was charged with the murder of a regular soldier, James Sydney Emden Shaw (23), in 1938. He was drunk at the time and stabbed Shaw in the neck after a street confrontation with another man. At his trial the judge's summing up appeared to suggest that Carraher's drunken state was a valid excuse for his behaviour. The jury took the hint and found him guilty of the lesser charge of culpable homicide. The lenient judge sentenced Carraher to three years.

He was now Killer Carraher, the man who had got away with murder. When he came out of prison he gloried in his hardman role, got drunk almost every day and went around with cronies beating up anyone he took a dislike to. On one such drunken rampage he attacked a man with a razor and was put away for another three years.

On a drunken night in November 1945 one of Carraher's pals got into a fight and Carraher joined the scene. Standing near, but not involved, was John Gordon (39). A regular soldier, he had only recently been released from a German prisoner-of-war camp, where he had been since his capture at Dunkirk in 1940. Carraher rushed up behind him and stabbed him in the neck with a wood-chisel. John Gordon died soon after being admitted to hospital. Patrick Carraher was arrested by the same detective who had arrested him for murder in 1938. He stood trial for murder again, in the same courtroom, and once again for stabbing a soldier in the neck. This time there was a difference: he was lound guilty as charged and sentenced to death.

Also hanged this day:

1752   at Castle Green, Oxford: Mary Blandy (31), gentlewoman, for poisoning her father with powder she believed was a love potion that would induce him to like her lover.

1943 G. H. Trenoweth for the murder of A. J. Bateman at Falmouth.

7 April

1903 NOT JACK THE RIPPER?
**George Chapman (37) (real name Severin Klosovski) hanged at
Wandsworth Prison, for poisoning three women.**
Hangman: William Billington. Assistant: Henry Pierrepoint

George Chapman is an unlikely candidate to be Jack the Ripper. He
was a suspect because he had been in Whitechapel at the time of the
Ripper killings in 1888 and had been a barber-surgeon as a young man
in Poland. Another reason is that Inspector Abberline of Scotland
Yard, who had been in charge of the Ripper investigation, remarked
to the officer who arrested Chapman, 'You've caught the Ripper,
then?'
Chapman was a poisoner, there was no doubt about that. When he
tired of them, he killed three barmaid-mistresses by feeding them
antimony: Mary Spink, Bessie Taylor and Maud Marsh. The jury
retired for only 11 minutes to find him guilty.
It seems unlikely that whoever *was* Jack the Ripper should have
indulged in the escalating frenzy of violent stabbing, bloodletting and
mutilation, only to calm down and carry out the cool, methodical
career of a poisoner.
Chapman almost collapsed on hearing the death penalty pronounced, and during his days in the condemned cell he got worse and
worse. He was partly carried to the gallows and had to be held upright
by a warder on each side of him while he stood on the trap door.

Also hanged this day:

1714 at Gloucester: Terence Macartney for murder, afterwards
gibbeted on the site of the murder on Durham Downs.

1749 at Canterbury, Kent: John Stone and Thomas Collington for
arson.

1819 at Old Bailey: Robert M'Vey and William Green for burglary.

1851 at Horsemonger Lane Gaol: Levi Harwood and James Burbage, for the murder of Reverend George Edward Hollest in the
vicarage at Frimley Green near Camberley.

1859 at Maidstone: Frederick Prentice (20), a farm labourer, for the

120

pistol-murder of his sweetheart, Emma Coppins (16), at Queenborough on the Isle of Sheppey. *Hangman: William Calcraft*

1983   at Sanayeh Park, Beirut, Lebanon: Ibrahim Tarraf Tarraf (36) publicly hanged where he had dumped the dismembered remains of his landlady and her son.

8 April

1930 20 MINUTES TO GO. . .
Sidney Harry Fox (31) hanged at Maidstone Prison for murdering his mother, Rosaline Fox (63), for the insurance.

Sidney Fox and his mother spent their time travelling around and staying at hotels, stealing odd items, signing dud or stolen cheques, and moving on without paying the hotel bills. His first attempt at more ambitious crime failed in 1927. He overcame his homosexual preferences to have an affair with a Mrs Marsh and insured her life for £6,000, but she woke up in her room gasping to find the gas tap turned on. Instead, Fox made off with her jewels. He was caught and sent to prison.

After he came out of prison, in March 1929, he took out a couple of accident policies on his mother, worth £3,000 if she died by accident. The policies were due to expire at midday on 22 October 1929, when the Foxes were staying at the Metropole Hotel in Margate, Kent. Fox had the policies extended for the suspiciously short period of 36 hours, until midnight on 23 October. The corpse of Mrs Fox was dragged from her burning room at 11.40 p.m. on the night of the 23rd, only 20 minutes before the policies would terminate.

Her death was attributed to shock and suffocation from the smoke, and she was buried at her home town in Norfolk. When Sidney Fox claimed the insurance money the insurance investigators were naturally suspicious; they called in the police, who had the body exhumed and examined by Sir Bernard Spilsbury. He declared that death was caused by manual strangulation and Sidney Fox was charged with her murder. *His* last 20 minutes were spent awaiting the hangman.

Also hanged this day:

1723   at Tyburn Tree: William Burke for highway robbery.

1806   at Horsemonger Lane Gaol: Richard Patch for the murder by shooting of Mr Bligh.

1870   at the Tombs Prison, New York, USA: Jack Reynolds for the

121

knife-murder of grocer William Townsend. Sneering on the gallows, he told the crowd 'This don't impress me much.'

1889   at Kilmainham Prison, Ireland: Peter Stafford for the murder of Farmer Crawley at Ballyhoo, County Meath.

1890   at Knutsford Gaol: Richard Davis (19) for the murder of his father (convicted with his brother George (16) who was reprieved). *Hangman: James Berry*

9 April

1945 ADMIRAL CANARIS DRAGGED TO GALLOWS
Admiral Wilhelm Canaris and Colonel Hans Oster hanged at Flossenburg concentration camp, for treason against Hitler in the 20 July plot.

Admiral Canaris had been chief of the *Abwehr*, the intelligence bureau of the High Command of the German forces, since 1934. Colonel Oster was his deputy. Various authors have alleged that Canaris was in contact with British Intelligence during World War Two, even that he was a spy for the British. This has never been proved.

Canaris was a brilliant spymaster for Germany, but *Abwehr* intelligence reports were frequently ignored by Hitler, because they were undermined by Himmler and Ribbentrop in the internal fighting among top Nazis. The rifts were further encouraged by propaganda schemes originating from the British Political Warfare Executive.

Canaris undoubtedly lost his enthusiasm for Hitler and the Nazi party as the war turned against Germany, but the extent of this loss is still the subject of controversy. He was not directly involved in the 20 July plot to blow up Hitler in 1944, but he was aware of it and of who the conspirators were. And he stayed silent. Colonel Oster, on the other hand, was at the centre of the plot.

Hitler survived the explosion in the conference room, and a bloody campaign of revenge was unleashed upon innocent and guilty alike. Seven thousand were arrested of whom nearly five thousand were tortured before a horrifying death (see 8 August). Canaris and Oster were scooped up in the terror that followed. Subjected to torture by the SS, they were eventually tried at Flossenburg concentration camp on 9 April 1945 and sentenced to death. Their subsequent fate was a mystery for ten years.

In 1955, at the trial of their prosecutor, witnesses were produced who were able to testify that they had seen Canaris and Oster hanged at the concentration camp on 9 April immediately after the trial. A

Danish witness, Colonel Lunding, described the brutal scene as the naked Canaris was dragged from his cell to the gallows.

Pastor Dietrich Bonhoeffer (39) was hanged with Canaris and Oster. He had been against Hitler from the start: only two days after Hitler seized power in 1933 a radio talk by Bonhoeffer was cut off in mid-broadcast. He had assisted Jews to escape with forged documents, conspired in contacting the British Foreign Office in 1942, and had taken part in an earlier attempt on Hitler's life. He was arrested in April 1943, held at Tegel army prison and had no part in the 20 July 1944 plot, but evidence against him was discovered. He was transferred to Flossenburg for trial and execution.

Also hanged this day:

1811 at Old Bailey: James Fadon. At Stafford: John Gould.

1830 at Old Bailey: James Sales for burglary.

1854 at Monaghan, Ireland: Grant, Quinn and Coomey for the murder of Thomas Bate.

1941 at Walton Gaol, Liverpool: Samuel Morgan (28) for the rape-murder of Mary Hagan (15) in a concrete blockhouse.

10 April

1739 DICK TURPIN AT YORK
Dick Turpin (34), most famous of all highwaymen, hanged at York for horse-stealing and murder.
Hangman: Matthew Blackbourn

Highwayman Dick Turpin is most famous for his legendary ride to York to establish an alibi; in fact it was another highwayman, John Nevison (see 15 March), who made the trip.

Dick was the son of a farmer in Hempstead, Essex, and served an apprenticeship to a butcher in London's Whitechapel. When a butcher in his own right, he took to cattle-thieving as a means of supply. He spent some time as a smuggler, burglar, deer stealer, and horse thief before taking up the highway robbery for which he was to be immortalised.

He was no gallant 'gentleman of the road', rather a callous and brutal robber who roamed the Epping Forest roads. He became a murderer in May 1737 when he shot Mr Thompson, who was a keeper of Epping Forest, who tried to arrest him. He was later to shoot and kill Tom King, another famous highwayman and confederate, but probably by poor aim rather than by intention. He had to get away from the vicinity of London and moved northwards, via Lincolnshire.

His luck ran out in Yorkshire and he was found guilty on two counts and sentenced to death. His last days as a condemned prisoner at York Castle were spent in some style. He joked about what awaited him, gave away gloves or hatbands to people who had pleased him, and ordered new clothes to wear at his execution.

He was taken to the place of execution in a cart, which was followed by five men he had hired as official mourners (at ten shillings each). He waved to the onlookers along the way. Climbing the ladder his right leg trembled, and he stamped it down angrily rather than have people think he was afraid. He calmly engaged in a 30-minute conversation with the hangman, with the noose around his neck. He did not wait for the hangman to 'turn him off' but threw himself from the ladder and died instantly. He may not have lived according to the legend of Dick Turpin, but he died in keeping with it.

Also hanged this day:

1745 at Tyburn Tree: Martha Tracy for robbery.

1777 at West Heath, Congleton: Samuel Thorley (50s) for the murder and cannibalism of Ann Smith (22). Afterwards gibbeted.

1876 at Hertford Gaol: George Hill for the murder of William George Thrussel.

1889 at Swansea Gaol, Wales: Thomas Allen (a Zulu) for the murder of Mr Kent, a publican.

1900 at Waterford County Gaol, Ireland: Patrick Dunphy for the murder of his two sons.

11 April

1863 AMBITION – TO BE HANGED
Robert Alexander Burton (18), smiling at the noose, hanged outside Maidstone Prison for the murder of Thomas Frederick Houghton (8) with the motive of getting himself hanged.
Hangman: William Calcraft

Burton was a self-pitying youth who was tired of life and murdered so that he would be hanged; he also blamed society for his crimes. He had been an apprentice carpenter at Chatham, but absconded to Canterbury to be a soldier, lost his nerve and ran all the way back home. He

124

soon pawned his tools and ran off again, this time to Portsmouth to be a sailor, but the navy rejected him. After eating a dinner at a Portsmouth inn he attacked the waiter when given the bill of two shillings and sixpence (12½p), knocking him down and throwing a pickle jar at him.

Back at Chatham his apprentice indentures were cancelled and his father threw him out of the house. Burton joined the West Kent Militia in Maidstone for the bounty, deserted and returned to Chatham to have a wild spree with the money. He worked for a while for a shoemaker before making off with some money, for which he was sent to prison for two months.

This was when he decided to commit murder so that he would be hanged. His first choice of victim was the shoemaker, but he was thwarted when the man left Chatham. He thought about killing a woman innkeeper in Chatham who had refused to serve him, but realised that her strength would be too much for him.

When he saw eight-year-old Tommy Houghton walking with his mother, on 23 July 1862, he followed them until Mrs Houghton went into her house leaving the boy to play on Chatham Great Lines (a large area of open land). Burton lured the lad to a nearby railway airshaft, beat him to the ground and jumped on him. After more struggling he pulled a knife from his pocket and cut the boy's throat. Tommy Houghton still put up a tremendous fight for his life, even with his windpipe severed, and Burton had to kneel on his chest to hold him down. He grabbed him by the throat and squeezed until blood flowed out of the boy's nose and eyes.

He gave himself up to a policeman, told how he had killed the boy, and took the police to the scene. He was tried at the Kent Spring Assizes in 1863, where he pleaded guilty but later retracted and an unsuccessful defence of insanity was attempted. When sentenced to death he replied 'Thank you, my lord' and revelled in his new found fame.

While waiting to be hanged he admitted a number of thefts, but blamed them all on a former master, a grocer, who had left the till unlocked, thereby tempting him to steal from it and to get into bad company. All of this, he claimed, had led him to his present situation. On another occasion he said he had become a criminal because he had 'been treated like a dog' and wanted to revenge himself upon his father for casting him out. He claimed this led to him killing the boy.

When Calcraft arrived in the condemned cell Burton said 'I am quite ready' and, almost eagerly, went to the scaffold and placed himself under the gallows' beam, smiling as he looked up at the hanging noose. When Calcraft released the bolt Burton plunged downwards and the leather strap fell away from his ankles, but he died without a struggle.

1820   at Boston, Massachusetts, USA: Michael Powers for the axe-murder of fellow Irish immigrant Timothy Kennedy who had refused to repay a loan.

1889   at Horfield Gaol, Bristol: John Withey for wife-murder.

12 April

1749 and 1751 INNOCENT COLEMAN AVENGED
In 1749 Richard Coleman was wrongly hanged at Kennington
Common, Surrey, for the murder of Sarah Green. He was innocent.
In 1751 Thomas Welch and Thomas Jones were justly hanged at
Kennington Common for the same murder.

Sarah Green was celebrating at a beanfeast in Kennington Lane on 22 July 1748 with others, including three men named Nichols, Jones and Welch. On her way home to Southwark in the early hours of the morning the three men attacked her and left her with severe injuries. Taken to St Thomas' hospital next day, she told that she thought one of her attackers was named Coleman.

Richard Coleman was a respectable brewer's clerk, married with two children. He was spoken to in the Queen's Head pub in Bandy Leg Walk, two days later, by a man who was hoping to ensnare him with some cunning questions. Coleman, who had been drinking heavily, answered angrily and with words that were ambiguous enough to convince the other of his guilt. The conversation was reported to a magistrate.

Coleman was questioned by the magistrate and taken to see Sarah Green in hospital. She did not recognise him but after a second confrontation the following day, by which time she was delirious, she said he was the man. She died soon after and the inquest jury named Coleman, and two other persons unknown, as the killers.

Two witnesses testified that Coleman was not one of the three men with Sarah Green at the beanfeast, at which he had not been present. Others swore that Coleman had been elsewhere at the time and could not have been guilty. It was no use, the jury believed the fevered identification by Sarah Green from her deathbed and the reported conversation at the Queen's Head. Coleman died on the gallows with resignation to his fate, although still solemnly declaring his innocence, and lamented that his wife and children would suffer unjustified distress (they were reduced to living off parish charity).

Two of the real killers, Thomas Welch and Thomas Jones, were hanged on the same scaffold two years later to the exact day. The third man, Nichols, had given King's Evidence and was not charged. Nichols also explained why Sarah Green had named 'Coleman' as one of her attackers: Welch and Jones had called Nichols by that name during the assault – it was an alias he sometimes used.

Also hanged this day:

1712   at Presteign, Radnorshire, Wales: Davy Morgan for robbery.

1715   at Newport, Rhode Island, USA: Jeremiah Meacham for the axe-murders of his wife and her sister.

1741   at Dorchester: Captain J. Smyth for murder following seduction.

1820   at Old Bailey: Henry Wilks, Charles Harris and John Smith for issuing forged notes.

13 April

1920 THE SHELL-SHOCKED OFFICER
Lieutenant Frederick Rothwell Holt (32), 4th Loyal North Lancashire Regiment, hanged in the Execution Shed at Strangeways Prison, Manchester, for the gun-murder of his mistress, Kitty Breaks (26).
Hangman: John Ellis

Lieutenant Holt had an excellent war record, having fought on the Western Front in France during World War One. He was invalided out of the army in a shell-shocked condition, suffering from amnesia and depression. He returned to his middle-class life in Lancashire on an inherited income of £500 a year, and settled down to live with Mrs Kitty Breaks, a woman six years his junior, who was separated from her husband. At his instigation, in November 1919, she insured her life for £5,000 and made a will in Holt's favour.

Kitty's body was found among the sand dunes at Lytham St Anne's, near Blackpool, on Christmas Eve 1919: she had been shot three times. Clear footprints in the sand, later found to match Holt's shoes, led away from the murder scene. Holt's buried Webley revolver and one of his blood-stained gloves were found near the track made by the footprints. These made clear the identity of Kitty's killer.

The shell-shocked officer appeared to be barely aware of his surroundings and of what was happening to him. He also had deluded ideas; he alleged that the police had sent mad dogs and germ-laden flies to attack him in his cell, and had tried to gas him.

Sir Edward Marshall Hall defended, claiming that Lieutenant Holt

127

was a man who had suffered in the service of his country to the extent that he had lost his sanity. The prosecution claimed that Holt had been living beyond his income and had planned, and deliberately carried out, the murder of Mrs Breaks for her insurance money, having tired of her.

Frederick Holt sat in court and took no notice of what was being said about him, his mind elsewhere. The jury may have interpreted his indifference as the callous officer-class lack of remorse. He was found guilty and sentenced to death and his only reaction was to remark 'Well, that's over, I hope my tea won't be late.'

Also hanged this day:

1731   at Chelmsford: William Smith for horse-stealing.

1829   at Old Bailey: Esther Hibner for the torturing to death of a female apprentice. She was so violent that she had to be hanged in a strait-jacket. *Hangman: William Calcraft*

1863   Dennis Delane who hired Beckham and Walsh to murder his landlord, F. Fitzgerald.

1888   at Fergus Falls, Minnesota, USA: Nels Olson Holong for the sickening murder of Lilly Field (15), his employer's daughter, whom he considered had insulted him. After cutting her throat he slit the body open and fed it to the pigs. The sheriff had to rescue him from a lynch mob on his way to the gallows.

1909   at Stafford Gaol: Joseph Edwin Jones (39) for wife-murder.

14 April

1792 ORIGIN OF BONE CHINA
Spence Broughton (45) hanged at York Castle for robbing the
Cambridge Mail coach.

The special interest in this case lies not so much in Broughton's crime as in what happened to him after execution. The judge had ruled that when he had been hanged, 'His body should be afterwards suspended betwixt Heaven and earth as unworthy of either, to be buffeted about by the winds and storms.' Accordingly, his dead body was encased in a specially-made iron cage and it was hung from a gibbet on Attercliffe Common. He was the last man to be gibbeted in Yorkshire, and he was to be 'buffeted by the winds and storms' for the next 36 years.

Sometime around 1825 a potter knocked off one of Broughton's finger bones and kept it. The following day he ground it to a fine dust and mixed it with his china clay paste, more as a grisly joke than for any practical purpose. To his surprise, the finished pot had a beautiful porcelain-like appearance. It was by this unlikely chance that bone china was invented, and bone ash has been used ever since to produce fine tableware.

Also hanged this day:

1828   at Old Bailey: Catherine Welch for the murder of her child.

1904   at Kilkenny County Gaol, Ireland: James Campion for wife-murder.

1920   at Cardiff Gaol, Wales: Tom Caler for the throat-cutting murders of a woman and her baby. *Hangman: John Ellis*

1926   at Pretoria, South Africa: Andries Van Niekerk (34) and Edward Markus (24) for the murders of two farmers who helped them.

1965   at Lancing, Texas, USA: Richard Eugene Hickock (33) and Perry Smith (36) for the murder of the Clutter family. Truman Capote used the case in his 'non-fiction' novel *In Cold Blood*.

15 April

1890 NO STEPS TO THE SCAFFOLD
Matthew William Chadwick hanged at Kirkdale Prison, Liverpool for the murder of Walter Davies.
Hangman: James Berry

This was the first time a newly designed, standardised scaffold was used. It had been installed at all prisons required to carry out executions. One of its main features was that there were no steps (American scaffolds were always built with 13 steps) to be climbed, instead the approach was made along either a flat or sloping gangway.

Also hanged this day:

1835   at Bristol: Mary Ann Burdock for poisoning.

1863   at Hereford: William Hope for the murder of Mary Corbett.

1878   at York Castle: Vincent Knowles Walker for the murder of Lydia Kells White in Hull. Hung for seven minutes before dying. *Hangman: William Marwood*

1881 at Semenovsky Square, St Petersburg, Russia: Sophia Perovskaya (26), Nikolai Rysakov, and Zhelyabov, for the bomb-assassination of Tsar Alexander II on 13 March 1881. A hundred thousand spectators watched the executions.

1904 at Kilkenny County Gaol, Ireland: John Kelly for wife-murder.

1942 C. Johnson for the murder of Maggie Smail at Ashford.

16 April

1947 THE BUTCHER OF AUSCHWITZ
**Rudolf Franz Hoess (47), Nazi concentration camp mass killer, hanged
at Auschwitz – the scene of his worst atrocities where he supervised
the murder of two-and-a-half million Jews, and the death by
starvation of another half million.**

Hoess was an ex-convict and convicted murderer who joined the SS in 1928. He received promotions and was Commandant of Auschwitz for three-and-a-half years, gassing six thousand Jews a day. His drive for greater efficiency in the extermination of Jews so impressed his Nazi masters that he was further promoted to Chief Inspector of concentration camps. He was sentenced by the Polish Peoples' Court in April 1947 and hanged a fortnight later.

Also hanged this day:

1703 at Thetford: Jack Withers and William Edwards for the murder of a penny-post man.

1841 at New Jersey, USA: Peter Robinson (32) hanged as bands played and families picnicked, for the murder of bank president Abraham Sudyam.

1935 at Wandsworth Prison: Percy Charles Anderson (21) for the shooting- and strangling-murder of Edith Constance Drew-Bear (21) on the East Brighton Golf Course.

1936 at Winsom Green Prison, Birmingham: Nurse Dorothea Nancy Waddingham (36) for murdering her patient Ada Baguley (50) and probably Ada's 89-year-old mother. *Hangmen: Tom and Albert Pierrepoint*

17 April

Hanged this day:

1816   at Old Bailey: John Franchett and George Thomas Turner for burglary; Thomas Cooper for cutting and maiming.

1847   at Bury St Edmunds: Catherine Foster for the murder of her husband.

1877   at Warwick Gaol: Frederick Baker for the murder of Maria Saunders.

18 April

1805 REPRIEVED – BUT HANGED
Mary Morgan (17) publicly hanged at Presteigne, Radnorshire, Wales, for the murder of her illegitimate child.

The tragic 17-year-old girl had been seduced by one of the local gentry at Presteigne. Abandoned and in despair, the poor girl killed her child. Her seducer was on the Grand Jury which found a true bill of murder against her. Tried before the severe (and notoriously incompetent) 61-year-old judge, Sir George Hardinge (1744–1816), she was sentenced to death. The judge fixed her execution for seven days hence and, although he had the power to reprieve her and to recommend Royal Clemency, he ignored all such pleas. Her young defending lawyer rode off to London in an attempt to gain her a reprieve, and succeeded. In furious haste he rode back to Presteigne, but arrived one hour after the execution had taken place.

There are two memorial stones to Mary Morgan in the churchyard at Presteigne, neither of which tells the full story of the drama of her tragedy. The first was donated by the Earl of Ailesbury, uttering pious hypocrisy:

To the memory of Mary Morgan who was young and beautiful, endowed with a good understanding and disposition, but unenlightened by the Sacred truths of Christianity, became the victim of sin and shame and was condemned to an ignominious death, on the 11th April 1805, for the murder of her bastard Child.

Rous'd to a first sense of guilt and remorse by the eloquent and humane exertions of her benevolent Judge Mr Justice Hardinge, she underwent the Sentence of the Law on the following Thursday with unfeigned repentance and a fervent hope of forgiveness through the merits of a redeeming Intercessor.

This stone is erected not merely to perpetuate the remembrance of a departed penitent, but to remind the living of the frailty of human nature when unsupported by Religion.
Thomas Brudenell Bruce, Earl of Ailesbury

The second, smaller stone is anonymous:

To the memory of
MARY MORGAN
who suffered April 18th 1805
Aged 17 years.
He that is without sin among you,
let him first cast a stone at her.
The 8th Chapter of John, part of ye 7th verse.

One wonders at the mentality of the noble Earl, if he considered Judge Hardinge to be humane and benevolent.

Also hanged this day:

1887 at Newgate Prison: Thomas William Currell for the murder by shooting of his sweetheart, Lydia Green.

1912 at Pentonville Prison: Frederick Henry Sedden (40) for poisoning Miss Barrow to acquire her assets. *Hangman: John Ellis, who claimed a record 25 seconds to carry out the execution*

19 April

1779 THE LOVELORN PARSON
Reverend James Hackman hanged at Tyburn Tree for the murder of Martha Reay, the mistress of the Earl of Sandwich.
Hangman: Edward Dennis

James Hackman, an officer of the 68th Regiment of Foot, went to Huntingdon on recruiting duties. While there he was invited to Hinchinbroke, the seat of the Earl of Sandwich who was First Lord of the Admiralty. He met and was besotted by the Earl's mistress, Martha Reay, who had been with the Earl since she was 18 and had had nine children by him. She was attracted to Hackman in return and encouraged him for the sake of an 'adventure'.

Hackman left the army in 1779, took holy orders and obtained the living at Wiveton in Norfolk. He and Martha exchanged passionate letters and he earnestly begged her to leave the Earl and marry him. He believed at one time that he had succeeded and that the marriage was imminent, referring to his Norfolk home as 'our parsonage' in a letter, but she had been deceiving him and had no intention of leaving Lord Sandwich.

When Hackman realised the true situation, that he had lost in the pursuit of the love of his life, he was suicidal. Seeing Miss Reay going to the Covent Garden Theatre in her coach, he followed to gaze at her for the last time, having resolved to kill himself that night. He went to his lodgings and collected two pistols, meaning to kill himself in her presence.

He waited at Covent Garden until she emerged after the play and then walked up to her. His actions were not according to his plan because, in what he described as a sudden and irresistible impulse, he shot her in the head and killed her. Pointing the other pistol at himself he fired again, but merely wounded himself. He was arrested at once. Having killed in front of witnesses in such a public place, and still wishing for death for himself, his trial and death sentence were almost formalities. Lord Sandwich wrote to him in Newgate and offered to do what he could to obtain a reprieve, if Hackman wanted to live. Hackman declined, saying that he wished for death and not for life.

Also hanged this day:

1662   at Tyburn Tree: three regicides, John Barkstead, Miles Corbet, and John Okey, hanged, drawn and quartered for their complicity in the death of King Charles I.

1875   at Kirkdale Prison, Liverpool: Alfred Thomas Heap for the murder of Margaret M'Kevett while trying to procure an abortion. At Cork County Gaol, Ireland: William Tobin for the murder of a farmer's wife to rob her of ten shillings (50p).

1878   in Malta: Guiseppa Azzopardi for the murder of Paoli Geanis.

1950   at Swansea Gaol, Wales: Albert Edward Jenkins (37) for the murder of his landlord, William Henry Llewellyn.

20 April

1849 SHE KILLED HER CRUEL MISTRESS
Sarah Thomas (17) publicly hanged at Bristol for the murder of her employer.
Hangman: William Calcraft

Sarah Thomas was a young maid servant who was badly ill-treated by her mistress: underfed, frequently beaten, and constantly driven by her demanding employer. One night, almost crazy with hunger and despair, Sarah crept into her mistress's bedroom and battered her head with a stone. The woman died and there was no doubt about who had done it. Sarah was charged and sentenced to death.

The scene at the execution was distressing for all concerned, and Calcraft said afterwards, 'I never felt so much compunction in having to bring that young girl to the scaffold.' The pretty 17-year-old was hysterical and had to be dragged to the scaffold, screaming 'I won't be hanged! I won't be hanged!' and weeping piteously 'Take me home!' Once they had got her on the drop, warders had to hold her in place and Calcraft hurriedly released the trap doors.

Also hanged this day:

1741 at Hatwells, Bristol: Captain Samuel Gooden, Matthew Mahoney, and Charles White for the murder of Captain Gooden's father.

1811 at York: Joseph Brown for murder.

1869 at Norwich Castle: William Sheward for the murder and dismemberment of his wife in a drunken row in 1851, having confessed to the police while drunk in London 18 years later. He tried to retract his confession when sober.

21 April

1849 THE KILLER IN THE FOG
James Blomfield Rush (49) publicly hanged at Norwich Castle for the gun-murders of Isaac Jermy, the Recorder of Norwich, and his son Jermy Jermy, at Stanfield Hall.
Hangman: William Calcraft

It was like a scene from a Victorian melodrama outside the moated Stanfield Hall, near Wymondham in Norfolk, at 8 p.m. on 28

November 1848. Out of the swirling Norfolk fog emerged a cloaked figure disguised with a red and black mask and long-haired wig, a pistol in each hand. He moved into the shadows of the porch at the front of the Hall.

Isaac Jermy heard a noise, went to investigate and was shot dead in the dark passageway by the front door. The younger Jermy left the dining room to find out what was happening and he, too, was killed with a single shot. The terrifying apparition in the Inverness cloak stormed through the ground floor of the Hall scattering legal papers and firing more shots, injuring Mrs Jermy and the maid Eliza Chesney, and threatening the other servants to stay in the kitchen. The cloaked killer, leaving terror and uproar in his wake, disappeared into the swirling fog whence he came.

James Blomfield Rush was a widower with nine children who lived with his housekeeper-mistress, the pregnant Emily Sandford, as tenant at Potash Farm. Recently bankrupt, he had previously been the tenant of Stanfield Hall Farm, but was evicted by Isaac Jermy because of various unsettled debts and poor farm management. More significantly, he was still heavily in debt to Isaac Jermy and his mortgage was due to expire within 48 hours. Rush was the only suspect and his guilt was never in doubt: not only did he have a motive, he had also been recognised during the rampage at Stanfield Hall despite his heavy disguise.

He was arrested at Potash Farm, but loudly protested that he had not left the house on the night of the murder. He also claimed that he had no quarrel with Mr Jermy and produced a certificate, bearing Isaac Jermy's signature, cancelling the mortgage. His alibi was not believed, and collapsed when Emily Sandford revealed his absence from Potash Farm on the murder night. As for the mortgage certificate, it was a simple forgery. The cloak, mask and wig were found at Potash Farm.

Rush conducted his own defence at the trial at Shire Hall in Norwich, where Isaac Jermy had once sat in judgement. His tactics were to deny everything bluntly, bully the witnesses, and hurl abuse at almost everyone in the court. The Stanfield Hall massacre had struck horror throughout the country; Queen Victoria followed the case closely. The Norfolk weekly newspapers printed special daily editions and posted them to distant subscribers hungry for the latest details. At the conclusion of the six-day trial, the jury retired for only six minutes, most of which was used in going to and from the jury room, and returned the inevitable verdict of guilty.

Hangman Calcraft had travelled from Bristol where he had hanged the 17-year-old Sarah Thomas the previous day. At a few minutes after noon he led the condemned man from the Castle gate to the waiting gallows, watched by a huge crowd. When Calcraft operated the drop a massive cheer echoed through the city centre.

The wax likeness of Rush dressed as at his trial, and the models of Stanfield Hall and Potash Farm used in the courtroom, were exhibited in the Chamber of Horrors at Madame Tussaud's for well over a century after his execution.

Also hanged this day:

1788   at Boughton, Cheshire: William Lownds (33) for highway robbery. Afterwards gibbeted.

1838   at Kirkdale Prison, Liverpool: William Hill for the murder of Betty Minshull.

1868   at Sydney, New South Wales, Australia: O'Farrell for the attempted assassination of the Duke of Edinburgh.

1876   at New York, USA: 'Dandy Johnny' Nolan (25) for the murder of factory owner James H. Noe, crushing his skull and gouging out his eyes with a special copper tool fitted on the thumb.

1882   at New York, USA: printer William Sindram for the gun-murder of his landlady, Mrs Catharine Craves at her boarding house. Calm on the gallows, Sindram yawned in the hangman's face when asked for his final words.

1928   at Benton, Illinois, USA: Charlie Birger publicly hanged for the murder of Mayor Adams of West City, Illinois. Approximately 50 people were gunned down in the 1920s gang-feud: Birgers versus Sheltons. The nattily dressed Birger chatted and joked on the scaffold as the last adjustments were made.

1949   at Pentonville Prison: Harry Lewis (21) for the panic-murder of cartoonist Harry Saul Michaelson during a burglary.

22 April

1904 CHICAGO TRIPLE HANGING
Early Chicago gangsters Gustave Marx, Harvey Van Dine, and Peter Neidermeier (all aged about 20), hanged together at Chicago Jail.

Three masked and merciless young thugs, all in their late teens or early 20s, were the first criminals to use the newly invented automatic pistols. Until their identities were discovered they were known as the 'Automatic Trio'. They committed a series of minor robberies, but would ruthlessly shoot and kill at the slightest sign of anything going wrong. With one exception, the pickings from their raids were meagre amounts of cash. The exception was a raid at the offices of the Chicago Street Railway barns at 3 a.m. on 30 August 1903, where staff were counting the previous day's takings.

The Trio got into the office, held the men at gun-point and gathered up the money, leaving a new member of the gang outside as lookout. He was a half-witted youth named Roeski. He banged on the door for no real reason and the noise panicked the killer-Trio and they started firing. The cashier and a conductor were killed and two assistant cashiers were seriously wounded. The gang fled, and from this night onwards would be known as the 'Car Barn Bandits'.

Clever detective work soon identified the most wanted criminals in Chicago. The leader was Gustave Marx, whose gleaming gold tooth had been apparent through a slit in his mask. The other killers were Peter Neidermeier and Harvey Van Dine. The lumbering Roeski was nothing more than a stooge. Marx was confronted by detectives in a saloon, one of whom he shot dead before being felled himself by a blow on the head from the butt of the other detective's gun.

The gang had a previously arranged plan to rescue Marx from the police station. The plan was for the captured gangster to insist on being taken to the captain's office to talk. At exactly 10 p.m. the rest of the gang would be in a room across the road with high powered rifles to shoot down the policemen in the office. If this failed they would blow up the police station with dynamite. When the rest of the gang failed to stage the rescue, an embittered Marx *did* talk. There had been more killings than the police knew about; Marx claimed that the total was 23.

The rest of the gang was surrounded at a shack outside Millers Station, about 40 miles from Chicago. The chase was not over: the desperate men escaped after killing one policeman and injuring another. They hijacked a train engine, after more killings, but were eventually cornered and first Van Dine and then Neidermeier surrendered. The half-wit Roeski escaped but was caught within the hour. The three killers were sentenced to death. Roeski, not actually charged with the murders, received a life sentence and went mad within a few weeks. Van Dine and Neidermeier were terrified as they awaited their deaths on the Chicago gallows, and both made unsuccessful suicide attempts.

Gustave Marx, the leader, was the only one who kept his nerve when the time came for the triple hanging. On the long walk from their separate cells to the execution chamber Van Dine went berserk and struggled so violently that he had to be tied to a chair and carried. Neidermeier, crying like a child, screamed for mercy and had to be supported in a state of near collapse. Marx stayed calm and showed no fear amidst the uproar.

Also hanged this day:

1745 at Kennington Common, Surrey: Donald M'Donald, James Nicholson, and Walter Olgive, for rebellion and treason in favour of the Jacobite Pretender.

1803 at Johnstown, New York, USA: Cato (a slave) hanged for the rape-murder of May Akins on a farm near Charlestown.

1831 at Ellis Island, New York Bay, USA: Charles Gibbs for piracy and murder.

1892 at Parish Prison, New Orleans, USA: Philip Baker for the murder of his female employer, a shopkeeper. *Hangman: Taylor*

1925 at Wandsworth Prison: John Norman Holmes Thorne (24) for the murder and dismemberment of his fiancée Elsie Cameron (26) at his chicken farm.

1930 at Winchester Prison: William Henry Podmore a.k.a. William F. Thomas (29) for the hammer-murder of Vivian Messiter (57) during a robbery.

1954 at Armley Gaol, Leeds: George Albert Hall (48) for the sex-murder of Mary Hackett (6). The body was hidden in the crypt of the Congregational Church at Halifax, buried under the floor beneath a pile of furniture, with the lids removed from two paint tins to mask the smell of decomposition. *Hangman: Steve Wade*

23 April

1784 'HANGED IN SO NEAT A MANNER'
A number of 'malefactors ordered for execution on the 18th inst' were brought out of Newgate Prison into Old Bailey and hanged on the new portable gallows which had been wheeled out into the street.
Hangman: Edward Dennis

The city aldermen were proud of their new gallows! It was kept in the Press Yard of the prison and wheeled out and placed in front of the Debtor's Door. The following day a broadsheet called *Street Literature* had this to say:

'The scaffold on which these miserable people suffered is a temporary machine which was drawn out of the yard of the sessions house by horses . . . being all calculated to take to pieces, which are kept within the prison.'

The public could, thereby, still watch hangings as they had done at

Tyburn until the end of the previous year. The first executions outside Newgate, at Old Bailey, had been on 9 December 1783, but it is believed that this was the first appearance of the 'portable machine'.

City records tell us about the new procedure: 'The criminals are not exposed to view until they mount the fatal stage.' The same record tells of a raised and covered platform for civic dignitaries and constables and then describes the active part of the gallows:

'In the middle of this machinery is placed a movable platform, in form of a trap-door, 10 feet long by 8 wide, on the middle of which is placed the gibbet, extending from the gaol across the Old Bailey. This movable platform is raised 6 inches higher than the rest of the scaffold, and on it the convicts stand; it is supported by 2 beams, which are held in their place by bolts. The movement of the lever withdraws the bolts, the platform falls in . . .'

This seems to be the first time that 'the drop' was used instead of a cart being pulled from beneath the feet of the condemned, or their being turned off a ladder. However it was to be more than a century before an efficient table of drops was developed to produce instantaneous death. Civic pride was shown in the new hanging machine:

'After hanging the usual time they were taken down, and the machine cleared away in half-an-hour. By practice the art is much improved, and there is no part of the world in which villains are hanged in so neat a manner, and with so little ceremony.'

Also hanged this day:

1833 at Old Bailey: George Coney for burglary.

1913 at Wakefield Prison, Yorkshire: William Sykes for the murder of two girls, aged 6 and 10.

1954 at Carlton Prison, Edinburgh: J. Lynch for the murder of M. Johnson and L. Sinclair.

24 April

1922 NAKED CORPSE IN GUN ALLEY
Colin Campbell Ross hanged at Melbourne Jail, Australia, for the rape-murder of Alma Tirtschka (12) in his wine bar.

Colin Ross was the first murderer to be convicted in Australia on forensic evidence: he was hanged thanks to the discovery of 22 reddish-blond female hairs on a blanket.

The naked body of Alma Tirtschka (12) was found on a drain grating in Gun Alley, in a sleazy part of Melbourne, shortly after 6 a.m. on 31 December 1921. The freshly washed body was laid on its back, the lower legs pulled back so that the feet were under the buttocks, and her red-blond hair was spread on the ground around the head like a golden halo. Blood seeping from the vagina indicated that it was a sex-crime (later confirmed by a vaginal swab-test). She had been bruised about the head, strangled, and the body had presumably been washed to remove blood and other traces.

Colin Ross had a wine bar 115 yards from where the body was dumped. He was a man with a powerful sex-drive and had a liking for young girls (he had joked to a drinking friend 'I like them without feathers', meaning pubic hairs). The police did not suspect him when they first questioned him, although they noted that the floor of the private room behind the bar had been recently scrubbed.

Once rewards totalling £1,250 had been offered, witnesses came forward from among the local criminals. Alma had been seen for the last time in the private room behind the wine bar on the afternoon prior to her body being found. Ross' former barmaid had challenged him about the murdered girl: she testified that Ross had replied by bursting into tears and admitting that he had lost control of himself and had killed the child before he knew what was happening.

Ross was arrested on 12 January and the blankets that had covered the settee in the private room were taken for scientific checks. The 22 red-blond hairs, matching Alma's hair, were found clinging to a corner of one of the blankets. While it was true that many of the witnesses were from unsavoury backgrounds and their evidence could not be relied on, the forensic evidence damned him.

Another witness, a down-and-out, claimed that he had seen Ross staggering under the weight of a blanket-wrapped bundle from his wine bar to Gun Alley at 2 a.m. If this was true it would mean that Ross had been hiding there, with the naked body, when a police patrolman had paused at the entrance to Gun Alley. The policeman's orders were to walk up Gun Alley, but he contented himself by merely flashing his torch up and down and then moving on. He could have caught the murderer in the act of disposing of the body. Ross must have been severely shaken by this close call. Instead of pushing the body down the drain as he had planned, he yanked the blanket from under the body, thereby pulling back the legs and splaying out the hair – and 22 red-blond hairs came away from the head and clung to the corner of the blanket. Those hairs hanged him.

1786   at Boughton, Cheshire: Peter Steer for wife-murder.

1818   at Old Bailey: John Ward and Hart Skelton for issuing forged notes.

1868   at Virginia City, Montana, USA: John Millain for the murder and robbery of popular prostitute and madam Julia Bulette (35).

1876   at Horfield Gaol, Bristol: Edward Deacon for wife-murder.

1889   at Dundee Prison: William Henry Bury for brutal wife-murder.

1940   W. C. Cowell for the murder of Anne Cook.

25 April

1901 'LET HER RIP!'
Black Jack Ketchum publicly hanged for train-robbery in front of a shocked crowd of cowboys at Clayton, New Mexico, USA.
Hangman: Sheriff of Clayton

Black Jack was eager to get the hanging over and done with. The crowd of tough westerners gathered for the execution were shocked to see the burly black-haired and moustached bandit, dressed in a black suit and waistcoat, eagerly leaping up the 13 steps to the gallows two at a time. As the noose was being hung round his neck, Black Jack shouted to the crowd 'I'll be in Hell before you start breakfast, boys!' The shocks weren't over yet. When everything was ready he twisted himself round towards the sheriff and roared, 'Let her rip!'

His last words were grimly accurate. The length of slack on the rope had been wrongly estimated and as he plunged downwards his head was ripped from his body, spraying his spurting blood over the scaffold as his head rolled across the ground.

Also hanged this day:

1822   at Massachusetts State Prison, Boston, USA: Samuel Green, one of America's first mass murderers, hanged for the clubbing-murder of informer Billy Williams, a fellow convict, in the prison.

1876   at Cardiff Gaol, Wales: Joseph N. Webber for the murder of Edward Stelfox.

1905   at Cork County Gaol, Ireland: former Police Constable Foster for the murder of William Regan.

1951 at Wandsworth Prison: Joseph Brown (33) and Edward Charles Smith (33) for the murder of 'Old Gossy' (79) in his shop at Clay Corner, Chertsey. Frederick Brown (27) was also charged but saved himself by giving prosecution evidence against his brother. *Hangman: Albert Pierrepoint. Assistants: Harry Allen (of Birmingham), Harry Allen (of Manchester) and Syd Dernley*

1952 at Walton Gaol, Liverpool: Edward Devlin (22) and Alfred Burns (21) for the brutal murder of Mrs Alice Rimmer (52) during a burglary. A callous pair of young thugs with many previous convictions, they played tough guys at their trial, railing against the judge and jury after the guilty verdict, and their relatives mounted an emotional campaign claiming that they were innocent. Sunday newspapers reported the following weekend that they had confessed in the condemned cells. *Hangman: Albert Pierrepoint. Assistants: Syd Dernley, Leslie Stewart, and Smith*

26 April

1929 IN THE MIND OF THE MURDERER
Vernon Booher (20) hanged at Fort Saskatchewan, Canada, for the shooting-murders at the Booher Farm of his mother, brother, and two hired hands. The case was solved by a doctor reading the murderer's 'thought-waves'.

Vernon Booher reported the murders at the Booher farm, near Mannville in Alberta, between 8.30 p.m. and 9 p.m. on Monday 9 July 1928. He said that after gathering in the cows that evening, he had discovered the bodies of his mother, brother, and a hired hand. But there were no cows in the farmyard when the police arrived; they returned from the fields by themselves the following morning.

Vernon later found a fourth body, another hired hand, after the police arrived. The victims were:

Mrs Eunice Booher who had been shot several times in the back of the head, and who sat slumped over the table in the living room where she had been working on a bowl of strawberries.

Fred Booher (24) had been shot twice, in the mouth and neck, and was laid on his back in the kitchen, still wearing his hat as though he had been shot as he entered the door.

Wasyl Rosyak, a Ukrainian hired hand who had been shot twice, in the face and stomach, was still holding a bucket of swill where he had been feeding the pigs in the barn.

Gabriel Goromby (30), a Hungarian hired hand, had been shot twice

142

The Idle 'Prentice Executed at Tyburn, the famous engraved cartoon by William Hogarth (1697–1764) showing the chaos and squalor of a hanging day at Tyburn.
(*Peter Newark's Historical Pictures*)

The scene outside Wandsworth Prison as the certificates of execution are displayed after the hanging of the traitor William Joyce ('Lord Haw-Haw'). See 3 January.
(*Press Association*)

'The Demon of the Belfry'. William Henry Theodore Durrant climbs the thirteen wooden steps to the gallows at San Quentin Prison. See 7 January.

The parents of 'Demon of the Belfry' Durrant enjoy a hearty dinner, sharing a private room in San Quentin Prison with the body of their son who has just been hanged.

Sheriff Henry Plummer was hanged on his own gallows. See 10 January.

Edward Pritchard killed a 14-year-old boy at Stroud in 1886 to rob him of the £200 factory wages he was carrying. See 17 February.

The front cover of John Lee's paperback book which was published circa 1908 after his release from life imprisonment. See 23 February.

The arrest of the archetypal Victorian villain, Charlie Peace. See 25 February. (*Peter Newark's Historical Pictures*)

The fearsome Charlie Peace at his trial. Parents threatened naughty children that 'Charlie Peace will come and get you!'

Habitual criminal Alfred Scandrett, hanged in 1888 for committing murder during a house robbery. See 20 March.

Mrs Elizabeth Berry killed her 11-year-old daughter for the £10 life insurance. She was hanged by James Berry. See 14 March.

The calling card of James Berry, who was public hangman from 1884 to 1892.

George Kelly, the Liverpool gangster. His tough-guy reputation did not survive the news of his messy last seconds on the gallows. See 28 March.

Below The Birger gang. About 50 were killed in the Birger–Shelton feud in the 1920s. Charlie Birger is sitting on the car roof, centre, in a bullet-proof vest and holding a Tommy gun. He was publicly hanged for murdering the mayor. See 21 April.
(*Peter Newark's Western Americana*)

Charlie Birger jokes with the hangman.

The hangman is about to place the noose around the neck of the black-hooded Charlie Birger. This picture was run in newspapers across America under the headline 'Birger's Last Stand'.

Norman Thorne at his chicken farm in Crowborough, Sussex, in 1925 while the police searched for his missing fiancée Elsie Cameron. He is standing on the spot where her dismembered remains were later found buried. See 22 April.
(*The Hulton-Deutsch Collection*)

'Black Jack' Ketchum was in a hurry to get the hanging done with and, when everything was ready, he yelled 'Let her rip!' His last words were grimly prophetic. See 25 April.

pencer Perceval (50), the only British
'rime Minister to have been
ssassinated. See 18 May.

Assassin John Bellingham in the dock
at the Old Bailey on 15 May 1812.
Four days earlier he had shot the
Prime Minister at the House of
Commons and three days later he was
publicly hanged. This engraving was
made at the time.

'rime Minister Perceval lies dying inside the entrance of the House of
Commons (from a contemporary print). That same morning Perceval had
old his family of the awful dream he had had the night before. He had
described this scene with eerie accuracy, even to the green coat with brass
buttons worn by his killer.

Hogarth's satirical invitation to the hanging of 'Thief-taker General' Jonathan Wild: thousands responded. See 24 May.
(*Peter Newark's Historical Pictures*)

Moses Shrimpton had a bloody hanging when he was given a 9-foot drop at Worcester for murdering a policeman. See 25 May.

Mary Lefley put arsenic in her husband's rice pudding. She shrieked all the way to the gallows at Lincoln Prison. See 26 May.

...antry boy Henry Jacoby (18) murdered Lady White (65) with several ...ammer-blows to the head at the Spencer Hotel near London's Marble ...rch. The jury's strong recommendation for mercy was ignored and his ...ecution caused a national outcry. See 5 June.

(Syndication International)

This pile of shaving and other brushes found at Auschwitz concentration camp represented the more modest end of the official programme of State robbery organised by the death camp's 'businessman' Oswald Pohl upon murdered victims. At the top end of the scale were their gold teeth, cash and jewellery. See 8 June.
(*Syndication International*)

Oswald Pohl hears his sentence of death by hanging at his trial at Landsberg, Germany, in 1951.
(*The Hulton-Deutsch Collection*)

Above Suleiman Daoud Sami hanged on the exact spot where he had ordered the destruction of Alexandria. See 9 June.
(*Peter Newark's Historical Pictures*)

Wife killer Walter Wood. See 30 June.

THE ILLUSTRATED POLICE BUDGET

THE LEADING ILLUSTRATED POLICE JOURNAL IN ENGLAND

No. 148.   SATURDAY, APRIL 4, 1896.   ONE PENNY

Trooper Wooldridge wore his best Royal Horse Guards uniform when he slit his wife's throat in a jealous rage because she had been seeing a corporal in the Life Guards. This type of murder was commonplace at the time but he was to be immortalised the following year as the condemned man in Oscar Wilde's *Ballad of Reading Gaol*. See 7 July.

eter Manuel (31) had a criminal
cord from the age of 12 for burglary,
neral thieving, robbery with violence,
decent assault, and rape. When he
rried out a string of 12 murders in
e 1950s it was often for the gloating
easure it gave him. See 11 July.
yndication International)

Soho drinking club hostess Ruth Ellis
(28) was the last woman to be hanged
in Britain, for the shooting-murder of
her estranged lover outside a
Hampstead Heath pub on Easter
Sunday 1955. See 13 July.
(*The Hulton-Deutsch Collection*)

ecutions at Old Bailey, outside the Debtors' Door of Newgate Prison, in
:09.
eter Newark's Historical Pictures)

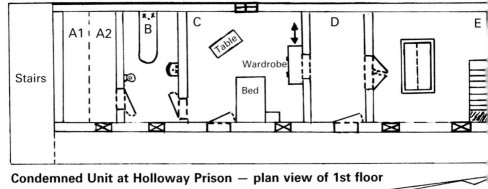

Condemned Unit at Holloway Prison — plan view of 1st floor

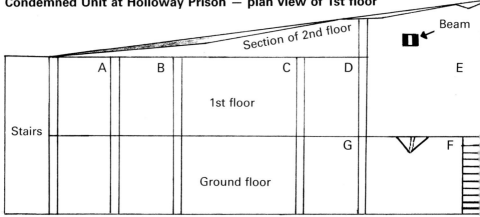

Condemned Unit at Holloway Prison — side view

The Condemned Unit at Holloway Prison. A1 and A2: Visitors' cell where the condemned person met visitors, separated by a glass partition. It was a single cell, 7 ft wide by 14 ft deep, and connected to B: Bathroom, a single 7 ft × 14 ft cell connected to C: Living Area, two cells combined into an area of 15 ft × 14 ft, where the condemned and the watching warders spent most of the time. It had an extra large window, fitted with one-way glass so that the occupants could not be seen. The wardrobe concealed the door to D: an empty 7 ft × 14 ft cell leading to E: Execution Chamber, two cells combined into a 15 ft × 14 ft area with the gallows beam set from wall to wall in what had been the cell above. Dominating the floor area were the flat double trapdoors. Stairs led down to F: 'The pit', which had originally been cells on the ground floor and was connected to G: Autopsy Room. ⊠ = original cell doors locked and sealed by being screwed to the doorframes. The only doors which could be opened were to C and D. When the hangmen entered C, the official witnesses entered D and took their places in E; usually the condemned died at the rope's end within 15 seconds of the doors being opened. See 13 July.

(Drawing by Mark Brice. Copyright © 1993 Rocky Stockman)

in the head and once in the chest. He was lying on the floor in the bunkhouse.

They had all been shot with a .303 rifle. The spent cartridge cases and the rifle had been taken away by the murderer, except for one casing found in a bowl of water in the kitchen. The Boohers did not own a .303 rifle, but one had gone missing with a box of cartridges from a neighbour's farmhouse between 11 a.m. and 1 p.m. the previous day while the owners were in church.

The first gunshots had been heard at about 6 p.m. Vernon said he had been out in the fields at that time, but he had spoken to family friend Councillor Scott at 6.30 p.m. at the farmyard gate. He had dissuaded Scott from going into the house, telling him that no one was at home. While they talked, Wasyl Rosyak was seen going towards the house and Vernon ordered him to go and feed the pigs in the barn, after which Scott departed. The police suspected Vernon Booher from the start, and held him in custody as a material witness.

The inquest was attended by Dr Adolph Maximilien Langsner, of Vienna, posing as a reporter. Dr Langsner claimed that he had the ability to interpret thought-waves emanating from a person's brain and he had been invited to attend, secretly, by the police. He closely studied Vernon Booher during the hearing and afterwards told the police that Vernon was the murderer. Langsner said that the rifle had been dumped in a clump of long grass and brush near the Booher farmhouse and to the west of it. He said he had obtained the image of the sun shining in that direction when he intercepted Booher's thought-waves while the young man was remembering the incident. A few hours later the rifle was found, 135 yards west of the house among long grass and brush.

Langsner sat silently outside Booher's cell for an hour. He reported that Vernon's mind was filled with hatred for his mother. Better still, he was able to recount for the detectives the sequence of events at the time of the murders. He next described a woman wearing a poke bonnet who had seen Booher leave the church service during the time that the rifle went missing; she was found and confirmed Langsner's 'vision'. Another witness was found who had seen Booher riding towards the neighbour's farm a little later.

Vernon Booher confessed when he knew that the rifle had been found. His statement confirmed Dr Langsner's report of the murder-sequence:

'I shot Mother as she sat at the dining room table with her back to me. Fred rushed into the house when he heard the gun go off and I shot him. Their bodies were lying in the house when Councillor Scott stopped in passing. I don't know what I would have done if he had attempted to go into the house. Rosyak came in from the fields while Scott was there. I sent him to the barn, so he would not see what was in the house. After Scott left, I went to the barn and killed Rosyak. Then, at about 8 o'clock, when Goromby came in from the tractor, I finished him. Mother was always nagging me about a girl I'm crazy about. And she threatened to tell something about her, if I didn't give her up. I had her murder planned for days.'

The confession was not allowed as evidence at the trial; the defence attorney claimed that Dr Langsner had hypnotised his client and the confession was the result of a post-hypnotic suggestion. Despite this, Langsner's guidance had led the police to discover other evidence and witnesses which was enough to convict Vernon Booher and have him sentenced to death. This conviction was later quashed on technical objections and a new trial ordered. He was convicted again at the second trial when a further confession was revealed. None of his surviving relatives claimed the body after execution and he was buried in the prison grounds.

Also hanged this day:

1749 at Tyburn Tree: Thomas Kingsmill, John Farrell, and Captain Richard Perrin, for burglary of the Customs House at Poole, Dorset. (See 18 January.)

1843 at Stafford, New York, USA: Benjamin D. White (39) for the murder of his father.

1858 at Old Bailey: G. Lani for murder.

1863 at Kirkdale Prison, Liverpool: George Woods and Duncan McPhail (40) for the robbery and murder of Ann Walne (79) at Ribchester. *Hangman: William Calcraft*

1875 at Horfield Gaol, Bristol: William Hale for wife-murder while they were both drunk.

1879 at Minden, Nebraska, USA: 'Nebraska Fiend' Stephen Lee Richards for the murder of five members of the Harlson family. He had committed at least nine other murders in the area of Lincoln, Nebraska.

1892 at Lewes Prison, Sussex: George H. Wood for the murder of Edith Jeal.

1905 at Pentonville Prison: Alfred Bridgeman for the murder of his girlfriend's mother.

1951 at Wandsworth Prison: James Virrels (55) for the stabbing- and axe-murder of his landlady, Mrs Alice Roberts. *Hangman: Albert Pierrepoint. Assistant: Syd Dernley.* Virrels stared wild-eyed at the

144

sight of the hangmen and his bowels opened on the short walk to the gallows.

27 April

Hanged this day:

1812   at Edinburgh: Hugh M'Donald, Neil Sutherland, and H. McIntosh.

1863   at Old Bailey: J. Brooks for the murder of Davy, a policeman.

1979   at Port of Spain, Trinidad: Stanley Abbott (40) for the murder of Gale Benson, an English girl, on the orders of racial fanatic Michael X. (See 16 May.)

28 April

1882 THE DEADLY MADEIRA CAKE
Dr George Lamson (30) hanged at Wandsworth Prison for the murder with an aconitine-laced Madeira cake of his crippled brother-in-law Percy John (18).
Hangman: William Marwood

Dr Lamson was addicted to morphia and had other expensive habits. Having squandered his own money he wrote worthless cheques on real and imagined bank accounts. Some £700 came his way after the death of a brother-in-law, Herbert John, which many later thought to be Lamson's first murder.

There was another brother-in-law, Percy John, an 18-year-old cripple at a private school at Blenheim House in Wimbledon. Percy would receive a £3,000 legacy when he became 21, but if he failed to live to maturity half of the money would go to his sister, Lamson's wife.

Lamson visited Percy at the school, bringing with him a Madeira cake in which he had inserted the vegetable poison aconitine. He induced Percy to eat a slice. The boy was violently ill soon after Lamson left, and died in agony before midnight. The school doctors suspected poison at once and the chemists who had sold the aconitine to Lamson came forward when they saw the newspaper report. Although he denied the charge, the jury took less than half an hour to find him guilty.

Without access to his morphia, his physical condition and his morale deteriorated as he awaited death in prison. He confessed to the killing of Percy, but denied killing Herbert. On the morning of his execution, wearing the same black suit he had worn at his trial, he was almost collapsing and had to be supported by two warders to the place of execution in the prison yard. He almost fell to the ground when, about 30 yards ahead of him, he saw the awful scene of the blackened scaffold and the freshly dug grave nearby.

He tried to compose himself but, time and again, his resolve left him. The two warders had to hold him upright as they stood on two planks placed across the trap door. Marwood signalled to the warders to let go of Lamson's arms as he pulled the lever, and the flaps opened and Lamson dropped through. Marwood was widely quoted afterwards as saying that Dr Lamson 'died like a gentleman'.

Also hanged this day:

1708 at Tyburn Tree: John Muggridge for murder, William Greig for treason.

1845 at Old Bailey: Thomas Henry Hocker (22) for the murder of Mr De La Rue (33). A crowd of ten thousand watched. *Hangman: William Calcraft*

1954 at Swansea Gaol, Wales: Thomas Ronald Lewis Harries (24) for the murder of farmer John Harries (63) and Phoebe Harries (54), his uncle and aunt.

1959 Joseph Chrimes (30) for the murder of Mrs M. Summerfield, battering her to death with a tyre lever, in the pursuance of theft.

29 April

1943 THE WIGWAM MURDER CASE
Private August Sangret (30), a French-Canadian half-breed Cree Indian, hanged at Wandsworth Prison for the 'Wigwam Murder' of Joan Pearl Wolfe (19).

Joan Wolfe was known as the 'Wigwam Girl' to police and soldiers in the Hankley Common area near Godalming in Surrey. She was a teenage runaway who lived rough in the woods sleeping in wigwams, which had been built for her by her Cree Indian boyfriend using branches, heather and grass. She was not a prostitute, but she spent her time with soldiers from the nearby training camps.

Two soldiers on a battle exercise on Hankley Common, on 7

October 1942, discovered a shrivelled arm sticking out from a mound of earth on the high ground. The police uncovered the rest of the decomposed body in the shallow grave and it was not long before it was identified as Joan Wolfe. Among the items found in the vicinity was a letter to August Sangret, her most frequent boyfriend, telling him that she was pregnant and expecting him to marry her.

Sangret had hidden a clasp-knife in the washroom of the Guard House just before he was questioned by the police. It was later discovered blocking a wastepipe and was proved to be the one used to stab the girl (it had an unusual hooked tip to the blade), before she was bludgeoned about the head and killed.

The murder spot, and a nearby blood-stained birch stump with strands of her hair sticking to it, was located 400 yards from where Joan Wolfe had been buried. Her body had been dragged to the high ground for burial, which was in keeping with Sangret's tribal ancestors who buried conquered enemies on a hilltop.

The forensic evidence of Dr Keith Simpson proved the guilt of Sangret. When the jury retired to consider their verdict they took with them two crucial exhibits: Joan's skull and the clasp-knife. Dr Simpson had explained to them that only one knife, with its tell-tale hook-tipped blade, could have inflicted the unusual stab wounds and the marks etched into the skull. They returned with a guilty verdict after two hours of close consideration, but with a surprising recommendation for mercy, which was not followed by the Home Office.

Also hanged this day:

1825   at Bath, New York, USA: Robert Douglass, notorious counterfeiter, for the stabbing-murder of Samuel H. Ives.

1902   at Wandsworth Prison: Charles Robert Earl (56) for the murder of Margaret Pamphilon.

30 April

1868 MURDER WHILE UNDER ARREST
Richard Bishop (21) hanged outside Maidstone Prison for the knifing-murder of Alfred Cartwright (24) while being taken to Sydenham Police Station on an assault charge.
Hangman: William Calcraft

Richard Bishop, ex-convict, was an iron-moulder by trade. He had coarse carrot-red hair and was well built, but had a brutal appearance. His wife kept a shop at Sydenham and a disturbance occurred outside it at midnight on 3 April 1868: the row was about a shilling (5p). Alfred Cartwright came on the scene to complain about the noise and, while the others quietened down, Bishop responded by hitting Cartwright in the eye. The constable was called and Cartwright insisted on Bishop being taken into custody. On the way to the police station, Bishop pulled a knife from his pocket, stabbed Cartwright and sneered that he 'won't get over that'. He didn't.

The hardened Bishop retained his callous attitude through his trial and while awaiting execution. He was the last person to be publicly hanged in Kent, from a scaffold erected on beams running out from the wall beside the prison gate. He climbed the steps with an almost jaunty manner, remained cool to the end, and died instantly when the drop was operated.

Also hanged this day:

1725   at Tyburn Tree: Vincent Davis for murder.

1796   at Boughton, Cheshire: James Price and Thomas Brown for highway robbery. Afterwards gibbeted.

1823   at Old Bailey: William Watts, William Hurd, James Brown, Robert Fuller, John Walker, James Aldridge, and Henry Seaton for burglary.

1855   Luigi Buranelli hanged for the murder of Joseph Lathan (or Lambert) in Foley Place, Marylebone.

1883   at Cork County Gaol, Ireland: Timothy O'Keefe for the murder of his uncle.

MAY

1 May

1820 THE CATO STREET CONSPIRATORS
The Cato Street conspirators were hanged and beheaded at Old Bailey for high treason – the last time this sentence was carried out.
Hangman: James Botting

The conspirators were a small group of radicals who met in a stable, which had a large loft above it, in Cato Street off the Edgware Road and, ominously, close to the site of the former Tyburn Tree of only recent memory. They were fired with the intention to overthrow the government, cut off the heads of ministers and parade them through London, abolish the monarchy and install their leader, Thistlewood, as President of the Republic. The authorities knew of the plot because one 'conspirator' was George Edwards, a government spy and *agent provocateur*.

As they met in the loft one night in February, they were surprised by a body of constables and soldiers bursting in on them, having been informed on by Edwards. A fight ensued and arrests were made, although some of the conspirators escaped and were rounded up later. While others were sentenced to transportation the main conspirators were sentenced to be hanged and then beheaded. They were: Arthur Thistlewood (50); James Ings, butcher and landlord; John Thomas Brunt (38), bootmaker; Richard Tidd (45), ex-soldier and habitual false enlister; William Davidson (34), cabinet maker.

On the morning of the execution five coffins were laid on the platform and part-filled with sawdust, to soak up the blood, and the headsman's block was set down by them.

Thistlewood, the leader, was brought out first and placed on the trap to have the noose fitted, and the others followed. They all seemed in good spirits, even sucking on oranges and making quips. When they were all arranged Hangman Botting released the trap. Thistlewood struggled slightly on the end of the rope, turning a full circle. Ings and Brunt suffered in agony and the assistant hangman had to pull on their legs to speed their deaths. Tidd died quickly, hardly moving. Davidson heaved three or four times before becoming still.

They hung for half an hour and were then cut down to be beheaded, but not by James Botting. A mystery man, possibly a surgeon, stepped on to the scaffold wearing a seaman's jersey, a dark hat pulled low over his face and a black mask that covered him down to the mouth where a coloured handkerchief was tied. The bodies were laid in the coffins with the heads hanging out, facing upward. The mystery man then started to cut Thistlewood's throat with a surgical knife, to the noisy disgust of the mob. When the head was cut off it was handed to the assistant hangman who held it up, proclaiming the traditional 'This is the head of Arthur Thistlewood, the traitor.' The others were similarly decapitated and displayed and, as Brunt's head was held up, the mystery man swiftly left the scaffold.

Many thought the mystery headsman must be a surgeon, or a medical student, because of the skill displayed. One rumour suggested that he was Thomas Wakley, who later founded the famous medical journal *The Lancet*: it was not him but Wakley was seriously injured when his house was set on fire that night by radical sypathisers. Another rumour identified him as a notorious bodysnatcher who specialised in severed heads!

Also hanged this day:

1701   at Tyburn Tree: George Griffiths for robbery.

1942   at Oxford Castle: Private Harold Hill (26), of the Royal Artillery, for strangling Doreen Joyce Hearne (8) and Kathleen Trundell (6) at Rough Wood, Penn, Buckinghamshire. At San Quentin Prison, California, USA: Robert 'Rattlesnake' James (a.k.a. Raymond Lisemga) for drowning his wife after attempts to kill her using rattlesnakes failed.

2 May

1837 'GREENACRE PIES'!
James Greenacre (52), a grocer and local politician, hanged at Old Bailey for the murder and mutilation of Mrs Hannah Brown (50).
Hangman: William Calcraft

It was a gruesome murder, with the body being cut up and distributed throughout south London, sending a shock of horror across London for months as each new grisly discovery was made.

The murderer was James Greenacre, already well known in political circles, but his notoriety made him a special attraction to the fashionable poseurs of the day including MPs and nobles, who flocked to visit him in the condemned cell at Newgate Prison. The scenes at his public execution were almost as sickening as his crime. When he stepped out on to the gallows he was met with furious howls from the mob. Shaken, he appealed to Calcraft 'Don't leave me long with that pack of ghouls.' Ghouls was an appropriate description. Ribald pie-sellers greatly increased their sales by calling the pies 'Greenacres'. The sickening association of the meat pies with the dismembered pieces of Hannah Brown somehow appealed to the grisly mob, and the piemen did a roaring trade.

1722   at Tyburn Tree: William Burridge for horse-theft.

1810   at Chester Castle: Thomas Done (20) for the murder of Betty Eckersley, probably on board his flat barge, and dumping her weighted body in the Bridgewater Canal.

1931   at Ratisbon, Germany: Kurt Erich Tetzner (26) for the murder of an unknown tramp (about 19) in a blazing car as part of an insurance swindle.

3 May

1934 THE OLD MAN'S BRUISE
Reginald Ivor Hinks (32) hanged at Horfield Gaol, Bristol, for the gas-oven murder of his father-in-law, James Pullen (85).

Reginald Hinks was a small-time crook, then working as a vacuum cleaner salesman, who turned into a killer of the most determined and callous type. Learning that divorcee Constance Jeffries, née Pullen, had an aged and senile father worth a few thousand pounds he wooed and married her within a few weeks.

Hinks' attempts to get 85-year-old James Pullen's money were thwarted by the solicitor but, via Constance, he used £900 to buy a mock Tudor villa in Englishcombe Lane, Bath. He decided to use more sinister means having realised that, if old James Pullen died, the money would come to him via Constance. He got rid of the helpless old man's male nurse and took control of Pullen himself, weakening him by reducing his diet and taking him out for vigorous walks. He would abandon the confused octogenarian on busy roads, hoping that he would get run over, but kindly passers-by repeatedly brought him home to Englishcombe Lane!

It was bath night in the mock Tudor villa on 30 November 1933. The same bath water was used successively for the baby, Constance, Hinks, and finally old Mr Pullen. Hinks staged an accident by allowing the old man to slide down under the filthy water until he passed out. The alarm was raised by calling out the police, a doctor, and the local fire brigade, for assistance with the accident. Hinks' timing was not quite right and the old man was revived.

The following night Hinks decided he would finish off his father-in-law for good and sent Constance out for the evening to a local cinema. He stunned the old man with a blow on the head, laid him on the kitchen floor with his head in the gas oven and turned the taps on full. When he called the firemen this time his victim was definitely dead.

153

He told the firemen that he had discovered the 'suicide' when he went to the kitchen for a drink of water. He told them that they might find a bruise on the back of the dead man's head, caused when he had dragged him away from the oven by his feet and his head had banged on the floor.

Medical examination at the post-mortem proved that the bruise had been inflicted while the old man was still alive, not after death. Plenty of witnesses volunteered information about the previous incidents, and Reginald Ivor Hinks's ambition to get James Pullen's money had failed again – and for the last time.

Also hanged this day:

1606 Father Henry Garnet (51) hanged, drawn and quartered for high treason as a conspirator of Guy Fawkes and the Gunpowder Plot on the previous 5 November.

1740 at Ovelchester, Somerset: Mrs Elizabeth Branch (67) and her daughter Mary Branch (24) for the beating to death of servant-girl Jane Butterworth.

1899 at Wandsworth Prison: Frederick James Andrews for the murder of a woman.

4 May

Hanged this day:

1722 at Tyburn Tree: John Hartley and Thomas Reeves, noted footpads, for robbery.

1762 at Tyburn Tree: John Rae for forgery; John Lewis for highway robbery.

1932 at Pentonville Prison: Maurice Freedman (36) for the throat-cutting murder of his former sweetheart Annette Friedson.

1934 at Wandsworth Prison: Frederick William Parker (21) and Albert Probert (26) for the murder of shopkeeper Joseph Bedford (80) to rob him of £6. *Hangman: Tom Pierrepoint*

5 May

1760 HANGED WITH A SILK ROPE?
The Fourth Earl Ferrers hanged at Tyburn Tree for murdering his estate steward, John Johnson.
Hangman: Thomas Turlis

There is a popular belief that if a lord is charged with murder he has the right to be 'Tried by God and my peers' in the House of Lords and, if condemned, be hanged with a silk rope. Lord Ferrers is the only peer of the Realm to have been hanged for murder and is, therefore, the only precedent. He was tried before the House of Lords assembled in Westminster Hall on 16 April 1760 and hanged with a common hemp rope at Tyburn on 5 May 1760. Afterwards he was taken to Surgeons' Hall to be anatomised.

The Fourth Earl had a history of violent behaviour, flying into rages especially when drunk. He was reportedly sober on 18 January 1760 when he summoned his steward, Mr John Johnson, to report to him at Staunton Hall, the Earl's family seat at Staunton Harold in Leicestershire. His lordship was in one of his rages. Having locked the door, he pointed a gun at Johnson and ordered him to sign a document admitting a series of illegal transactions. The honest Johnson refused. Furiously waving the gun, he forced his steward to kneel on the floor in front of him and then shot Johnson in the stomach. The poor man died 17 hours later.

The next day Staunton Hall was beseiged by the villagers and Lord Ferrers was arrested and charged with murder. When he chose to be tried by the House of Lords he was taken to the capital, driven in his own landau with six horses and with a large escort, and imprisoned in the Tower of London. His defence at the trial was that he was of unsound mind, but his peers would have none of it: he was found guilty and sentenced to death. One of the biggest crowds ever turned out for the execution, as Ferrers remarked to the sheriff: 'They have never seen a lord hung before.' He wore a white suit trimmed with silver, the clothes he had worn at his wedding.

His behaviour on the three-hour journey, in his own landau and six, from the Tower to Tyburn was impeccable. The same could not be said of the hangmen. On the black-clothed scaffold Ferrers handed a purse containing five guineas to the assistant hangman and an unseemly brawl took place between Turlis and the man. The sheriff intervened and gave Turlis the purse. It took some minutes for Ferrers to die, with Turlis and the assistant pulling down on his legs to speed his demise. His body was taken to Surgeons' Hall in a coffin lined with white satin. There it was cut open and put on public display until 8 May, when it was handed over to his friends for burial.

Also hanged this day:

1820   at Old Bailey: Henry Hawkins for burglary; William Saunders for horse-stealing, and William Arnold for extortion.

6 May

1902 NEWGATE'S LAST HANGING
The despicable George Woolfe (21) was the last person to be hanged in Newgate Prison, for the murder of his girlfriend, Charlotte Cheeseman, whose body he afterwards dumped in the evil-smelling Tottenham Marshes.
Hangman: William Billington. Assistant: John Billington

Woolfe was a callous and vindictive Hoxton lad. He seduced factory girl Charlotte Cheeseman, but soon tired of her. He wrote her a series of cruel letters, and another to her employers alleging a string of entirely false crimes and giving false character details. Charlotte, incredibly, was still besotted by him and implored him to see her again. No longer wanting her, he told his cronies he 'would get shunt of her'. They were seen together in a pub, the Rosemary Branch in Southgate Road, on the night of Saturday 25 January 1902. His method of getting 'shunt' of her was savagely to kick her repeatedly and inflict 17 stab wounds with a broken file or chisel, afterwards dumping her corpse in Tottenham Marshes.

The body was found next morning by a boy playing football on the marshes, whose ball had rolled into the ditch where Charlotte's body lay. Her face and hands were covered with blood, her nasal bones were broken, her brain had been battered in, and her hair was matted with frozen blood. Despite these awful injuries, the doctor considered that death had been only gradual and, therefore, the poor girl must have lain there dying in the freezing marsh-ditch for some hours. When discovered, there was still some warmth in the corpse and the process of rigor mortis had just started.

The police search for George Woolfe was not successful until 6 February. He had disappeared, but was found to have enlisted in the Surrey Regiment under the false name of Private Slater, as revealed by his father. He was brought to trial and condemned, to the satisfaction of a disgusted public. The delay between his trial and execution was because of new regulations that required three Sundays to pass to allow the condemned to make his peace with his maker.

His hanging, in the Execution Shed, was the last at Newgate and the prison was closed later that month. The occasion, as had been customary, was marked by the flying of a black flag from the prison

156

mast and the sound of the dreaded death-knell from the bell of St Sepulchre's.

After the closure of Newgate Madame Tussaud's Waxwork Museum bought many items including the bell of St Sepulchre's for £100. It can be heard, tolling the death-knell, as visitors enter the Chamber of Horrors. Another purchase was the complete condemned cell from which Jack Sheppard made his last and most celebrated escape (see 16 November), which remained in the Chamber of Horrors until the 1970s.

Also hanged this day:

1958 Vivian Teed (24) for the murder, by 27 hammer-blows, of postmaster W. Williams (73) during a robbery.

7 May

Hanged this day:

1809   at Old Bailey: John Nicholls for forgery.

1829   at Blackwell's Island, New York, USA: Catharine Cashiere, a moronic, alcoholic and syphilitic black woman, for the stabbing-murder of another alcoholic, Susan Anthony, in a bar-room brawl. Richard Johnson for the gun-murder of his mistress Ursula Newman because she would not name him as the father of her illegitimate child.

1883   at Lincoln Prison: Thomas Garry for the murder of John Newton.

1896   at Moyamensing Prison, Philadelphia, USA: Mass murderer Dr H. H. Holmes (36) (real name Hermann Webster Mudgett) hanged for the murder of Benjamin F. Pitezel as part of an insurance fraud. Holmes had built a 'Murder Castle' in Chicago with secret passages, a gas chamber, and a dissecting room. Estimates of the numbers of his murder victims range from the two he confessed about on the scaffold to two hundred.

8 May

1959 TEN PINTS – AND A TEN-INCH KNIFE!
Ronald Henry Marwood (25) hanged at Pentonville Prison for the knife-murder of PC Raymond Summers (23) during an affray.

Ronald Marwood had drunk ten pints of brown ale when he and his friends arrived at a fierce street fight outside a dancehall in Seven

Sisters Road, Holloway, North London. About twenty youths were engaged in battle on 14 December 1958, using choppers, knives, bottles and knuckle-dusters, as well as their boots and their fists. Marwood and his friends were not connected with either gang, but they seemed to have joined in anyway.

PC Summers tried to stop the affray and may have been in the act of arresting Marwood's best friend when Marwood hit him from behind. The fact is that Marwood had a ten-inch knife in his hand when he struck Summers, and the constable fell to the ground. The fighting lads ran away, leaving only two teenage girls trying to comfort the dying policeman. Marwood was one of the many rounded up and questioned, but he told the police that he had not been at the scene of the affray and he was allowed to go.

It was later established that he had lied about his whereabouts on the night of the murder, but, on 20 December, when investigators went to question him further, he had disappeared. It was not until 27 January that he came out of hiding, reported to a police station, and admitted that he had stabbed PC Summers. He tried to retract his confession at his trial, but there was little doubt that he had stabbed PC Summers to death.

It is strange that the undoubted killer of a policeman should have attracted such a large crowd of sympathisers (about a thousand) outside Pentonville Prison on the morning of execution. They were in an ugly mood, screaming abuse and threats at the mounted policemen who were trying to maintain order.

Also hanged this day:

1811   at Tortola, West Indies: The Hon Arthur William Hodge for the flogging to death of a negro slave.

1883   at Chester Castle: Patrick Casey for the murders of Samuel Earlham and Mary Moxam during robbery.

1951   at Strangeways Prison, Manchester: James Inglis (29) for the murder of Alice Morgan because he did not have enough money to pay for sex. He ran to the gallows and only seven seconds elapsed from the hangmen entering his cell to the drop being opened. *Hangman: Albert Pierrepoint. Assistant: Syd Dernley*

9 May

1726 SHRIEKING IN THE FLAMES!
Thomas Billings hanged at Tyburn Tree for the murder of John Hayes. The murdered man's wife, Catherine Hayes (36), was burned alive for petty treason*.
Hangman: Richard Arnet

Catherine Hayes was a former whore from Worcestershire who achieved respectability by marrying John Hayes. They lived in Tyburn Road (now Oxford Street). She tired of her husband and took to her bed with two young lodgers, Thomas Billings and Thomas Wood. Hayes was the dominant one and had soon ensnared Billings and Wood to murder her husband. In March 1725 Catherine let Billings into the master bedroom and he bludgeoned his landlord's head with a coal-axe. With help from young Wood, they cut off the head and threw it into the Thames and hoped that it would be washed out to sea. The rest of the body was dismembered and dropped into a pond at Marylebone.

A watchman found the bloody head lying in the mud at Westminster. It was washed, the hair was combed, and it was publicly displayed in an effort to discover the identity of the murdered man. It was soon realised that the head was that of John Hayes, despite his wife's lies about him being elsewhere. Hayes, Billings and Wood were arrested and questioned and Thomas Wood broke down and confessed the whole story. Billings and Wood were sentenced to be hanged for murder, but Catherine Hayes was condemned for petty treason and sentenced to burning at the stake. She screamed all the way back to her cell when she realised what her fate would be.

Thomas Wood died of jail fever. After Billings had been hanged (his body was afterwards hung in chains at the Marylebone pond where he had dumped the remains of John Hayes) Catherine Hayes was tied to the stake with an iron chain, and dry faggots were piled around her. It was customary for the hangman to attach a rope round the neck of the person to be burned and, after the fire had been lit but before the flames reached her, to strangle the petty traitoress. Hangman Arnet might have been drunk or he may have accidentally dropped the rope when the flames scorched his hand but, for whatever cause, he failed to strangle her.

Her shrieks of terror were loud and shrill, and she kicked the flaming faggots away from her. Arnet and others threw the faggots back but her screams continued and the faggots were kicked back and forth. The records do not say how long her screams continued, but it is clear that she was a long time in dying and it was three hours before her body was reduced to ashes.

Also hanged this day:

1800   at Philadelphia, USA: Joseph Baker, Canadian mutineer and murderer, and his accomplices Berrouse and LaCroix, for piracy.

1924   at Amite, Louisiana, USA: six men publicly hanged in pairs starting at midday: Leona and Deamore, Giglio and Rini, and two others. *Hangman: 'Joe'*

10 May

1477 PAWNS IN ROYAL DEATH-GAME
Thomas Burdet and John Stacy hanged at Tyburn for sorcery and having 'composed the death of the king in treasonous rhymes'.

Here were two victims of the royal intrigues during the War of the Roses. The plot and counter-plot between the factions supporting Edward IV and his brother George, Duke of Clarence, resulted in the ignominious deaths of many lesser men.

The Woodvilles, the queen's powerful family, in a bid to discredit Clarence, had an Oxford clerk named John Stacy arrested for sorcery and tortured. In his agony he denounced one of Clarence's household, Thomas Burdet. Burdet and Stacy were tried at Westminster for treason and witchcraft by having 'composed the death of the king'. It was alleged that Clarence's man, Burdet, had induced Stacy and another sorcerer to calculate the astrological omens for the king and the Prince of Wales and that they had published a prediction of the king's death, in treasonable rhymes, which concluded that Edward IV would be succeeded by a king whose name would begin with G: George, Duke of Clarence?

Burdet and Stacy were tried by the king's men who were determined to undermine the prestige of Clarence and, inevitably, they were pronounced guilty and hanged; unlucky pawns in a struggle between their powerful superiors.

What about the accuracy of the 'treasonous prediction'? The following year Edward IV had Clarence charged with treason and imprisoned in the Tower of London where he was drowned in a barrel of Malmsey wine.

Edward IV died in 1483 and should have been succeeded by his 13-year-old son as Edward V, but the lad was king in name only: on the journey to London he and his younger brother, the Duke of York

(9), fell into the hands of their uncle Richard who seized the Crown and became Richard III.

The boys were removed to the Tower of London and, a few months later, disappeared and were never seen again. What happened to the so-called princes in the Tower is still the subject of heated controversy between historians.

Was their uncle Richard, Duke of Gloucester, the 'G' predicted in the 'treasonous rhyme'?

Also hanged this day:

1702   at Tyburn Tree: John Smith for murder.

1703   at Tyburn Tree: Thomas Istrick for house-breaking.

1880   at Aylesbury Prison: William Dumdleton for the murder of John Edmunds.

1898   at Nauplin, Greece: Karditzi and Kyriakos for the attempted assassination of the King of Greece.

1909   at Swansea Gaol: William Joseph Foy for the murder of Mary Ann Rees. He walked to the scaffold smoking a cigarette and wearing a fern in his buttonhole. *Hangman: Henry Pierrepoint. Assistant: John Ellis*

11 May

Hanged this day:

1880   at York Castle: John Henry Wood, claiming his innocence to the end, for the murder of John Coe.

1920   at Walton Gaol, Liverpool: Bert Salisbury for the gun-murder of his common-law wife Alice; William Waddington for the murder of an Oldham girl aged 7. *Hangman: John Ellis*

12 May

1936 BUCK RUXTON'S SEALED CONFESSION
Dr Buck Ruxton (36) hanged at Strangeways Prison, Manchester, for the murder and mutilation of his wife and his children's nursemaid.

Dr Buck Ruxton, a Parsee who had Anglicised his name, lived with his common-law wife, Belle, at 2 Dalton Square, Lancaster. Dr Ruxton

(36) and Belle (34) had lived as man and wife for eight years and had three children. A local girl, Mary Rogerson (20) was hired to work as the children's nursemaid. Ruxton built up a large and successful medical practice in Lancaster, but his relationship with Belle was often stormy. He was intensely jealous and Belle was something of a playful flirt; this was an explosive mixture of personalities.

Belle returned home from a trip to Blackpool, to see the illuminations, in the early hours of Sunday 15 September 1935. The strict, authoritarian doctor must have had a furious row with his wife which he concluded by strangling her. At some time later he also killed Mary Rogerson; if she had been present in the room during the row she may have been killed immediately after Mrs Ruxton. What is known is that he cut up both bodies into a mass of small pieces, wrapping them in newspaper or bits of cloth, but permanently removing the parts he thought might lead to identification.

He hired a car and dumped the parcels into a ravine at Moffat, Dumfriesshire, Scotland. There was a lot of cleaning to do back at 2 Dalton Square: the carpets were drenched with blood, and the walls and floors had to be washed down. Foolishly, he engaged others to help him with the job; they were later to give evidence at his trial.

When Mary Rogerson's parents reported her missing he had to report Belle's disappearance as well, although he suggested that she had left him and was with relatives in Scotland. The parcels of dismembered human remains were discovered at Moffat at the end of September. One of the newspaper wrappings was found to be a 'slip edition' of the *Sunday Graphic*. A slip edition is one that is produced for a specific area and contains local news. This slip edition was for the Morecambe and Lancaster area. When the police in Dumfriesshire contacted their colleagues in Lancaster, the mystery of the parcels of parts of two females was soon linked with the two missing women from Lancaster.

The game was up, but Dr Buck Ruxton vehemently denied his guilt. Police discovered plenty of blood stains in the house despite the combined cleaning efforts, and more bits of human remains in the wastepipes. The massive forensic investigation included the superimposing of a photograph of Mrs Ruxton's head on to an x-ray of one of the Moffat skulls.

Nonetheless, Ruxton continued his denials at his trial. When it was put to him that he had killed Belle after she returned from Blackpool, he became wild and emotional: 'It is a deliberate, fantastic story. You might just as well say the sun was rising in the west and setting in the east!'

It was then suggested to him that he had killed Mary Rogerson that same morning: 'That is absolute bunkum with a capital B, if I may say it. Why should I kill poor Mary?'

The real answers emerged two months after his trial in March 1936, when he was found guilty and sentenced to death. The following confession, in Ruxton's neat handwriting, was written and signed on 14 October 1935, the day after he was charged with murder, and then sealed in an envelope. It was published in a newspaper on the Sunday after his execution:

'I killed Mrs Ruxton in a fit of temper because I thought she had been with a man. I was mad at the time. Mary Rogerson was present at the time. I had to kill her.'

Also hanged this day:

1828 at Old Bailey: young brothers Charles and William Melford, and Dennis Sullivan, for burglary.

1868 at Dumfries Prison, Scotland: Robert Smith (19) for the sex-murder of a little girl named Scott. *Hangman: Thomas Askern.* This was the last public execution in Scotland, although the crowd could see little because of the arrangement of barricades to hold them a long way back from the scaffold.

1892 at Parish Prison, New Orleans, USA: Dr Etienne Deschamps (61) for the seduction and chloroform-murder of Juliette Deitsch (12) on 30 January 1889. *Hangman: Taylor*

1903 at Strangeways Prison, Manchester: William George Hudson (26) for the murder of Harry Shoot, his friend and fellow soldier.

13 May

Hanged this day:

1803 at Dover, New Jersey, USA: Peter Stout for the axe-murder of Thomas Williams (14). Stout considered himself to have been somehow insulted by the youth whereupon he immediately killed the boy with an axe in the street at Dover.

1828 at Old Bailey: John Brown for burglary; Russell Brown for highway robbery; John Baker for horse-stealing; Hanby Price for coining and John Roberts for robbery.

1945 Private G. E. Smith for the murder of Sir E. Teichman.

14 May

1959 HOMICIDE ACT OF 1957
Michael Tatum (24) hanged for the murder of an 85-year-old man during a robbery.

Tatum had battered the old man to death with a blunt instrument during a robbery, therefore it was a capital offence under the 1957 Homicide Act (see the British Hanging Chronology and 23 July) whereby murder was punishable by death in five categories, including in the course or furtherance of theft.

Also hanged this day:

1880   at Armagh County Gaol, Ireland: Peter Conway for the murder of his brother-in-law, Mr Millar.

1883   at Kilmainham Prison, Dublin: Joe Brady for the murder of Mr Burke.

15 May

1888 'A BODY NEVER KNOWS. . .'
John Alfred Gell hanged at Strangeways Prison, Manchester, for the murder of Mrs Mary Miller at Moston, Lancashire.
Hangman: James Berry

Gell was reported to have said 'I die an innocent man' as he stood beneath the gallows' beam. A more remarkable statement was that made by Warder Webb while talking with Hangman Berry. Shaking his head sadly, Warder Webb remarked: 'A body never knows who will be next.' Within three months Berry was back at Strangeways to hang a convict named John Jackson (see 7 August) who had committed a murder during an escape and had actually managed to get outside the prison, but was recaptured. The man he had murdered was Warder Webb.

Also hanged this day:

1815   at Old Bailey: William Sawyer for murder.

1826   at Old Bailey: Peter Neader and William Leach for highway robbery; Robert Savage and James Bonfield for burglary.

164

1873 at Sacramento, California, USA: Charles Mortimer for the throat-cutting murder of bar owner Mary Gibson.

16 May

1975 'MICHAEL X' HANGED
Would-be black power leader Abdul Malik (41), a.k.a. Michael X (original name Michael de Freitas), hanged at Port of Spain, Trinidad, for the murder and decapitation of fellow criminal Joseph Skerritt. Also involved in other murders.

17 August 1933 Michael de Freitas was born in Trinidad, son of a Portuguese planter and a local black woman.
1960s He was living in the Notting Hill area of London and working as an 'enforcer' for the evil racketeer landlord Peter Rachman.
1963 De Freitas became fascinated by Black Power politics, converted to the Muslim faith and changed his name to Abdul Malik.
1965 He was so impressed by the visit to Britain of Malcolm X* preaching racial hatred that he formed the Racial Advancement and Action Society (RAAS) and changed his name again, this time to Michael X. His antics attracted much attention from the media and from 'trendy' socialites.
1967 He was jailed for a year under the new Race Relations Act, after a fiery speech inciting his followers to shoot any white man seen with a black woman. In another speech he said 'Fear of the white monkeys is nothing . . . Before I killed for the first time I wondered if I would have a conscience, but I slept well.'
1969 He was charged with robbery and demanding money with menaces. He jumped bail and fled, apparently to the relief of the British authorities who did not try to get him back.
1970 He resigned from all of his Black Power offices, including that as chairman of RAAS. Moved into a luxurious bungalow at Christina Gardens in La Chance, a rich suburb in Port of Spain, Trinidad, and set up a political-religious commune including:

Hakim Jamal (40), a black American activist.
Gale Benson, a beautiful white girl from an upper-class British background, who was Jamal's girlfriend. Michael X described her as the prettiest girl he had ever seen. She apparently had a masochistic streak: despite her love for Jamal, she was completely under the domination of Michael X who claimed that he once tied her to a bed, naked, and beat her until he became tired.
Joe Skerritt, a cousin of Michael X and the commune's odd-job man.

Stanley Abbott (34), a former borstal boy and accomplice to Michael X's activities in London.
Edward Chaddee (20), an accomplice.
Steve Yates, an accomplice.
Adolphus Parmasser (21), an accomplice.

(These are the names which will be used here; some of the participants had different original names and assumed yet more.)

2 January 1972 Michael X had decided that Gale Benson must be killed. She was resented by the other black activists because she was white and he thought that she was causing a rift between him and Hakim Jamal. He ordered Abbott and Yates to dig a pit in the garden and Yates lured her out to it. Abbott grabbed her and muffled her screams while Yates set about her with a machete or cutlass. She was thrown into the pit and the attack with machete and cutlass continued until she was helpless; then they filled in the pit, burying her while still alive.

20 January 1972 Hakim Jamal had reported Gale Benson as missing to the police and was now fearing for his own life. He left for the USA.

8 February 1972 Michael X ordered another killing, this time of Joe Skerritt for refusing to raid a police post. Skerritt was told to join some others digging a drainage trench and was there set upon with knives and cutlasses. Michael X delivered the cutlass blow which killed him, almost cutting off Skerritt's head in the process. The body was dumped in the trench and covered with soil. The mound was smoothed over and lettuces planted on it.

10 February 1972 Steve Yates drowned during a commune bathing party at Sans Souci Bay, a death which has never been satisfactorily explained.

18 February 1972 The commune dispersed and Michael X fled to Guyana with his wife and four children.

19 February 1972 The bungalow at Christina Gardens caught fire and was gutted by dawn. The police, possibly following up a tip-off from a rival local gang, attended with the fire service.

20 February 1972 From Guyana, Michael X ordered his lawyer to take out an injunction to prevent the police from entering his property. It was too late, they were already digging.

22 February 1972 Joe Skerritt's body unearthed.

24 February 1972 Gale Benson's body found. A cutlass wound in the throat had probably been inflicted as she lay wounded in the pit, to hold her down as the earth was shovelled on to her. Particles of soil found in her throat and lungs proved that she had been buried alive and died from suffocation.

1 March 1972 Michael X arrested in Guyana while fleeing for the Brazilian border and deported to Trinidad.

166

August 1972 Michael X and Stanley Abbott tried at Port of Spain for the murder of Joe Skerritt. Michael X was found guilty and sentenced to death, but his appeals delayed his execution until 1975. Abbott was found guilty of the lesser charge of manslaughter.

May 1973 Hakim Jamal shot to death by five gunmen in front of his family in Boston, Massachusetts, USA, purportedly on a contract organised by Michael X from the condemned cell.

July 1973 Stanley Abbott and Edward Chaddee were found guilty of the murder of Gale Benson and sentenced to death. Abbott was hanged on 27 April 1979 and Chaddee was reprieved. Adolphus Parmasser was not charged, having agreed to give prosecution evidence.

16 May 1975 The end of Michael X.

* Malcolm X, American Black Power leader and agitator, was murdered in 1965 at Harlem, New York City, USA, by other Black Muslims.

Also hanged this day:

1873 at New York, USA: Michael Nixon for the gun-murder of Charles H. Phifer during a Bowery hold-up.

1882 at Durham Gaol: Thomas Fury for the murder of Maria FitzSimmons in 1869.

1887 at Dorchester Castle: Henry William Young for the murder of his wife's illegitimate child.

17 May

1871 INTELLECTUAL'S OBSCENITIES ON GALLOWS
Edward Rulloff (52) the 'intellectual killer' hanged after a 30-year career of killing, at Binghampton, New York, USA, mouthing obscenities at the crowd that stopped only when he dropped through the trap.

Born with the name Edward Howard Rulloffson in 1819, he belonged to a poor and hard working family in Hammond River, Canada. He had only a few years of formal education, but he read every book, on any subject, which came his way and absorbed the contents into his astonishing memory. His appearance was distinctly odd: a huge head quite out of proportion to his muscular body, and wide-set blazing blue eyes.

He worked as a shop assistant. It was at the age of 20 that he first fell

167

foul of the law after an outbreak of burglaries in the district, one of which had been at the home of his employer. The employer was staggered to see young Rulloffson calmly at work in the shop, brazenly wearing a suit that had been stolen in the burglary! For this he was sentenced to two years in prison.

His avid reading continued while in prison and, by the time of his release, he was an expert in a bewildering number of languages as well as in the law, medicine, and botany. He went to Dryden in New York State and became the town's school teacher, calling himself Professor Rulloff, and becoming a popular and respected figure. By the end of 1843 he had married one of his young students, Harriet Schutt, and set himself up in a medical practice as Dr Rulloff.

Although he was successful he resented the opposition from Harriet's family, and moved to Lancing on the shore of Lake Cayuga, New York. His local fame as a doctor and herbalist ensured his success, but it was there that he committed his first murders. He treated the wife and child of Harriet's brother, William Schutt, who were suffering from a mysterious illness from which they died. Twenty-seven years later, as he awaited execution, he admitted that he had poisoned them in revenge for the Schutt family's opposition to his marriage.

In 1845 Harriet and their daughter Dorothy disappeared. Rulloff told various people that they were away visiting friends, or relatives, at different places. The Schutt brothers were suspicious and, after Rulloff fled, went after him and brought him back to be charged with Harriet's murder. The lake had been dragged without success; hardly surprising in the light of discoveries made years later, that Rulloff had sold the bodies to a medical school. The charge of murdering his wife failed because, as the law stood at that time, a body had to be produced. He was charged only with abduction and sentenced to ten years' imprisonment.

In Auburn Prison he served his time as a model prisoner, reading thousands of books and teaching fellow convicts. After his release he again faced charges for the murders of Harriet and Dorothy, it now having been discovered that he had sold the bodies to the medical school. The charge of killing Harriet had to be dropped because he had already been acquitted for this once, and could not be charged again. However, he was found guilty of murdering his daughter and sentenced to death, but escaped to Pennsylvania.

While free he worked as a scientist at Allegheny College, calling himself Professor James Nelson, but many lawmen were on his trail and he had to move on. He was caught in Ohio and brought back to New York State. His appeal succeeded and he was cleared of the murder of Dorothy, again because the body could not be produced after all those years. The police had to save him from an enraged lynch mob. He was charged with the Schutt deaths, but had to be set free when the exhumations proved inconclusive. He had officially got away with four murders!

Rulloff then organised a fiendishly efficient burglary squad in New York City for six years. When he was not masterminding this criminal source of income, he worked with feverish intensity perfecting a language teaching method and gave talks before learned societies. But it all went wrong during the night robbery of the Halbert Brothers Silk Shop at Binghampton on 21 August 1870.

William T. Dexter and Albert Jarvis, Rulloff's men, were surprised to discover two shop assistants living on the premises: Fred Mirrick and Gilbert Burrows. Mirrick and Burrows struggled with the intruders when a third man, Rulloff, walked into the shop with a gun and shot the defenders. Mirrick was killed, but Burrows was able to stagger away and raise the alarm. Local residents quickly formed into groups to hunt down the killers and Dexter and Jarvis were found that night – floating lifeless in the river after being beaten to death and dumped in the water.

Rulloff was soon in police custody, and identified by Burrows. Dexter's family revealed details of Rulloff's amazing intellectual lifestyle: how he had passed himself off under different identities to different societies at the same time, despite his top-heavy appearance with his oddly shaped head. The newspapers reported every angle of the astonishing story of the 'Educated Murderer' before and during his trial, which inevitably ended with him being sentenced to death.

A large crowd was waiting in front of Binghampton Prison on the morning of the hanging. Rulloff walked to the gallows arrogantly, loudly boasting of his mental superiority compared with that of the mob. This large-brained genius – who was familiar with perhaps 30 languages and was a master of many other subjects – interspersed the bragging with streams of the crudest gutter language. His obscenities were directed at the crowd and he railed at them with the foulest of oaths. His tirade of full-throated verbal filth continued as he stood with the noose around his neck. It was stopped only when the drop opened below him.

Also hanged this day:

1881   at Maidstone Prison: Private Albert Moore (23), an officer's batman, for the throat-cutting murder of Mary Ann Marsh (74) in the officer's house. *Hangman: William Marwood*

18 May

1812 PRIME MINISTER DREAMED HE WOULD BE SHOT IN THE HOUSE OF COMMONS

John Bellingham hanged in front of Newgate Prison, for murdering Prime Minister Spencer Perceval (50) in the House of Commons.
Hangman: William Brunskill

Spencer Perceval had a dream the night before he was killed. In the dream he was shot in the lobby of the House of Commons by a man wearing a green coat with brass buttons and, after being shot in the chest, everything went black. In the morning he recounted the dream to his horrified family, and later to friends.

Perceval had been Chancellor of the Exchequer since 1807, a title he retained when, in 1809, he became Prime Minister and First Lord of the Treasury. He was married and had six sons and six daughters. His family was fearful about the vivid dream he had described and pleaded with him not to go to the House that day, but an urgent appeal arrived from his colleagues that the government was in difficulties in the debate on the Peninsular War and he was needed. He left at once.

He entered the House of Commons via the lobby of St Stephen's Chapel at a little after 5 p.m. on 11 May 1812. It was then that John Bellingham stepped out from behind some folding doors, wearing a green coat with brass buttons, and fired a pistol at the Prime Minister. Perceval staggered back, shot in his left side, and exclaimed 'Oh, I am murdered!' He died within a few minutes.

Bellingham surrendered without fuss and another loaded pistol was found in his pocket. He was a deranged man with a grudge who was convinced that he was entitled to a government pension for losses he had sustained in Russia. Irony was added to the tragedy when it became apparent that the assassination was a case of mistaken identity; Bellingham thought he had shot Lord Leveson Gower, a former ambassador to Russia. Justice was swift. Bellingham committed his crime on the evening of 11 May, he was tried at the Old Bailey and the jury took 14 minutes to find him guilty on 15 May. He was hanged as the clock was striking the hour at 8 a.m. on 18 May. A week is not always a long time in politics.

Spencer Perceval is the only British Prime Minister to have been assassinated.

Also hanged this day:

1835 at Maidstone: Patrick Carrol (32) for the stabbing-murder of Elizabeth Browning, landlady of the Britannia pub in Woolwich.

Carrol died after two or three 'convulsive struggles' at the rope-end. *Hangman: William Calcraft*

1885   at Chelmsford Gaol: James Lee for the murder of a police inspector.

1932   at Strangeways Prison, Manchester: Charles James Cowle (19) for the sex-murder of Naomi Annie Farnworth (6). *Hangman: Tom Pierrepoint*

19 May

Hanged this day:

1829   at Old Bailey: William Henry Carr for forgery; John Shaw and John Hawkins for burglary; Thomas Crowther, John Turner, and John Martelly for highway robbery.

1882   at the Tombs Prison, New York, USA: Augustus D. Leighton for the murder of his mistress Mary Dean. She had ordered him out of their Manhattan home after a row and, inflamed, he cut her throat in front of a crowd of witnesses who were watching the commotion.

1891   at Strangeways Prison, Manchester: Alfred Turner for the murder of Mary Moran, his sweetheart.

20 May

1909 NO MERCY!
The brothers Morris and Marks Reuben hanged at Pentonville Prison for the Rupert Street Murder in Whitechapel of William Sproull (35).

William Sproull was the powerfully built Second Engineer of the SS *Dorset*, which had arrived at Victoria Dock in the East End of London on 15 March 1909. That night he set out with Second Mate McEachern to have a good time. They met a couple of young prostitutes, Ellen Stevens and Emily Allen, and enjoyed a drinking bout lasting for about five hours. During this time they were taken by the girls to their sleazy rooms at 3 Rupert Street. Around 1 a.m. the door burst open and the Reuben brothers, Morris and Marks, came in and immediately attacked the seamen. The Reuben brothers were the girls' ponces and would use the girls to lure newly paid sailors to the house so that they could be beaten up and robbed.

Sproull was not so drunk that he couldn't defend himself, to the surprise of the cowardly Reubens. McEachern was able to escape, dazed and bloody, while Morris Reuben flailed at Sproull with his swagger stick. Marks Reuben snapped open his clasp-knife and stabbed the fighting sailor about the body; a stab wound over the heart was to prove fatal. The brothers pushed Sproull out of the house, after emptying his pockets of cash and relieving him of his watch and chain. Sproull staggered across the road and collapsed on the pavement opposite. He was dead when found by a policeman half-an-hour later.

The constable followed the trail of blood to the door of 3 Rupert Street. The brothers and the two prostitutes were arrested and there was evidence aplenty: Marks Reuben's blood-stained knife was found hidden behind a metal sheet on the wall by the stove; Morris Reuben had Sproull's watch and chain hanging from hooks inside his trouser-leg; there was the stick he had broken over Sproull's head, as well as scattered blood stains inside and outside the house. As if this was not enough, the prostitutes were allowed to give King's Evidence against their ponces.

There was no hope for Marks Reuben at the trial but an attempt was made to save Morris Reuben, as he had not struck the actual deathblow. This was not accepted by the judge and jury because he was clearly guilty of what has sometimes been called 'constructive murder', that is where robbers conspire to use violence upon their victims and where one of them kills in the process.

Morris Reuben showed his terror throughout the trial and at one stage collapsed on the floor of the dock and had to be attended by a doctor. When the jury had given its verdict, after a ten-minute retirement, Morris went white. With his eyes popped in his terror, and both arms extended towards the jury he whined, 'Vot gentlemen? No recommendation? Oh my poor mother! Vot, no recommendation?' The jurymen ignored him, and there was to be no recommendation for mercy for the evil brothers who had shown no mercy to their victims. His hopes of a reprieve were dashed too: the Home Secretary also had no mercy.

The hanging of the Reuben brothers had a salutary effect on the criminal fraternity of the East End. Robbery with violence had been prevalent, especially upon visiting seamen. Divisional Detective Inspector Frederick Wensley, who had been in charge of the case, was able to report later that this type of crime sharply declined after the double hanging.

Also hanged this day:

1827 at Old Bailey: James Wingfield for rape; Royal Keats (known as the 'Wooden-Legged Drover') for sheep-stealing.

172

1879 at Strangeways Prison, Manchester: William Cooper for the murder of Ellen Mather.

21 May

Hanged this day:

1722 at Tyburn Tree: John Hawkins and James Simpson for mail-robbery.

1883 at Taunton Prison: George White for wife-murder; Joseph Wedlake for the murder of Mark Cox.

22 May

1866 MURDER ON THE BRIDGE
Joseph Bell publicly hanged outside Perth Prison, Scotland, for the murder and robbery of Alexander M'Ewan.
Hangman: William Calcraft

Alexander M'Ewan was a baker's roundsman who was shot ('. . . his head veritably riddled with pellets') and robbed of all the money on him – his own and his employer's – at Vicars Bridge in Blairingone. Joseph Bell, a potter and poacher, was accused but protested his innocence to the end. The jury was satisfied of his guilt and he died 12 days after the trial. William Calcraft was brought from London to perform the hanging, and the scaffold was borrowed from Aberdeen. Two thousand people saw the execution, the last to be held fully in public in Scotland, although there was a later 'nominal' public execution in 1868. (See 12 May.)

Also hanged this day:

1822 at Old Bailey: George Adams, William Bartholomew, John Close, John Anson, Edward Ward – all for burglary.

1894 at Kirkdale Prison, Liverpool: John Langford for the murder of Elizabeth Steven.

1900 at Newgate Prison: Henry Grove for the murder of an old man at Enfield.

23 May

1701 DRUNKEN HANGING OF CAPTAIN KIDD
Captain William Kidd (56) with accomplices Nicholas Churchill, James Howe, Gabriel Loff, Hugh Parrot, Abel Owens, and Darby Mullins, hanged at Execution Dock, Wapping, for piracy.

Captain Kidd had been given commissions from the king to hunt down pirates but, in 1697 when he reached the pirate haven of Madagascar, he turned pirate himself. His career as a pirate lasted a mere five months and yet he became one of history's most notorious buccaneers. He was arrested in Boston, Massachusetts, and sent to England. He faced four separate trials for piracy and murder, on succeeding days at the Old Bailey, and was sentenced to death with his accomplices.

He had been drinking heavily and was drunk by the time he arrived at Execution Dock. He noticed a former lover in the crowd and growled 'I have lain with that bitch three times and now she has come to see me hanged!' It was a bungled execution. Kidd was hanged with the Irishman, Darby Mullins. Mullins died almost at once but the rope on Captain Kidd snapped and he fell to the ground. Kidd was so intoxicated, and dazed from his fall, that he seemed not to realise what was happening. He was forced up the gallows steps again. The rope was re-knotted and he was pushed off for the second time, and again the rope snapped.

By now the crowd were howling for him to be set free, fearing that the snapping ropes were a sign from Heaven, but the sheriff would have none of it. He was taken up and pushed off for the third time and it was third time unlucky for the pirate captain. The others were hanged without any further mishaps.

The corpses were left hanging on gibbets on the shore until they had been covered by three Thames tides washing up and over them. Afterwards they were 'hung in chains', at some distance from each other, along the bank of the Thames where they stayed for some years. The 'chains' were actually the bands of an iron suit which served to hold the body together as the flesh and bones rotted away.

Also hanged this day:

1842 at Old Bailey: Daniel Good for the ghastly murder of Jane Jones.

1876 at Newgate Prison: Matteo Corgalis, Pascaler Caladis, George Kadi, and Gioranni Cacaris, for murder and mutiny on board the ship *Lehnie*.

1882 at Norwich Castle: George Abigail for the murder of Jane Plunkett.

1888 at Armley Gaol, Leeds: James William Richardson (23) for the murder of his bullying foreman, William Berridge. *Hangman: James Billington*

1892 at Melbourne, Australia: Frederick Bailey Deeming (about 40), swindler and mass murderer.

1905 at Wandsworth Prison: Alfred (22) and Albert Stratton (20) for the murders of shopkeeper Thomas Farrow (69) and his wife Ann (60s) in Deptford in south-east London. They were the first murderers to be convicted on the evidence of fingerprints. *Hangman: William Billington. Assistant: John Billington.* Two brothers hanged by two brothers!

24 May

1725 THE FIRST 'MASTER CRIMINAL'
'Thief-taker General' Jonathan Wild (43) hanged at Tyburn Tree, for receiving stolen lace.
Hangman: (probably) Richard Arnet

Jonathan Wild lived respectably enough as a buckle maker in Wolverhampton until he was 24, when he deserted his wife and went to London. He was soon in debt and was thrown into prison for four years, and it was then that he learned about crime from the inside. He studied the subject well and graduated to be, probably, the first master criminal.

Thieves would deliver their booty to him, there being no law against receiving at that time, and he would offer to restore it to the original owners for half the value plus his handling fee of five shillings (25p). He and the thief would share the sum for the restored goods fifty-fifty. He grew rich at no risk to himself. He did not have to go out to find the victims of burglaries; he had opened an office and they would come to him to report the theft and say how much of a reward they would give to recover the items. He soon had the thieves organised into areas. They would bring the goods to his warehouses to await the owners who would claim them back and pay the rewards. Anything not claimed would be sent on one of Wild's ships to the Continent for sale there. On the homeward journey the ship would be loaded with bolts of lace and barrels of spirits, to be smuggled ashore without duty being paid, for sale on the home market.

He had an arrangement with the City Marshal. Wild knew who all the thieves were; after all, most of them worked for him! Wild and the Marshal received a bounty of up to £40 for each thief who was turned in and convicted. This was not only an easy form of extra income for Wild, it also gave him more power to keep the thieves in order. Burglary was a capital crime. Criminals who failed to share their ill-gotten gains, or who tried to cheat him, would find themselves handed over to the authorities for an early trip to Tyburn Tree.

When the Marshal fell out of favour with the Lord Mayor, and was later imprisoned, Jonathan Wild styled himself 'Thief-taker General for Great Britain and Ireland' and strutted around London with a silver-topped staff of office. The underworld feared and hated him, yet he continued to live his double life, as master thief and Thief-taker General, without retaliation from these tough and violent outlaws. During his thief-taking years he was responsible for 67 criminals being convicted and executed: 35 highwaymen, 22 burglars, and 10 returned transportees. To the ordinary public he was a respected figure, although the authorities knew all about him. It is amazing that he got away with it for so many years.

His downfall came about over 50 yards of stolen lace, valued at £40, which he sold back to the owners on behalf of the thieves. He was charged under an Act of Parliament that had been passed with him in mind, which made it a capital offence to receive stolen goods and to attempt to obtain a reward for returning them. In this case the burglars gave evidence against Wild and other cases were added; in all he was charged on 11 counts. It was the end of the surprisingly long criminal career of the thief-taking master thief.

In the condemned cell at Newgate, during the early hours on the morning of the last day of his life, Jonathan Wild swallowed a massive dose of laudanum. Somehow or other, his constitution survived and he had to face the awful journey to Tyburn. He was slumped in the back of the cart, drowsy and mostly insensible of what was happening around him on the way. It was just as well. One of the biggest crowds ever seen in London attended his execution, lining the route from Newgate and at Tyburn itself. He was now a publicly hated figure. The mobs shouted abuse all the way to Tyburn and pelted the cart with stones, rotten vegetables, dung, and anything else handy. When he arrived at Tyburn he showed some signs of recovery from the poison. The crowd was impatient to see the end of him and would permit him no delay for taking prayers. They even threatened to kill the hangman unless he did the job immediately, which he did.

In the midst of these scenes of mob hatred from the general public of London there was a contrary example of the mentality of the criminal classes towards Wild. He had lived off them, terrorised them, and sent 67 of their kind to die on the gallows. Despite all of this, seven of his 'employees' were to be hanged with him – and they considered it an honour to be hanged on the same scaffold (see 1725, opposite).

Wild was buried in St Pancras churchyard and within days his grave had been robbed for the anatomists. The skeleton turned up years later and was presented to the Royal College of Surgeons of England in 1847 and placed in their museum at Lincoln's Inn Fields. It shares a glass case with the skeleton of Red Barn murderer William Corder (see 11 August) and the skull of Eugene Aram (see 6 August).

Also hanged this day:

1725 at Tyburn Tree: Robert Harpham for coining. Also seven robbers and murderers who considered it an honour to be hanged with Thief-taker General Jonathan Wild: Edward Burnworth, William Blewitt, Emanuel Dixon, Thomas Berry, William Shelton, John Legge, and John Higgs.

1752 at Bristol: Richard Mooney and John Jones for highway robbery.

1876 at Holly Springs, Mississippi, USA: John Eli Cannaday (a.k.a. John Sneedom) for the axe-murder of Marcus Lucas while robbing him. Cannaday had anticipated a hoard of gold in the house, but found only $2.

25 May

1885 A BLOODY HANGING
Moses Shrimpton hanged at Worcester Prison for the murder of PC Davis.
Hangman: James Berry

Moses Shrimpton was an 'old lag' who had spent many years locked up in prisons. He had killed a policeman who interrupted him during a poaching foray, which brought his long career of crime to an end. Berry gave him a nine-foot drop, which almost ripped the head from the body and splashed blood on the wall and floor of the pit below the gallows.

Also hanged this day:

1752 at Chester: John Connolly and John Morgan for burglary.

1831 at Old Bailey: John Broach for stealing from a dwelling house.

1874 at Newgate Prison: James Godwin (27) for wife-murder. *Hangman: William Calcraft in his last appearance on the scaffold after 45 years as Public Hangman*

1910   at Wandsworth Prison: Thomas W. Jessops, a fireman, for the murder of John Healey, stage carpenter at the Empire Music Hall, Camberwell. The first execution held during the reign of King George V.

26 May

1868 BRITAIN'S LAST PUBLIC EXECUTION
The Fenian, Michael Barrett (27), publicly hanged at Old Bailey for the murder of Sarah Ann Hodgkinson in the ghastly Clerkenwell explosion.
Hangman: William Calcraft

Michael Barrett, an Irish stevedore, was convicted for taking a leading part in the bomb outrage at the Clerkenwell House of Detention the previous December. He belonged to the Fenian Society, or Irish Republican Brotherhood, formed in 1858 to fight for an end to British rule in Ireland. They organised acts of terrorism in Canada and England to draw attention to their cause.

A Fenian gang, led by Barrett, attempted to rescue Richard O'Sullivan Burke and Joseph Casey, two of their members, from Clerkenwell Prison on 12 December 1867. They placed a dynamite charge against the wall, but the fuse failed. They tried again at 3.45 p.m. the next day, when Burke and Casey should have been taking exercise in the yard. However, the police had heard that a rescue was to be attempted, and the two men had been removed. A wagon with a large cask of dynamite was placed against the wall and a white ball was thrown over the wall to warn their men to stand clear. It was Barrett himself who set the fuse, and this time it worked. The massive explosion tore a great gap in the prison wall, but it also wrecked the tenements opposite, killing 12 and injuring 120 of the women and children there.

Five men and a woman were soon arrested and charged with the murder of Sarah Ann Hodgkinson, one of the victims. Two of the men were quick to offer to turn Queen's Evidence and have their charges dropped. Barrett was found guilty and the others were acquitted for lack of evidence.

At Britain's last public execution* Michael Barrett was led out of the prison at 8 a.m. by the priest. His appearance was at first greeted with cheers, but these were replaced by hisses, which continued for a few minutes. As they mounted the steps to the gallows, Barrett walked with a firm tread, deathly pale of face but showing no signs of fear. He prayed fervently with the priest, after which Hangman Calcraft slipped the white cap over his head and put the noose around his neck. Barrett

178

turned round and spoke through the cap asking for the rope to be adjusted, a request with which Calcraft complied. Within a moment Barrett was dead: when the bolt was withdrawn he fell through the trap and hung there motionless. The body was cut down and removed at 9 a.m.

* Three days after his hanging a new law received the royal assent. Thereafter all executions were to be held privately inside official prisons.

Also hanged this day:

1738   at Tyburn Tree: Joan Toon and Henry Blastock for robbery.

1822   at Old Bailey: Thomas Lomas and John Nunbria for issuing forged notes; Robert Crawley for burglary.

1828   at Old Bailey: Samuel Wadden for burglary; Ephraim Slater for issuing forged notes.

1879   at Taunton Prison: Catherine Churchill for the murder of her husband.

1882   at Armley Gaol, Leeds: Osmond Otto Brand for the murder of William Pepper.

1884   at Lincoln Prison: Mary Lefley for husband-murder, having laced his rice pudding with arsenic. When Hangman James Berry entered the condemned cell she threw up her arms and screamed 'Murder! Murder!' and had to be dragged to the scaffold shrieking all the time.

1938   at Durham Gaol: Robert Hoolhouse (21) hanged, on very slight evidence, for the murder of Mrs Margaret Jane Dobson (67).

1961   at Wandsworth Prison: Victor John Terry (20) for the gun-murder of a Worthing bank guard an hour after hearing on his car radio that his friend 'Flossie' Forsyth had been hanged at Wandsworth (see entry for 10 November). Terry's defence included the claim that he was possessed by the spirit of American gangster 'Legs' Diamond. He had led a life of criminal violence from the age of eight.

27 May

Hanged this day:

1727   at Tyburn Tree: Edward Bellamy for house-breaking.

1844   at Old Bailey: W. Crouch for wife-murder.

1862 at Albany, Oregon, USA: Andrew J. Pate for the gun-murder of George Lamb in a fight after Lamb had called him a 'Southern son of a bitch'.

1879 at York Castle: John Darcy for the murder of William Metcalf.

28 May

1686 HANGMAN HANGED
Pascha Rose, butcher and public hangman, hanged at Tyburn Tree for house-breaking and theft.
Hangman: Jack Ketch

Pascha Rose had assisted Jack Ketch at hangings, including some for the infamous 'Bloody Assizes' in the West Country. Jack Ketch was dismissed at the beginning of the year for insulting the Sheriff of London and was replaced by his former assistant, Pascha Rose. Rose's reign on the scaffold did not last for many months, but he did end on the scaffold. Jack Ketch was reinstated to his old job to hang his successor. Ketch had been the public hangman since 1663 and was to die by the end of 1686.

Also hanged this day:

1733 at Tyburn Tree: Henry Hart, John Davis, and John Jones hanged. *Hangman: John 'Laughing Jack' Hooper*. John Davis was unshackled because he had pretended to be ill for some days and, on the way to Tyburn, he made an escape bid but was chased and recaptured.

1828 at Old Bailey: William Wyell for highway robbery.

1879 at Kirkdale Prison, Liverpool: Thomas Johnson for the murder of Eliza Mary Patten.

1884 at Durham Gaol: Joseph Lawson for the murder of Sergeant Smith. He started towards the scaffold full of bravado, even joking and laughing. Then he changed mood and maintained a stream of obscene and blasphemous language, drowning out the words of the chaplain, until he fell through the trap. *Hangman: James Berry*

1888 at Tralee County Gaol, Ireland: Daniel Moriarty and Daniel Hayed for the murder of James Fitzmaurice at Lixnan, County Kerry.

29 May

Hanged this day:

1818   at Schoharie, New York, USA: Abraham Casler, a farmer, for the poisoning-murder of his wife at an inn.

1827   at Old Bailey: George Williams for sheep-stealing, Benjamin Sanders for highway robbery, and John Eagles for letter-stealing.

30 May

1690 END OF THE ROAD FOR 'OLD MOBB'
Thomas 'Old Mobb' Sympson hanged at Tyburn Tree for 32 indictments of highway robbery.

Sympson enjoyed a long career as a highwayman, cloaked in respectability. He robbed many famous people of the day including the infamous Judge Jeffreys, whom he relieved of 56 guineas at gun-point. Another famous victim was the Duchess of Portsmouth, mistress of King Charles II, who sharply asked him if he knew who she was. He told her 'As it is my trade to rob one whore to supply another, I must presume to take what you have' and took £200 in gold and a bag of jewellery given to her by the Merry Monarch. Sympson was finally captured in Westminster.

Also hanged this day:

1807   at Stafford: George Holden for the murder of his three children.

31 May

1928 SHOT IN THE EYES
Two violent criminals, executed at the same moment, for the murder of a policeman in such horrific circumstances that it appalled the whole country: the shockingly brutal gun-murder of PC George William Gutteridge in an Essex lane. Frederick Guy Browne (47) hanged at Pentonville Prison. William Henry Kennedy a.k.a. Patrick Michael Kennedy (36) hanged at Wandsworth Prison.
Hangmen: Robert Baxter at Pentonville and (probably) Robert Wilson at Wandsworth

Browne and Kennedy, ex-convicts, were on the Romford-Ongar road in Essex at 4 a.m. on the morning of 27 September 1927, in a Morris

Cowley car stolen from a doctor in Billericay. Police Constable Gutteridge had dismounted from his bicycle and was standing at the side of the road, waving a lamp at them to stop. Browne, at the wheel of the stolen car, ignored the signal and drove past. When they heard Gutteridge blowing on his police whistle, Kennedy told Browne to stop.

PC Gutteridge asked Browne, the driver, a series of questions and was not satisfied with the answers. He took out his notebook and was about to start writing when Browne fired two shots from an old fashioned Webley pistol. Both bullets hit Gutteridge in the left cheek, and he staggered across the road and fell down. 'Get out, quick!' said Browne, 'I'll finish the bugger.' They both jumped out of the car and went over to the fallen constable, who was still alive. 'What are you looking at me like that for?' snarled Browne at the dying policeman. He stooped down and shot a bullet into each of Gutteridge's eyes. The killers fled to London and abandoned the car in Brixton, stained with the blood of the murdered policeman. The body of PC Gutteridge was found at 6 a.m; he was still clutching his pencil in his right hand. His bicycle, helmet and notebook were lying nearby.

Browne was the first to come under suspicion, while the police were investigating stolen cars. They kept a watch on his premises at the Globe Garage in Northcote Road, Battersea, and saw him drive up at 7.50 p.m. on 20 January 1928. Knowing of his fondness for firearms and that he had vowed not to be taken alive 'next time', they waited until he had got out of the car before six policemen rushed in and arrested him. Their caution had been wise. The loaded Webley pistol was found in the car, with more bullets in Browne's pocket. Browne admitted that had they rushed him while he was in the car he would have shot the policemen and then himself, adding 'I shall have to have a machine gun for you bastards next time!'

Medical instruments which had been taken from the Morris Cowley, used in the Gutteridge killing, were found in Browne's garage. Other guns and ammunition were found at his flat. The old-fashioned Webley pistol was proved to be the murder weapon. Kennedy was arrested five days later in Liverpool in connection with the car thefts. His reaction was to point a gun and try to shoot the detective, but he had left the safety catch on and the only sound he could produce was a 'click'. (This action undermined his later claim to have been a passive partner in the murder.)

Kennedy gave a full account of the murder to the police in a vivid description of the events of the morning of 27 September. At the trial he tried to give the impression that he was terrified of Browne and had taken no active part in the murder. Browne flatly denied the charge and conducted himself throughout the trial like an overbearing bully. After being found guilty they made speeches from the dock before being sentenced to death, both admitting that they had had a fair trial.

From the condemned cell, Kennedy wrote a final emotional letter to his wife, whom he had married only eight days before his arrest, suggesting that such was his need for her that she should commit suicide and join him.

Browne was a difficult prisoner. In a rage he wrecked his cell, exhibiting fearsome strength. He tried to commit suicide by hanging himself and by cutting his throat, but was prevented each time. He even went on a hunger strike and had to be forcibly fed. When the time for execution came he was composed and went to his death calmly. In his last few hours he had written a letter to the newspapers and, literally with gallows humour, had given his return address as 'the Prison Mortuary'.

Also hanged this day:

1718   at Bunhill Fields, London: John Price, a hangman, taken from Newgate to a specially erected scaffold at the scene of his murder of an old woman. He was afterwards hung in a suit of iron on the gibbet at Holloway Fields. *Hangman: Bailiff Banks*

1876   at Barlinnie Prison, Glasgow: Thomas Barr for the murder of his wife and mother-in-law.

1878   at Carlton Prison, Edinburgh: Eugene Marie Chantrelle for wife-murder.

1881   at Kirkdale Prison, Liverpool: Joseph Patrick M'Entee for wife-murder.

1886   at Winchester Prison: Albert Edward Brown for the murder of a youth; James Whelan for murder on the high seas.

1904   at Walton Gaol, Liverpool: William Kirwan for the murder of his sister-in-law; Pong Lun for the murder of another Chinese, Go Hing. *Hangman: John Billington. Assistant: Henry Pierrepoint*

1922   at Gloucester Prison: Major Herbert Rowse Armstrong (52) hanged at 8 a.m. for poisoning his wife, Katherine. *Hangman: John Ellis. Assistant: Edward Taylor*

1962   at Ramleh Prison, near Tel Aviv, Israel: Karl Adolf Eichmann (56), Nazi war criminal responsible for the administration of the Nazi 'final solution to the Jewish problem' whereby six million European Jews were exterminated in the death camps. He was captured in Argentina on 11 May 1960 and smuggled to Israel for trial. The execution took place at 11.53 p.m.

JUNE

1 June

1571 TYBURN'S NEW TRIPLE-TREE GALLOWS
Catholic John Storey hanged, drawn, and quartered on the new triangular gallows at Tyburn.

According to a contemporary broadsheet '. . . the saide Storey was drawn upon a herdell from the Tower of London unto Tiborn, where was prepared for him a newe payre of gallowes, made in triangular manner'. The broadsheet also claimed that during the post-hanging drawing when the hangman was 'rifling among his bowels' Storey got up and hit the hangman a severe blow. Having been confined in the Tower, dragged to Tyburn on a hurdle, and suffered hanging, drawing and quartering, his crime was probably treason. Storey's place in the history of Tyburn executions is that he was the first to be hanged on the infamous Triple Tree. (See British Hanging Chronology for details.)

Also hanged this day:

1821 at Norfolk, Virginia, USA: Manuel Philip Garcia and Jose Castillano for the murder of fellow burglar Peter Lagoardette. The first time that laundry marks were used to trace killers.

1824 at Old Bailey: John Reading for robbery.

1831 at Rhode Island, USA: Narraganset Indian half-breed, Amasa Walmsley, for the clubbing-murders of John Burke and Hannah Prank after a drunken party.

1840 at Bodmin Gaol, Cornwall: James and William Lightfoot for the murder of Neville Norway. *Hangman: George Mitchell*

2 June

1903 THE *VERONICA* MUTINY-MURDERS
Gustave Rau (28) and Willem Smith (30) hanged at Walton Gaol, Liverpool, for the murders of Captain Shaw after mutiny on board the *Veronica*. Another six were murdered during the mutiny.
Hangman: William Billington

Captain Alexander Shaw of the *Veronica*, a British-owned sailing barque, set out from the Gulf of Mexico bound for Montevideo in October 1902. His crew were described as 'the dregs of the Gulf waterfront', and so it proved to be! Gustave Rau (28), Willem Smith (30), Otto Monsson (18), and Harry Flohr (19) mutinied in December and took over the ship, using guns smuggled aboard by Rau and Monsson. At different times they killed seven of the officers and crew, including Captain Shaw. The only non-conspirator spared was the cook, Moses Thomas. They set the barque on fire and got away on the ship's boat, taking Thomas with them. After they were picked up by a tramp steamer, claiming to be survivors of a shipwreck, Moses Thomas was able to report what had happened.

The mutineers were taken to Liverpool where they were charged with a string of offences including piracy and seven murders but, at their trial in May 1903, they faced a single charge of murdering Captain Shaw. Harry Flohr turned King's Evidence and supported the testimony of Moses Thomas. Rau, Smith, and Monsson were all found guilty and sentenced to death. The jury recommended mercy for Monsson because of his youth and previous good character, and he was reprieved.

Also hanged this day:

1818   at Old Bailey: George Claxton for issuing forged notes.

1845   at Old Bailey: J. Conner for the murder of Mary Brothers. The rope slipped and Conner had to be hanged again, before which he asked the hangman (possibly John Thrift), 'What do you call this, murder?'

1936   at Pentbridge Jail, Melbourne, Australia: Arnold Sodeman (36) for the murder of June Rushmer (6) at Leon Gatha, 67 miles from Melbourne, in December 1935. He also confessed to the killings of: Mena Griffiths (12) at St Kilda, Melbourne, in November 1930; Hazel Wilson (16) at Ormond, Melbourne, in January 1931; and Ethel Belshaw (12) at Inverloch, Melbourne, in January 1935. His autopsy revealed that he had suffered from leptomeningitis, an inflammation of the part of the brain called meninges. This led to genuine insanity when Sodeman took any alcohol.

3 June

1691 As clever Tom Clinch, while the rabble was bawling,
   Rode stately through Holborn to die at his calling,
   He stopt at the 'George' for a bottle of sack,
   And promised to pay for it when he came back.
   Jonathan Swift (1667–1745)*

Tom Cox (26) hanged at Tyburn Tree for highway robbery.

Tom Cox was the youngest son of a landed family from Blandford, Dorset. Traditionally, younger sons of the gentry did not get much of

188

the family fortune when they reached maturity, and this was the case with Tom Cox. He moved to London and became a highwayman, but had only a short career before being caught and condemned.

He was a handsome young man, with money, and had lived a flamboyant life style that continued even after being sentenced. His last days in Newgate were spent riotously, with good food and wine brought in to entertain his visitors. He scorned the beseeching of the prison chaplains to repent and maintained his boisterous bravado throughout his last journey, on the road to Tyburn Tree. Nor did his nerve give on arrival at the gallows. When the chaplain asked if he would join in final prayers with the other condemned prisoner he kicked the cleric off the cart, and when the hangman tried to intervene, kicked him off too!

It is almost certain that Jonathan Swift's satirical poem, 'Clever Tom Clinch', written in 1727, was based on Tom Cox.

Also hanged this day:

1852 at New York, USA: Maurice Antonio for the clubbing-murder of Ignacio Pinto after fighting over their mutual mistress.

4 June

Hanged this day:

1813 at Albany, New York, USA: Private Thomas Burns for the drunken and random shooting of a civilian, John E. Conkling.

1857 at Maidstone: Jesse George Bave (27), a sailor, for the bayonet-murder of Samuel Long, ship's corporal, on board the hulk *Hebe* at Woolwich. *Hangman: William Calcraft*

1895 at Liverpool: William Miller for the murder of Edward Moyce.

5 June

1922 'HE WAS NOBBUT A CHILD'
Henry Julius Jacoby (18) hanged at Pentonville Prison for the Spencer Hotel murder of Lady White (65) in London's West End.
Hangman: John Ellis

Henry Jacoby was a slightly built, fair-haired lad of 18 with a pleasant smile. He had been working as a pantry boy at the Spencer Hotel in

Portman Street near Marble Arch in London's West End for only three weeks when, during the early hours of 14 March 1922, he told the porter that he had woken and heard whispering and thought that intruders had broken in. They made a search and, finding nothing suspicious, Jacoby returned to his bed in the basement.

At about 2 a.m. he was still awake and decided to steal from one of the rich guests. He took a torch from a workman's toolbag, and a hammer – 'to use if necessary' as he later told the police. The first unlocked door he found was that of Lady (Alice) White, the widow of the former chairman of London County Council Sir Edward White. Shining the torch around the room he saw Lady White in one of the single beds; she woke up and began to scream. Jacoby hit her several times on the head with the hammer and then fled back to the basement in panic. He washed the blood off the hammer and wiped it dry with two of his handkerchiefs, then returned it and the torch to the toolbag.

Lady White's body was discovered in the morning and the police immediately realised that it was an 'inside job' and all of the staff were questioned. Jacoby told a stream of lies, adding his own misleading theories, before eventually admitting the crime. His blood-stained handkerchiefs were found in his room. At his Old Bailey trial he retold the story of the whispering intruders and tried to explain his attack on Lady White as mistaking her for an intruder: no one believed this. The judge explained the law that, if Jacoby had hit Lady White intending grievous bodily harm which resulted in death, then it was murder and not manslaughter. He was found guilty and sentenced to death, the jury adding a strong recommendation for mercy because of his youth.

There was a great public outcry for a reprieve. At this time another murderer, the ex-Royal Flying Corps officer Ronald True*, was being examined for insanity after being convicted for murdering a prostitute. Furious allegations of class prejudice in favour of the moneyed True, who had killed an 'unimportant whore', and against the working-class Jacoby who had killed a titled lady, were added to the campaign without success.

The official view was that Henry Jacoby had committed a brutal killing of a defenceless old lady during a robbery and was undeserving of mercy. The view of H. R. Oswald, the London County Coroner, was that Jacoby enjoyed all the attention he was getting as he listened to the witnesses and smiled to the spectators in the crowded courtrooms. He was always asking the warders what the newspapers were saying about him. Oswald concluded, 'I am convinced from my own contact with this young ruffian that he would have developed into a dangerous criminal, with a tendency towards robbery and violence.'

Others in official positions, who had contact with Jacoby in Pentonville, were moved to sympathy. Hangman Ellis saw Jacoby playing cricket with other prisoners the day before the execution and he later recalled, in an article in *Empire News*, 'I saw t'poor lad the day before

190

his death. He was nobbut a child. It was t'most harrowing sight I ever saw in my life. And I 'ad t'kill him next day.' Jacoby told one of the warders in the condemned cell 'I've told all my friends to buy up all the ropes there are, so that Ellis will have to use a rubber one tomorrow. So I shall bounce back and have a look at him again!'

The Governor of Pentonville Prison, Major Frederick Wallace Blake, described Jacoby as 'a thorough little gentleman' during his time in prison. While being led to the gallows, Jacoby said to Major Blake 'I want to thank you, sir, and everybody here, for all your kindness to me.'

* True was reprieved three days after Jacoby was hanged, and the public fury continued. True and Jacoby had met in prison while awaiting their trials: True had boisterously slapped Jacoby on the back and shouted 'Here's another for our murderers club, only those who killed outright accepted!' True was committed to Broadmoor and was kept there until his death from a heart attack in 1951.

Also hanged this day:

1797   at Old Bailey: James Mackley and Martin Clench, who may both have been innocent, for the murder of Sydney Fryer, Esq. The execution was bungled and the hangmen and two clergymen fell through the trap with the prisoners. *Hangman: William Brunskill. Assistant: James Langley*

6 June

1935 JUSTICE DELAYED
Mrs Mary (May) Carey, and her son Howard Carey (27), hanged in the yard of Georgetown Jail, Delaware, USA. The murder was committed for gain and out of resentment of her brother's action seven-and-a-half years earlier.

Robert Hitchens lived on his own in a wooden two-storey house across the road from his sister, May Carey, and her sons, at Omar in Delaware. Outwardly, May Carey gave the appearance of being loving and caring towards her brother but, within the family, she harboured a festering grudge. She resented Robert claiming everything for himself as the eldest child when their mother had died. She knew he had a $2,000 life-insurance policy, too.

For four weeks she plotted with her sons to kill her brother. She would talk it over with Howie and James (then 20 and 17) when her youngest son, Lawrence (then 14), had gone to bed. She promised to buy Howie a car if he did the killing. It was all planned for a Saturday night, 5 November 1927, when they knew Rob returned home late. They let themselves in to Rob's house, using their key, and waited in the dark. Rob came home and let himself in and, as he was holding a match and about to light the lamp in the living room, he heard a sound and turned around. At that moment Howie hit his uncle on the head with a heavy club, but Rob's last-minute movement spoiled his aim. Rob Hitchens staggered to the door, but May Carey got there first and battered him about the head with a 3lb hammer: he sank to the floor under the rain of blows.

Blood was splashed everywhere, even on the ceiling. May took the pistol which James had been holding and gave it to Howie, ordering him to finish off his uncle to 'spare him any further suffering'. Howie protested at first but, after she threatened to get James to do it, he fired one shot into his uncle's brain. They let themselves out and locked the door. They had to get rid of their blood-drenched clothes and wash themselves clean. The club, hammer, and pistol, were washed down and buried. Rob Hitchens' body was discovered a few days later when a friend called at the house and couldn't get an answer.

The police got to work, assisted by most of the outraged neighbours, but no one suspected the grieving relatives across the road. Robert Hitchens' estate was settled and there was not much left to divide between the beneficiaries, May and two nieces. After debts and expenses had been paid, each received about $200.

The police investigation failed to solve the mystery of the 'man with no enemies', despite intense inquiries by the local force. Rewards were offered by newspapers and local citizens. The famous Pinkerton Detective Agency sent one of their best men who carried out a vigorous investigation, but he too got nowhere. As the months, and then the years, went by the local detectives kept the case in mind and followed up on any leads that might help them to solve this baffling blot on Omar's reputation.

Seven years and a month passed. On 5 December 1934 Lawrence Carey, by then aged 21, was suspected of an attempted armed robbery a few miles from Omar. (He was later sentenced to seven years' imprisonment.) The detectives who questioned him were the same ones who had investigated the murder of his uncle, and they remembered. After asking a few carefully worded questions they were astonished how easily the truth began to emerge. Young Lawrence had not gone to sleep when he had been packed off to bed seven years before, he had listened to what was being said downstairs – and he remembered it all. The rest of the murdering family were arrested and questioned.

James was first, and he soon broke down and confessed. Howard was presented with his brother's evidence and before long was in tears and confessing his part although, in a muddled way of thinking, he was of the opinion that since it had all happened so many years before, and because he was now married with three children, he should no longer be held responsible.

May Carey was questioned last and she held out longest, until the exhumed murder weapons – the club, hammer, and pistol – were brought in and laid on the table. Then she confessed and said that she was the one to blame and not the boys, who would not have done it had she not ordered them to.

The trial was held in Georgetown in April 1935. James was found guilty of second degree murder and given an automatic life sentence. May and Howard were guilty of first degree murder. Mrs Carey had to be held upright to be sentenced to death and, upon hearing the dread words from the judge, began to scream hysterically before falling down in a faint. Howard sobbed and was soon screaming like his mother. When he heard his own death sentence he collapsed.

The night before the double execution was an awful experience for everyone in Georgetown Jail. May Carey's screaming fit went on and on. As well as horrifying everyone within the prison, it was heard up to three blocks away on the outside. She was the first to be hanged in the morning. She was by now a frail and old-looking woman whose weight had shrivelled away to a skeleton-like six stones. Numb and by then silent, she was taken out to the specially erected scaffold in the yard. It was not until six or seven minutes after the drop that she was pronounced dead. Howard followed, as silent and trance-like as his mother had been a few minutes earlier. Justice may have been delayed, but it had eventually been done.

Also hanged this day:

1816   at New London, Connecticut, USA: racist Miner Babcock for the murder of a free negro named London.

1818   near Chester, Pennsylvania, USA: John H. Craig (31) for the murder of Edward Hunter. He was given permission to walk to the scaffold, about a mile from Chester, and perhaps originated the phrase about 'walking the last mile' to the gallows.

1928   at Pentonville Prison: Frederick Stewart for the gun-murder of Mr Webb while robbing his flat. *Hangman: Tom Pierrepoint*

1944   at Wandsworth Prison: Private Ernest James Harman Kemp (21), Royal Artillery, for rape-murder of a WAAF, Leading Aircraftwoman Iris Miriam Deeley (21), on allotments at Eltham in south-east London on 14 February, St Valentine's Day, strangling her with her own scarf.

7 June

1798 THE 'SECRET' PUBLIC HANGING
John James O'Coigley hanged and beheaded at Penenden Heath, Maidstone, Kent, for high treason.

The French Revolution had reached its peak with the fall of Robespierre and the Jacobins in 1794, but the revolutionary ferment carried on as late as 1799. The disruption and slaughter that accompanied the French Revolution had alarmed the ruling classes of other European countries, not least the British.

O'Coigley had been on his way to France, but was captured at the King's Head in Margate in February 1798. In a pocketbook found in his great coat was a letter from 'The Secret Committee of England, to the Executive Directory of France'.

It alleged that England was ready for revolution, with disaffection among the people, the army, and the fleet, and exhorted the French army to invade where 'Myriads will hail their arrival, and they will soon finish the campaign.' He was tried for high treason and sentenced to be hanged, drawn, and quartered: King George III respited this to hanging and beheading.

O'Coigley was told at 5 p.m. on Wednesday 6 June that he would die the following day. The authorities, fearing riot, kept secret from the public the date and time of execution: 'Very few knew of it in London, very few in Rochester and Canterbury, and even in Maidstone on Wednesday night. . .'

On the morning of the execution, at Penenden Heath:

'. . . at half past ten there were only three people on the ground. The place is an eminence that overlooks a common: a gibbet stands always fixed upon the spot. About eleven o'clock a deal coffin, not painted, together with the platform &c were brought upon a cart to the ground . . . the platform was put up . . . it is what is called a drop . . . it was tried by the men.' (The *Morning Post*, Friday 8 June.)

The cavalcade, including a few hundred soldiers, left Maidstone Prison at 11.15 a.m. and moved slowly to Penenden Heath, about a mile away, arriving at 12.15 p.m. There were, by then, about a thousand spectators including the military. The condemned man spent some time in prayer and delivered a long speech in which he denied ever carrying a letter to France or ever belonging to a political society. He accused the witnesses at his trial of perjury. He was hanged at 12.45 p.m. and there were no struggles for the first two minutes, then he began to convulse and the hangman pulled on his legs to speed the death:

'After the body had hung about twelve minutes, it was lowered, the executioner holding it in his arms, till it was laid gently on the platform. A young man, a surgeon, put on a yellow linen dress, and prepared to cut off the head, the other part of the sentence being remitted. The coat, waistcoat, and shoes, were taken off, and the cap was taken from his face, which lately so comely (for he was a very handsome man, with a good complexion) was now the colour of lead. He appeared to be quite dead. The surgeon felt if there was any pulse, and took out a large knife, like a bill hook: the head was laid so as to hang over the edge of the platform, and the surgeon began to cut it off; he had considerable difficulty in cutting through the windpipe. When the head was severed from the body, the executioner held it up to the spectators, and turning round to shew it to them all, said three times, "This is the head of a Traitor". At this time the blood was streaming from the head, which now began to change from blue to white. The head was laid down on the scaffold, and it, together with the body, were allowed to bleed about ten minutes, when the body was stripped quite naked, put into the coffin together with the head; the coffin was nailed up, and the whole was buried in a grave under the gallows (at 1.15 p.m.), it being against the law on this occasion, to allow the friends to take the body away.' (The *Morning Post*, Friday 8 June.)

Also hanged this day:

1753 at Tyburn Tree: Jacobite rebel Dr Archibald Cameron hanged, drawn, and quartered. *Hangman: Thomas Turlis*

1826 at Old Bailey: James Johnson for robbery.

1897 at Barlinnie Prison, Glasgow: George Paterson for the murder of a woman.

8 June

1951 THE DEATH CAMPS 'BUSINESSMAN'
General Oswald Pohl hanged at Landsberg Prison, Germany, for war crimes.

Pohl, a naval officer before joining the SS, was the chief of the Economic Office of the SS and was personally in charge of the working-to-death programme for the inmates of the concentration camps. This programme was a part of the evil final solution to the Jewish question (meaning extermination) and Pohl was the first captured war criminal to reveal the full meaning of the phrase during questioning by Allied officers. He was also in charge of the project for robbing the dead bodies of concentration camp victims of their gold teeth and other valuables.

Also hanged this day:

1810   at Cincinnati, Ohio, USA: William Clutter for the axe-murder of his employer, John Farmer, on board his boat.

1866   at Philadelphia, USA: Anton Probst for the murder of the Dearing family.

9 June

1896 NEWGATE'S LAST TRIPLE EXECUTION
Henry Fowler (31), Albert Milsom (33), and William Seaman hanged at Newgate Prison, all murderers.
Hangman: James Billington. Assistant: William Warbrick

Fowler and Milsom broke into a decayed mansion, Muswell Lodge, in the Muswell Hill district of north London during the early hours of 14 February 1896. The noise of the break-in roused retired engineer Henry Smith (80), who came down to the kitchen dressed only in his nightshirt. Fowler and Milsom beat the old man about the head, at least 12 blows being struck, and then cut up a tablecloth with their pocket-knives and bound him without realising that he was already dead from the head-blows.

They emptied Smith's safe of a believed sum of £700, although Fowler told Milsom it was £112. Carelessly, the pair left behind the two knives used to cut the tablecloth and, even more damning, a damaged toy lantern. They buried the rest of the house-breaking tools in the grounds and hid in the woods until daylight. They got away and (making another mistake) disappeared from their normal haunts.

When Fowler, a 'ticket-of-leave man' who had been released from prison the month before, failed to report to the police he was at once suspected of the nearby Muswell Hill robbery-murder. There was no direct evidence against him at the time, but the crime fitted his modus operandi and Smith's neighbours described two rough looking strangers seen in the street two days earlier – descriptions which could have fitted Fowler and his known associate, Milsom.

It was the toy lantern that positively linked them to the killing. The police induced a child to play with it so that it would be seen by Milsom's brother-in-law, Henry Miller (15). 'That's mine' exclaimed

196

Miller. When asked if he could prove it by a passer-by (actually a plain-clothes policeman) the earnest young man pointed out the cracked green glass, some dents and marks, and the home-made wick that he had cut from a piece of tartan cloth. This conclusively linked Milsom to the crime, and Milsom was the link to Fowler.

Fowler and Milsom were tracked through Liverpool, Manchester, Cardiff, London, Swindon, and finally Bath where they were arrested late at night on 12 April. Fowler was so violent in resisting arrest that he had to be knocked down with a series of blows to the head from a policeman's revolver.

The case against them at their trial was complete. There was the lantern, the identification of the pair by Smith's neighbours, a £10 note taken from Smith's safe which was traced to Fowler by its serial number – and the testimony of Milsom. He tried to blame the killing on Fowler after he (Milsom) had left the house. Fowler, in turn, claimed that Milsom had killed the old man by standing on his neck until he died. The judge, Mr Justice Hawkins, deduced that because they had both used their pocket-knives to cut the tablecloth to bind the old man after he was in fact dead, it followed that they were both present when he was killed.

The murderous partners were left waiting in the dock while the jury considered their verdict. Fowler suddenly sprang at Milsom, grabbing him by the throat and wrestling him to the floor. The fight lasted for a violent 12 minutes as warders and constables joined in to try to restore order. The dock was rocked from side to side and its glass partition was smashed. It did not delay the verdict or the inevitable sentencing of them both to death by Mr Justice Hawkins.

William Seaman was another burglar-murderer. Earlier in the year he had broken into the Whitechapel home of an underworld 'fence', John Goodman Levy (77) who was reputed to have a hoard of cash, and battered and stabbed the old man to death. He also killed Levy's housekeeper, Mrs Sarah Gale (35). He had been seen breaking into the house and was still in the loft when the constables arrived and found the bodies. He escaped through a hole in the roof and was confronted with the sight of a large crowd gathered below. Yelling curses, he jumped off the roof and fell on to some of the onlookers 40 feet below, breaking both thighs as he landed.

It was feared that the mutual hatred between Fowler and Milsom might result in a violent scene on the scaffold*. To prevent an untoward mishap, four warders were positioned on stout planks across the trap doors. As a further precaution, Seaman was made to occupy the central spot so as to keep Fowler and Milsom separated. 'It is the first time I've ever been a bloody peacemaker!' growled Seaman.

Nonetheless, there was a mishap, caused by the extra precautions. When Billington was ready he glanced over his shoulder, but failed to see that his assistant, kneeling behind the screen of warders, was still fixing the strap around the legs of one of the trio. Billington operated the lever and Warbrick heard the bolts moving below the traps. He fell headfirst into the opening void, but managed to grab the legs of the man he had been pinioning, and was unhurt.

A number of books incorrectly refer to this occasion as being Britain's last triple hanging: the following month the same hangmen carried out another triple at Winchester (see 21 July).

Also hanged this day:

1883 at Alexandria, Egypt: Suleiman Daoud Sami sentenced to death by court martial two days earlier for treason. He was hanged at 5 a.m. in an open space on the exact spot where he had ordered the firing and destruction of the city the previous year. In an abject state of collapse, he had to be supported by his guards and placed in a chair on a table below the gallows. He died with a placard on his chest bearing the Arabic inscription 'This is the punishment of the guilty'. His body was left hanging for some hours amid the ruins he had created. During the country-wide anarchy that year the British took control of the governing of Egypt to bring stability and safeguard passage through the Suez Canal. The British presence remained until 1956.

10 June

1896 THE EVIL 'BABY FARMER'
Mrs Amelia Elizabeth Dyer (57) hanged at Newgate Prison for the 'baby-farming' murder of Doris Marmon (aged 4 months) – but there were others.
Hangman: James Billington

On the afternoon of the same day that Henry Fowler and Albert Milsom had been sentenced to death (see above), Mrs Dyer went on trial for murder at the Old Bailey before the same judge, Mr Justice Hawkins. Mrs Dyer had been a baby farmer (see 3 February) for 20 years. Her downfall began with the discovery of the dead body of baby Helena Fry, in the River Thames at Reading. The child had been strangled with a length of white tape* and was wrapped in a weighted brown-paper parcel. The brown paper had a name and address on it: the name was proved to be one of Dyer's recent aliases and the address was one from which she had recently moved.

The police had that area of the Thames dragged and a total of seven babies were found, three of whom were never identified. A weighted carpet bag was pulled from the river with two babies in it, both

198

strangled with white tape, and they were identified as Doris Marmon (4 months) and Harry Simmons (12 months). They were traced to Mrs Dyer who had received £10 to 'adopt' each one.

She was charged only with the murder of Doris Marmon, even though there was plenty of evidence that the other identified babies had been given into her care. Identical white tape to that used in the stranglings was found at her house. She refused to reveal how many babies she had killed although she did later say 'You'll know all mine by the tape round their necks.' The only defence offered at the trial was insanity, and that was rejected. The jury found her guilty after only five minutes.

* *The tape that Mrs Dyer used to strangle Helena Fry is now an exhibit at Scotland Yard's Black Museum, as is the rope with which Billington hanged Dyer at Newgate.*

Also hanged this day:

1692 at Gallows Hill, Salem, Massachusetts, USA: Bridget Bishop, the first of the supposed Salem witches to be hanged (see 19 August).

1890 at Wandsworth Prison: Daniel Steward Corrie for the murder of J. Furionger.

11 June

1954 THE 'UNCOMMON' ACCIDENT
G. Edward Grammer hanged at Maryland Penitentiary, USA, for the bludgeoning-murder of his wife.

It was a common enough wife-murder with a common enough motive: another woman. Grammer hit his wife on the head and killed her, placed her in the car, rammed a rock on to the accelerator pedal and got out, allowing the car to travel on at full speed and crash. He had hoped that the further injuries to his wife would mask the real death blow, and everything would look like a common-place road accident.

When the police arrived at the crash they immediately realised that there was something decidedly uncommon about this one: lady motorists, or gentlemen motorists for that matter, do not usually drive along the road with a heavy stone holding down the accelerator pedal. Investigators, their suspicions aroused, checked everything closely. They called Grammer in for questioning and he was no match for them: he admitted second degree murder.

He later made a deadly mistake: he retracted his confession and pleaded not guilty. Instead of resulting in a formal conviction for second degree murder and a prison term, his trial had all the prosecution evidence paraded and this included clear proof of premeditated murder. He was found guilty and sentenced to death by hanging.

Also hanged this day:

1780 at Tower Hill, London: William McDonald, Charlotte Gardiner, and Mary Roberts. At Bishopsgate: William Brown. At Coleman Street: William Pateman. These five were all hanged for their parts in the Gordon Riots of 4 to 9 June, and especially the burning of Newgate Prison and the freeing of the prisoners on 6 June. Five hundred were estimated to have been killed in the riots and great damage was done to property. In consequence, 59 were sentenced to death and executions were carried out at various street sites to strike terror into the mob and restore order.

1878 at Pottsville, Pennsylvania, USA: Dennis 'Buckey' Donnelly for the 'Molly Maguire' murder of Thomas Sanger (see 21 June). *Hangman: Sheriff William Matz*

12 June

1931 ACQUITTED TO KILL AGAIN
Stephanus Louis Van Wyk hanged in Pretoria, South Africa, for the murder of farmer Cyril Tucker.

Van Wyk was a hardened professional criminal, usually working as a fraudster. It was for fraud that he was sentenced to 18-months' hard labour in 1929 and he told fellow convicts that he would have his revenge on his nephew, John Moller (28), whom he thought had informed on him. Within days of Van Wyk's release from prison his nephew had been killed.

Van Wyk had been seen near to where Moller's body was found in a pit (the case became known as the 'Jackal Pit Murder'), and a pick and shovel were found nearby, as was a pair of discarded socks with a sewn-on label marked 'S van W'. Van Wyk was arrested, charged with the murder, and went on trial in October 1930 at Bloemfontein. He claimed that, while he and Moller were digging for a stashed £3,000, he accidentally hit his nephew with the pick. He claimed that Moller had fallen into the pit and died from hitting his head in the fall. Van Wyk said that he then panicked and buried the body in the pit. He was acquitted.

Three months later he negotiated the purchase of a farm from Cyril Tucker but, instead of paying, hammered Tucker to death as the farmer lay in bed and buried the body in a field. While being questioned by the police on another matter, questions were inevitably asked about the missing Tucker. Van Wyk's story was that Tucker had attacked him with a gun during an argument and he had hit the man in self-defence. Once more he trotted out the story that he had panicked and decided to bury the body. The same excuse didn't work twice and this time he was convicted of murder and condemned to death. Before being hanged he admitted that both killings had been murders.

Also hanged this day:

1780   at Bow Street, London: Thomas Taplin and Richard Roberts; at Holborn: James Henry. All three were executed for their parts in the burning of Newgate Prison on 6 June.

1801   at Chesterfield, New Jersey, USA: slave Cyrus Emlay (35) for the axe-murder of his master Humphrey Wall whose house he then burned down. It was reported that the slave 'was most agreeable to his execution'.

1906   at Boston, Massachusetts, USA: Charles Louis Tucker (26) for the knife-murder of Mabel Page (41) at her home.

13 June

1930 DEATHWISH?
Albert Edward Marjeram (23) hanged at Wandsworth Prison for the stabbing-murder of Edith May Parker.

Albert Marjeram had a morbid fascination for knives. Since childhood he would stare fixedly at a knife, or at a number of them lined up in a row on the table. At other times he would stand and, wordlessly, slowly draw them across his throat. At least, all of this was claimed by his mother, as a defence witness at his trial for murder in support of a plea of insanity.

He bought a butcher's knife for two shillings (10p) and, on 11 April 1930, went for a walk on Dartford Heath, Kent. He saw two sisters, Edith May and Eva Parker, walking ahead of him. Without a word, he stabbed Edith in the back. The police had captured him within a few hours and he confessed and made a statement, a part of which read 'I was on the heath when the two girls came along. I never spoke to them. I just up and done it with a knife.' And, later in the statement, 'I forgot to add the motive. It was robbery, as I was out of work and wanted money.'

It was almost as though he wished to be hanged. At his trial the doctors called by the prosecution had no doubt that he was sane and the insanity plea failed. He was sentenced and hanged, whether or not that had been his wish.

Also hanged this day:

1748 at Tyburn Tree: George Cock for stealing.

1932 at Fremantle Prison, Western Australia: John Thomas Smith a.k.a. Stanley 'Snowy' Rowles for the murder of Louis Carron (27) in the bush. The case was known as the 'Murchison Mystery' and it is almost certain that Smith murdered two other bushmen.

14 June

1856 THE RUGELEY POISONER
Dr William Palmer (32) publicly hanged outside Stafford Gaol for the murder of John Parsons Cook. He probably poisoned 13 others as well.
Hangman: George Smith

William Palmer came from a wealthy family of drunkards and moral degenerates. He inherited about £9,000, but the money did not last long, being squandered on gambling and drunken living. Palmer accumulated debts and got into deeper trouble trying to raise the necessary funds by further unsuccessful gambling.

He turned to poisoning his creditors to remove them from his list of problems. The first was a man named Bladon who was invited to stay at Palmer's house, where he was promptly taken ill and died. Mrs Bly, the widow of another creditor that he had poisoned, approached Palmer with the news that Bly had told her before he died that the doctor owed him £800. Palmer replied that, on the contrary, Bly had owed *him* the £800 and he would be obliged if Mrs Bly would settle the debt.

He next turned to poisoning his kin. Four of his legitimate children died of convulsions in infancy and more of his numerous bastard offspring went the same way. He poisoned members of his family, either for inheritances or for insurance benefits totalling tens of thousands of pounds. It was not enough and his debts continued to spiral.

His final murder, probably the 14th, was of a fellow gambler and drunkard named John Parsons Cook at the Talbot Arms, opposite Palmer's house in Rugeley. The motive this time was to enable Palmer to go to London, while Cook lay stricken in bed, and collect Cook's winnings from bets on his horse Polestar, which had won a race at Shrewsbury. Palmer immediately used the money to pay off some of his own debts. He had a shock when he returned to Rugeley and found that Cook was up and dressed and on the way to recovery. Substituting some pills left by another doctor, he dosed the unsuspecting Cook with prussic acid and strychnine and he died within minutes.

Cook's stepfather was suspicious and demanded an investigation. Palmer was arrested and the bodies of his wife and a brother were exhumed. He was charged only with the murder of Cook, found guilty at the Old Bailey (a special law had been passed allowing him to be tried away from Staffordshire where public feeling was strongly against him) and sentenced to death.

He was returned to Stafford Gaol for the execution. His trial and the sensation of his mass poisoning in the quiet country town of Rugeley had excited the nation. It is thought that as many as twenty thousand people gathered for the spectacle of his hanging.

Rugeley has never lived down the notoriety of being 'Palmer's Town'. An attempt to change its name was made by leading townsmen in an appeal to the Prime Minister of the day. The PM was agreeable. 'Why not name it after me?' asked Lord Palmerston: that was the end of that!

Also hanged this day:

1716   at Tyburn Tree: Colonel Henry Oxburgh, hanged, drawn and quartered for high treason.

1816   at Old Bailey: Philip Street for burglary.

1892   at Armley Gaol, Leeds: Harry Pickering for wife-murder.

15 June

Hanged this day:

1710   at Tyburn Tree: Daniel Demaree for treason.

1886   at Gloucester Prison: Edward Hewitt for wife-murder.

16 June

1702   at Tyburn Tree: Mary Adams, a Drury Lane whore with many rich customers, for cashing cheques stolen from one of them.

1747   at Tyburn Tree: the popular 'Gentleman Harry' Simms for highway robbery. *Hangman: John Thrift*

1754   at Edinburgh: Nichol Brown for wife-murder.

17 June

1924 THE TREACHEROUS BRIDE
Ralph Waller hanged at Walla Walla, Washington, USA, for double murder.

Ralph Waller, after a two-year love affair with his wife's sister Ida that destroyed his own marriage, received a love letter from her that closed with:

'. . . love and kisses from your sweetie. Ida.'

The letter arrived on 19 February 1924, which was the same day, he later found out, that Ida had married a farmer named Alfred Waldeman.

When he learned of her treachery, and burning with jealousy, he travelled from Butte, Montana, to the Waldeman Ranch at Pomeroy in Washington State; a distance of 250 miles by train across the Bitterroot Mountains. After buying a gun and some bullets in a local hardware store for $7, he walked to the ranch and arrived as it was getting dark on 3 April. There he shot and killed his sister-in-law and her new husband, while they were still on their honeymoon.

Mrs Barbara Waldeman (69), Alfred's mother, was also in the house and was the third victim. Although shot six times and left for dead, she was able to identify the killer at his trial. Waller confessed and revealed the pitiful tale of Ida's double-crossing, first of her own sister and then of him. He made no appeal against his death sentence.

Mrs Waldeman died of her wounds one day short of a year later and so became his third murder-victim*, but by then Waller was long dead.

* *Most countries legally define murder as being when death occurs within a year and a day of the injury being inflicted.*

Also hanged this day:

1751 at Tyburn Tree: Thomas Quin, Joseph Dowdell, and Thomas Talbot for murder and robbery.

1825 at Buffalo, New York, USA: brothers Isaac, Israel, and Nelson Thayer for the murder of moneylender John Love to whom they had rented a room at their farmhouse. After shooting Love for his money they cut up his body and fed it to their pigs.

1937 at Johannesburg, South Africa: so-called 'Torch Murderer' Andries Stephanus Du Plessis (21) for five murders.

18 June

Hanged this day:

1712 at Tyburn Tree: Elizabeth Mason for murder.

1895 at Wandsworth Prison: Joseph Canning (52) for the murder of Jane Youell.

1924 at Armley Gaol, Leeds: William Horsely Wardell, a swindler who preyed on lonely women, for the murder of Mrs Elizabeth Reaney (60). *Hangman: Tom Pierrepoint. Assistant: William Willis*

19 June

1962 SUICIDE BY PROXY – OR MURDER?
Marthinius Roussouw (23) hanged at Cape Town, South Africa, for the gun-murder of his employer, Baron Von Schauroth (36).

The Baron Dietrich Joachim Gunther Von Schauroth was a farmer whose habit it was to carry large amounts of money on him, probably for illicit diamond dealing. His title came from his late father who had settled in South Africa after World War Two.

During 1960 Von Schauroth had taken out additional life insurance policies so that he was insured for over £200,000. In March 1961 his body was found at a roadside near Vissershoek in Cape Province; he had been shot twice in the back of the head. His bodyguard, Marthinius Roussouw, was quickly arrested as he had been seen with the Baron on the night of the murder and it seemed like a straight-forward case of killing to rob the victim of the money he had been carrying.

This all altered when Roussouw changed his story: he claimed that he was only carrying out his employer's own orders to shoot him. He said that the Baron was troubled by debts, was unhappy with his wife, and had told him that he was 'tired of life'. Von Schauroth could not commit suicide because it would invalidate the insurance policies, and he wanted his wife to inherit the £200,000. So he wanted Roussouw to shoot him, as a kind of suicide by proxy!

There was no corroboration to Roussouw's fantastic story. The Baron and his 20-year-old wife appeared to be happy and often went out together: nor had he appeared to be depressed on the day of his death. The murder was more likely to have been for the robbery of the large amount of cash and illicit diamonds that the Baron was carrying on him. An uncut diamond had been dropped and was found near the body.

Whatever the circumstances, it was clearly murder and the jury at the trial in September 1961 took only an hour to return their guilty verdict. When asked if they had found any extenuating circumstances the foreman replied that they had found none. Roussouw's execution was delayed for nine months by his lawyers's post-trial attempts to save his life. He walked calmly to the scaffold singing 'Nearer my God to Thee'. The insurance companies contested paying out the £200,000, because of the alleged 'suicide by proxy'. It was not until a year after Roussouw's execution that the Baron's widow received an ex gratia award of £10,000.

Also hanged this day:

1738 at Tyburn Tree: John Johnson (76) for robbery, after 50 years as an 'expert and successful robber'.

1850 at New Haven, Connecticut, USA: Henry L. Foote for the rape and throat-cutting murder of Emily H. Cooper.

20 June

1679 RELIGIOUS PERSECUTION
Jesuit priests Thomas Whitbread, William Harcourt, John Fenwick, John Gavan, Antony Turner, and a number of unnamed Roman Catholics, hanged, drawn and quartered at Tyburn Tree, for treason.
Hangman: Jack Ketch

These were all victims of religious persecution in the wake of the 'Popish Plot' scare (see 21 February).

206

Also hanged this day:

1780 at Old Bailey: John Glover, James Jackson and Benjamin Bowsey; at Whitechapel: Samuel Solomons; at Bethnal Green: John Gamble. All hanged for their parts in the burning of Newgate Prison on 6 June.

21 June

1877 THE 'MOLLY MAGUIRES'
The first hangings of 'Molly Maguire' murderers in Pennsylvania, USA. Hugh McGehen, James Boyle, James Carroll, Thomas Munley, Thomas Duffy and James Roarity hanged at Pottsville; John 'Yellow Jack' Donaghue, Alex Campbell, Edward Kelly (19) and Michael J. Doyle hanged at Mauch Chunk.
Hangmen: Sheriff Werner at Pottsville and Sheriff Raudenbush at Mauch Chunk

The Molly Maguires were a secret Irish-American terrorist group which sought to control the workers and the profits in the Pennsylvania coalfields by a campaign of murder, violence and extortion upon both workers and managers of the mines.

Most of the working population in the coalfields were of English, German, or Welsh extraction; those of Irish descent were very much a minority group. The members of the Molly Maguires were a small minority within the Irish community. But they held such power through terror and political corruption that, for a few violent years, there was no effective law enforcement in parts of Pennsylvania.

They began by posing as campaigners seeking to improve the awful working conditions of the miners. They infiltrated, and eventually controlled and perverted, a number of lodges of the Ancient Order of Hibernians and used its structure for their power base. Even if they had started with good intentions, which is doubtful, they soon gave way to corruption and extreme violence and became a greater evil than that which they were supposed to cure.

Arson, dynamiting, beatings, and murder were committed against any mine or 'boss' who offended a 'Molly' for any real or imagined act. Sacking a Molly miner who was drunk was enough. The violence was often committed publicly, but very few people were willing to act as witnesses for fear of becoming victims themselves. It was a classic reign of terror.

The group was exposed and brought to justice almost single-handedly by a remarkably courageous Pinkerton Detective, James McParlan (33), who spent five years working under cover in their midst. His evidence identified many of the killers of coalfield foremen, supervisors and managers. The conspiracy of silence that had thwarted the authorities' efforts to restore law and order was broken, and arrests were made followed by trials and convictions. The first hangings were held on 21 June, starting at 10 a.m. at Pottsville and a little later 40 miles away at Mauch Chunk.

In May 1877 the Ancient Order of Hibernians had revoked the charters of those lodges under the control of the Mollies. With their leaders and the most violent of their enforcers under arrest, the 'secret society within a secret society' was wiped out. Another ten Mollies were hanged later:

18 January 1878 'King of the Mollies', Jack Kehoe, at Bloomsburg.
25 March 1878 Pat Hester, Pat Tully, and Pete McHugh at Bloomsburg.
28 March 1878 Tom Fisher at Mauch Chunk.
11 June 1878 Dennis 'Buckey' Donnelly at Pottsville.
15 January 1879 James McDonnell and Charles Sharpe at Mauch Chunk.
16 January 1879 Martin Bergen at Pottsville.
9 October 1879 Peter McManus, the twentieth and last, at Sunbury.

Also hanged this day:

1780   at Old Street, London: Thomas Price, James Burns and Benjamin Waters; at Coleman Street: George Staples; at White's Alley: Jonathan Stacy. All hanged for their parts in the burning of Newgate Prison on 6 June.

1832   at Philadelphia, Pennsylvania, USA: Lino Amalia Espos y Mina for the arsenic-murder of Dr William Chapman, headmaster of a Philadelphia school.

1913   at Dorchester Prison: William Walter Burton (29) for the murder of Winifred Mary Mitchell (23). *Hangman: Henry Pierrepoint. Assistant: Brown*

22 June

1535 HENRY VIII'S BROKEN PROMISE
John Fisher, Bishop of Rochester, hanged, beheaded, and quartered at the Tower of London for high treason.

Henry VIII had proclaimed himself head of the Church and Defender of the Faith with his Act of Supremacy, as a part of his plan to divorce

Catherine of Aragon and marry Anne Boleyn. Many highly placed men could not reconcile this with their religious consciences. Henry asked the Bishop for his true feelings on this issue and promised him complete indemnity against the penalties of the new Act. Bishop Fisher replied that he still had 'grave doubts' on the matter, and Henry immediately had him arrested and sent to join Sir Thomas More in the Tower of London!

Pope Paul III elevated Bishop Fisher to Cardinal during the month of May. A furious Henry VIII swore 'The Pope might send Fisher a Cardinal's hat but that the Bishop should never have a head to wear it on' and ordered his trial for 17 June. The jury were given more than a broad hint by the Lord Chancellor: 'That the offence is so heinous and dangerous a treason that they could easily perceive what verdict they must return.' Found guilty by a loyal and no doubt fearful jury, the Lord Chancellor pronounced sentence: 'That you be hanged by the neck, taken down while you are still half alive, thereafter your head smitten off, and your body divided into four quarters.'

Five days later he was woken and told by the Lieutenant of the Tower that 'it was the King's pleasure' that he should suffer death at 9 a.m. that morning. 'What hour is it now?' asked the Bishop. 'It is now about five' he was told. 'Well then, let me by your patience sleep an hour or two for I have slept very little this night.' He slept soundly for another two hours.

After execution, his naked and headless corpse was left on show until nightfall. His head was exposed on a pike above London Bridge for a fortnight but, because it attracted huge crowds amidst reports that rays of light could be seen shining from it, it was then thrown into the Thames. He was canonised St John, four hundred years later in 1935. Sir Thomas More was beheaded at the Tower 14 days after Bishop Fisher and was also canonised in 1935.

Also hanged this day:

1752   at Tyburn Tree: Thomas Wilford (17) a one-armed cripple for the murder of his wife Sarah. Wilford was the first to suffer under a new act of Parliament that required that after they had been executed murderers should be either hung in chains or anatomised. He was anatomised.

1780   at Bloomsbury Square, London: Charles Kent, John Gray, and Latitia Holland for their parts in the burning of Newgate Prison on 6 June.

1954   M. Taylor for the murder of Mrs M. Bradshaw.

23 June

1649 TYBURN TREE, FULL!
Twenty-three men and a woman, burglars and robbers, hanged at
Tyburn Tree.
Hangman: William Lowen

The condemned were taken to Tyburn in a convoy of eight carts. They
were arranged eight to each beam of the famous triangular Tree – its
maximum capacity – and hanged simultaneously. William Lowen was
described as the new hangman, but it is not known if this was his first
execution: if so it was a spectacular introduction to his new career for
the former street sweeper.

Also hanged this day:

1819   at Old Bailey: Thomas Jeffcott and Nicholas B. Aubin for
letter-stealing; William Ambrose for malicious shooting.

24 June

Hanged this day:

1811   at Old Bailey: Richard Armitage, a bank clerk; Charles Thomas for forgery.

1942   D. Edmondson for the murder of Miss O. M. Osliff at
Southport, Lancashire.

25 June

1942 TERROR OF THE PROSTITUTES
Leading Aircraftman Gordon Frederick Cummins (28), an RAF
aircrew trainee, hanged at Wandsworth Prison during an air raid for
the Jack-the-Ripper style murder of London prostitute Evelyn Oatley
a.k.a. Nita Ward (35).

Cummins strangled and mutilated four women in London's West End
in four days of mayhem that sparked off a terror among prostitutes
similar to the heyday of Jack-the-Ripper. His victims were:
Evelyn Hamilton (42), found strangled in an air raid shelter in

210

Montagu Place W1 on the morning of Sunday 9 February 1942. Her handbag containing £80 had been stolen. There had been no sexual assault.

Evelyn Oatley a.k.a. Nita Ward (35), found naked in her flat in Wardour Street on Monday. Her throat had been cut, and her vagina mutilated with a tin-opener.

Margaret Lowe (43), strangled on Tuesday in her flat in Gosfield Street W1 and mutilated with a razor blade. Her body was discovered by her 14-year-old daughter a few days later.

Doris Jouannet a.k.a. Doris Robson (32), strangled and her genitals savagely mutilated in a Paddington hotel on Wednesday.

Cummins was interrupted in the course of another assault, on Margaret Hayward, on Friday 14 near Piccadilly Circus, by the arrival of a delivery boy on his rounds. Cummins fled leaving his gas mask with his RAF number, 5259878, marked on the bag. Before he was traced he attacked another prostitute, Mrs Mulcahy a.k.a. Kathleen King, a few hours later in her flat in Southwick Street, Paddington. He gripped her throat and squeezed, but she resisted by kicking him in the shins and screaming. He gave her an extra £5 and ran off in panic.

He was arrested on Sunday 16 February and found to be in possession of different items stolen from his victims. These and the fingerprints he had left behind were enough to hang him, although he never admitted any of his crimes. Two earlier unsolved murders were attributed to Cummins: those of Maple Church (19), whose body was found in a bombed house near Euston Station in October 1941, and of Mrs Humphries in Gloucester Crescent near Regent's Park.

Also hanged this day:

1716 at Tyburn Tree: Richard Gusiane, hanged, drawn and quartered for high treason.

1875 at Maine, USA: Louis Wagner for the axe-murder of Mrs Anethe Christensen, his former employer's wife during a robbery, and triple killer John True Gordon. They were the last men hanged in Maine.

1902 at Heidelburg, Transvaal, South Africa: Solomon Van Aan for the murder of Captain Mair in September 1901 during the Boer War. The Boers had displayed a flag of truce and Captain Mair went forward to negotiate when he was treacherously shot by Van Aan.

26 June

1926 THE UNPREGNANT MURDERESS
Louie Calvert (33) a.k.a. Louise Jackson a.k.a. Gomersal hanged at
Strangeways Prison, Manchester, for the murder of Mrs Lily
Waterhouse (40).

Louie Calvert used many names. The police knew her as Louie
Gomersal, prostitute, but she attended Salvation Army meetings as
Louise Jackson (wearing a stolen bonnet). Among other names she
used was Edith Thompson, who had been hanged for murder in 1923
(see 9 January).

It was as Louise Jackson that she became housekeeper for night-
watchman Arthur Calvert at 7 Railway Place, Hunslet, near Leeds.
Her young son went to live with her while her daughter stayed with
Louie's sister in Dewsbury, Wiltshire. Louie was a small, thin,
toothless woman with a vile and violent temper. It seems, however,
that she and Arthur Calvert had a sexual relationship. When she told
him that she was pregnant, he believed her and married her: from then
on she was Louie Calvert.

She strung the expectant father along for months, even though there
were no obvious signs that the baby was on the way. She announced
that she was going to her sister in Dewsbury for the 'confinement' and
set off on 8 March 1926. She went there all right, stayed long enough
to send Calvert a telegram of her safe arrival, and then travelled back
to Leeds.

She moved in as a lodger with Mrs Lily Waterhouse in Amberley
Road, only a few miles from Railway Place. She placed a newspaper
advert, offering to adopt a newly born baby. A 17-year-old girl from
Wrangford agreed to hand over her illegitimate baby girl a few weeks
hence, on 31 March. During this waiting time she continued to stay
with Mrs Waterhouse.

Small possessions went missing and Mrs Waterhouse realised that
Louie was a thief but, because of her lodger's foul temper, she was at
first fearful of mentioning it. More went missing and the police were
informed. Louie Calvert was issued with a summons to appear in court
on 1 April, Maunday Thursday. The Wednesday before, Louie
Calvert attacked and savagely battered her landlady with extreme
violence, then finished her off by strangling her. Whether the murder
was before or after taking delivery of the baby is not clear, but she left
the house in Amberley Road that day and went back to Railway Place
to present Arthur with 'his' daughter.

Louie was up and about at 5 a.m. on Thursday morning and went
back to Amberley Road. She let herself into the house where her
victim's battered body still lay and, ever the petty thief, filled a

212

suitcase with some more of her late landlady's few pitiful belongings: odd items of crockery (some cracked), cutlery, some linen. Neighbours saw her as she left to go back to Railway Place.

The crime was discovered when the police called to find out why Mrs Waterhouse had not appeared in court. Their first call after that was to 7 Railway Place where the door was answered by Louie Calvert – wearing Mrs Waterhouse's boots which were several sizes too large for her. She was arrested and charged with murder.

While under sentence of death she also confessed to the earlier murder of her employer John William Frobisher in 1922, to whom she had been housekeeper (as Louise Jackson). She made another claim to being pregnant, in an effort to avoid the hangman's rope. The prison authorities were not as gullible as Arthur Calvert: medical tests proved that it was just a sham – her last one.

27 June

1777 THE KING'S CHAPLAIN
Reverend Dr William Dodd (48), former Chaplain to the King, hanged at Tyburn Tree for forgery.
Hangman: Edward Dennis

William Dodd was the son of a clergyman and became a leading churchman in his own right. He was appointed Chaplain in Ordinary to King George III in 1763, 12 years after his ordination. He was a promoter of Magdalen Hospital and the Humane Society, became tutor to the son of Lord Chesterfield, accepted numerous clerical offices, founded two private chapels and published many literary works including his own sermons (one of which argued against capital punishment although he was to be the chief witness at the trial of a highwayman who had robbed him and the man was hanged!). When his former pupil succeeded to the title the new Lord Chesterfield became Dodd's patron.

Dodd had a taste for the high life and was popularly know as the 'Macaroni Parson' because of his foppish dress. His accomplishments did not include solvency and it was his extravagance – and pressing creditors – that caused his downfall.

Seeking the rich pastoracy of St George's, Hanover Square, which was the gift of the king, he wrote a letter offering a £3,000 bribe to a lady of the Court. The king was outraged and had Dodd removed from his list of chaplains. When the news became public it increased the pressure from his creditors.

In a desperate measure he forged a £4,200 bond in the name of Lord Chesterfield, received payment and calmed his creditors. The forgery was revealed as soon as the brokers referred it to Lord Chesterfield, who repudiated it. Forgery was a capital offence in those days, as being 'indispensable to protect commercial credit' in the city of London.

By selling up his property and furniture, Dr Dodd was able to restore all of the sum, but Lord Chesterfield refused to help his former tutor and Dodd was charged before the Lord Mayor. The jury took only five minutes to find Dodd guilty and he was sentenced to death.

Dr Johnson and others made great efforts to have him reprieved, but George III would not be moved. Dodd was driven to Tyburn in a mourning coach and the route was thronged with more sightseers than ever before, greater even than for Jonathan Wild and Lord Ferrers. Following the coach was the common cart, carrying 15-year-old Joseph Harris (see 1777 opposite), from which they would both be 'launched into eternity'.

Dr Dodd faced his death with dignity, even doing his best to comfort young Harris right up to the awful moment. Rumours gripped the enormous crowd* that a conspiracy was afoot to cheat the gallows from claiming Dr Dodd's life. Just before the cart was driven off from beneath them, Dodd was seen to whisper to Hangman Dennis and this was seen as further proof that Dennis had been bribed to fix the noose wrongly. It is true that Dennis' first action, once the cart had been removed, was to steady the legs of Dr Dodd.

Another story had it that he was hanged with a silver tube in his windpipe so that he could survive the hanging and be revived. After being cut down his body was rushed to a doctor in Goodge Street and given the following treatment:

'Air mixed with *volatile alkali* was pumped into the doctor's lungs by a double bellows, spirits of hartshorn being held in front of the bellows air-inlet. His spine and oesophagus were pressed and massaged. Blankets had to be held in such a way that they hardly touched him, while steam of hot balsam was circulated round his body and forced up his anus. Peppermint water, horseradish juice and turpentine were applied. . .'

It was all to no avail; even so, rumours continued that he had been revived and had gone abroad.

* *Present at the execution was another clergyman, the Reverend James Hackman, who was hanged two years later for murdering the mistress of the Earl of Sandwich (see 19 April).*

Also hanged this day:

1777   Joseph Harris (15) hanged at Tyburn Tree for theft, alongside Dr Dodds (see above). *Hangman: Edward Dennis.* Harris was sentenced for stealing two half-sovereigns and some silver coins. When the noose was draped round his neck before the journey from Newgate to Tyburn, he collapsed and had to be lifted into the cart. He cried throughout the journey with his head lying in his father's lap. At the gallows Dr Dodd tried to comfort the lad. Joseph's father stayed with the boy until Hangman Dennis removed the cart from under him. The sight of the weeping grey-haired old man aroused much sympathy.

1825   at Old Bailey: Edward Davis Dunn and James Goff for burglary.

28 June

1797 HANGED FROM THE YARDARM
Sailors Thomas Ashley and Robert Johnson hanged from the yardarm on board HMS *Le Pompee* at Portsmouth, Hampshire, following the Mutiny at the Nore.

Four condemned mutineers stood on the deck of *Le Pompee*, eyes bandaged and each with a noose around his neck, awaiting the sound of the gun to signal that the time of their appointment with death had arrived. They were Thomas Ashley, Robert Johnson, William Guthrie, and James Galloway.

Two mutinies in the Royal Navy had rocked the Government. First there had been the Spithead Mutiny of the Channel Fleet in April, settled when the sailors' demands for better pay, food and medical attention were agreed in May.

No sooner had this situation been calmed than a far more serious one occurred involving the North Sea Fleet. This became known as the Mutiny at the Nore, a sandbank near Sheerness in the Thames Estuary. The instigator was Richard Parker (30) who eventually had 13 ships of the line plus frigates under his orders. The mutiny was crushed on 13 June, with the ringleaders being rounded up, tried, and condemned. Parker was hanged two days after the *Le Pompee* mutineers. (See 30 June.)

On the deck of *Le Pompee* the gun fired and two gangs of heaving sailors pulled the ropes and hoisted Ashley and Johnson slowly upwards towards the yardarm, to suffer death by strangulation. Guthrie and Galloway stood fast awaiting their own doom, but their nooses were removed and they were informed that they had been pardoned and were to return to their ships.

1812 at Newton, New Jersey, USA: Mary Cole for the throat-cutting murder of her mother, Agnes Teaurs.

1898 at Cambridge Prison: Walter Horsford for the murder of Mr Holmes, his cousin.

29 June

1809 DEATH OF A BULLY
Captain John Sutherland hanged at Execution Dock, Wapping, for stabbing to death his negro cabin boy.
Hangman: William Brunskill

Captain Sutherland was commander of the British armed transport *The Friends* as the ship lay in the Tagus off Lisbon, Portugal. While on board he had routinely ill-treated his negro cabin boy and, finally, stabbed him to death. On his return to England he was tried and convicted of the murder, much to the disgust of fellow seamen of all ranks that an Englishman should be hanged for killing 'a mere nigger boy'.

Hangman Brunskill removed the body when the first tide reached the gallows instead of allowing three tides to wash over the gallows as was usual at Execution Dock.

Also hanged this day:

1809 at Shooter's Hill, Eltham, Kent: George Webb for burglary. Shooter's Hill Police Station now stands on the site of the gibbet.

1874 at Newgate Prison: Francis Stewart (43) for the murder of her baby grandson.

30 June

1936 A CONFESSION TOO MANY
RAF deserter, Frederick Herbert Charles Field (32), hanged at Wandsworth Prison for the murder of Mrs Beatrice Vilna Sutton.

In 1931 Field had confessed to murdering prostitute Norah Upchurch (20), but withdrew the confession at his trial and was acquitted. He was arrested as a deserter in 1936 and surprised his captors by immediately confessing that he had killed Beatrice Sutton in her flat at Clapham. He again denied his confession at this second trial for his life, but his cocky luck had run out because his description of her injuries were too accurate. The jury took 15 minutes to find him guilty. Had he not confessed he would almost certainly have got away with it again.

Also hanged this day:

1797 at Portsmouth, Hampshire: Richard Parker (30) for leading the Mutiny at the Nore (see 28 June).

1806 at Clarksburg, Virginia, USA: farmer Abel Clemmons for the murder of his wife and eight children.

1825 at Old Bailey: William Sergeant, James Harper, and William Probert for horse-stealing. (Probert had been an accessory to the sensational murder of William Weare, but had turned King's Evidence and was not charged. John Thurtell was hanged for this crime on 9 January 1824.)

1826 at Fairfax, Virginia, USA: William F. Hooe for the murder for robbery of plantation owner William Simpson who he had lured to Centreville on a dark night to buy contraband slaves.

1829 at Old Bailey: Ann Chapman for murder.

1882 at Washington DC, USA: Charles Guiteau for the assassination of President Garfield. Garfield was shot on 2 July 1881, lingered, and died of blood poisoning on 19 September probably from unsterile instruments used in his surgery.

1887 at Strangeways Prison, Manchester: Walter Wood for wife-murder. *Hangman: James Berry*

JULY

1 July

1774 THE FLYING HIGHWAYMAN
**William Hawke, popularly known as the 'Flying Highwayman',
hanged at Tyburn Tree for the theft of some linen.**
Hangman: Edward Dennis

There were a number of 'gentlemen of the road' styled the Flying Highwayman, but the best known was William Hawke. He operated with three speedy horses, at different times, and further aided his getaways by 'flying' over turnpikes.

Most highwaymen were unimaginative and had short careers before being caught and hanged; Hawke was an exception being more lively and ingenious. The *Annual Register*, 13 years earlier, had this to say of him:

'. . . (he) engrosses the conversation of most of the towns within twenty miles of London, as he has occasionally visited all the public roads around the Metropolis, and has collected several considerable sums. He robs upon three different horses, a grey, a sorrel, and a black one, the last of which has a bald face, to hide which, he generally hangs on a black cat's skin; he has leapt over the Colnbrook turnpike a dozen times within this fortnight, and is now well known by most of the turnpike men in the different roads about town.'

After such a long and famous career it was for the ignominious theft of a small amount of linen that he was condemned to the gallows. His last days in Newgate were spent entertaining a stream of visiting notables and gentry, all wanting to meet the legendary Flying Highwayman. They found him brave, witty and cheerful to the end. Colonel George Hanger (later Lord Coleraine) secretly provided him with £50 to use as bribes in order to escape, but Hawke was unsuccessful with the turnkeys, and returned the money to the colonel with gracious thanks. His last night was spent in prayers and singing psalms with fellow prisoners.

He was firm throughout the last journey on the road to Tyburn and did not flinch at the gallows, where he saw the hearse waiting with his own coffin, coloured black, studded with yellow nails, and bearing a plate engraved with his name and the date of his death. He died bravely and, after he was cut down, the coffin was taken to Uxbridge and a large crowd attended a splendid funeral service, to pay their final tributes to the popular Flying Highwayman. One of the mourners was his hangman, Edward Dennis.

1896 at Muskogee, Arkansas, USA: five half-black half-Cree Indians Rufus Buck (20), Lucky Davis, Sam Sampson, Maomi July, and Lewis Davis, for a two-week murder–rape–robbery rampage.

2 July

Hanged this day:

1739 at Tyburn Tree: William Caldough for robbery.

1778 at Worcester, Massachusetts, USA: Mrs Bathsheba Spooner (30), Sergeant James Buchanan (30), Private William Brooks (27) and Private Ezra Ross (18) for the murder of Bathsheba's ageing husband Joshua Spooner.

1895 at Wandsworth Prison: Henry Tickner (42), a soldier, for wife-murder.

3 July

Hanged this day:

1753 at Tyburn Tree: Christian Johnson and John Stockdale for murder.

4 July

1839 SERGEANT MAJOR SHOT ON PARADE
Private George Willis, Royal Artillery, hanged outside Maidstone Prison for shooting Sergeant Major William Shepherd on parade at Woolwich Barracks.
Hangman: William Calcraft

The role of sergeant majors is to instil discipline, and maintain it at all times. They are perfectionists, demanding the highest standards in personal turnout, equipment, and the instant obedience of orders. The aura of the sergeant major in any barracks is formidable: legend has it that they can freeze a lake at a single glance! They have been perceived by the lower ranks as ogres in human form ever since there have been regiments.

Private Willis had belonged to the Royal Artillery for a year, having joined at an early age. He apparently came from a decent and loving family, had regularly attended Sunday school as a boy, and his conduct since enlisting had been good.

Then came the day when he was the focus of the steely scrutiny of Sergeant Major Shepherd, and was reprimanded for being 'dirty on parade'. Private Willis was so upset that he brooded about his disgrace and, had he not been prevented by comrades, would have committed suicide. His brooding continued until, on the parade ground at Woolwich, he raised his carbine and deliberately shot and killed his sergeant major.

He was tried at the Old Bailey, condemned to death, and returned to Maidstone Prison. On the night before his execution he was convinced that the sentence would not be carried out. He told the chaplain that even before his trial he had had a dream that he would be found guilty, sentenced to death, taken out to the scaffold and even have the nightcap and noose round his neck when, as he was about to be dropped, a pardon would arrive.

He slept well on his last night, ate a good breakfast and walked around the prison yard with the greatest indifference. After being pinioned he walked so fast towards the scaffold that he was requested to walk slower. He mounted the scaffold showing no fear and gazed calmly at the watching crowd. The cap and noose were put in place. . .

The blatant shooting of a sergeant major, the personified symbol of military authority, represented more than a threat to good order and discipline in the army. 1839 was a troubled year in the country, with the Chartist movement prominent in civil disturbance throughout the land and revolution a dire possibility. The action of Private Willis could cast doubt upon the reliability of the army; an example 'to encourage the others' was needed. There could be no chance of mercy. Calcraft pulled the bolts and Private Willis, whose dream had been an accurate prediction of everything except this last moment, fell through the trap doors and struggled for a short time before hanging still.

Also hanged this day:

1821   at Old Bailey: John Snipe for forgery; Matthew Prescott for extortion; Charles Waite and Robert Goulding for burglary.

1828   at Old Bailey: William Rea for highway robbery; James Harpham for burglary.

1851   at Downieville, California, USA: the first woman tried and hanged in California: Mexican ex-prostitute Juanita for the knife-killing of a roughneck forcing himself upon her in her cabin. It was almost certainly self-defence, but she was convicted after a quick trial in the local saloon.

5 July

1691 UNWISE CHANGE
Thomas Collett a.k.a Thomas Cole hanged at Tyburn Tree for burglary.

Tom had spent a happy and more or less successful career as a highwayman, but a new career as a burglar did not last long. This Tom Collett should not be confused with the more famous highwayman of the same time also named Thomas Collett (a.k.a. Jack Cottengen, but more famously called 'Mulled Sack') who was hanged in 1694.

Also hanged this day:

1723   at Kent Street, Southwark, London: Thomas Athol and his son, Thomas Athol for murder.

1824   at Old Bailey: George Davis and Williams for burglary.

6 July

1961 IDENTIKIT MURDERER
Eurasian Edwin Albert Bush (21) hanged at Pentonville Prison for the murder of Mrs Elsie May Batten with two antique daggers, in an antique shop in Charing Cross Road.

Bush was the first murderer in Britain to be caught as a result of the Identikit system. Identikit was a set of transparencies of drawings of variations of facial features: face and head shape, hair, nose, mouth, eyes, ears, etc. A composite face would be assembled by a witness sitting with a policeman as the different features were overlaid until a likeness was achieved. It has since been replaced by Photofit.

As a variation on the cliché of a murderer returning to the scene of the crime, Bush visited the scene the day before the murder. He went into an antique shop at 23 Cecil Court, an alley off Charing Cross Road in London's West End, on Thursday 2 March 1961 to look at a dress sword. Then he went to another shop across the alley to ask if the owner would buy a sword.

The following day he returned to 23 Cecil Court and was attended by shop assistant Elsie May Batten. Bush's statement to the police after arrest gives the best description of what happened next:

> 'I went back to the shop and started looking through the daggers, telling her I might want to buy one, but I picked one up and hit her in the back. I then lost my nerve and picked up a stone vase and hit her with it. I grabbed a knife and hit her once in the stomach and once in the neck.'

He took a dress sword and went across to the other shop to sell it for £10 so that he could buy his girl an engagement ring. Mr Roberts, the proprietor, was out so Bush left the sword with the son, Paul Roberts. Bush had blood on his clothes and had left behind finger, palm, and footprints. Mr Roberts and his son helped the police compile an Identikit portrait and, from this, PC John Cole recognised and arrested Bush while on his beat in Soho the following Wednesday, 8 March.

At his trial at the Old Bailey Bush claimed that Mrs Batten had said 'You niggers are all the same. You come in and never buy anything.' He said 'I lost my head . . .' and continued by repeating the description of his murderous attack. He had had two months to think up this racial ingredient as mitigation, but there was abundant evidence that the crime had been planned.

Also hanged this day:

1725 at Tyburn Tree: John Johnson for robbery.

1750 at Tyburn Tree: 'three gin-ridden hags' – Elizabeth Banks for stripping a child, Catherine Conway for forging a seaman's ticket and Margaret Harvey for robbing her master. *Hangman: (probably) John Thrift*

1840 at Old Bailey: Francis Benjamin Courvoisier (23), Swiss valet, for murdering his master Lord William Russell (73) at Norfolk Street off Park Lane. A huge crowd watched the execution including Charles Dickens and William Makepeace Thackeray, who each recorded his personal impressions of it. *Hangman: William Calcraft*

1857 at Maidstone, Kent: Private Thomas Mansell (29) for the murder of Corporal Alexander McBurney at Hougham, near Dover. *Hangman: William Calcraft*

1860 at New Jersey, USA: Reverend Jacob S. Harden for the arsenic-murder of his young wife.

7 July

1896 THE CONDEMNED MAN IN OSCAR WILDE'S *BALLAD OF READING GAOL*
Trooper Charles Thomas Wooldridge (30), of the Royal Horse Guards, hanged at Reading Gaol for the murder of his wife, Laura Ellen Wooldridge (23), while in a jealous rage.
Hangman: James Billington

While stationed with his regiment at Windsor, Trooper Wooldridge met and courted Miss Laura Glendell who was assistant at the post office in Eton High Street. They married secretly, because Wooldridge did not have his commanding officer's permission to marry, and Miss Glendell continued to be known by her maiden name. There were other difficulties.

They lived at 21 Alma Terrace in Arthur Road, Windsor, near the railway station, but they did not live happily. Wooldridge would lose control of his temper during differences and hit his young wife. They became estranged. When his regiment was ordered to Regent's Park Barracks he had to leave Laura behind because, as far as the army was concerned, they were not married. He visited her at Alma Terrace, but he was not made welcome and this was another occasion when he struck her and bruised her face. He became contrite and asked her to meet him outside the barracks on Sunday; she probably agreed for no other reason than to get rid of him.

He dressed up in his best uniform and waited on that fateful Sunday afternoon, 29 March 1896, and he waited in vain. He had heard that she had been seeing a corporal of the Life Guards who was stationed at Windsor. Jealousy and anger welled up and he borrowed a cut-throat razor from a comrade and departed for Windsor. He gained admittance to 21 Alma Terrace by saying that he had some papers for Laura to sign. Soon she was heard screaming and neighbours saw her run into the road, her face streaming with blood from a razor slash. Her husband grabbed her and they struggled until he made two more slashes and she crumpled into the middle of the road with her throat fatally cut. People rushed to the scene and Wooldridge quietly gave himself up to one of them, PC Henry Miles, with the words 'Take me, I have killed my wife.'

Tragic as it was with the death of a young wife and the inevitable later death by judicial hanging of the husband, as a criminal case it was an unremarkable wife-murder, albeit brutal and premeditated. Unremarkable, and it would have been unremembered, but for a coincidence of timing.

Wooldridge was remanded to await his trial at Reading Gaol and, in the exercise yard, he was seen (from afar) by Oscar Wilde who was serving a two-year sentence for homosexuality. A year later, after his release, Wilde wrote his haunting poem of more than a hundred verses, *The Ballad of Reading Gaol*, with its repetitive theme:

> The man had killed the thing he loved,
> And so he had to die.

The book included a plate showing a wreath enclosing the words 'In Memoriam C. T. W. sometime Trooper of The Royal Horse Guards OBIIT H. M. Prison Reading Berkshire July 7th 1896'. *The Ballad* was Wilde's last, and one of his best, literary works and was immediately successful.

He had only seen Wooldridge in the exercise yard, surrounded by warders, prior to the trial. He never saw him while under sentence of death, but he did see the grave being prepared. Without realising it at the time, adjacent to the exercise yard he also saw the Execution Shed; he was later to tell a friend in a letter:

'The shed in which people are hanged is a little shed with a glass roof, like a photographer's studio on the sands at Margate. For eighteen months I thought it *was* a studio for photographing prisoners. There is no adjective to describe it. I call it "hideous" because it became so to me after I knew its use.'

At 7.45 a.m. on the morning of the execution, the bell of the nearby St Lawrence's Church began its awful death-knell which was to continue until 8.15 a.m. At 8 a.m. Hangman James Billington despatched Wooldridge with a drop of six feet seven inches.

Also hanged this day:

1703 at Fulham, London: John Peter Dramatti for murder.

1736 at the Market Place, Edinburgh: Captain John Porteous for murder; he ordered soldiers to fire into a rioting mob, killing and wounding many.

1813 at Northampton: Huffey White and Richard Kendall for robbery of the Leeds Mail.

1820 at Old Bailey: Thomas Cumber for extortion; Peter Miller, Henry Brown, and James Gardner for issuing forged notes.

1826 at Frankfort, Kentucky, USA: lawyer Jereboam O. Beauchamp (23) for the murder of Colonel Solomon P. Sharp. His wife, Ann Cooke Beauchamp, visited him in jail as he awaited death and they mutually plunged daggers into each other: Ann died, but not Jereboam, and he was hanged with the knife-cut still bleeding.

1827 at Old Bailey: George Warner Griffiths and William Cundell for burglary.

1865 at the Arsenal, Washington DC, USA: Lewis Paine (20), Mrs Mary Surratt (48), George Atzerodt, and David Herold for complicity in the assassination of President Abraham Lincoln.

1903 at Chelmsford Gaol: Charles Howell, a soldier, for the murder of Maud Luen.

1950 at Winchester Prison: Roman Redel (23) and Zbigniew Gower (23) for the shooting-murder of Robert Taylor (30) during their escape after a bank robbery in Bristol. *Hangman: Albert Pierrepoint. Assistants: Harry Kirk, Harry Allen and Syd Dernley*

1986 at Pudu Prison, Kuala Lumpur: Kevin Barlow and Brian Chambers for drug-trafficking. Kevin Barlow, from Britain, and Australian Brian Chambers became the first foreigners to be hanged under Malaysia's tough, and vigorously enforced, anti-drug laws. (See 21 July.)

8 July

Hanged this day:

1771 at Hare Street, Spitalfields, London: Henry Stroud and Campbell, ringleaders of a riot resulting in the murder of Daniel Clarke.

1796 at Woodbury, New Jersey, USA: Abraham Johnstone for the stabbing-murder of another slave.

1839 at Old Bailey: John W. Marchant for the murder of another young servant.

9 July

1912 THE TRAGEDY OF 'FIRST LOVE'
Arthur Birkett (22) hanged at Strangeways Prison, Manchester, for the throat-cutting murder of Alice Beetham (18).

Arthur Birkett was a decent, popular, and hard-working lad employed as a weaver at the Jubilee Mill in Blackburn. He supported his widowed mother, grandmother, and younger sister in their tiny terraced house. He regularly followed the fortunes of Blackburn

Rovers, who had won the Football League championship that season, and belonged to the North Lancashire Territorials.

Arthur Birkett (22) had never had a girlfriend until he went out with Alice Beetham (18) in April 1912. She was a pretty girl, not the 'flighty' kind, and had worked at Jubilee Mill since she was 14. They went out together a few times during the following month, but Alice began to lose interest and then tried to avoid even casual encounters with him. Arthur, in contrast, had fallen hopelessly in love with Alice. Hopeless love like this will always be a shattering experience for the one who loves. Unable to cope with his agony, Arthur bought a razor, as he said later, to kill himself.

On the Monday morning at Jubilee Mill, 20 May 1912, Arthur tried to speak to Alice as she passed his loom, but she quickly walked on without responding. He followed and threw an arm around her neck and, with all his strength, drew the razor across her throat. It cut deeply, severing everything from ear to ear and all the way back to the bone, even nicking the bone itself. She fell to the floor, streaming with blood, and died. Birkett slashed the razor across his own throat, but not with the same force. He staggered away, bleeding, pushing people out of his way, until he was held by two men at the mill's gate. He later told policemen 'I've been off my head for two days. I've been crazy.'

The tragedy of a rejected first love was an experience that Arthur Birkett could not cope with: he killed Alice and was hanged because he killed her. Alice was Arthur's first – and only – love. Poor Alice had never loved at all. The tragedy was complete.

Also hanged this day:

1701 at Bedford: Thomas Dunn for robbery.

1709 at Guildford: Christopher Slaughterford for the murder of Jane Young.

1832 at Old Bailey: John Drewitt for burglary.

1858 at Geneseo, New York, USA: Isaac Wood for the poison-murder of his wife and child. He had previously poisoned his brother David and his wife and three children to inherit their property, and had got away with it.

1886 at New York, USA: Cuban Miguel Chacon for the gun-murder of his mistress, prostitute Maria Williams. Chacon was hiding from the police and was handed over by the leader of the Cuban Revolutionary Society for the good of the Cuban community.

1901 at Bodmin Gaol, Cornwall: Valeri Giovanni for the murder of a man on the high seas.

10 July

1919 MASSACRE OF THE CORNISH FAMILY
Private Henry Perry a.k.a. Beckett (38) hanged at Pentonville Prison
for the murder of the Cornish family in Forest Gate, London.

Private Perry had been a soldier for eight years and had seen active service during World War One in the Middle East. He had been badly injured about the head and suffered torture as a prisoner of the Turks. About to be demobbed, he stayed as a lodger with the Cornish family, to which he was related by marriage, at Stukeley Road in Forest Gate, East London. He was ordered to leave after a row.

A few days later, on 28 April 1919, he returned between 2 p.m. and 3 p.m. when Mrs Alice Cornish (43) was alone in the house. After some more sharp words were exchanged he went berserk, hitting her about the head with the kitchen poker. He carried her to the garden shed while she was still alive and hit her again, this time with a pickaxe. As she was still not dead he stabbed her in the throat with a carving knife.

He waited in the house until little Marie (6) came home from school and hit her a number of times on the head with a hammer, afterwards picking her up and throwing her down the cellar steps. The eldest daughter, Alice (15), arrived soon after and she was attacked with the hammer until she fell to the floor. He finished her with an axe-blow to the throat and threw her body into the cellar. When Mr Walter Cornish (48) got home from work Perry struck him down with the axe.

Perry ransacked the house, taking any money and valuables he could find, and cut off Mrs Cornish's finger to get at her wedding ring. He was seen fleeing with blood on his face and hands. Mr Cornish managed to stagger outside and, before being taken to hospital, was able to tell neighbours he had been attacked by 'that soldier' who had been his lodger. He died two days later. Perry was captured a few days later in East Ham, still in possession of the items stolen from the house. He admitted everything, but claimed that he was obeying voices in his head. His insanity plea failed at the Old Bailey trial and the jury needed only ten minutes to find him guilty.

Also hanged this day:

1700   at East Smithfield, London: Matthew and Cuthbert Vanberger, and Gerard Dromelius for the murder of Oliver Morris.

1722   at Tyburn Tree: Nathaniel Jackson and Thomas Bullock for highway robbery.

1840   at Chicago (on the lake shore), Illinois, USA: John Stone (34) was the first man to be hanged in the new city, for the rape-murder of Lucretia Thompson who spurned him.

1910 at Durham Gaol: Thomas Craig for the jealousy inspired murder of Thomas Henderson.

11 July

1958 TALKED HIMSELF TO DEATH
Peter Thomas Anthony Manuel (31) hanged at Barlinnie Prison, Glasgow, for seven murders (but there were more).

Peter Manuel was a full-time criminal who had been in continuous trouble with the police since the age of 12. He had a string of convictions for burglary, general thieving, robbery with violence, indecent assault and rape. He also committed a string of murders, not always with robbery, some of which were undoubtedly carried out for the gloating pleasure that it gave him.

His victims were:
In *September 1954*: 'Red Helen' Carlin, prostitute, at Pimlico, London.
On *4 January 1956*: Anne Kneilands (17) at East Kilbride.
On *11 January 1956*: Anne Steele (55).
In *June 1956*: Ellen Petrie.
On *17 September 1956*: Mrs Marion Watt (45), her sister Mrs Margaret Brown, and daughter Vivienne Watt (16) at Burnside, Glasgow*.
From 2 October 1956 to 30 November 1957 Peter Manuel served 13 months of an 18-month sentence in Barlinnie Prison for housebreaking.
On *7 December 1957*: Sydney Dunn (36), taxi driver, at Newcastle.
On *28 December 1957*: Isabelle Cooke (17) at Mount Vernon, near Glasgow.
On *1 January 1958*: Peter James Smart (45), Mrs Doris Smart and Michael Smart (11) at Uddingston near Glasgow.

Manuel talked too much. He contacted Mr Watt's solicitor from Barlinnie Prison offering information about the murders. He claimed he had met the murderer, and described the inside of the Watts' house so accurately that he attracted suspicion on to himself. He gave himself away after the murder of the Smart family by recklessly spending new banknotes in a pub. They were a new issue of banknotes which were proved by the serial numbers to have been issued to Peter Smart shortly before he was shot with his family.

Manuel was arrested on 13 January 1958 and immediately talked further, in fact a lot more, about eight of his murders. He tried to retract his confession at his trial, sacked his defending lawyers during the trial so that he could conduct the defence, and do all the talking, himself. He was found guilty of seven of the eight murder charges, being acquitted of killing Anne Kneilands because of lack of supporting evidence to his confession. While awaiting his execution he confessed to some of the other murders.

* *The tragically bereaved William Watt (45) was away on a fishing holiday when his family was shot to death. A ferryman mistakenly believed that Mr Watt had used his ferry on the murder night, and Watt was held in Barlinnie Prison on suspicion of murder for 67 days until early December 1956. Manuel was in Barlinnie at the same time.*

Also hanged this day:

1768 at Tyburn Tree: James Murphy and James Duggan for riot.

1806 at New York City, USA: John Banks for wife-murder.

1832 at Old Bailey: Thomas Reilly for wife-murder.

1863 at Norfolk, Virginia, USA: Dr David M. Wright (60) for the gun-murder of Lieutenant A. L. Sanborn. Lieutenant Sanborn was in command of black troops marching through Norfolk to the fury of the racist doctor.

1899 at Northampton Prison: Joseph Cornelius Parker for the murder of his sweetheart.

1940 V. Ostler and W. Appleby for the murder of PC W. R. Shiell.

12 July

1726 CAPTAIN FLY AND *FAME'S REVENGE*
Captain William Fly and two accomplices hanged at Nix' Mate Island, Boston, USA, for mutiny, piracy and murder on the high seas.

William Fly's short and bloody career as a pirate began on 27 May 1726 on board the slave trader *Elizabeth*. During the nightwatch he and other mutineers seized control of the ship and murdered Captain John Green, and three other sailors, by tossing them overboard. They renamed the ship *Fame's Revenge*.

Captain Fly captured a sloop, the *John and Hannah*, off the coast of North Carolina, but wrecked it on a sandbank by poor seamanship. In a terrible rage he blamed the *John and Hannah*'s captain, John Fulker,

232

and had him stripped and flogged with the cat o' nine tails until his flesh was reduced to bloody tatters.

He forced the surrender of another ship, the *John and Betty*, robbed it of valuables, pressed six of its crew into joining them, and then let it sail away. He captured another ship, the *James*, and manned it with some of his pirates.

As his two ships sailed towards some unarmed fishing schooners, he himself succumbed to a mutiny from sailors he had captured who were now on board the *Fame's Revenge*. Under Captain William Atkinson, who had been with Fulker on the *John and Hannah*, the *Fame's Revenge* sailed for Boston with Captain Fly and three other pirates clapped in irons. Captain Fly was hanged with two of his brutal followers exactly 46 days after his career as a pirate captain began.

Also hanged this day:

1899 at Winchester Prison: Charles Maidment for the murder of his sweetheart.

1904 at Pentonville Prison: John Sullivan, a sailor, for the murder of a cabin boy.

13 July

1955 RUTH ELLIS AND THE END OF THE HOLLOWAY GALLOWS
Ruth Ellis (28) hanged at Holloway Prison for the murder of her lover, racing driver David Moffat Drummond Blakely (25).
Hangman: Albert Pierrepoint

Ruth Ellis was the last woman to be hanged in Britain and it was the occasion of a newspaper uproar. All kinds of emotional arguments were applied about the 'brutality' of hanging a woman. The furore was an example of press hypocrisy that had little to do with hanging, as such, or even the hanging of a woman. It was about the hanging of a young and 'glamorous' woman. It was what the Americans call a 'sob story', which could (and did) sell more newspapers.

Significantly, at the same time that Ruth Ellis was in the condemned cell at Holloway, a 40-year-old woman awaited a similar fate at Strangeways Prison in Manchester. This woman was completely ignored by the newspapers (she was reprieved two days before she was due to hang). Nor had there been any professional sobbing by the newspapers when two other women had been hanged in recent years:

the cruel Blackpool poisoner Mrs Merrifield (46) on 18 September 1953, and the callous Mrs Christofi (53) on 13 December 1954.

Ruth Ellis was a part of sleazy Soho nightlife and had been hostess at a drinking club. She had had a stormy affair with racing driver David Blakely, but he had cooled of late, in fact he was pointedly avoiding her, while she was becoming obsessed and bitter at the rejection. During this estrangement she continued her association with other men.

On Good Friday she had caused a disturbance outside the Hampstead flat where Blakely was staying with friends and the police were twice called as a result. She made a number of telephone calls to the flat, but Blakely would not come to the phone.

On Easter Sunday she went looking for him, with a loaded revolver in her handbag. Shortly after 9 p.m. she saw him through a window of the Magdala Tavern, on the edge of Hampstead Heath. She waited outside.

Blakely left with his friend at 9.20 p.m., saw Ruth Ellis but ignored her. She fired a shot and he ran for cover, her second shot hit him and he fell, face down, on the roadside. She stood over him and fired four more bullets at him, still pulling the trigger after the gun was empty. An off duty policeman came from the pub and took the revolver from her; she offered no resistance.

David Blakely had been hit four times and was dead on arrival at the hospital. Of the two shots that had missed Blakely, one had ricocheted and hit and injured a woman who had been walking down the road with her husband.

Ruth Ellis made no attempt to avoid the consequences of her crime. A newspaper paid for two defending barristers, but she did little to support their efforts to save her. The prosecutor at the trial asked her only one question:

'Mrs Ellis, when you fired that revolver at close range into the body of David Blakely, what did you intend to do?'
    Ellis replied: 'It is obvious that when I shot him I intended to kill him.'

She was, of course, found guilty and condemned to death. Newspapers clamoured for a reprieve but the Home Secretary announced, on 11 July, that the execution would go ahead as planned.

She was calm and brave in her final moments, fortified by a nip of brandy and a crucifix. She was required to wear canvas knickers for the execution, as had all females since the execution of Edith Thompson on 9 January 1923.

At Holloway the execution chamber was connected to the condemned cell by an opening hidden behind a wardrobe. The wardrobe was on wheels and would be slid aside when the hangmen entered the cell. Until that instant the condemned was unaware of the closeness of the gallows.

Ellis said nothing when the hangmen arrived, and walked firmly and silently to her death. She was buried within the prison grounds later that day. Her grave had to be moved in the late 1960s to make way for an access road to the prison jam factory. Her body was reburied in 1971 at St Mary's in Amersham, Buckinghamshire; Blakely's grave is a few miles away at Penn.

Also hanged this day:

1807 at Wisbech: Richard Faulkner (15) for the murder of George Burnham (12).

1860 at Bedloe's Island, New York, USA: Albert E. Hicks, who has described himself as the worst man in the world, hanged in front of a cheering crowd of twelve thousand. He had looted a sloop moored in New York Harbour and killed Captain Burr and crewmen Oliver and Smith Watts as they slept in their bunks.

1885 at Old Bailey: Henry Alt for the jealousy inspired murder of Charles Howard.

1904 at Northampton Prison: Sam Rowledge (37), a carpenter, for the murder of a servant-girl, Alice Foster.

1950 at Horfield Gaol, Bristol: Ronald Atwell (24) for the murder of Lily Palmer in a Somerset field. *Hangman: Albert Pierrepoint. Assistant: Syd Dernley*

14 July

1903 FORCED GALLOWS CONFESSION
Samuel Herbert Dougal (57) hanged at Chelmsford Gaol for the Moat Farm murder of Miss Camille Holland (55).
Hangman: William Billington. Assistant: John Billington

Dougal was a cockney ex-soldier with a high sex-drive, and a ruthless quest for money. He had served a prison term for forgery, being released in 1898, after which he met Miss Camille Holland (55) and set out to get her money. At his suggestion, Miss Holland bought Moat Farm at Clavering, Essex, and they moved in. She was last seen on 19 May 1899 when they both set out on a supposed shopping trip. He shot her in the head and buried her in a drainage ditch on the farm, and gave out a thin story that she had gone away on a yachting holiday.

Dougal lived off her money, his old forgery skills coming in useful for this. He lived well with his third wife, who had joined him at Moat Farm after Miss Holland's departure, and bought himself a motor car (the first in that district). He still enjoyed himself with any likely lass who seemed willing and was said to have held orgies with nubile young women. A group of them were supposed to have ridden bicycles naked in a field.

It is remarkable that he got away with all this for three years; the police were suspicious about Miss Holland's prolonged 'yachting holiday', but they had no hard evidence on which to proceed with an investigation. Then one of Miss Holland's cheques was exposed as a forgery and Dougal was arrested. The police started a search of Moat Farm and they eventually found Holland's decomposed body in the ditch. The bullet that had killed her was proved to have been fired from Dougal's own revolver. When asked whether he pleaded guilty or not guilty at his trial, he replied 'Absolutely not guilty' in a firm voice. He made a bold defence, claiming that the shooting had been an accident, and he appeared confident. The jury needed just under an hour to declare him guilty.

Dougal insisted that he was innocent until the moment before Billington operated the lever to hang him. The prison chaplain, Mr Blakemore, delayed the execution as the condemned man stood beneath the gallows' beam, with the rope around his neck and the white cap covering his face. 'Dougal,' he shouted, 'are you guilty or not guilty?' There was no answer. 'Dougal, are you guilty or not guilty?' A moment's pause, and then Dougal answered in a quiet voice, 'Guilty!'

Billington operated the lever as Dougal spoke, the trap doors opened and he dropped: the rope spun violently at first and became still. Questions were asked in Parliament about the chaplain's behaviour and the Home Secretary issued instructions to prevent such a harrowing scene being repeated at future executions.

Also hanged this day:

1798 at Heidelburg, Pennsylvania, USA: John Hauer and Charles M'Manus for the murder of Hauer's brother-in-law, Francis Shitz, and the attempted murder of Peter Shitz, in an inheritance swindle.

1910 at Chelmsford Gaol: Frederick Foreman, a labourer, for the murder of Elizabeth Eley with whom he had been living.

15 July

1845 FALSE WITNESSES
Brothers Stephen and William Hodges publicly hanged at West Point, Iowa, USA, for the murder of German settlers John Miller and his son-in-law Leicy in their log-cabin.

On the night of 10 May 1845 three men, one of them wearing a fur-trimmed cloth cap without a peak, entered the cabin where the elderly Miller and young Leicy were sleeping with their wives on the floor. The raiders believed that Miller had his life-savings, with which he intended to buy land, hidden in the cabin.

Miller and Leicy struggled fiercely with the raiders, both being stabbed repeatedly. Miller forced one raider out of the door before a final knife-thrust killed him. Leicy, grappling with one man, was stabbed in the back and head by the third man who was carrying a lantern. Then as Leicy ran for the door, he was shot and mortally injured in the abdomen. The sound of the fighting, and the accompanying screaming of Miller's and Leicy's wives, prompted the murderers to depart without their intended loot.

The murderers were traced by Edward Bonney, a keen private investigator, to the nearby town of Nauvoo. The fur-trimmed cap had been dropped during the flight from the crime, and Bonney found witnesses who had seen William Hodges wearing it in Nauvoo prior to the murder. His brother Stephen Hodges was seen the morning after with a bloodstain on his shirt. The third man was a notorious criminal, Robert Birch a.k.a. Thomas Brown among other aliases, but this was not known at the time.

Stephen and William Hodges were taken to the cabin where Leicy identified Stephen as the one who stabbed him and William who shot him. Leicy died soon after. The Hodges brothers were put on trial. A number of men testified at the trial that the Hodges were in Nauvoo at the time of the murder*, but the evidence against them was too strong. They were publicly hanged at West Point, only three-and-a-half miles from the scene of the log-cabin murder.

* *Four of the witnesses were John and Aaron Long, William 'the Judge' Fox, and Robert Birch – all members of the same gang. See 19 October.*

Also hanged this day:

1749 at Slendon Common, Sussex: John Mills for burglary.

1936 at Exeter Gaol: Charlotte Bryant (33) for the murder of her husband Frederick Bryant (39). *Hangman: Tom Pierrepoint. Assistant: Albert Pierrepoint*

1953 at Pentonville Prison: John Reginald Halliday Christie (55) for mass murder. He was an isolated and broken man at his execution, but he took enough interest to eat a final breakfast and, although a teetotaller, drink a glass of whisky. *Hangman: Albert Pierrepoint.* (See also 9 March.)

16 July

1909 ONLY THE BOSS HANGED
Black Hand gang leader, Leonardo Gebbia, publicly hanged at New Orleans, Louisiana, USA, for the kidnap and murder of Walter Lamana (7) whose father Peter Lamana was a rich New Orleans undertaker.

A $6,000 ransom had been demanded. Informants revealed that the boy had been strangled by Angelo Incaratero, but the gang boss Gebbia was the only one ever caught. It is rare to hear of a case where the minions escape and only the boss is punished; it is usually the other way round. Standing on the gallows with the noose round his neck, Gebbia wailed 'Why ain't they caught the others? How about Tony Gendusa, Incaratero, Monfre, and Frank Luchesi? . . . but they are satisfied just so long as they are hanging me!'
    The bereaved undertaker, Peter Lamana, and his supporters stood at the gallows feasting on roast beef and wine as they watched Gebbia hang. Lamana was afterwards given the hanging rope as a souvenir.

Also hanged this day:

1880 at New York, USA: Chastine Cox for the murder of Mrs Jane De Forest while robbing her home.

17 July

Hanged this day:

1857 at New York, USA: John Dorsey for the throat-cutting murder of his prostitute wife, Ann McGirr a.k.a. Hopkins, in front of a crowd of witnesses.

1900 at Newgate Prison: Alfred Highfield for the murder of a young woman.

18 July

Hanged this day:

1701   at Tyburn Tree: Herman Strodman, a young apprentice, for the murder of another apprentice.

1716   at Tyburn Tree: John Hall, Esq. and the Reverend William Paul hanged, drawn and quartered for high treason.

1811   at Cambridge: Daniel Dawson for poisoning horses.

1893   at Northampton Prison: Richard Sabey for the murder of Louisa Johnson.

1894   at Winchester Prison: Samuel Elkins.

19 July

1899 THE HANGING OF SIMPLE MARY
Mary Ann Ansell (22) hanged at St Alban's Prison for poisoning her sister with a cake made with phosphorus.
Hangman: James Billington

Mary Ansell was a simple-minded girl who talked to herself and suffered from hallucinations. The family had a history of mental illness and it was for the murder of her sister Caroline, an inmate of Leavesden Asylum at Watford, that Mary Ann was convicted.

A cake was delivered by post to Caroline at the Asylum, which she quickly and greedily ate. It contained phosphorus and poor Caroline collapsed and died in agony. Mary was convicted on circumstantial evidence, allegedly to claim on an insurance policy for about £10. Their brother reputedly confessed to the murder on his deathbed some years later.

Also hanged this day:

1893   at Worcester Prison: Amie Meunier for the murder of an old woman.

1911   at Leicester Prison: William Henry Palmer (50) for the murder of Mrs Ann Harris, a lonely old widow of Walcote, Leicestershire. *Hangman: John Ellis.* Leicester is just over 40 miles from Stafford where a more famous William Palmer, the Rugeley mass-poisoner (see 14 June), was hanged half a century earlier. This William Palmer also protested his innocence to the end, but in a less refined manner. He yelled 'Are you going to let these fellows murder me?', and threw himself at Hangman Ellis and the warders. A furious scramble took place on the floor of the condemned cell until Ellis and four warders dragged Palmer to the gallows 40 yards away, still cursing and struggling. Ellis enjoyed the scrap, in retrospect at least, when he later said that 'It was the most exciting execution of my long career'!

1951 at Norwich Castle: Dennis A.R. Moore (22) for strangling his fiancée Eileen Cullen (21), and Alfred G. Reynolds (24) for the gun-murder of his girlfriend Ellen M. Ludkin (19). These two labourers murdered their pregnant girlfriends in otherwise unrelated crimes. *Hangman: Albert Pierrepoint. Assistants: Harry Allen (Manchester), Syd Dernley and Leslie Stewart*

20 July

1934 NEIGHBOURS
William Alfred Bayly (28) hanged at Auckland Prison, New Zealand, for the murder of neighbours Samuel Pender Lakey and his wife Christobel Lakey. Bayly might have killed before.

Bill Bayly, married with two children, worked a dairy farm owned by his father at Ruawaro, about 60 miles south of Auckland. His father had sold an adjoining farm to Sam and Christobel Lakey some years before. Bill Bayly resented the sale, thinking that his father should have kept both farms for him.

He made himself as objectionable as possible to the Lakeys. It was more than neighbourly bickering: there was a dispute about a boundary, about the terms for Bayly's sheep grazing on the Lakey farm, even about the Lakeys' dog chasing Bayly's bull. Bayly threatened to get his friends, Lakey's creditors, to force the Lakeys off the farm and out of the district: 'You won't see the next season out, Lakey!'

The Lakeys were capable of harsh words too; Christobel snapped at Bayly 'You murdered Elsie Walker* and your conscience is hurting you. I wouldn't be surprised if we got the same treatment!' Murder them he did. On Sunday 15 October 1933 he shot Sam Lakey in a shed by Lakey's farmyard, as was later proved by blood stains on boxes and the inside wall of the shed. He then battered Christobel about the head until she was almost dead, stuffed her body into mutton sacks and dumped it face down in the duckpond.

Bayly carted Sam's body away and took it to his own cowshed, where he burnt it to ashes in an oil drum. Another farmer later reported that he had seen the smoke billowing out from Bill Bayly's

240

cowshed that Sunday evening: 'It seemed to go up about 20 feet in the air. It hung low and did not blow away.'

Bayly had also taken some guns belonging to Sam Lakey, a suit, and all the men's shoes in the cupboard, probably hoping that Sam's disappearance would cause the police to suspect that he had murdered his wife and fled.

Christobel's body was found on the Monday morning and the police were called. One of the pairs of missing shoes belonged to another neighbour and Sam would not have taken those with him as they were much too small for him to wear. The police now realised that Sam may also have been killed. Other evidence was gathered to support the theory of a double murder. Bill Bayly's obstructive attitude to the investigators at his farm made him a suspect, but there was not yet enough to arrest him. He went into hiding in December and the search of his property was intensified.

Hundreds of items were found that forensic investigators proved to be the remains from Sam Lakey: tiny bits of scorched bone, some hair and burned scalp, buttons, part of Lakey's cherrywood pipe, part of his cigarette lighter (with a distinctive homemade wick matching wool from Christobel's workbox). The ashes had been hidden in different places on Bayly's farm, including the sheepdip pit. Lakey's guns were found submerged in the swamps bordering the two farms.

Bill Bayly surrendered himself to a solicitor and he was charged. He went on trial at Auckland on 21 May 1934 and it lasted until 23 June. The prosecution called over 70 witnesses and produced more than 250 forensic exhibits. The defence called no witnesses. The trial lasted five weeks, but the jury needed less than an hour to find its verdict: guilty of double murder. Bayly never made a confession. Petitions for clemency were rejected and he was hanged at 8 a.m. on 20 July.

* *Bayly had been arrested five years earlier and held on suspicion of murdering his cousin, Elsie Walker, but had to be released because of lack of evidence.*

Also hanged this day:

1729 at Tyburn Tree: John Everett for highway robbery.

1802 at York: Martha Chappell for the murder of her new-born child.

21 July

1989 MALAYSIA'S ANTI-DRUG LAWS
Derrick Gregory (38) of Richmond, Surrey, hanged in Malaysia for drug-trafficking.

Importing narcotics into Malaysia is a capital offence and is vigorously enforced, as a huge multi-languaged notice at the airport makes clear. There was no doubt that Gregory was guilty of the crime, having been caught in possession of the drugs. It was contended by his defender that Gregory was retarded, with the mental development of a minor.

In 1987 six Malaysian drug smugglers were hanged in one month and international coverage was given to the similar conviction and hanging of the British Kevin Barlow and Australian Brian Chambers at Pudu Prison in Kuala Lumpur the previous year (see 7 July).

Also hanged this day:

1700 at Stafford: George Caddell for the rape and murder of Miss Price.

1823 at Old Bailey: John Wilford for burglary; Robert Rowe for house-breaking; William Samuel Mills and John Smith for issuing forged notes.

1891 at Wandsworth Prison: Franz Joseph Munch for the murder of James Hickey.

1896 at Winchester Prison: probably Britain's last triple hanging. Frederick Burden (24) for the throat-slitting murder of his mistress, Angelina Faithful, an adulterous married woman. Phillip Matthews (32) for the murder of his child, Elsie Gertrude Matthews (4). Private Samuel Edward Smith, King's Royal Rifles, for the gun-murder of Corporal Robert Payne in the barracks. *Hangman: James Billington. Assistant: William Warbrick, for some reason using his original name of Wilkinson for this execution.*

1903 at Leicester Prison: Porter and Preston for the murder of a policeman at Sileby.

22 July

Hanged this day:

1818 at Old Bailey: Thomas Clark for highway robbery.

242

1829 at Old Bailey: Charles Jones for issuing forged notes.

1870 at Atlanta, Georgia, USA: James Jeter Phillips confessed on the gallows to the murder of his wife Mary.

1902 at Winchester Prison: William Churcher for the murder of Sophia Jane Hepworth at Gosport. In accordance with new regulations, the prison bell was tolled after the execution, but the black flag was not hoisted.

23 July

1957 MURDER DURING BURGLARY
John Vickers (22) hanged at Durham Gaol for the murder of a 72-year-old woman, a shopkeeper, during a burglary.

Vickers was the first person to be hanged since August 1955. He was, therefore, the first person to be executed under the Homicide Act of 1957 whereby five types of murder carried the death penalty. For further details of the Act see the British Hanging Chronology.

Also hanged this day:

1812 at Chester: Jane Lomas for the murder of her husband.

1880 at Toronto, Canada: Bennet a.k.a. Dickson for the murder of Senator George Brown.

24 July

1735 WAYWARD PURITAN
Patience Boston (22), a Puritan, hanged at York, Maine, USA, for the murder of Benjamin Trot (8).

Patience Boston was a decidedly unusual young Puritan who lived in Falmouth in Maine. She was either mad or had set out to disobey everything that was required of a Puritan. She smoked, drank, lied, cursed, and was a thief. Her final transgression was the murder of eight-year-old Benjamin Trot. She was seen to pick him up from where he had been playing and, clearly in a violent fury, hurl him down a well-shaft where he drowned. Some say it was a random attack although she claimed that he had walked on her toe. She was hanged at York, the first woman to be hanged in Maine.

Also hanged this day:

1829   at Glasgow: Mr and Mrs Stewart for murder.

1880   at Calcutta, India: George Nairns for the murder of a native policeman.

25 July

1961 A DRUNKEN RAGE
Samuel McLaughlin (40) hanged at Crumlin Road Gaol, Belfast, Northern Ireland, for the murder of his wife Nellie (32).
Hangman: Harry Allen. Assistant: Rickard

Sam McLaughlin's marriage with Nellie was going through a bad time. She had moved to a cottage at Lislaban near Cloughmills in County Antrim and he hoped to get her to take him back. He was a rough, tough, foundry worker who spent a lot of his wages on drink. It was the drinking that caused most of his matrimonial difficulties and, there is little doubt, was to lead to him murdering his wife.

He spent the night of 17 October 1960 drinking with Nellie and they went back to her cottage and went to bed. An argument developed and he attacked her with a broom handle as she lay in bed. He stood over her and, in his drunken rage, battered her head time and time again. She moved her head from side to side trying to avoid the blows, but they continued to rain down. Her blood was splashed over the wall behind her and on the pillow and bedclothes. Before she was quite dead, he strangled her with one of her stockings. Then he got up and left.

Nellie's mother called round on the morning of 19 October and could get no answer. The blinds were still drawn and she feared the worst. A policeman was called and he had to break a window to get in: then the worst was confirmed. McLaughlin was arrested the same day.

At the first trial the all male jury failed to agree. At the second trial a defence of insanity was put forward, claiming that his alcohol-befuddled mind prevented him from knowing what he was doing or that what he was doing was wrong. Drunkenness has never been an acceptable excuse for murder, or any other crime for that matter, and he was found guilty and sentenced to death. Three appeals failed. It was reported that he shook hands with Hangman Harry Allen before being pinioned. His was the first hanging at a Belfast gaol for nearly 20 years.

Also hanged this day:

1723   at Execution Dock, Wapping: Captain John Massy for piracy.

1893 at Old Bailey: PC George S. Cooke for the murder of Maud Merton.

1899 at Lincoln Prison: Edward Bell for wife-murder.

1941 D. M. Jennings for the murder of Albert Farley at Dorchester.

1952 at Bordeaux Jail, Montreal, Canada: the cripple Genereux Ruest for his part in the 'Love Bomb Murder' (see 12 January). He arrived at the gallows in his wheelchair and was transferred to a stool on the trap doors. The hangman miscalculated the length of drop, and Ruest took 21 minutes to die by strangulation.

26 July

1736 OPEN THE BOX!
Thomas Reynolds hanged at Tyburn Tree for highway robbery.
Hangman: John Thrift

After being cut down his body was placed in the waiting coffin. The hangman's assistant fell into a faint as he was nailing down the lid – Reynolds had revived and, pushing aside the lid, had grabbed his arm! The hangman, John Thrift, considered it his duty to hang Reynolds again but the mob seized the unfortunate fellow and took him to a nearby house. One of the broadsheets of the day claimed that Reynolds then 'vomited three pints of blood, but on giving him a glass of wine he died'.

Also hanged this day:

1815 at Old Bailey: Eliza Fenning (21) for administering arsenic with intent to kill her employers. Hanged with her were Abraham Adams and William Oldfield. *Hangman: John Langley*

1817 at Meadville, Pennsylvania, USA: George Speth Vanhollen for the axe-murder of Hugh Fitzpatrick in the victim's log cabin while robbing him of $40. Vanhollen threw the hangman over the side of the scaffold seconds before being executed!

1833 in the USA: Joel Clough for the murder of Mrs Mary W. Hamilton, who had laughed at his declaration of love.

1876 at Durham Gaol: John Williams for the murder of his brother-in-law.

1892 at Devizes Prison: John Gurd (a.k.a. Louis Hamilton) for the murder of Henry Richards.

1904 at Glasgow: Thomas Gunning for the murder of his sweetheart Agnes Allen.

1944 at Strangeways Prison, Manchester: James Galbraith for the axe-murder of another merchant seaman, James William Percey, on board the *Pacific Shipper* in Salford Dock.

27 July

1820 THE WICKED SQUIRE'S VALET
Stephen Sullivan (32), hanged at Gallows Green, Limerick, Ireland for the murder of Ellie Hanley (15). He was the valet and accomplice to John Scanlan (26), Squire of Ballycahane Castle.

Squire Scanlan had been hanged at Gallows Green immediately after his trial on 10 March 1820, to prevent his influential family and friends obtaining a reprieve or pardon. The Squire's family may have been unable to prevent the execution, but for 12 months they succeeded in suppressing the story from being reported in the newspapers.

Meanwhile, the man who had actually beaten Ellie Hanley to death in such a cruel manner had escaped from the scene of the murder, at Glin in July 1819, and was still at large. This was Stephen Sullivan, the Squire's valet and former army batman. That he had eluded justice for so long was undoubtedly because the news of the murder was known only by word of mouth in the immediate area of Glin and Limerick, thanks to the determination of the Scanlans to avoid disgrace and scandal.

The authorities wanted him, but where was he? It was known that Squire Scanlan had rejoined the army soon after the murder, and had just as quickly deserted, but Sullivan had not been with him then. Most people believed that he had gone abroad. In fact the audacious villain was only 30 or so miles away, at Scartaglen, where he was living comfortably under a different name. The 'luck of the Irish' was with him, or so it seemed, because at about the time that Scanlan was being tried and hanged the former valet was marrying a local heiress!

His luck deserted him in May 1820. He was charged with being a counterfeiter, of which he was probably innocent, and held in Tralee County Gaol. If this were not bad enough, someone there recognised him as the wanted murderer of Ellie Hanley. A message was sent to the Knight of Glin, who had Sullivan taken to Limerick to face the murder charge.

Stephen Sullivan had to stand in the same courtroom and the same dock as had his master, Squire Scanlan. Like his late master, he was found guilty and sentenced to die on the same gallows. However, their

246

final exits were not identical: whereas Scanlan had insisted to the end that he was innocent, Sullivan made a full written confession, and this was later to be widely published.

Almost exactly a year after the crime, Sullivan stood awaiting execution on Gallows Green and uttered his final words: 'I declare before Almighty God that I am guilty of the murder, but it was Mr Scanlan who put me up to it.'

Copies of his verbatim confession were avidly read across Ireland and filtered to mainland Britain, eventually being repeated in the *Newgate Calendar*. In 1824 the story of the murder was thinly disguised as fiction and 'The Poor Man's Daughter' was included in the two-volume *Tales of Irish Life* by Michael James Whitty. In 1829 the novel *The Collegians* by Gerald Griffin was based on the murder.

In the 1840s there were operas, *The Bohemian Girl* by Michael William Balfe and *Maritana* by William Vincent Wallace. Then came a successful stage play, *The Colleen Bawn* by Dion Boucicault, and by now Ellie was lifted almost to saintliness. *The Lily of Killarney* was the most famous work based upon the murder of young Ellie. It was an 1862 opera by Julius Benedict that was still being performed in the early decades of the twentieth century.

Also hanged this day:

1816 at Old Bailey: Joseph Boyce, William Gregory, and George Haycock for issuing forged notes.

1817 at York: William King for murder.

1875 at Warwick Gaol: Jeremiah Corkery for the murder of Mr Lines.

1880 at Maidstone Prison: Thomas Berry (37) for the murder of his estranged mistress, Caroline Adams, at the Leather Bottle tea-garden at Belvedere. *Hangman: William Marwood*

1886 at Shrewsbury Prison: William Samuels for the murder by poisoning of William Mabbots at Welshpool.

1897 at Lincoln Prison: Joseph Bowser for wife-murder.

1920 at Pentonville Prison: Arthur Goslett (a.k.a. Captain Arthur Godfrey RN), conman and bigamist, for wife-murder.

1926 at Pentonville Prison: Johannes Josephus Cornelius Mommers for the murder of Augusta Violette Pionbini.

1928 at Horfield Gaol, Bristol: William John Maynard (36) for the murder of wealthy recluse Richard Francis Roadley (84).

28 July

1865 'YE SHOULD HAVE SEEN PRITCHARD'S!'
Dr Edward William Pritchard (40) hanged at Glasgow Jail Square, the last person to be publicly hanged in Glasgow, for the poisoning of his wife and mother-in-law (70).
Hangman: William Calcraft

Dr Pritchard served as an assistant surgeon in the Royal Navy for five years. He married and went into general practice in Yorkshire for some years but was strongly disliked for his arrogant behaviour, bragging, lying and womanising. He had to move on.

He moved with his wife and five children to start afresh in Glasgow in 1860, but he didn't change his unpleasant ways. He apparently had a high sex-drive. He preyed on servant-girls and his wife caught him in a compomising situation with one of them, Mary M'Cleod (15). When Mary M'Cleod became pregnant Pritchard performed an abortion and obtained her silence by promising to marry her if Mrs Pritchard died. Another servant-girl died in a fire at his house in 1863 and, strangely, she had made no attempt to get out of bed to avoid the flames. There was a suspicion that she may have been unconscious at the time.

Pritchard moved his family and practice to Sauchiehall Street, Glasgow, using money provided by his mother-in-law Mrs Taylor. His wife, Mary Jane, became ill in November 1864 and went to stay at her mother's house in Edinburgh, where she recovered. Back in Glasgow, in February she became ill again and Dr Pritchard declared that she was too ill to be moved to hospital. He must have been dismayed when her formidable mother came to nurse Mary Jane.

The robust mother-in-law soon fell ill herself, and died on 24 February 1865. Dr Pritchard signed the death certificate, giving the cause of death as apoplexy. Mary Jane lasted until 18 March and her death certificate was also signed by Pritchard, with gastric fever being given as the cause. The circumstances were very suspicious and an anonymous letter started an investigation. The bodies were exhumed and found to contain fatal quantities of the poisons aconite and antimony. Chemists' records revealed that Dr Pritchard had bought quantities of both poisons in the months since December and he was charged with the murders.

He was tried at Edinburgh in July 1865 and he was found guilty by the jury, who had retired for an hour. He confessed to both killings on the day before his execution. A hundred thousand watched the hanging in Jail Square, the last public execution in Glasgow. Pritchard was given the short drop, usual at that time, and his death was by strangulation.

Dr Dunlop, the Glasgow surgeon, often told audiences of hanged corpses being found to have firm erections and even to have ejaculated where death did not come instantaneously. He would finish his tales with the punchline 'Ah man, ye should have seen Pritchard's!'

Also hanged this day:

1721 at Tyburn Tree: Matthew Clark for the murder of a young woman while kissing her.

1809 at Chester: William Proudlove and George Glover for robbery and shooting.

1819 at Old Bailey: Charles Wright and Benjamin Noble for burglary.

1838 at the Tombs Prison, New York, USA: Edward Coleman for the throat-cutting murder of his bride of a few days, in the middle of a Manhattan street. This was the first hanging at the Tombs Prison.

1870 at Richmond Prison, Dublin: Andrew Carr for the infamous Bull Lane murder of prostitute Margaret Murphy. Carr was decapitated by the hanging, followed by a grisly three minutes of the body twitching.

1891 at Lincoln Prison: Arthur Spencer for the murder of Mary Ann Garner.

1903 at Lincoln Prison: Leonard Pachett for wife-murder.

1908 at Strangeways Prison, Manchester: Fred Ballington for the knife-murder of his wife Ann in front of witnesses in the compartment of a train waiting at London Road station in Manchester. *Hangman: Henry Pierrepoint. Assistant: William Willis*

29 July

1879 KATE WEBSTER'S DRIPPING
Kate Webster a.k.a. Catherine Lawler (30) hanged at Wandsworth Prison for the murder and dismembering of her employer Mrs Julia Martha Thomas, in response to being sacked.
Hangman: William Marwood

The hard-drinking Irishwoman, Katherine Webster, convicted thief and prostitute, was employed as cook-housekeeper to the crotchety old Mrs Thomas at No 2 Vine Cottages in Park Road, Richmond, Surrey in January 1879. On the night of Sunday 2 March, when Kate had been drinking, Mrs Thomas returned from church and a fierce argument developed which resulted in Kate Webster being sacked.

Webster hit her mistress with an axe and continued until she had killed her. This she followed up by cutting her mistress to pieces on the kitchen floor. Even this gruesome task was interrupted by a quick visit to a local pub for refreshment. She boiled most of the dismembered bits in the kitchen copper, throwing others on the fire.

She set about distributing different parts of her former employer around London, throwing some in the Thames. She is also reputed to have sold two large jars of dripping to someone in a nearby pub. Then she sold her victim's furniture and clothes wherever she could find a buyer and fled back to Ireland.

She was found in her home town of Killane in County Wexford, still wearing Mrs Thomas' clothes and with some of the jewellery that she had not been able to sell. Charged with theft from, and the murder of, her employer, she screamed and raged at her accusers, denying everything and throwing counter accusations at others. Her trial at the Old Bailey was the sensation of the day, and when she was found guilty and sentenced to death, she still denied it all and raged at her treatment.

During her last night as she awaited death in Wandsworth, with all chance of reprieve gone, Kate Webster made a full confession of her awful crimes. She went to bed at 10 p.m. and slept reasonably well, rising at 5 a.m. The prison bell started to toll the death-knell at 8.45 a.m. and the condemned woman was taken to the scaffold in the prison yard by the southern entry gate. Her last words were 'Lord have mercy upon me' as Marwood drew the bolt releasing the trap upon which she stood.

Also hanged this day:

1818   at Old Bailey: William Loish for wife-murder.

1834   at Chatham Lines, Kent, with the two thousand-strong garrison and twelve thousand civilians watching: Private Benjamin Gardiner (29) for the murder of Sergeant Patrick Feeney, both of the 50th Regiment. *Hangman: William Calcraft*

30 July

1924 ON THE BEAM
Lance Corporal Abraham (Jack) Goldenberg (22) of the East Lancashire Regiment hanged at Winchester Prison for the murder of bank clerk William Edward Hall (28) during a robbery.

Lance Corporal Jack Goldenberg entered the sub-branch of a bank near Bordon Camp, Hampshire, shortly before 2 p.m. on an April afternoon in 1924. He had stolen an officer's revolver and he shot the lone bank clerk in the head, twice, and at point-blank range. He left with between £500 and £1,000, locking the door of the small building as he left. The body of William Hall was discovered about an hour later.

It was realised that the bullets used in the murder were of War Office issue and an immediate roll call was carried out among the six thousand soldiers at Bordon Camp, but there were no absentees. All leave was cancelled. The camp was gripped with nervous tension, every soldier aware that there was probably a murderer in their midst. But who was it? Everyone watched the behaviour of everyone else.

Goldenberg attracted attention to himself in this tense atmosphere. He volunteered the information to the police that he had been to the bank to cash a cheque for ten shillings (50p) at 1.45 p.m. A few days later he went to them again and said 'No further developments have come to my knowledge. If anything does crop up, I'll at once notify you.' He spoke to reporters, offering theories and telling them that he had given important information to the police that should lead to the murderers being arrested.

A few days later a sergeant major observed Goldenberg behaving furtively in the vicinity of a latrine. The sergeant major went into the hut and noticed footprints on a windowsill. When he climbed on to the windowsill himself his head was level with the roof beams and, hidden on a beam, he saw a brown-paper parcel. The parcel contained about £500 in banknotes.

Goldenberg was arrested within minutes and confessed right away. He told the police everything: how he had killed Mr Hall, where he had hidden the revolver, and where the rest of the money (including bags of silver coins) were to be found. He said that he had wanted the money so that he could marry his girlfriend, explaining that he couldn't make much money in the army. A further £37 was found in his pockets and he insisted that it was his own money and had not come from the robbery; in fact he became very excited that the police should believe him on that point.

At his trial, at Winchester Assizes in June, he retracted his confession and a plea of insanity was made, but he was found guilty as charged. After the sentence of death had been intoned the hushed court was amazed when Goldenberg, seemingly oblivious of his awful situation, earnestly asked the judge for assurance that the £37 would be declared as his property!

An appeal, again pleading insanity, failed. The evidence that led to his discovery had been found on a beam and his life ended on another beam, this time in the execution chamber at Winchester Prison. In the pit below the gallows' beam, a coffin was waiting for him.

Goldenberg's coffin had been intended for another lance corporal. Albert Edward Dearnley had been sentenced to death at Winchester the previous November for the murder, during a sado-masochistic bondage game, of his friend Drummer James Frederick Ellis (21), of the Leicestershire Regiment. On the day before Dearnley's execution a reprieve arrived. Lance Corporal Jack Goldenberg, therefore, was buried in a second-hand coffin.

Also hanged this day:

1746   at Kennington Common, Surrey: Francis Townley, Esq., John Dawson, Esq., T. Chadwick, Esq., Thomas Deacon, Andrew Blood, David Morgan, and George Fletcher, for rebellion and treason. They had taken part in the Jacobite revolt in Scotland the previous year, supporting Bonnie Prince Charlie.

1794   at Boston, Massachusetts, USA: pirates John Baptist Collins, Augustus Palacha, and Emanuel Furtado, for the murder of passenger Enoch Wood on board the brig *Betsey*.

1878   at Durham Gaol: Robert Vest for the murder of a ship's pilot.

1901   at Maidstone Prison: Charles Watkins for the murder of his brother-in-law.

1902   at Derby Gaol: John Bedford for the murder of his mistress, Mrs Nancy Price.

1953   at Armley Gaol, Leeds: Private Philip Henry (25), of the King's Own Yorkshire Light Infantry for the murder of Flora Jane Gilligan (76).

31 July

1940 THE BITTER MEMORY OF AMRITSAR
Udham Singh (37), a Sikh fanatic, hanged at Pentonville Prison for the assassination inside Caxton Hall of Sir Michael O'Dwyer (75), a former Governor of the Punjab.
Hangman: Tom Pierrepoint. Assistant: Albert Pierrepoint

Udham Singh joined the audience of 160 people in the Tudor Room at Caxton Hall, in Westminster, to hear a lecture on Afghanistan. The meeting was jointly organised by the East India Association and the Royal Central Asian Society. Udham Singh knew that there would be distinguished British men of Indian affairs on the platform including the Secretary of State for India, Lord Zetland, but especially there would be Sir Michael O'Dwyer.

 Although he was in Britain as an engineer and living in Mornington

Crescent near Regent's Park, Udham Singh's life was dominated by his hatred of the British. He hated them for the continued occupation of his homeland, but there was an even more personal, and burning, hatred that the years had not mellowed: the bitter memory of the Amritsar Massacre in the Punjab 21 years earlier, when his brother had been one of 379 killed.

Sir Michael O'Dwyer had been the Governor of the Punjab when the Amritsar riot and massacre occurred, but he was not responsible for the killings. It was General Dyer who overreacted and ordered his troops to fire into the crowd in the Sikhs' holy city. A note about Sir Michael in Udham Singh's diary referred to him as 'O'Dyer': had Singh mistakenly believed that he was the hated General Dyer?

When the lecture had finished and everyone was leaving, Udham Singh went to the platform and produced his .45 Smith & Wesson revolver and fired six times at extremely close range upon the distinguished party. Sir Michael fell dead with two shots in the back, one going through the heart and lungs and the other into the kidney. Lord Zetland was more shaken than injured even though he was hit twice in the chest: he was saved by the thickness of his clothes and the fact that Singh was using ill-fitting .44 bullets which were 30 years old and had lost much of their power. Two others on the platform were injured.

Singh was overpowered before he could leave the room, and taken away to be charged with murder. His hatred had not abated: 'I did it because I had a grudge against him, he deserved it. I don't belong to any society or anything else. I don't care, I don't mind dying . . . Is Zetland dead? He ought to be, I put two in him . . . Only one dead, eh? I thought I could get more.' At his trial in June he claimed that the shooting was an accident. Nobody believed him.

Also hanged this day:

1741   at Tyburn Tree: Richard Eades for street-robbery.

1807   at Monmouth, Wales: Martha Holden for the murder of her husband.

1894   at Strangeways Prison, Manchester: William Crossley for the murder of Mary Ann Allen.

AUGUST

1 August

1831 THE SADDEST STORY IN THIS BOOK
John Any Bird Bell (14) publicly hanged at Maidstone, Kent, for the murder of Richard Faulkner Taylor (13) to rob him of his father's sickness allowance of nine shillings.
Hangman: William Calcraft

Richard Faulkner Taylor (13) was a small boy, described as being 'possessed of peculiar intelligence and an amiable disposition'. His father was a poor tallow chandler of Stroud (now Strood) near Rochester in Kent, who had been unable to work for some time because of sickness. The family were reduced to living on a weekly handout from the parish.

It was young Richard's weekly task to walk from his home in Stroud to Aylesford, about six miles to the south, to collect his father's sickness relief money of nine shillings (45p). When he set out on Friday 4 March 1831 he was wearing shoes, stockings, brown breeches, shirt, waistcoat, neckerchief, blue jacket, a sou'wester hat – and a pair of mittens. The mittens were important: his father had shown him how to conceal the money in them.

Richard arrived in Aylesford as usual and received the nine shillings from the Parish Relief Officer, Mr Cutbath, who watched as the lad carefully dropped the silver coins into a small bag and tucked it into the palm of his hand, under a mitten.

Richard set off for home but, after a couple of miles, his life's journey came to an end shortly after meeting the Bell brothers.

John Bell (14) and James Bell (11) were boys with a fair complexion and of slight but wiry stature. Their father was a menial woodgrubber who, when in work, was usually employed uprooting the stumps of felled trees. The family lived in the Poor House at Bridge Woods, about two miles north of Aylesford.

Although Mr Bell sang in the church choir and read the bible to his family on the sabbath, his religious leanings did not seem to influence his sons. John and James were rough young villains, both illiterate, and John was the worst; he had been expelled from school for threatening a teacher with violence.

The Bell brothers had met Richard Taylor on some of his earlier journeys from Stroud to Aylesford. They had learned of his reason for the weekly visits and they hatched a plan to kill the boy to get the nine shillings. They had been prevented, by unfavourable circumstances, from carrying out the plan until that awful Friday 4 March.

They met their victim on his way back, on the high road from Aylesford. They told him that they knew a track that would shorten his journey and thereby lured him into Bridge Woods. After a while they told him that they were lost and the frightened Richard Taylor lay down and began to cry.

The younger Bell, James, went off to the edge of the trees and kept watch while John cut a stick with a bone-handled pocketknife. As Richard Taylor lay sobbing, John Bell jumped on him and, after a short struggle, killed him with one stabbing cut into the throat. He encountered more difficulty in removing the money from the tightly clenched deathgrip of his victim than he had had in killing him. Once he had the money he pushed the body into a ditch and then washed the blood from his hands in a pond. He gave his brother a shilling and sixpence (7½p) as his share.

Mr and Mrs Taylor were worried when Richard did not arrive home at 3 p.m., his usual time. A search was made, but there was no trace of the missing boy. Meanwhile, near the lonely track in Bridge Woods, the Bell brothers (as they later admitted) walked past the body of their victim on most days without a care*.

The body was discovered after ten weeks; it was greatly decomposed and maggots had destroyed the face. It was clear that the boy had been murdered and it was not considered necessary to carry out a medical examination, or even search the rotting and stinking clothes. The body was quickly buried in the condition in which it had been found.

A search of the immediate area of the ditch uncovered a rusting bone-handled knife which the constable established belonged to John Bell. Mr Bell and his sons were arrested, but the father was soon released even though he was suspected of being at least an accessory after the fact. John and James had been seen with Richard Taylor by two witnesses.

The boys denied any involvement in the murder during questioning by Rochester magistrates. Two macabre incidents were staged so that the boys' reactions could be observed.

They were taken to the graveyard for the exhumation of Richard Taylor's body and when the grave was opened they were asked to search the pockets of the corpse. John remained still, maintaining a sullen silence. James cheerfully jumped into the pit and emptied the pockets, finding only Taylor's knife; the absence of the nine shillings being deemed as proof that robbery had been the cause of the murder.

John Bell had said he was hungry and some bread and cheese, with the murder knife, were placed on the table before them. John flinched and refused to touch the knife, but James picked it up and cut himself a hearty meal.

They were questioned by the magistrates again and then remanded to be held at Maidstone Prison until the trial. The younger brother, James, then broke down and tearfully admitted that John had committed the murder while he had kept watch. John confessed to the constable on the journey to Maidstone:

'It was me who committed the murder in the wood; while I cut his throat my brother went back to the gate . . . I had not much difficulty in cutting his throat; I did it at one cut; the boy was crying when I did it. He squeaked; not much, but as a rabbit would squeak . . . Torment will come to me for this, and I know I shall be hanged for it.'

(Later on the journey) 'That is the road which leads to the place where I killed the poor boy; don't you think that he is better off than me now, sir?'

John Bell was tried for murder on Friday 29 July, with James being used as chief prosecution witness. The jury found him guilty within two minutes without retiring from the courtroom, but they added a recommendation for mercy '. . . on account of his deplorable state of ignorance and the barbarous manner in which he had been brought up'. John appeared indifferent to the proceedings until that part of the sentencing to death when it was said that his body would afterwards be given to the surgeons for dissection, when he cried for the first time.

The execution was fixed for the following Monday and it was to be the first time that the new drop would be used, outside the gate of Maidstone Prison instead of at Penenden Heath. During the morning he was visited by the father of Richard Faulkner Taylor, who told the boy-murderer that he had come to give both his and Mrs Taylor's forgiveness.

The prison bell began the death-toll at 11 a.m. and John Bell fell to his knees, crying and offering up prayers. He stood firm as Hangman Calcraft pinioned his arms, but cried on the way to the scaffold and looked wildly around him when he saw the five thousand-strong crowd gathered outside to see him die.

He walked firmly, but had to be assisted on to the trap door. When a woman in the crowd was seized with a fit of hysterics he looked in her direction with alarm on his face and said 'Pray for a poor boy, pray for me.' Asked if he had anything else to say he replied 'All you people take warning by me, take warning!'

After a further slight pause, Calcraft pulled the bolt and the boy died almost without any struggling at the end of the rope. His body hung for an hour and was taken down and handed over to a surgeon. A large number of ghoulish viewers, men and women, watched the dissection in Rochester.

* *There was an unlikely story told at the time that the brothers had visited Taylor each day and that the lad was still alive on the third day.*

Also hanged this day:

1701 at Edinburgh: Reverend Thomas Hunter for the murder of his two children.

1712 at Tyburn Tree: Elizabeth Chivers for husband-murder.

1870 at Old Bailey: Walter Millar for the murder of the Reverend Elias Huelin and Ann Boss at Chelsea. *Hangman: William Calcraft*

1876 at Maidstone Prison: James Parris (32), a labourer, for the murder of William Crouch (6) by battering him on the head with a piece of iron at Ryarsh. *Hangman: William Marwood*

1887 at Lancaster Castle: Alfred Sowrey (24) for the murder of his sweetheart Annie Kelly (19). Sowrey was in a state of terror for days before the execution and had to be carried screaming to the scaffold. In the struggle he kicked Hangman James Berry's leg, which left Berry scarred for life.

1905 at Maidstone Prison: Ferat Mohamed Benali for the murder of a fellow Algerian.

2 August

1929 THE SILENCER GAVE HIM AWAY!
Russell St Clair Beitzel a.k.a. Russell Burholme (30) hanged at San Quentin Prison, California, USA, for the murder of his 'wife' Barbara Mauger (a.k.a. Mrs Barbara Burholme, a.k.a. Mrs Barbour), and her unborn baby.

The pregnant woman known as Mrs Barbara Burholme lived with her 'husband' in a flat on Golden Avenue, Los Angeles. They had met the year before, in 1927, when they both worked at a store in Philadelphia and when he was using his real name, Russell Beitzel. He got into some trouble at the store and they moved to Los Angeles and adopted the name of Burholme.

Barbara didn't know it, but Beitzel was already married. When she became pregnant she begged him to marry her, but all he would say was that he wasn't ready for it. The begging developed into nagging and, like many other men before (and after), he decided to get rid of the troublesome woman in his life. He phoned Barbara on Saturday 23 June 1928 when a neighbour, Mrs Burns, happened to be in the flat. They had arranged to go on a picnic to Stone Canyon the following day. He said he wanted to buy some ammunition so that he could practise with his gun, a .38 revolver, when they were at the canyon. He told her to get the gun from the dresser and read him the numbers on it. Barbara complied and, unwittingly, gave him the information he needed to buy the correct sized bullets with which to kill her.

They went on the picnic next day and he shot her three times and then stripped the body, leaving it to be devoured by coyotes. He went back to the flat that Sunday evening and told an unlikely story, that Barbara had suddenly decided to go and stay with relatives until the baby was born. He cleared her things out and gave up the flat a week later. The body was discovered on 2 August by two men who were driving by, and investigated when they saw buzzards circling over a part of the canyon. They found her badly decomposed, and partly devoured, naked body. Not far away a portion of a premature baby's skull was also found. The Los Angeles detectives soon linked the body to two missing persons' reports that had been anonymously filed on Barbara.

The first and only suspect was Russell Beitzel/Burholme. He told a string of lies and denied all accusations. There was plenty of circumstantial evidence, but what really sealed his conviction were the bullets recovered from Barbara's body. His revolver had a partly sawn-off muzzle, to allow him to fit a silencer. This caused distinctive markings on bullets fired from it; comparisons from test firings matched the bullets found in the body. The silencer had given him away. Russell Beitzel was hanged exactly a year to the day after the buzzards had been seen circling over his victim's torn body in Stone Canyon.

Also hanged this day:

1831   at Sterling, Connecticut, USA: Oliver Watkins for the murder of his wife by strangling her with a horsewhip. It was the last public hanging in Connecticut.

1875   at Durham Gaol: William M'Hugh for the murder by drowning of Thomas Mooney; Michael Gilligham for the murder of John Kileian; Elizabeth Pearson for the murder of her uncle, James Watson, by mixing rat poison with his medicine.

1904   at Durham Gaol: footballer George Breeze for the murder of a married woman with whom he had become involved.

3 August

1916 'TAKE ME BACK TO IRELAND'
Roger David Casement (52), formerly Sir Roger Casement, hanged at Pentonville Prison for treason.
Hangman: John Ellis

Roger David Casement was born near Dublin in 1864 when Ireland, since the Act of Union in 1800, was still a part of the United Kingdom of Great Britain and Ireland. It was to remain so until the partition of

Northern and Southern Ireland in 1921 when Southern Ireland became the Irish Free State, with Dominion status, within the British Empire. Therefore, throughout his lifetime Roger Casement was a British subject owing full allegiance to the king.

Casement joined the British consular service in 1892 and was to achieve fame after he was sent to the west coast of Africa. His dispatches to Whitehall about the plight of the oppressed natives of the Belgian Congo caused a scandal in 1903, and acclaim for himself from influential persons. In 1910, when he was serving in Brazil, he exposed more outrages; this time upon the native Indians working on rubber plantations in the Putumayo River valley in Peru and Brazil. He became a hero to many British people and was knighted the following year. Soon after the knighthood, Sir Roger Casement retired from the consular service for medical reasons and received a monthly pension. He took up the Irish cause and became a fervent nationalist, but retained his knighthood, pension and, inevitably, his British citizenship.

The war between the United Kingdom and Germany began on 4 August 1914. Sir Roger Casement went to Germany on 15 October 1914 and spent 18 months in Berlin trying to persuade the German government to support an armed rebellion in Ireland. During this time he toured prisoner-of-war camps addressing Irish prisoners and trying to enlist them into his Irish Brigade to fight on the side of the Kaiser. Most gave him a hostile reception.

He thought he had achieved some success when he learned that the Germans were sending a shipment of arms to Ireland for an armed uprising in Dublin on Easter Sunday. In fact the arms shipment was a collection of obsolete weapons that the Germans had captured from the Russians earlier in the war. Casement sent a message to the rebels warning them of the inferior weapons: the message was intercepted by the British, and so was the ship carrying the arms.

Sir Roger Casement arrived in a lonely part of Tralee Bay from a German U-boat on Good Friday and was captured within a few hours. He was taken to Dublin and on to London, for trial at the Old Bailey where he was charged with treason and, being a British subject who had conspired with the king's enemies against the king in time of war, there could be only one verdict: guilty.

Many persons of national influence attempted to win Casement a reprieve, but without success. Transcripts from his private diaries were circulated by the government to prominent people, including British and American journalists, which revealed the completely irrelevant matter of his homosexual relationships.

Shortly before the execution the king revoked the knighthood that had been awarded only five years before. Therefore it was as plain Roger David Casement that the six-foot-four-inch condemned traitor accompanied Hangman Ellis to the scaffold, 'with a brave and soldierly bearing' according to Ellis. The large crowd waiting outside Pentonville Prison cheered when the certificate of execution was fixed on the gate; after all, it was wartime and Roger Casement was a traitor and a pervert as far as the British were concerned.

To the Irish, or some Irishmen at any rate, he was a national hero and martyr. Over the decades there were demands for his body to be returned to his homeland. While at Pentonville he had said, 'Don't let my body lie in this dreadful place, take me back to Ireland.' He had been buried within the prison in unconsecrated ground, as is usual with executed criminals. It was not until nearly half a century later, in February 1965, as a political move on the part of Prime Minister Harold Wilson, that his body was exhumed and sent back to Ireland. He was reburied in Glasnevin Cemetery in Dublin.

The prison officer in charge of the grim task of digging up the body found the coffin in remarkably good condition. He later received an anonymous gift of a full set of Waterford crystal from Ireland.

Also hanged this day:

1795   at Kennington Common, Surrey: Jeremiah Lewis Avershaw (22), flamboyant highwayman, for the murder of a policeman. His body was afterwards hung in chains on Wimbledon Common.

1818   at Maidstone: Charles Hussey for the murder of Mr Bird and his housekeeper at Greenwich.

1820   at Godalming: John Chennell Junior and Thomas Calcraft for the murder of John Chennell Senior.

1885   at Nottingham Prison: Joseph Tucker for the murder of Elizabeth Williamson.

1898   at Carnarvon Prison, Wales: Thomas Jones for the murder of a woman at Festining.

1943   at Winsom Green Prison, Birmingham: William Quayle (52) for the murder of Vera Clark (8).

4 August

1862 THE MURDER STILE
George Jacob Gilbert (30) hanged at the gate of Winchester Prison, Hampshire, for the savage murder of Miss Mary Ann Susan Hall (23), a virgin, on her way to church.
Hangman: William Calcraft

George Gilbert was a rough brute with a criminal record of rape, burglary, highway robbery, poaching and lesser offences. Mary Hall was a virtuous young lady who lived with her father and stepmother at Midgham Farm a mile or so away from Fordingbridge. She was engaged to a cousin.

It was a part of Mary's Sunday routine to attend two services at Fordingbridge Church, each time walking along a path through the fields from her home to the church. She had been accosted more than once on these journeys by George Gilbert uttering coarse remarks to her, which she tried to ignore.

On the last day of her life, Sunday 22 June 1862, Mary left Midgham Farm alone at 10 a.m. and, as was usual in those days when attending church, she was wearing her best clothes: a white bonnet with green flowers, a cloak with silk tassels, and kid gloves. She was also carrying a parasol and two religious books. When she reached the stile separating her father's farm and a neighbour's she was intercepted and savagely attacked by George Gilbert*.

Mary responded with a spirited resistance, but Gilbert's greater strength prevailed and he dragged her to a more secluded spot 138 yards away. The last 15 yards was along a foul-smelling ditch hidden by furze bushes on either side.

A second fierce struggle ensued with Gilbert tearing at Mary's clothing and reducing her underwear to tattered rags. Denied his aim of sexual gratification by Mary's fight to retain her virginity, he ended the attack by partly strangling her and pressing her head down into the mud and slimy water.

George Gilbert was seen in the area by various people, and his clothes were wet and muddy. In an attempt to cover up his own involvement, he went to the local constable at 4 p.m. with the parasol. He reported finding it while out walking across the fields and said that he had discovered a woman's body in the nearby ditch. But it was no good: witnesses came forward to report his previous behaviour towards Miss Hall on that path. Others said that they had seen him in the vicinity of the crime at the time of the murder. Gilbert could not satisfactorily explain his soaked and muddy trousers, nor the similarly wet and stained boots and stockings found at his lodgings. (Months later, during repairs to the roof of Gilbert's lodgings, a workman found some trinkets hidden in the thatch which had been worn by Mary on the day she died.) The sexton of Fordingbridge Church had particularly noticed that Gilbert's boots were hobnailed all around the soles, and not, as was usual, on just the heels and toes. At the murder scene he saw footprints corresponding to the pattern of Gilbert's unusual hobnailed boots.

There were 22 prosecution witnesses at the trial; the defence called none, not even the accused, and the jury needed only 15 minutes' retirement to find him guilty. Sentencing him to death, the judge told Gilbert: 'Time will be given to you, that time and opportunity which you denied to your unhappy victim . . . you shall have some time at least to think over your past career in this world and to prepare for that which is to come.' Only a few days before her death, Mary Hall had had a fearful dream. The next morning she told the family, 'I dreamt that I was going to be put to death by someone who would not give me time to say my prayers, even though I earnestly begged for time to do so.'

George Gilbert must have heeded the judge's words during his 16 days in the condemned cell, which included the three sabbaths that the law now required between sentencing and execution. During that time he received visits from the chaplain and made a full confession to the murder.

The murder of Mary Hall had aroused enormous interest and a reported ten thousand gathered to see Gilbert hanged at the gate of Winchester Prison. The authorities feared that there would be a disturbance, such were the feelings against the murderer, but the well-dressed crowd, which included an unusually large number of women, was orderly, and there was no trouble.

Hangman Calcraft did not pinion Gilbert in the condemned cell. He walked freely and unaided, with the chaplain at his side, from the cell to a room behind the gate. Calcraft then fixed a leather belt around Gilbert's waist and pinioned the arms just above the elbows with shorter straps attached to the main belt. When the trap was released there was only a short drop and George Gilbert died after a series on muscular convulsions which lasted some little time.

The crowd watched more or less silently. One man fainted and was carried away, but the women were reported to have watched with greater calm than the men.

* *The stile is still there to this day, separating Midgham Farm and Harding's Field. It is now known by local people as the murder stile.*

Also hanged this day:

1896   at Strangeways Prison, Manchester: Joseph Hirst for the murder of a child.

1908   at Durham Gaol: Matthew James Dodds for wife-murder.

5 August

1931 'MOOSH' AND 'TIGGY'
William 'Moosh' Shelley (57) and Oliver 'Tiggy' Newman (61) hanged for the murder of Herbert William 'Pigsticker' Ayres (45).

The world depression, which began in America in 1929, reached Britain in 1931 and the number of unemployed doubled to nearly three million. The nation faced bankruptcy and hard times were experienced by everyone but, as always, the ones who suffered most were those who were already at the lowest social level. Among them were the central characters in this story.

An area of wasteland between the Watford and Barnet bypass roads was inhabited by tramps, the occasionally employed, the permanently unemployed, and society's unemployable misfits. They lived among the weeds and sprawling brambles, in any rough shelter they could construct from waste material scavenged from the nearby rubbish tip at Scratchwood Sidings. There was no camaraderie among these down-and-outs: it was a hostile environment where each man looked after his own interests. Real names were hardly used; most were known by nicknames.

Moosh and Tiggy (William Shelley and Oliver Newman) were one step up the social scale, sometimes getting casual work with gangs of navvies and consequently living better than many others: in a wooden hut with floorboards and a canvas roof. They were a belligerent and beer-sodden pair who kept three fierce dogs to guard their hut and who were feared by the others.

When Moosh and Tiggy caught Pigsticker (William Herbert Ayres) stealing some of their tea and sugar they gave him a peremptory beating and sent him on his way. They permitted a fellow navvy, John Armstrong, to bed down for the night on the floor of their hut on 30 May 1931. He was woken late at night when Moosh and Tiggy returned from a pub. Looking out he saw them bludgeoning Pigsticker to the ground and then loading him into a sack and carrying him away on a pole. Fearing for his own life, Armstrong went back to bed and pretended to have been asleep all the time.

Moosh and Tiggy took Pigsticker to Scratchwood Sidings and buried him in the smouldering rubbish. The body was found on 2 June, badly burned, and was almost unrecognisable. However there was a tattoo of a red heart transfixed with a sword on the unburned left forearm. From the tattoo, and the surviving tatters of his clothes, he was identified by some of the watching inhabitants.

When questioned by the police, Armstrong told them about the fight he had witnessed. Moosh and Tiggy were arrested and the murder weapon, a blood-stained axe, was found hidden under the floorboards of the hut. The pair cheerfully admitted that they had killed Pigsticker. Why? An amount of bread and bacon was missing from the hut and they had assumed that Pigsticker had been stealing from them again. But had he? Armstrong was revealed as a thief during the murder trial at the Old Bailey: while giving evidence he produced an alarm clock from his pocket and Moosh exclaimed, 'Blimey, Tiggy! Look at that, he's pinched our clock!' Perhaps they had killed the wrong man! After being sentenced to death, Moosh made the strange comment that it was 20 years late. Had he murdered before?

Also hanged this day:

1678 at Westover, Virginia, USA: Thomas Hellier, a slave, for the axe-murder of his master and his wife and their maid.

1723 at Execution Dock, Wapping: Philip Roche for piracy and murder.

1870 at New York, USA: Cab driver John Real for the gun-murder of policeman John Smedick, who he claimed demanded payments not to harrass him.

1896 at Derby Gaol: William Pugh (21) for the murder of Elizabeth Boot (19).

6 August

1795 SLAVE'S REVENGE FOR NAKED WHIPPING
Pomp, a slave, hanged at Ipswich, Massachusetts, USA, for the axe-murder of his master Captain Charles Furbush.

Captain Furbush caught Pomp in the act of trying to run away. He had the slave stripped naked and cruelly flogged as an example to the other slaves. Then he had Pomp suspended from a beam in the barn and left there all night to suffer at the end of the rope.

Pomp took his revenge one night when his master was asleep in bed, hitting him repeatedly on the head with an axe.

Also hanged this day:

1759 at Tyburn Field, York: Eugene Aram (55) for the murder of a shoemaker, Daniel Clark, 14 years earlier in Knaresborough. Eugene Aram's skull survives to this day, in a glass case at the museum of the Royal College of Surgeons of England at Lincoln's Inn Fields, London. The case also holds the skeletons of 'Thief-taker General' Jonathan Wild (see 24 May) and Red Barn murderer William Corder (see 11 August).

1811 at Salisbury, Wiltshire: Samuel Tucker.

1883 at Durham Gaol: James Burton for the murder of Elizabeth Sharpe.

7 August

Hanged this day:

1834   at Maidstone: Thomas Hammond (21) for the rape-murder of Mrs Sarah Rigden at Wingham, halfway between Sandwich and Canterbury. *Hangman: William Calcraft*

1888   at Strangeways Prison, Manchester: John Jackson for the murder of Warder Webb during an escape attempt. *Hangman: James Berry.* (See 15 May.)

1907   at Walton Gaol, Liverpool: Charles Paterson for the murder of Mrs Lilian J. Charlton.

8 August

1944 HITLER PLOTTERS HANGED WITH PIANO WIRE IN PLOTZENSEE PRISON, BERLIN

This was the first trial of conspirators in the failed plot to blow up Hitler at his headquarters on 20 July. Hitler survived and a reign of terror followed. The Gestapo recorded seven thousand arrests and the ensuing death-roll is believed to have been 4,980.

The trial had been the usual bitter mockery of justice for which the Reich Peoples' Court in Berlin, under its fanatical President Dr Ronald Freisler*, had become infamous. The eight German army officers on trial had already been expelled from the army and had suffered torture by the SS. They were further humiliated at this travesty of a trial by being forced to wear oversized civilian clothes, without belts or braces, and having to hold up their trousers as the president and prosecutor ranted at them.

Field Marshal von Witzleben was reduced from the proud man he had once been to a toothless wreck, his false teeth having been taken from him. Shaking and trying to keep his trousers from falling down, he was shouted at by the sneering Freisler, 'You dirty old man! Why do you keep fiddling with your trousers?'

Even the so-called defence attorneys, appointed by the court, railed against their 'clients'.

The defendants were:

Field Marshal Erwin von Witzleben. Had the July 20 plot succeeded he would have become Commander in Chief of the German army.

Colonel General Erich Hoeppner. Former chief of the home army,

268

to have been Commander in Chief of the reserve army after the plot.

Lieutenant General Paul Von Hase

Lieutenant General Bernardis

Major General Hemuth Stieff

Reserve Lieutenant Colonel Dr Hans Von Hagen

Captain Karl Klausing

Reserve Lieutenant Count Peter Yorck Von Wartenburg. To have been Secretary of State in the Reich Chancellery after the plot.

'They must be hanged like cattle' were the orders from Hitler: they were. A mere two hours after the trial they were hanged in a small room in Plotzensee Prison, Berlin. They died by slow, agonising strangulation in nooses made with piano wire, and suspended from butcher's hooks. To add to their wretchedness some of them were naked when they were brought into the room. Others were stripped to the waist before being suspended on the hooks but, denied the use of braces or belts, they died with their trousers round their ankles.

The cruel mode of the hangings was personally devised by Hitler and filmed, with sound, for a special film show for the *Fuehrer* that same night. Hitler then gave orders for special showings of the film to troops and party officials throughout the Reich. In addition to the death sentences, all the officers' property and estates were confiscated.

* *The venomous Judge Freisler was killed by an American bomb that fell on his court on the morning of 3 February 1945.*

Also hanged this day:

1826　at Old Bailey: Charles Butcher for sheep-stealing; John Hayes for burglary.

1870　at Aylesbury Prison: John Owen for the murder, in March, of the Marshall family at Denham. Marshall was the village blacksmith, and Owen's employer. *Hangman: William Calcraft*

1923　at Nottingham Prison: Albert Edward Burrows (62) for the murder of his mistress Hannah Calladine (28), her children, and of a four-year-old boy three years later. He threw all the bodies down the same mineshaft. *Hangman: Tom Pierrepoint*

1940　G. E. Roberts for the murder of A. J. Allen.

1944　W. A. Cowle for the murder of Miss N. E. Payne; W. F. G. Meffen for the murder of Miss N. E. Stanley.

1952　at Darwin Jail, Australia: Jerry Coci (20) and Jonus Nopoty (19), Czech and Romanian immigrants, for the gun- and stabbing-murder of taxi driver George Grantham. Coci had been on the run for killing a child on the road. Right up to the day of execution, Coci and Nopoty were in danger of being lynched by the incensed public, and special guards manned the prison.

1955 at Winsom Green Prison, Birmingham: sex pervert Ernest Charles Harding (42) for the murder of Patsy Higgins (10).

1960 at Nairobi Prison, Kenya: Peter Harold Poole (28) for the murder of Kamawe Musunge. The first white man to be hanged in Kenya for the murder of a native.

9 August

1905 ONE-ARMED BIGAMIST
William Alfred Hancocks (35) hanged at Knutsford Gaol, Cheshire, for the murder of his daughter Mary Elizabeth Hancocks (15).
Hangman: John Billington. Assistant: Henry Pierrepoint

Hancocks was a one-armed sheriff's officer, and bigamist, convicted for murdering his daughter. When he went to be hanged, he left behind in the condemned cell a letter addressed to each of his wives. For this execution Henry Pierrepoint used his own innovation of a specially made leather strap for pinioning a one-armed man.

Also hanged this day:

1813 at Woodford, Essex: William Cornwell for the murder of Mrs Stephens, a local shopkeeper, watched by three thousand local people.

1856 at Dorchester: Elizabeth Martha Brown (45) for the murder of John Anthony Brown (25), her husband. *Hangman: William Calcraft.* At York: W. Dove for wife-murder by poisoning.

1867 at the Tombs Prison, New York, USA: Jeremiah O'Brien for the knife-murder of prostitute Lucy McLaughlin for stepping on his toes at a dance.

1875 at Lincoln Prison: Peter Blanchard for the murder of Louisa Hodgson.

1886 at Strangeways Prison, Manchester: Mary Ann Britland (38), first woman to be hanged at Strangeways, for the poisoning-murder of Mary Dixon at Ashton-under-Lyne. She had also poisoned her own husband and daughter, all in the hope of marrying Mary Dixon's husband (unknown by him). At her trial she interrupted the judge during sentencing with screams for mercy. Her last hour before execution was spent in continuous groans and weeping, and was still moaning weakly as she was part-carried to the scaffold and held up by warders until the trap doors were opened. *Hangman: James Berry*

1899   at Nottingham Prison: Elias Parr for murdering his daughter.

1910   at Armley Gaol, Leeds: John Raper Coulson for the throat-cutting murders of his wife and child.

10 August

1949 THE ACID BATH KILLER
John George Haigh (39) hanged at Wandsworth Prison for the gun-murder of a wealthy widow, Mrs Olive Durrand Deacon (69).
Hangman: Albert Pierrepoint

Although convicted of the murder of only Mrs Durrand Deacon, Haigh confessed to nine murders, all for monetary gain. Afterwards he disposed of the bodies in vats of sulphuric acid.

On the day before his execution he arranged for his clothes to be bequeathed to Madame Tussaud's Chamber of Horrors so as to clothe the wax model of himself. Aware of his fate, but apparently unconcerned, his gallows' demeanour has been described as 'smiling and imperious to the end'.

Also hanged this day:

1752   at Tyburn Tree: John Smith and James Butler for robbery.

1812   at Old Bailey: Thomas Bowler, described as a rich farmer, for 'maliciously shooting' and injuring Mr Burrows, another wealthy farmer of Harrow. At Maidstone: William Brown for the murder of his child.

1832   in front of Leicester Prison: James Cook for the murder and butchery of Mr Paas.

1874   at Exeter Prison: MacDonald for the murder of Bridget Welsche.

1888   at Chesterfield Prison: Arthur T. Delaney for wife-murder after repeated drunken beatings. *Hangman: James Berry*

1893   at Shepton Mallet Prison: Charles Squires for the murder of a child.

1909   at Wandsworth Prison: Julius Warmer for the gun-murder of Cissie Archer.

1910 at Newcastle Prison: John Alexander Dickman for the murder on a train of colliery cashier John Innes Nisbet, and the robbery of his bag containing £370 in wages.

1922 at Wandsworth Prison: IRA gunmen, Reginald Dunne (a.k.a. John O'Brien 24) and Joseph O'Sullivan (a.k.a. James Connelly 24), for the assassination of Sir Henry Wilson (58) outside his home in Eaton Place, London.

1926 at Durham Gaol: James Smith for wife-murder.

11 August

1828 MURDER IN THE RED BARN
William Corder (24) publicly hanged at Bury St Edmunds, Suffolk, for the 'Red Barn Murder' of Maria Marten (26), which became a popular melodrama.
Hangman: James Foxon

The story of Maria Marten and her murder in the Red Barn has been the base for countless plays, blood and thunder melodramas, penny dreadful broadsheets, books and fireside stories.

The heroine was presented as a poor-but-honest mole catcher's daughter, pure in body and heart, cruelly used by the wicked squire who had his wicked way with her. The villain was portrayed as a hulking brute of a man who spurned the innocent girl he had defiled. The baby was born, and killed by the father. The heroine was lured with a false promise to the Red Barn, Polstead, Suffolk, and horribly murdered and buried in the earth floor.

The heroine's weeping mother had a thrice-dreamed vision of the murder and secret burial which, when investigated, revealed the body to be exactly where she had dreamed it to be. The murderer was arrested and the final dramatic scene was the just retribution of the villain on the scaffold.

The facts are slightly different. Maria Marten (26), mole catcher's daughter, was living in her father's cottage near the Corder Farm. However, she was not the pure and innocent maid of legend, having had amorous affairs and an illegitimate daughter before meeting William Corder.

The villain of the piece, William Corder (24), was not the squire but a tenant farmer and son of a prosperous local landowner. He was only five foot four inches tall, of slender build and gentle appearance. He had an affair with Maria that resulted in the birth of a baby boy, who did not live long. Corder arranged a secret burial for the baby, the location of which he never revealed. His family were opposed to him

272

marrying Maria and so, most likely, was he.

Corder was under pressure from Maria and her parents to marry. On 18 May 1827 he told her that he had arranged a secret marriage in Ipswich, and that his family might try to stop the wedding. He also told her that she was about to be arrested on a bastardy warrant and must disguise herself in male clothes and meet him at the Red Barn.

Corder shot Maria in the Red Barn and buried her body in the earth floor at the furthest wall from the door. The earth was hard and dry and he had to leave the Barn to get a pick-axe and a better shovel. Maria's stepbrother saw Corder walking back to the Red Barn with the pick-axe and shovel on his shoulder. The body was buried at a depth of about 18 inches.

Corder told the Martens that Maria was lodging elsewhere to conceal the secret marriage. He remained at Polstead until September and then departed with money borrowed from his mother. He wrote to the Martens that he and Maria were living happily on the Isle of Wight, but all the letters were postmarked in London. He advertised for a wife and married, afterwards running a school for young ladies near Brentford.

Maria's stepmother claimed to have seen the murder of Maria in a dream on three successive nights in March 1828, and indicated where the body was hidden. Maria's father dug up the floor* where his wife said that Maria's body was buried and both the location of the grave and the method of murder were as she had said: was this a genuine psychic revelation, or did the Martens know more about the death than they admitted? An order was then dispatched to London for the arrest of William Corder.

Mr Lea, a police officer from Lambeth Street, traced Corder to the Brentford school and arrested him. He was taken to Bury St Edmunds and his trial began on Thursday 7 August 1828. He claimed that he and Maria had met in the Red Barn and that a bitter argument had ensued about the burial of the baby. Corder said that as he walked out of the barn, Maria had shot herself and that, in a panic, he had buried her. His story was not believed.

Corder made a written confession shortly before midnight on Sunday 10 August in the condemned cell. He was hanged in front of Bury St Edmunds Prison at midday on 11 August, watched by a crowd of seven thousand.

While James Foxon was preparing the noose, one of the officiating worthies remarked that there was too much slack rope and ordered Foxon to shorten it. Foxon had allowed that length for the drop and was offended at having his work interfered with. He obeyed, but with bad grace. As soon as Foxon had completed the adjustments, still angry, he climbed down from the platform and immediately cut the rope that held the trap door. Corder plunged through the trap while the chaplain was still building up to his final prayer.

Although Corder was therefore hanged earlier than expected, he died later than planned. Foxon had probably been right about the length of the drop because Corder struggled at the rope's end, raising his arms time and again in his death agony, and Foxon jumped and grabbed him at the waist to quicken the end. Even so, it took ten minutes for Corder to die.

William Corder's skeleton survives at the museum of the Royal College of Surgeons of England at Lincoln's Inn Fields, London. Sharing the case are the skull of Eugene Aram (see 6 August) and the skeleton of 'Thief-taker General' Jonathan Wild (see 24 May).

The following items are on public display at Moyse's Hall Museum in Cornhill, Bury St Edmunds: an account of the trial bound in Corder's skin; his scalp including one ear, and the 'mole catcher's spud', which Maria's father used to dig up her body.

Also hanged this day:

1705 at Tyburn Tree: Thomas Cook for murder and riot; Nan Holland for robbery.

1729 at Execution Dock, Wapping: Captain John Gould for piracy.

1875 in Jersey, Channel Islands: Joseph Philip Le Brun for the murder of his sister.

1879 at Exeter Gaol: Annie Tooke for the murder of an infant.

1882 at Limerick County Gaol, Ireland: Francis Hynes for the murder of Dougherty.

1896 at Nottingham Prison: Samuel Wilkinson for the murder of an old woman named Kaye; John Rose for wife-murder.

1903 at Wandsworth Prison: William Joseph Tuffen for the murder of his wife, Caroline Tuffen.

1926 at Winchester Prison: Charles Edward Finden for the murder of John Richard Thompson (15) and stealing the lad's wages of 15 shillings (75p).

1954 at Wandsworth Prison: Chelsea artist, William Sanchez de Pina Hepper (62), for the rape-murder of Margaret Rose Louise Spevick (11) at his Hove studio.

12 August

1958 KILLER FREED TO KILL AGAIN
Matthew Kavanagh (32) hanged at Winsom Green Prison for the capital murder in the course of robbery of a fellow lodger, Isaiah Dixon (60).

This was Matthew Kavanagh's second murder charge within little more than a year. He had been charged in 1957 with the murder of Mrs Evelyn Ulla (35) on wasteland near a pub in Sheldon, Birmingham. Kavanagh claimed that she had fallen down dead while he was adjusting her scarf. She was found to have died by vagal inhibition whereby pressure applied to the vagus nerve, a cranial nerve in the neck, had caused instant death. The murder charge was reduced to manslaughter. The judge stopped the trial, ruling that there was no case to answer, and Kavanagh was allowed to go free.

In the summer of 1958 he had moved to Rugby and was out of work. Broke and unable to pay his rent, he was turned out of his lodging house. He spent an evening with friends who paid for his drinks and, drunk, he returned and broke into the lodging house. Another lodger, Isaiah Dixon, was also drunk and Kavanagh decided to rob him; in the process he strangled the drunken old man with his own tie. Taking nearly £5 in notes and silver coins he went back to town and started spending some of the money. He confessed what he had done to a cafe owner, who called the police.

At his second murder trial the jury were not told of the Evelyn Ulla case, but only the facts of the Isaiah Dixon killing. The defence was that Mr Dixon may have died by accident during a struggle, vagal inhibition being suggested! The jury returned a guilty verdict within 40 minutes and, murder in the course of robbery being a capital offence at that time, Kavanagh was sentenced to death. There was no reprieve.

Also hanged this day:

1716 at Tyburn Tree: John Goodman for horse-stealing.

1749 at Tyburn Tree: William Bowen and Thomas Neale for highway robbery, with Thomas Neale raging and cursing at the spectators as he was about to be 'turned off'. Neale's burglar brother was hanged at Guildford two days later.

1844 at Bodmin Gaol, Cornwall: Mathew Weeks (22) for the murder of Charlotte Dymond (18). *Hangman: George Mitchell*

1878 at Nottingham Prison: Thomas Cholerton for the murder of Jane Smith (after which he attempted suicide).

1895 at Invercargill, New Zealand: Minnie Dean for baby-farming murders. The only woman to have been hanged in New Zealand.

1896 at the large Parade Ground, Teheran, Iran: Mirza Riza publicly hanged in front of a large crowd of troops and civilians for the assassination of the Shah of Persia, Nasr-ed-Din (65), who had reigned for 48 years.

1902 at Stafford Gaol: William Lane for the throat-cutting murder of Elizabeth Dyson.

1924 at Wandsworth Prison: Jean-Pierre Vaquier (45) for the strychnine-murder of Alfred Poynter Jones, landlord of the Blue Anchor Hotel at Byfleet, Surrey, so that he could have Mrs Jones. He had obtained poisons from a chemist in Southampton Row and signed the register as J. Wanker. *Hangman: Tom Pierrepoint*

1927 at Pentonville Prison: John Robinson for the 'Charing Cross Trunk Murder' of Mrs Minnie Bonati.

1955 at Armley Gaol, Leeds: Alec Wilkinson (22) for the murder of his mother-in-law, Clara Farrell (50), a prostitute known as the 'Green Linnet'.

1957 at Cape Town, South Africa: William Lawrence Warren Nicholson (31) for the murder of his wife Sylvia.

13 August

1868 BRITAIN'S FIRST 'PRIVATE' HANGING
Thomas Wells (18) hanged inside Maidstone Prison, for the murder of the stationmaster, Edward Adolphus Walshe, at Dover Priory railway station.
Hangman: William Calcraft. Assistant: George Smith

Thomas Wells was employed as a carriage cleaner at Dover Priory station, then a part of the London, Chatham and Dover Railway. After 18 months his work became unsatisfactory and he was often reprimanded by the stationmaster, Mr Walshe.

Wells bought a gun, which he used for shooting birds. One morning, at the end of April 1868, he indulged in target practice and the explosions could be heard all over the station. Mr Walshe was furious and told Wells that he would be reported. Wells told his workmates that he would shoot Mr Walshe. Thomas Wells was summoned to the stationmaster's office and interviewed by Mr Walshe and Mr Cox, his supervisor. He was informed that if he made a full apology to

276

Mr Walshe the matter would be closed; failing that he would either be fined or dismissed from the company. He was given ten minutes to think it over. He returned, sullen and aggressive, and said he would not apologise. He then left. While Cox and Walshe discussed what the punishment should be, Wells returned once more. He raised his gun and shot Mr Walshe in the head at point-blank range. He ran off through the station and across the lines, but was captured about 20 minutes later.

He appeared before the magistrates at the Dover Sessions and was committed to the Kent Summer Assizes at Maidstone. He was found guilty after the jury's retirement of only five minutes. When being sentenced to death he was warned not to hold out any hope for a commutation of the sentence.

Thomas Wells was the first to be hanged in a non-public execution under the Capital Punishment Within Prisons Act (which had received the royal assent on 29 May 1868). The gallows were repositioned in the former timberyard within the prison, under an iron roof against a high wall to keep it out of sight of both the cells and the nearby houses. During the morning of the execution Wells was twice treated with stimulants to prevent him fainting. When Hangman Calcraft and Smith arrived he willingly shook hands with them, but collapsed in a faint while being pinioned. He walked to the gallows wearing a blue porter's uniform with a flower in his buttonhole.

On the scaffold he was supported by a warder on each side while Calcraft fixed the noose and white hood. In a croaking voice, the boy responded to the chaplain's ministrations and tried to join in the singing of the final hymn. Calcraft signalled to Smith to pull the lever and the drop opened at 10.30 a.m., Thomas Wells fell to the newly dug pit below and his body jerked half round and then swung back again, where the waiting Calcraft steadied it. The 18-year-old boy died by slow strangulation, his strapped legs rising and lowering and his fists clenching tightly. Awful gurglings were heard coming from beneath the white hood. He took a few minutes to die with his neck and clenched hands turning first red and then blue, accompanied by convulsive shuddering of the muscles.

Also hanged this day:

1817   at Monmouth: James Harry for wife-murder.

1872   at Maidstone Prison: Royal Marine James Tooth (42) for the murder of Drummer-boy George Stock (17); Private Francis Bradford (20) for the bayonet-murder of fellow 3rd Buffs soldier Daniel Donohue in Dover Barracks; labourer Thomas Moore (42) of Ashford for wife-murder. *Hangman: William Calcraft. Assistant: George Smith*

1877 at Chester Castle: Henry Leigh for the murder of Alice Ann Haltoh (8) after robbing her.

1895 at York Castle: Robert Hudson for the murder of his wife and child.

1902 at Wandsworth Prison: George William Hibbs for the murder of Miriam Jane Tye at Battersea.

1907 at Wandsworth Prison: 'Croydon Poisoner' Richard Brinkley (53) for the prussic acid murder (by mistake) of Mr Richard Beck and Mrs Elizabeth Beck. The poisoned beer was intended for someone else. *Hangman: Henry Pierrepoint*

1915 at Maidstone Prison: George Joseph Smith (43) for the 'Brides In The Bath' murders. During his last days in the condemned cell he was frequently weeping and in terror of what was awaiting him. Despite the overwhelming proof of his crimes, he never showed remorse or admitted his guilt: his last words were still 'I am innocent'. *Hangman: John Ellis*

1937 at Pentonville Prison: Leslie George Stone (24) for the murder of Ruby Anne Keen (23).

1964 at Walton Gaol and Strangeways Prison: Peter Anthony Allen (21) and Gwynne Owen Evans (24) (real name John Robson Welby) for the murder during a robbery of John Alan West (53). They were the last men to suffer judicial hanging in Britain; others were subsequently condemned to death, but reprieved. *Hangmen: Robert Leslie Stewart in Liverpool; Harry Allen in Manchester*

14 August

Hanged this day:

1723 at Tyburn Tree: Daniel Williams, James Butler, and Wade Means, for murder and robbery.

1738 at Wicklow, Ireland: George Manley for murder.

1749 at Guildford: Benjamin Neale for burglary. His highwayman brother had been hanged at Tyburn two days earlier.

1876 at Kirkdale Prison, Liverpool: William Fish (26) for the rape-murder of Emily Mary Holland (7). At Cork County Gaol, Ireland: Richard Thompson for the stabbing-murder of John Henry Bluudel.

1877 at Horsemonger Lane Gaol: Caleb Smith for the murder of Eliza Osborne.

1894   at Newgate Prison: Paul Koczula (24) for the murder of Mrs Rasch in Shaftsbury Avenue, London.

1900   at Newgate Prison: William James Irwin hanged for wife-murder.

1907   at Cardiff Gaol: Rhoda Willis (44) for child-murder. *Hangmen: Henry and Tom Pierrepoint*

1959   at Armley Gaol, Leeds: Rotherham Technical College lecturer Bernard Walden (33), for the shooting-murder of a female student, Miss J. Moran, and her boyfriend Mr N. Saxton. Jealousy was the motive; Walden had proposed to the girl, but had been rejected. Murder by shooting was a capital offence under the 1957 Homicide Act.

15 August

1905 SUSPICIOUS MOTHER-IN-LAW
Arthur Devereux (24) hanged at Pentonville Prison for the 'trunk-murder' of his wife Beatrice (25) and their twin babies.

Mrs Gregory was with her daughter in Hastings when the girl met chemist's assistant Arthur Devereux. Young Beatrice and Arthur fell in love, married, and were soon the parents of a baby boy, Stanley. Times were hard and Arthur's income was too small to permit the three of them to live in any comfort. When Beatrice had a second pregnancy Arthur was at a loss as to how to support his growing family. It became more urgent when Beatrice was delivered of twin boys, Laurence Rowland and Evelyn Lancelot. Arthur could not earn enough money to keep a family of five.

He loved his eldest son Stanley with an intensity that excluded the undernourished Beatrice and the twins. In January 1905 he bought a tin trunk and started looking for work elsewhere. He brought home a bottle of 'cough mixture', laced with chloroform and morphine, which he induced Beatrice and the twins to swallow. They died quickly and he stuffed the bodies into the trunk, sealing the top with a layer of glue to keep the air out – and to keep in any smell of decomposing bodies. He had the trunk collected and taken to a furniture repository in Harrow. He took Stanley to live in another part of London and his wages were now enough to give them a better life style. Until his mother-in-law found them.

Mrs Gregory demanded to know why Beatrice and the twins were not with him, and was not satisfied with his feeble answers. She returned to the original Devereux neighbourhood and made enquiries.

She eventually heard about the trunk loaded on to the furniture repository's van. When she located the warehouse she informed Scotland Yard of her suspicions, and an order was issued for the trunk to be opened: the bodies were revealed.

Arthur Devereux, in the meantime, had moved on with the six-year-old Stanley and left no forwarding address. He was traced by Scotland Yard to Coventry, where he had obtained another job as a chemist's assistant. When confronted by the detective, and before the purpose of the visit was explained, he gave himself away by blurting out, 'You have made a mistake. I don't know anything about a tin trunk!' He was arrested and charged with murder. At his trial at the Old Bailey in July his defence was that Beatrice had poisoned the twins and then herself and that, finding the bodies, he had panicked (the old story!) and hidden them in the trunk. It was unlikely that the jury would have believed his story, but when it was revealed that he had applied for a job and described himself as a widower while Beatrice was still alive there was no doubt that the murders were premeditated.

Also hanged this day:

1878 at Bodmin Gaol: Selina Wadge for the murder of her illegitimate baby son.

1881 at Nottingham Prison: Thomas Brown for the murder of Elizabeth Caldwell while they were both drunk.

1893 at Stafford Gaol: John T. Hewitt for the murder of William Masfen.

1905 at Armley Gaol, Leeds: Thomas George Tattersall for wife-murder.

16 August

1264 SAVED!
Inetta De Balsham hanged at exactly 9 a.m. and seconds before the arrival of a reprieve from King Henry III.

Inetta De Balsham's crime is not known, but it may have been concerned with the civil war between King Henry III and Simon de Montfort. The king's courier arrived on horseback only seconds after De Balsham had been 'turned off'. The hangman glanced at the reprieve, ran up the steps and cut the rope with his sword. De Balsham by now had a ghastly blue face, but could still breathe and survived.

Also hanged this day:

1830   at York: William Shaw for murder.

1875   at Lancaster Castle: William M'Cullogh for the murder of William Watson; Mark Fiddler for wife-murder.

1880   at Derby Gaol: John Wakefield for the murder of a nine-year-old girl because he was tired of his own life.

1887   at Knutsford Gaol: Thomas Henry Bevan (20) for the murder of his aunt, Mrs Sarah Griffiths (59), to steal 17 shillings and 6½ pence (88p). *Hangman: James Berry*

1892   at Newgate Prison: John G. Wenzel for the murder of PC Joseph Joyce; James Taylor for wife-murder.

1893   at Chelmsford Gaol: John Davis for the murder of Police Sergeant Eves.

1900   at Armley Gaol, Leeds: Charles Buckhouse for the gun-murder of PC John Kew at Swinton; Mellor for the murder of his two children. *Hangman: James Billington. Assistant: William Billington*

17 August

1904 BUSY BILLINGTON BROTHERS
John Thomas Kay (52), a labourer, hanged at Armley Gaol, Leeds, for the murder of his mistress, Jane Hurst. Samuel Holden hanged at Winsom Green Prison, Birmingham for the murder of *his* mistress, Susan Humphries.
Hangmen: William Billington in Leeds and John Billington in Birmingham

There is a story that Holden, a market porter, walked to the scaffold smoking an expensive cigar. Apart from that, the only notable point about these executions is that the brothers Billington hanged two men in separate prisons, at the same time, each for murdering his mistress.

Also hanged this day:

1789   at Northampton: Thomas Gordon (19) for the murder of a constable.

1866   at the Tombs Prison, New York, USA: Bernard Friery for the stabbing-murder of barkeeper Henry Lazurus.

1885   at Stafford Gaol: Thomas Boulton for the murder of his niece, Elizabeth Bunting.

1892   at Kirkdale Prison, Liverpool: Patrick Gibbons for the murder of his mother.

1897   at Armley Gaol, Leeds: Joseph Robinson (33) for wife-murder; Walter Robinson for the murder of his cousin, Sarah Pickles.

18 August

Hanged this day:

1874   at York Castle: William Jackson (29) for the murder of his sister.

1891   at Armley Gaol, Leeds: Walter Lewis Turner (32) for the rape-murder and mutilation of Barbara Waterhouse (5). At Chelmsford Gaol: Thomas Sadler for the murder of William Wass.

1892   at Armley Gaol, Leeds: Moses Oudworth for wife-murder.

1897   at Walton Gaol, Liverpool: Thomas Lloyd for wife-murder.

1901   at Wandsworth Prison: Ernest Wickham for the murder of a young woman.

19 August

1692 SALEM WITCHES
Reverend George Burroughs (42), and others, hanged at Gallows Hill, Salem, Massachusetts, USA, for witchcraft.
Hangman: Sheriff John Corwin

A mad fever of hunting down supposed witches gripped the people of Salem in 1692. It all started when clergyman Samuel Parris (39) invited a group of young girls (aged 9 to 20) to his house to hear stories from his slave, Tituba. The stories involved witchcraft from her African and West Indian background and some of the girls became hysterical, or bewitched according to Parris. The girls told wild stories of witchcraft within the Puritan community of Salem and the fiery Samuel Parris led a witch-hunt, based mostly on the ravings of Anne Putnam (12).

   The colonists' mania was further inflamed by the anti-witchcraft rantings of the two prominent American divines Increase Mather (53) and his son Cotton Mather (29), especially those of the latter. The mad denunciations led to 150 innocent people being accused, of which 25 women, six men (and two dogs) were put on trial, found guilty and sentenced to death. Nineteen were hanged, two died in jail, and Giles Corey (who was in his 80s) was pressed to death. The two dogs were also hanged. The first to be hanged was Bridget Bishop on 10 June 1692, on Gallows Hill.

On 19 August 1692 the former Salem parish minister, the Reverend George Burroughs (42), was hanged with others on Gallows Hill, Salem, on the 'evidence' of Anne Putnam. After the hanging the minister's body was dragged to a grave and buried but, as a further example of the Salem madness, one hand, one foot, and his chin were left uncovered by the earth.

Another victim was Deputy Constable John Willard, for refusing to make any more arrests. One of the religious persecutors was Nicholas Noyes, who railed at Sarah Good as the poor woman stood on the gallows*:

Nicholas Noyes: 'You are a witch, confess and repent!'
Sarah Good: 'You are a liar. I am no more a witch than you are a wizard and if you take away my life, God will give you blood to drink!'
(Years later Noyes choked to death on a flow of blood from his mouth.)

During 1693 and 1694 the fever abated and the remaining accused were released. Increase Mather, not so fiery as his son, wrote a calming book. In 1697 Samuel Sewell made a public 'confession of error and guilt' for his part in condemning the 19 alleged witches who were hanged. Finally, on 17 October 1711, Governor J. Dudley signed the Order of Compensation, reversing all convictions and granting compensation to the heirs of those hanged.

* *Hanged with Sarah Good were Susanna Martin, Rebecca Nurse, Elizabeth 'Goody' How, and Sarah Wild.*

Also hanged this day:

1829 at Libberton's Wynd, Edinburgh: blacksmith John Stuart and his wife Catherine for the murder and robbery of Robert Lamont, a rich farmer, on board the River Clyde ferryboat *Toward Castle*.

1884 at Kirkdale Prison, Liverpool: Peter Cassidy for wife-murder.

1891 at Wandsworth Prison: Robert Bradshaw for wife-murder.

1922 at Winchester Prison: Thomas Henry Allaway (36) for the rape-murder of Irene Wilkins at Bournemouth. Allaway, employed as a chauffeur, responded by telegram to an advertisement placed by Irene Wilkins in the *Morning Post* seeking employment as a cook, intending to rape her.

20 August

**1857 AND 1863 TWO DOUBLE PUBLIC HANGINGS AT
MAIDSTONE**
**In 1857 George Kebble Edwards (18) was hanged for the axe-murder
at Maidstone of his brother, Thomas Edwards. Stephen Fox (23)
hanged for the gun-murder of his sweetheart, Mary Ann Hadley (25),
at St Mary Northgate, Canterbury.**
**In 1863 Alfred Eldridge (33), a labourer, was hanged for the murder
by kicking of Richard Steed (55) at Herne. Private Alfred Holden (25),
Royal Artillery, hanged for the throat-cutting murder of his infant
son, Alfred James Holden, at Gillingham.**
Hangman: William Calcraft on both occasions

Alfred Eldridge was a former soldier of good character who had
served in the Crimean War and during the Indian Mutiny. He
murdered the former 'Herne carrier', Richard Steed, at whose home
he had lodged. Eldridge was enraged when Steed took out a summons
because of a dispute about a shilling (5p). He kicked Steed to death
after an evening in a pub at Herne. Steed's nose was broken, the bones
on one side of his face were smashed, an eye was knocked out, and his
blood was spread all about him. Although Eldridge had washed his
boots, blood, hair, and red wool from Steed's scarf were found sticking
to them. While awaiting execution he wanted to dig his own grave, but
was refused permission.

Also hanged this day:

1812 at Stafford: William Booth for forgery.

1813 at Warwick: John Brittain for wife-murder.

1817 at Old Bailey: John Wilkins, James Fitzwilliam, and William
Ball, for burglary.

1891 at Kirkdale Prison, Liverpool: John Conway for the murder of
Nicholas Martin (10). The day before execution he confessed, 'I was
impelled to the crime while under the influence of drink, by a fit of
murderous mania, and morbid curiosity to observe the process of
dying. A moment after the commission of the crime I experienced the
deepest sorrow of it, and would have done anything in the world to
undo it.' *Hangman: James Berry*. There was an argument between
Berry and Dr Barr about the length of the drop, the latter insisting on
an extra two feet. As a result, the hanging almost decapitated Conway,
his head held to the body just by tissue, and his blood splashed around
the pit; this led to Berry's resignation a few months later.

1895 at Stafford Gaol: Thomas Bond for the murders of Frederick Bakewell and George Hackett.

1901 at Winsom Green Prison, Birmingham: John Joyce for the murder of an old man.

21 August

Hanged this day:

1749 at Kennington Common, Surrey: Hugh Dawson and John Gummel for highway robbery.

1750 at Kennington Common, Surrey: James Cooper for murder.

1877 at Kirkdale Prison, Liverpool: John Golding for the murder of Daniel Lloyd; M'Govern for the murder of John Campbell.

1882 at Kirkdale Prison, Liverpool: William Turner for wife-murder.

1888 at the Tombs Prison, New York, USA: Danny Lyons (28) for the gun-murder of another pimp, Joseph Quinn, in an argument about a prostitute.

1894 at Armley Gaol, Leeds: Alfred Dews for the murder of his baby son.

1900 at Cardiff Gaol: William Lacy for wife-murder.

22 August

1887 THE WHITECHAPEL MYSTERY
Israel Lipski (22) hanged at Newgate Prison for the killing of Mrs Miriam Angel (22).
Hangman: James Berry

A year before the Whitechapel furore created by the murders of Jack the Ripper, the press and Parliament concentrated their attention on the murder of Mrs Angel in her bed at 16 Batty Street, off the Commercial Road. It was known as the 'Whitechapel Mystery'.

A total of 15 people lived at 16 Batty Street, the attic being occupied by Israel Lipski. The room below his was taken by Mr and Mrs Angel. Isaac Angel left for work at 6.30 a.m. on the morning of 28 June 1887, leaving his pregnant wife asleep in bed and with the door unlocked.

Israel Lipski was starting a new business that day, using his room to make walking sticks for which he employed two other men: Isaac Schmuss and Simon Rosenbloom. Lipski had been in and out of the house a few times, to nearby shops, the last being to buy nitric acid at 9 a.m. Mrs Angel usually had breakfast at her mother's house at 9 a.m. and, when she did not arrive, the mother went to 16 Batty Street. The door to her daughter's room was locked, with the key in the lock on the inside, and there was no answer to her knocking. The door was broken open and Mrs Angel was found dead in her bed, her face bruised. A doctor was called who confirmed death and had the room searched: Lipski was found under the bed, unconscious from swallowing nitric acid. Mrs Angel's death was later shown to be from nitric acid.

At first it seemed a clear case: that Lipski had bought the nitric acid, entered the room and locked the door with the intention of raping and/or robbing Mrs Angel, had attacked the young woman and punched her three or four times in the face, then poured the nitric acid down her throat. When he heard the banging on the door he must have hidden under the bed. Realising that discovery was certain, he swallowed the remaining poison to commit suicide.

The case became the famous mystery when Lipski alleged that Mrs Angel and himself were attacked by his two new employees, Schmuss and Rosenbloom. The two journeymen gave unsatisfactory accounts of their movements that morning, and some doubts were aroused. Even so, the coroner's jury gave a verdict of wilful murder against Lipski and he was tried at the Old Bailey where the trial jury needed only eight minutes to convict him.

The press, parliamentarians, and some members of the legal profession were of the mind that Lipski was innocent. All manner of locked room theories were put forward; speculations about the 'Whitechapel Mystery' reached heated levels of argument. A concerted campaign was organised, involving telegrams to and from Queen Victoria herself. Royal questions to the Home Secretary caused the execution to be delayed for a week from the original fixed date of 15 August.

When all arguments had been considered the Home Secretary was unconvinced and decided that the law must take its course. While he was drafting notice of this decision, Israel Lipski confessed his guilt! It began:

'I will not die with a lie on my lips. I alone was guilty of the murder of Miriam Angel. I thought the woman had money in her room. So I entered, the door being unlocked, and the woman asleep. I had no thought of violation. She woke up, I hit her . . .'

Hangman Berry had told reporters that he would give Lipski a drop of six feet. The following year, one of the three doctors in attendance at the execution revealed that the drop had been nearer eight feet and that Lipski was nearly decapitated. He also revealed that it took 13 minutes for Lipski's heart to stop beating.

Also hanged this day:

1852 at Richmond, Virginia, USA: slaves Jane and John Williams hanged separately from the back of a cart for the axe-murders of their owner Mrs V. B. Winston and her child. John Williams was hanged after Jane, and was whipped off the tail of the cart.

1876 at Armagh County Gaol, Ireland: Stephen Mackeson for the murder of Mary M'Shane.

1882 at Cork County Gaol, Ireland: Thomas Haynes for wife-murder.

1887 at Armley Gaol, Leeds: Henry Hobson for the murder of Ada Stoddart at Sheffield.

1890 at Knutsford Gaol: Felix Spicer (60) for the murders of his sons William (14) and Henry (4). *Hangman: James Berry*

1947 at Armley Gaol, Leeds: John Edward Gartside (24) for the murder of Mr and Mrs Percy Baker.

23 August

1305 Scots, wha hae wi' Wallace bled,
Scots, wham Bruce has aften led,
Welcome to your gory bed,
Or to victory!
Robert Burns (1759–96)

Scottish patriot William Wallace (33) hanged, drawn, beheaded and quartered at the Elms, Smithfield, London, for high treason.

Wallace was Scotland's greatest patriot and its chief champion for independence from England and King Edward I. He led and inspired a number of victories until Edward invaded Scotland with ninety thousand men in 1298. In the Battle of Falkirk Wallace was abandoned by his cavalry and the rest of his army was cut down by the English archers and routed.

Wallace evaded capture, possibly by hiding abroad, until he was betrayed near Glasgow in early August 1305. He was taken to London and tried at Westminster Hall and, inevitably, condemned. He was hanged at the Elms at Smooth Field (now Smithfield) in the City of

London, then drawn, beheaded and quartered. His head was spiked on a pole and fixed above London Bridge and his quartered remains were put on public display in Newcastle, Berwick, Perth and Stirling – the scenes of earlier glories.

Also hanged this day:

1808 at Burlington, Vermont, USA: smuggler Cyrus B. Dean for the murders of revenue agents Asa Marsh and Jonathan Ormsby.

1813 at Penenden Heath, near Maidstone: Philip Nicholson for the murders of his employers Mr and Mrs Thomson Bonar (or Bonner).

1881 at Maidstone Prison: George Durling (36) for the murder of his mistress Fanny Musson a.k.a. Frances Vincent. *Hangman: William Marwood.* After the drop of eight feet, death appeared to have been instantaneous but, after a few seconds, Durling struggled violently at the rope-end and frightful gurgling sounds were heard for some minutes.

24 August

1953 DIFFICULT TO GET ON WITH
John Balaban (29) hanged at Adelaide Prison, South Australia, for wife-murder; but there were others.

Balaban had led a very disturbed life from an early age. His mother deserted him and his father when Balaban was an infant. When he was six years old his father committed suicide: the boy had the awful experience of waking up to see his father's body hanging from a rafter. He was a loner for most of his life and appears to have been a difficult man to get on with. An analytical chemist, he was an immigrant to Australia from Romania, arriving in 1951. Two years later he was convicted for the murder of his wife (they married in 1952), but made a voluntary statement admitting other killings.

In 1947 he had strangled Hungarian Reva Kwas, in Paris. On 5 December 1952 in Melbourne he had strangled prostitute Zora Kusic, followed by frenzied slashing of her torso. Then, on 11 April 1953, his wife Thelma, his mother-in-law, and his stepson (6), were all battered to death with an iron bar while they slept.

It would appear that he gave way to violent rages if he felt that he was being rejected by anyone. Although he may have suffered from some aspects of paranoia, he was adjudged to be legally sane and aware of what he was doing and that what he was doing was wrong. As

288

he was led to the execution chamber, with the chaplain trying to give him last-minute comfort, he shouted 'Why don't you shut up?' To the last, he couldn't get on with people.

Also hanged this day:

1808 at Armagh, Ireland: Archibald Campbell, Esq., for murder.

1827 at Albany, New York, USA: Jesse Strang a.k.a. Joseph Orton for the murder of his employer John Whipple. Seeing the execution, Levi Kelley was filled with horror and yet became a murderer himself soon after (see 21 November).

1829 at Old Bailey: James Butler for arson; James Brown for burglary.

1853 at Taunton, Somerset: John B. Bicknell for the murder of his grandparents.

1874 at Usk Prison, Monmouthshire: James Henry Gibbs for wife-murder.

25 August

Hanged this day:

1810 at York: Ann Barber for murder.

1825 at Malone, New York, USA: Stephen Videto for the gun-murder of Mrs Fanny Mosely who had spurned him.

1854 at Harrisburg, Pennsylvania, USA: wealthy Courtland C. Johnson for the gun-murders of his wife and her lover Nathaniel Colyer. Having surprised them frolicking naked in the garden, he chased the still-naked couple through the house until he had shot them both.

1866 at New Bailey Prison, Manchester: James Burrows for the murder of J. Brennan in a barn near Slattocks.

1876 at Cork County Gaol, Ireland: Thomas Crowe for the murder of John Hyland.

1879 at Newgate Prison: James Dilley for the murder of his illegitimate child. At Cork County Gaol, Ireland: Guiseppe Pistoria for murder and mutiny on board the ship *Caswell*.

1896 at Armley Gaol, Leeds: Joseph Robert Ellis (22) for wife-murder.

26 August

1884 ENTER HANGMAN BILLINGTON
Joseph Laycock hanged at Armley Gaol, Leeds, for the murder of his wife and four children.
Hangman: James Billington

Laycock was a Sheffield hawker who had killed his wife and four children. He cried at the gallows and asked Billington if he was going to hurt him. Billington's comforting reply was that he would never feel it because he would be out of existence in two minutes. This was Billington's first execution and he gave Laycock a drop of eight feet four inches, reduced from nine feet because Laycock had attempted suicide by cutting his throat. Although Laycock twitched slightly as he hung at the end of the rope, the watching officials were satisfied with Billington's first hanging and were to use him often thereafter.

James Billington hanged 147 persons, the last on 3 December 1901. He died ten days later, of bronchitis, leaving three of his sons as hangmen: Thomas, William, and John.

Also hanged this day:

1738 at Tyburn Tree: William Newington for forgery.

1791 at Stephentown, New York, USA: Whiting Sweeting for the murder of posse-man Darius Quimby.

1873 at Omagh Prison, Ireland: Sub-Inspector Thomas Hartley Montgomery (33), Royal Irish Constabulary, for murder and robbery of bank official William Glass. *Hangman: William Marwood*

1876 at Cork County Gaol, Ireland: Emmanuel Christos Bombas for murder and mutiny on the ship *Caswell*.

1879 at Warwick Gaol: John Ralph for the murder of Sarah Alice Vernon.

1884 at Wexford County Gaol, Ireland: James Tobin for the murder of Elizabeth Moore.

1887 at Lewes Prison: W. Wilton for wife-murder.

1891 at Winchester Prison: Edward H. F. Watts for wife-murder.

27 August

Hanged this day:

1827   at Old Bailey: Thomas Norton for highway robbery.

1861   at Chester: Martin Doyle for 'barbarous attempted murder'. This was the last execution for the crime of attempted murder.

1890   at Newgate Prison: Francois Manteau for murdering Francois De Grave.

28 August

1724 LEGACY OF LUMLEY DAVIS
Lumley Davis hanged at Tyburn Tree – after giving his unused escape equipment to the 'great escaper', Jack Sheppard, in Newgate.

Lumley Davis was a condemned criminal of little note, we do not even know for which crime he was hanged. He was a failed escaper as well; although he had secreted tools and equipment while in the condemned hold at Newgate Prison he was unable to get away. His claim to our notice is that before he was taken to Tyburn he gave his equipment to the youngster, Jack Sheppard. Sheppard had already made two escapes from prison, but it was to be his daring third escape on 31 August, using the gear left by Lumley Davis, that was to make him a hero of the working classes and of prison folklore. See 16 November for Jack Sheppard's story and an account of his even more sensational fourth escape.

Also hanged this day:

1811   at Old Bailey: Joseph Antonio, Joseph King, and Thomas Mann.

1885   at Duluth, Minnesota, USA: Finnish immigrant John Waisenen for the murder of Joseph Farley while robbing and burning his house. He died at the rope's end by slow strangulation, his hands and grimacing face turning blue.

1888   at Winsom Green Prison, Birmingham: George Nathaniel Daniels for the murder of his sweetheart; Harry Benjamin Jones for the murder of a child.

1890   at Winsom Green Prison, Birmingham: Frederick Davis for wife-murder. At Armley Gaol, Leeds: James Harrison for wife-murder.

1900   at Armley Gaol, Leeds: Charles Blewitt for wife-murder.

29 August

1783 'HE WILL LIVE TO BE HANGED'
William Wynne Ryland, engraver to King George III, hanged at
Tyburn Tree for forgery.
Hangman: Edward Dennis

William Wynne Ryland was the most respected and famous engraver of his time. As well as the business for which he had achieved his fame, engraver to the king among others, he forged bills of exchange with great skill: his downfall came only when a papermaker proved that the paper of one such bill had not been in existence at the date showing on it. When arrested Ryland attempted to commit suicide by cutting his throat, but survived to face his trial and execution.

   When the famous poet, artist, and mystic, William Blake (1757–1827), was a lad of 14 his father took him to meet Ryland with a view to Blake being taken on as a pupil. When they left Blake had this to say: 'Father, I do not like the man's face. It looks as if he will live to be hanged.'

Also hanged this day:

1876   at Newgate Prison: John Eblethrift for wife-murder.

1927   at Dublin: chauffeur and odd-jobman Gerard Toal (18) for the murder of housekeeper Mary Callan (36).

30 August

1850 THOSE HARVARD PROFESSORS!
Professor John White Webster (57) hanged in the courtyard of
Leverett Street Jail, Boston, Massachusetts, USA, for the murder of
miserly financier and prominent Bostonian Dr George Parkman.

Dr Webster was an eminent Professor of Chemistry and Mineralogy at the Massachusetts Medical College at Harvard. His extravagant life-style in the 1840s meant that he was always short of funds, and had to borrow. One of his creditors was fellow academic Dr George Parkman, the head of one of Boston's first families. Parkman had moved into real estate and amassed a large fortune. When he failed to return from a pre-lunch walk on Friday 23 November 1849 his disappearance caused a sensation.

A few days later the Parkman residence was visited by Dr Webster with the story that he had only just heard about the disappearance. He said he had met Dr Parkman at 1.30 p.m. on the Friday and repaid a debt, and that when he last saw him he was walking away clutching the $483, suggesting that he must have been waylaid by robbers. It was true that Webster had seen Parkman on the Friday, when the furious financier had visited Webster's laboratory demanding repayment. When Webster had obtained the loan from Parkman he had pledged his famous mineral collection as security and Parkman had discovered that it had been sold. The acid comments of Parkman during the meeting, including 'I got you into your office, Sir, and now I will get you out of it!', sent Dr Webster into a rage.

As Parkman turned to leave, the livid Webster struck him on the head with a piece of timber, killing him with the single blow. Dr Webster then locked the laboratory and worked through the night dissecting the body and burning pieces in his furnace; other parts he dropped into a sewer under the building.

Dr Parkman's arrival at Webster's laboratory had been observed by the janitor, Ephraim Littlefield. The janitor disliked Dr Webster and he pursued his suspicions with great zeal. When Dr Webster was absent, Littlefield used a crowbar to make a hole in the wall: when he had broken through the five layers of bricks the first things he saw were parts of a leg and an arm. Dr Webster was arrested and teeth from the ashes in the furnace were proved from dental records to be those of the missing Dr Parkman.

Professor John White Webster's trial in March 1850 was a sensation across the country. It lasted 11 days and the witnesses for both prosecution and defence included the nation's top people. Such was the demand for the public seats that spectators were only admitted for ten minutes at a time, thus sixty thousand people are reported to have watched the trial in relays. After being found guilty and sentenced to hang, Webster continued to insist on his innocence. Near the end he confessed, claiming that he had flown into a rage when cruelly provoked by the insulting words of Dr Parkman.

Harvard academics, as a species, lost much of the awe that had previously been accorded to them, especially in snobbish New England. One of them had been hanged as a common murderer!

By 1880, 30 years after the Webster trial, society matriarch Mrs Perry of Williamstown, Massachusetts, was asked to take in a guest for the duration of a conference being held there. Her proposed guest was the revered James Russell Lowell, distinguished diplomat and man of letters, currently lecturing at Harvard. Mrs Perry refused at once: 'I could not sleep if one of those Harvard professors were in the house!' (See also 1 February.)

Also hanged this day:

1898 at Swansea Gaol, Wales: Joseph Lewis for the murder of a gamekeeper.

31 August

1909 KENSINGTON ASSASSINATION
Madar Lal Dhingra (25) hanged at Pentonville Prison for the assassination of Sir William Hutt Curzon Wyllie and Dr Cowas Lalcaca.
Hangman: Henry Pierrepoint. Assistant: Tom Pierrepoint

Madar Lal Dhingra was a Parsee Indian student studying engineering at University College, London. He hated the British for occupying his country. He had been invited to attend a concert at the Imperial Institute in Kensington on 1 July 1909. It was sponsored by the National Indian Association, a benevolent organisation for the care and assistance of Indian students. He went to the concert armed with a Colt automatic, a Belgian pistol, and a dagger.

Sir William Wyllie was a distinguished civil servant in Indian affairs, and Honorary Treasurer of NIA, who was attending the concert with his wife. As the audience was dispersing after the performance, at about 11 p.m., Madar Lal Dhingra approached Sir William in the vestibule and engaged him in what appeared to be a genial conversation. Suddenly the student pulled the Colt from a pocket and fired five shots at close range, four of them hitting Sir William in the head and killing him instantly.

Dr Lalcaca, who had been standing nearby, moved to disarm the gunman, but another two shots killed him on the spot. With one bullet left, Dhingra turned the Colt on himself, but it misfired. Onlookers swamped him before he could grab another of his weapons.

Dhingra was tried at the Old Bailey and found guilty of double murder. He was unrepentant, declaring 'It is perfectly justifiable to kill the Englishman who is polluting our sacred soil.' The murderer was of slender build, weighing only seven stone. He was given a long drop of eight feet three inches at his execution.

Also hanged this day:

1874 at Kirkdale Prison, Liverpool: Mary Williams and Flanagan for the murder of a man and his aunt.

SEPTEMBER

1 September

1538 at Clerkenwell, London: Cratwell, who had been the public hangman since 1534, hanged at the Wrestling Ground for having robbed a booth at St Bartholomew's Fair.

1749 at Winchester: Robert Cox for forgery.

2 September

1724 HANGED BY MISTAKE 1724 – DIED 1749!
Margaret Dickson (23) hanged at Gallows Stone in the Grassmarket,
Edinburgh, for infanticide.
Hangman: John Dalgleish

Meg Dickson's husband had deserted her and their two children. In 1723 she left the children with relatives at Musselburgh, near Edinburgh, and set off to obtain help from other relatives. On the journey she was offered domestic work at a house in a village near Kelso on the border, and later became pregnant by one of the sons of the house.

She concealed the pregnancy and gave birth without assistance, but the child died. A few days later, on 9 December 1723, she abandoned the body on the bank of the River Tweed where it was found the same day. She was found to have been recently pregnant, which she admitted, but her story that the child had been still-born was not believed. At her trial, in Edinburgh in July 1724, she was found guilty and condemned on dubious evidence.

Meg Dickson was hanged in front of a large crowd in the Grassmarket. Hangman Dalgleish pulled on her legs to hasten the death and her body was left hanging for the usual time, probably about 30 minutes, and then taken down.

She was put into a coffin which was then placed on a cart. Her coffin was damaged when medical students unsuccessfully tried to seize the body for experiments. The cart, with the broken coffin no longer airtight, was taken along the uneven and pot-holed tracks for burial at Musselburgh, about five miles away. The driver stopped at the top of Pepper Hill for a rest and a swig from his bottle. The bumpy ride may have jerked Dickson's heart and lungs back into action but, for whatever cause, she recovered and was heard making noises as she tried to climb out of her coffin, to the profound shock of the cart driver! Meg was pardoned and lived for another 25 years. It later transpired that she was innocent of the charge anyway.

3 September

1803 NOT A HOPE
Regency conman John Hatfield (44) a.k.a. 'Colonel the Hon.
Alexander Augustus Hope MP' (and other aliases) hanged beside the
River Eden near Carlisle for impersonation and forgery.

Hatfield was a swindler who preyed on moneyed women, business-men, country gentry – anyone who would fall for the confident and charming ploys that he worked in different parts of the kingdom.

In his final year his efforts were conducted in the Lake District as 'Colonel the Hon. Alexander Augustus Hope, MP for Linlithgowshire and brother of the Earl of Hopetoun', extracting funds from false notes and by loans. He was not discovered for many months until a visiting magistrate, who knew the real Colonel Hope MP, had him arrested. Hatfield escaped, but the chase was on and he became nationally famous. He was caught in Swansea and taken to London but later sent for trial at Carlisle. After the six-hour trial the jury took a mere ten minutes to find him guilty and he was sentenced to death.

At his public execution he looked much older than the handsome swindler of a few months earlier. His final words were 'My spirit is strong but my body is weak' and he faced his death with cool dignity. There was a mishap during the hanging when the rope twice slipped so that Hatfield's feet nearly touched the ground, but he was already dead when that happened.

Also hanged this day:

1782   at Tyburn Tree: George Weston (29) for frauds; his brother Joseph Weston (23) for attempted murder. They were highwaymen famous for the Royal Mail Robbery of the previous year, but acquitted for lack of evidence.

1803   at Dublin: Robert Emmett Esq. (barrister) and Edward Kearney for high treason (the first of several cases during September and October 1803).

1810   at Horsemonger Lane Gaol: T. R. Valentine for forgery.

1811   at Shrewsbury: John Taylor, James Baker, Isaac Hickman, William Turner, and Abraham Whitehouse.

1925   at Armley Gaol, Leeds: Alfred Bostock, a married man who battered his pregnant mistress Elizabeth Sherratt and threw her body in the river at Rotherham; and Wilfred Fowler (23), a Sheffield gangster, for the murder of William Plommer (Fowler's brother was hanged the following day). *Hangman: Tom Pierrepoint*

1958 Frank Stokes (44), a hotel porter, for the hammer-murder during a robbery of Mrs L. V. Ash, a 75-year-old widow. A part of his fury was due to the fact that she had offered him work as a gardener at sixpence (2½p) an hour, which he considered insulting.

4 September

Hanged this day:

1817 at Lancaster: John Nuttall for the murder of Ann White.

1860 at Horsemonger Lane Gaol: William Godfrey Youngman for the murders of his sweetheart Mary Streeter, her mother and two brothers, on 16 August at Manor Place, Walworth.

1925 at Armley Gaol, Leeds: gang-leader Lawrence Fowler, whose younger brother was hanged the previous day for the same crime, the murder of William Plommer in a street ambush. *Hangman: Tom Pierrepoint*

1941 John Smith for the murder of Miss M. E. Knight.

5 September

1930 DESTRUCTIVE URGE
'I wish the whole world had but a single throat and I had my hands around it.'

Carl Panzram (39) hanged in the prison yard at Fort Leavenworth Prison, Kansas, USA, for the murder of the prison laundry superintendent Robert Warnke. He had committed 20 other murders.

Carl Panzram was the son of Prussian immigrants to America. In trouble with the authorities from the age of eight, he was driven by a destructive urge that apparently had no limit.

He was a violent boy, brutally beaten in return by his captors which prompted even further violent outrages. He devoted his life to destructive criminal acts inside and out of prison. He served time in different American states and extended his murderings to Africa, where he hired six blacks for a crocodile-hunting trip and sodomised and killed them all before feeding them to the crocodiles.

In 1928 Panzram was sentenced from 20 years to life in Leavenworth for a series of burglaries and murders carried out in Baltimore and Washington DC. He vowed that he would kill the first man who bothered him and, the following year, he used an iron bar to smash the head of Robert Warnke in the laundry. He was convicted and sentenced to hang.

He wrote a contemptuous letter to an organisation campaigning for his reprieve: 'I wish the whole world had but a single throat and I had my hands around it . . . the only way to reform people is to kill them.'

His life of crime is summarised by his admission*:

'In my own lifetime I have murdered 21 human beings, I have committed thousands of burglaries, robberies, larcenies, arsons and last but not least I have committed sodomy on more than a thousand male human beings. For all these things I am not in the least sorry.'

Panzram's destructive urge continued up to his execution, only now it was directed against himself. He ran up the steps to the gallows, dragging the hangman with him, yelling 'Let's get going! What are you stalling around for?' On the platform he was asked if he wanted to say anything. Panzram grabbed the rope and fixed it around his neck and snarled 'Hurry it up, you bastard! I could hang a dozen men while you are fooling around!'

* Panzram completed his autobiography while on Death Row at Leavenworth. Its descriptions of his savage brutality and its sexual frankness was much too shocking to be published at the time, but it appeared in 1970 as Killer: A Journal of Murder edited by Thomas E. Gaddis and James O. Long.

Also hanged this day:

1803   at Dublin: James Byrne for high treason.

1817   at Old Bailey: John Coffin for rape.

1875   at Kirkdale Prison, Liverpool: William Baker for the murder of Charles Langan.

6 September

1902 THE UNDERCOVER SHERIFF
Jim Fleming hanged in Montana, USA, for the shotgun-murder of Oliver Dotson in an attempt to get Dotson's son freed from a murder sentence.

Clint Dotson was starting a life sentence in Deer Lodge Prison, Montana, for the August 1899 shooting to death of Gene Cullinane, a prospector. His accomplices, Oliver Benson and Ellis Persinger, each received ten-year terms. In prison Clint Dotson met Jim Fleming and they became best friends: such good friends that Fleming agreed to kill Clint's father when he got out. Clint had no special grudge against his father, but the circumstances of his death could be useful.

Clint told Fleming about an imaginary $50,000 that he had stashed away on the outside, from a supposed railway robbery. The gullible Fleming believed it, and also believed that Clint would share the haul with him if he did as Clint suggested. The plan was for Fleming, when released from prison, to arrange for the killing of Clint's father, Oliver Dotson, who was another prospector. The death had to look like suicide, with a false note from the old man confessing to the murder of Cullinane. This would thereby procure the release of the 'innocent' Clint Dotson.

Jim Fleming left Deer Lodge and went looking for Oliver Dotson and, in September 1901, found him. They had a drinking session in the old man's cabin, but Fleming made sure that Oliver Dotson did most of the drinking. He even managed to get old Oliver, as part of a joke, to write a letter confessing that it was he who had killed Cullinane and not his son Clint. Fleming killed old Dotson with a shotgun blast into the heart and then rigged the gun on a wood frame so that it was aiming at the dead body, with string running from the trigger to Dotson's hand.

When the body was found it looked like suicide, and the note alongside the body seemed to confirm it. However, Sheriff Robinson was not so easily convinced; it was he who had originally arrested Clint Dotson, Benson and Persinger. The facts as he knew them did not fit properly with the 'suicide note'. He checked with Benson and Persinger in Deer Lodge Prison and was left in no doubt that it was young Clint who had shot Cullinane. Sheriff Robinson also discovered that Clint had befriended Jim Fleming, and that Fleming had recently been released.

Robinson went looking for Jim Fleming, disguising himself as a tramp. When he found the ever-gullible Fleming he was able to gain his confidence and it was not long before the foolish killer was telling him the whole story. The tramp thereupon broke his cover, reverted to being Sheriff Robinson and arrested Fleming for the murder of Oliver Dotson. Jim Fleming was hanged and his scheming best friend remained in Deer Lodge Prison for the rest of his life.

Also hanged this day:

1803   at Dublin: Felix Roarke for high treason.

1817   at Lancaster: Henry Schofield for the murder of his two children.

1833   at Hartford, Connecticut, USA: convict William Teller for the clubbing-murder of Guard Ezra Hoskins during an escape bid at the State Prison at Wethersfield. At Morristown, New Jersey, USA: Antoine Le Blanc, French immigrant, for the murder of his employers Mr and Mrs Sayre and their black maid.

1875   at Kirkdale Prison, Liverpool: Edward Cooper for the murder of Edward Jones while on a British ship.

7 September

1685 THE BLOODY ASSIZES
The Bloody Assizes following the Monmouth Rebellion began in Dorchester, Dorset, and the following 13* men were the first (of hundreds) to be hanged, drawn and quartered: Matthew Bragg, John Foane, Henry Ford, John Game, Ben Gray, Samuel Hilliard, Philip Levermore, Robert Pinney, George Seaward, Thomas Smith, Joseph Speed, Thomas Welch and John Wills.
Hangman: Jack Ketch. Assistant: Pascha Rose

The Protestant Duke of Monmouth, illegitimate son of Charles II, landed at Lyme, Dorset, on 11 June 1685 with the aim of overthrowing the Catholic King James II. Six thousand west-countrymen flocked to his banner and he was proclaimed as king at Taunton on 20 June. His army was defeated at the Battle of Sedgemoor in Somerset on 5 July and he was captured and taken to London. Monmouth was beheaded at the Tower of London on 15 July (executioner Jack Ketch having to strike several times with the axe before the head was severed).

   The Royal revenge upon the west-country rebels was ruthless. More than a hundred were savagely put to death without trial at Taunton. Then followed the Bloody Assizes of Judge Jeffreys in September. Throughout Dorset, Devon and Somerset, approximately 2,600 men and women were charged with high treason. Five hundred or more were sentenced to death of whom 320 were actually executed, being

Dr Edward William Pritchard (40) was the last man to be publicly hanged in Glasgow, for poisoning his wife and mother-in-law. After the slow hanging, the City surgeon had a remarkable tale to tell about Pritchard's corpse. See 28 July.

e ghastly scene at the execution
Andrew Carr at Richmond
son, Dublin, as it was shown
the *Illustrated Police News* in
70. See 28 July.

Above James Bell (11) and his brother John Any Bird Bell (14) murdered Richard Faulkner Taylor (13) in the woods near where Kent's Rochester Airport now stands. John Bell was publicly hanged. See 1 August. (*Brian Lane Collection*)

The title page of a contemporary printed account of the murder of Richard Faulkner Taylor by John Any Bird Bell. (*Brian Lane Collection*)

A NARRATIVE
OF THE
FACTS
RELATIVE TO
THE MURDER
OF
Richard Faulkner Taylor,
IN THE WOODS BETWEEN ROCHESTER AND MAIDSTONE,
On Friday the 4th of March, 1831,
WITH THE
PROCEEDINGS ON THE CORONER'S INQUEST;
THE HIGHLY
INTERESTING EVIDENCE OF JAMES BELL,
NOT ADDUCED ON THE TRIAL,
COMPRISING A COMPLETE AND CIRCUMSTANTIAL
History of the Diabolical Affair,
TOGETHER WITH
THE TRIAL
OF
JOHN ANY BIRD BELL
FOR THE MURDER;
INCLUDING
The Confession
OF THE PRISONER,
AND AN ACCOUNT OF HIS BEHAVIOUR AFTER CONDEMNATION.
Also an Abstract from the very excellent
DISCOURSE OF THE REV. J. WINTER,
BEING
THE CONDEMNED SERMON
Preached at the Chapel of the Gaol on the Sunday previous to the Execution.
TO WHICH IS ADDED,
A SKETCH OF THE PRISONER'S LIFE.

Rochester :
PRINTED AND SOLD BY S. CADDEL ; AND MAY BE HAD
OF EVERY BOOKSELLER IN THE COUNTY.
SOLD ALSO IN LONDON BY T. CADDEL, 65, RATCLIFF-HIGHWAY.

Price One Shilling.

Above left   Alfred Sowrey (24) murdered his fiancée on the morning of their wedding day. In blind terror he fought all the way to the gallows at Lancaster Castle and kicked Hangman Berry so violently as to inflict a lifelong scar. See 1 August.

Above right   John Jackson, who was hanged for killing a prison officer at Strangeways Prison. A remarkable comment linked two hangings: see 15 May and 7 August.

Left   Mrs Mary Ann Britland (38) was the first woman to be hanged at Strangeways Prison and had to be carried to the scaffold. See 9 August.

Maria Marten (26), the vic
in the famous 'Murder in t
Red Barn' case. See 11
August.

William Corder (24),
the killer in the famous
'Murder in the Red
Barn' case.

Above   The public execution of William Corder at Bury St Edmunds in 1828.

The gibbet. This 1810 woodcut by George Hodder, Liverpool, shows a pirate being so-called 'hung in chains', but in reality encased in a metal-banded 'suit', and left hanging on the foreshore as a warning to others. After being hanged in the normal way, the body was then encased in hardened pine resin or pitch to delay decomposition. In this way a body could be left hanging for years until it disintegrated or had been pecked away by birds. Gibbeting was abolished in England in 1834.

Mirza Riza hanged on the large parade ground at Teheran for the assassination of the Shah of Persia. See 12 August.
(*Peter Newark's Historical Pictures*)

Below left John Conway was almost decapitated as a result of an argument between Hangman Berry and the prison doctor. See 20 August.

Below right Israel Lipski (22) hanged for the 'Whitechapel mystery' killing of Miriam Angel (22). See 22 August.

In the back garden of the cottage at The Crumbles, near Eastbourne, pathologist Sir Bernard Spilsbury sorts out and identifies some of the cut and sawn pieces of human flesh that had once been 38-year-old spinster Emily Kaye. Spilsbury described the scene inside the bungalow as the most gruesome he had ever seen. He also performed the autopsy on Miss Kaye's murderer, after Patrick Mahon had been 'doubly hanged' at Wandsworth. See 9 September.
(*Syndication International*)

The evil Mrs Brownrigg of Fleet Street who flogged and starved her apprentice girls. She is shown here whipping Mary Clifford (16), who subsequently died, and Mrs Brownrigg was hanged at Tyburn Tree for murdering her. See 14 September.

John Wiggins struggled fiercely with Hangman Calcraft and four warders (not three as shown here) on the scaffold outside Newgate Prison, shouting that he was innocent. Despite the crowd shown in this drawing, there were fewer people in Old Bailey than on a normal working day. See 15 October.

Twenty Nazi leaders in the dock at the International Military Tribunal at Nuremberg charged with crimes against humanity in a trial which lasted almost a year. *Back row:* Erich Raeder, Baldur Von Schirach (standing), Fritz Sauckel, Alfred Jodl, Franz Von Papen, Artur Von Seyss-Inquart, Albert Speer, Konstantin Von Neurath, Hans Fritzsche. *Front row:* Hermann Goering, Rudolf Hess, Joachim Von Ribbentrop, Wilhelm Von Keitel, Ernst Kaltenbrunner, Alfred Rosenberg, Hans Frank, Wilhelm Frick, Julius Streicher, Walter Funk, Hjalmar Schacht. Those hanged suffered brutal deaths at the hands of bungling US Army hangman, Master Sergeant John Woods. See 16 October.
(*The Hulton-Deutsch Collection*)

A contemporary reward poster for Australia's most celebrated criminals, Ned Kelly and his gang. The rewards totalled £8,000 before the gang's final shoot-out in 1880. See 11 November.
(*Peter Newark's Historical Pictures*)

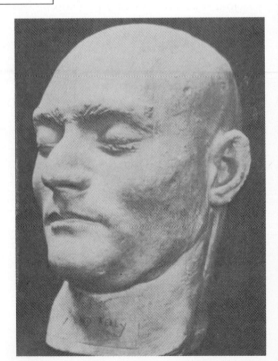

Ned Kelly's deathmask, taken after his hanging in 1880.
(*Peter Newark's Historical Pictures*)

'The Great Escaper' Jack Sheppard (22) was only 5 ft 4 in tall but it was his slender build, and his great strength, which enabled him to perform his amazing escapes – including two from the condemned cell at Newgate. He was the original 'Jack-the-lad' and his drinking and whoring led to his recapture after the last escape. He had a fifth escape planned, on the cart journey from Newgate to Tyburn! See 16 November.

'The Murder of the Century'. Dr Hawley Harvey Crippen hanged by John Ellis at Pentonville Prison in 1910. This was not the end of the amazing story – there was a sensational sequel in 1985. See 23 November.
(*Peter Newark's Historical Pictures*)

The Caxton Gibbet is a grim reminder of times past for present-day
travellers; it stands at the point where the north–south A14 is intersected by
the A45, seven miles west of Cambridge. The present gibbet is not the
original, more a copy of a copy of a copy. Made in 1934 from 400-year-old
oak beams from a demolished house at Baldock, it is believed to be an
exact replica of the ancient gibbet which stood at the Caxton crossroads as
long ago as 1346 and was still in use in 1753. Its hangings this century have
been in effigy only; notable 'victims' have been Kaiser Wilhelm II during
the 'hang the Kaiser' furore in 1919 and Arthur Scargill during the
coalminers' strike in October 1984.
(*Patrick Thurston*)

This profile of the slightly built 'Chinless Killer' was printed in the *Daily Telegraph* in 1881 and then used in a Scotland Yard poster offering a £200 reward for his capture. It brought dubious fame to Percy Lefroy Mapleton (22), who had robbed and killed Isaac Gold (64) on a train on the Brighton line. See 29 November.

Flamboyant highwayman '16-string Jack' Rann, so called because of the eight silk strings he wore at each knee. See 30 November.
(*Peter Newark's Historical Pictures*)

The first executions in Old Bailey, outside Newgate Prison, when ten men and women were hanged on 9 December 1783.

he horrific scene at one of Belsen's many mass graves. British troops
>und 13,000 decaying corpses unburied amid appalling filth when they
itered the camp in 1945. Thirteen of the evil killers were hanged by Albert
ierrepoint: see 13 December.
Syndication International)

he blonde-haired Irma Grese (21) killed as many as 30 prisoners a day at
Belsen concentration camp during World War Two, often whipping them to
eath. Commandant Josef Kramer (39) was known as the 'Beast of Belsen'.
Grese was the first of 13 guards to be hanged on Friday 13 December 1945.

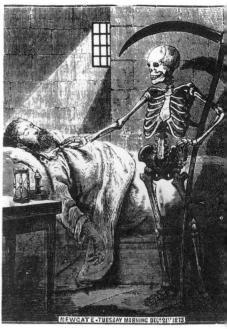

John Amery, the son of cabinet minister Leo Amery and elder brother of war hero Julian Amery who also became a cabinet minister. A silly and wayward young man with no redeeming qualities, John Amery brought continual distress to his family: their final grief was when he was hanged for treason at the end of World War Two. See 19 December. (*Syndication International*)

How the *Illustrated Police News* depicted Death waiting to meet Henry Wainwright on the morning of his execution at Newgate. Wainwright might have avoided the meeting had h not gone to get a cab. . . . See 21 December.

Mary Eleanor Wheeler (24), better known as Eleanor Pearcey, was hanged for a double-murder in 1890. Her father had been hanged for murder ten years earlier. See 23 December.

The ghastly mutilation of Sweet Fanny Adams (8). See 24 December.

The Montfaucon Gallows on the outskirts of Paris was built in the 1200s and lasted until 1761. After being hanged the bodies were left as a grim warning to the townspeople; sometimes there were as many as 80 corpses at a time. After rotting and being pecked by birds, the bodies would disintegrate and (mostly) fall into the walled enclosure at the base. This unidentified engraving is from the early 1800s.

Dead Man's Walk inside Newgate Prison. Executed murderers were buried under the flagstones.

hanged, drawn and quartered in groups of varying sizes in different towns. The heads and quarters were displayed on poles in the towns and at crossroads in country areas. The rotting remains reduced the West Country into a stinking shambles.

Between eight hundred and a thousand were transported and sold as bondslaves for ten-year terms in the West Indies. Others were fined or whipped, or both. A few were acquitted. King William III pardoned eight hundred of them in 1690.

* Originally 29 were sentenced to be executed on 7 September but Hangman Jack Ketch protested that it would be impossible for him and his assistant to hang, cut up and quarter so many men in one day.

Also hanged this day:

1945   at Armley Gaol, Leeds: Thomas Richardson (27) for the axe-murder of Dr David Dewar, his rival for sexual favours from a married woman. *Hangman: Tom Pierrepoint*

8 September

1868 FIRST 'PRIVATE HANGING' IN NEWGATE
Alexander Mackay hanged in the Execution Shed at Newgate Prison for the murder of his mistress at Norton Folgate, Shoreditch, London.

Mackay had battered his mistress to death with a rolling-pin and a furnace rake. The prison officials did not like the new procedure of a private hanging within the prison. In the past they had handed over the criminal, at the Press Yard Gate, to City of London officials for the execution and the gathered crowd had been the official witnesses. Now they were responsible for all the final activities within their own precinct.

Instead of a yelling and festive mob, an awful silence enveloped the whole of Newgate. Within the execution shed, officials spoke in whispers and the strained silence was too much for many of them; some were physically sick when the great bell of St Sepulchre began its fearsome death-knell. Alexander Mackay lost all composure in this frightening atmosphere and had to be dragged to the gallows 'whimpering like a crippled puppy'.

Also hanged this day:

1803   at Dublin, Ireland: T. Maxwell Roche and Owen Kirwan for high treason.

1817   at Lancaster: James Ashcroft senior (53), his brother David Ashcroft (48), his son James Ashcroft junior (32), their kinsman William Holden (47), and John Robinson (53) for the murders of servants Margaret Marsden (74) and Hannah Partington (19).

1961   at Wandsworth Prison: Henryk Niemasz for the murder of Hunert Roderick Twells Buxton and his wife Alice Buxton.

9 September

1924 ANOTHER CRUMBLES MURDER
Patrick Herbert Mahon (34) hanged at Wandsworth Prison for the murder and dismembering of Emily Beilby Kaye (38) at the Crumbles, Eastbourne.
Hangman: Tom Pierrepoint

Three and a half years earlier Tom Pierrepoint had been at Wandsworth to hang Field and Gray for the murder which first focused attention on the Crumbles (see 4 February), a desolate stretch of shingle beach between Eastbourne and Pevensey Bay. The return of Tom Pierrepoint to Wandsworth to hang Patrick Mahon was for an even more horrific and sensational murder. In a way it, too, was a double hanging.

Patrick Mahon was a married man with a good job as sales manager for Consols Automatic Aerators Ltd of Sunbury-on-Thames. He was handsome, well dressed, popular; even animals came running when he whistled. To offset these advantages he was vain, a womaniser, a gambler, and had a criminal record: in 1911 he had been bound over for forging cheques. In 1912 he had been sentenced to 12 months' imprisonment for embezzlement and in 1916 he was sentenced to five years' imprisonment for robbery with violence after a hammer attack on a girl at a bank.

The crime that brought him to the gallows at Wandsworth was the killing and cutting-up of another woman, in a bungalow on the Crumbles. The great pathologist Sir Bernard Spilsbury, so used to seeing the results of sudden death in all of its most horrific ways, described the scene inside the bungalow as the most gruesome he had ever seen.

Mahon had enjoyed a sexual fling with Emily Kaye, a middle-class spinster. When she became pregnant and insisted on him leaving his wife, he decided to get rid of her. After she had cashed her investments of about £600 he installed her in a holiday bungalow, the Officer's House of the former Langney Coastguard Station on the Crumbles. Ominously, it was close to the spot where

Irene Munro's body had been found in the 1920 Crumbles murder case.

Mahon bought a large cook's knife and a tenon saw on 12 April 1924 and went to join Emily Kaye at the bungalow. At some time during that weekend before Easter he killed her, probably with an axe-blow of such violence that the shaft of the axe was broken. Her body was cut and sawn into pieces; some parts were boiled in two large saucepans and other bits were burned in the fireplaces. Large pieces were stored in a fibre trunk; a biscuit tin contained internal organs, and a hat box held 37 pieces of human flesh that had been boiled. The head was never found.

Mahon's downfall was brought about, unwittingly, by his wife. Suspecting that he was involved with other women again, she searched his suits in the wardrobe at home. She found a left-luggage ticket for Waterloo Station and asked a friend to take a look. He was a former railway policeman, and when he saw that the Gladstone bag held blood-stained clothing and a cook's knife, he informed Scotland Yard. The Gladstone bag was returned and police kept a watch at Waterloo. When Mahon tried to reclaim it, on 2 May, he was arrested.

On Saturday 4 May Sir Bernard Spilsbury spent eight hours in the bungalow at the Crumbles, sorting and identifying the human remains which included nearly a thousand bits of human bone among the ashes. The only parts unaccounted for were the head, upper part of the neck, lower part of one leg, the uterus and one ovary. It was Spilsbury's evidence at the trial which doomed Mahon.

One of Mahon's many lies was just how Emily Kaye had died: he said that during a furious row she had attacked him and, during the struggle, she had fallen back and struck her head on the coal-scuttle. When he realised that she was dead he had panicked etc., etc. (how often that story has been heard at murder trials!). Spilsbury revealed that the coal-scuttle was too flimsy to cause 'rapidly fatal injuries'. Mahon was found guilty and sentenced to death.

Spilsbury also performed the postmortem on Mahon, after the execution, and described him as having been 'doubly-hanged'. When the white hood and the noose had been adjusted as he stood at the chalk marks on the centre of the scaffold trap doors, Mahon had sensed when Pierrepoint was releasing the lever. In a desperate last-second attempt to avoid hanging, he had leapt forward so that his pinioned feet might land on the firm floor beyond the trap doors.

It didn't work and his body fell backwards at speed: the lower part of his spine hit the sharp edge of the opened platform with such force that it fractured, and instantly killed him. A fragment of a second later the spine was again fractured, this time at the neck, as his falling body was jerked to a halt at the end of the rope.

1723 at Tyburn Tree: Henry Argur for robbery.

10 September

1818 'IT IS A DESPERATE LIFE . . .'
Joseph Thompson Hare hanged at Baltimore, Maryland, USA, for robbing a mail coach.

Hare began his criminal career as a thief in the slums of Philadelphia and graduated later to armed robbery and murder. He led a gang of robbers who more or less regularly plundered the stagecoaches on the Natchez Trace, the trail between Natchez and Nashville. He lived a miserable life on the run; stealing wherever he could and committing murder as well, until he was caught and given five years in 1813.

Shortly after his release he robbed a Baltimore mail coach, a capital crime, and got away with $17,000 in March 1818. He was caught two days later. During his time in prison awaiting trial and execution, he wrote his life story and confession, which was published after his death. In it he summed up: 'Let not anyone be induced to turn highwayman by reading this book and seeing the great sums of money I have robbed, for it is a desperate life, full of danger, and sooner or later ends at the gallows.'

Also hanged this day:

1801 at Dedham, Massachusetts, USA: sickly cripple Jason Fairbanks (21), for the frenzied pocket-knife murder of the beautiful Elizabeth Fales (19), for whom he had yearned in vain.

1845 at Troy, New York, USA: Henry G. Green for the arsenic-murder of his wife.

1864 at Armley Gaol, Leeds: Sargisons and Myers for murder.

1940 J. W. Wright for the murder of Mrs A. Wright.

11 September

Hanged this day:

1721 at Tyburn Tree: John Meff for robbery.

306

1857 at Liverpool: Captain H. Rogers for the murder of A. Rose, a blackamoor.

1863 at Liverpool: Thomas Alvarez Hughes and O'Brien for murder. *Hangman: William Calcraft*

12 September

1942 CASUAL MURDER
Sammy Dashwood (22) and George Silverosa (23), ex-Borstal boys, hanged at Pentonville Prison for the murder of Shoreditch pawnbroker Leonard Moules (71).

Two former Borstal boys, Sammy Dashwood and George Silverosa, met and had a midday dinner in a Bethnal Green cafe on Thursday 30 April 1942. Dashwood produced a .45 revolver and said he was going to 'do a job'. 'Where?' asked Silverosa. 'Anywhere, I don't care as long as it's something.'

They passed a pawnbroker's as they walked along Hackney Road and Dashwood casually remarked 'We might as well go and do this if you are coming.' Silverosa just as casually agreed. As Thursday was early closing day, they waited until the old man came out to put up the shutters at 1 pm.

They followed him into the shop and between them they battered the old man into unconsciousness. It was probably Dashwood who struck the deathblows; he had the revolver and the injuries to the head were consistent with being hit with the two-and-a-half pound weapon. There were signs of a heavy blow, which was most likely the first, and which would have disabled Moules. Another five scalp wounds were found parallel and close together; these could only have been inflicted if the head was held firm and there was no movement.

Dashwood and Silverosa robbed the safe and departed, leaving a palm print on the inside of the safe. Leonard Moules never regained consciousness and died nine days later in Bethnal Green Hospital. A soldier told the police that he had seen two men in a cafe on the day of the murder and one of them had had a gun; he thought their names were George and Sam.

The police recognised the descriptions and thought it well worth-while questioning George Silverosa and Sammy Dashwood. Silverosa was found first and he immediately admitted that he was involved, but blamed the violence on Dashwood. When Dashwood was arrested and told of Silverosa's statement he claimed that it had been Silverosa who was fighting the old man when he went down. The palm print inside the safe was Silverosa's. They were both found guilty and condemned and, despite their youth, there was to be no clemency for two such hardened criminals and brutal casual killers.

13 September

Hanged this day:

1703 at Tyburn Tree: Edward Jeffreys for murder.

1811 at Penenden Heath, Kent: Frederick Bardie.

1942 at Winsom Green Prison, Birmingham: H. O. Merry for the murder of Joyce Dixon.

14 September

1767 THE EVIL MRS BROWNRIGG
Mrs Elizabeth Brownrigg (47) hanged at Tyburn Tree for the cruel ill-treatment and murder of a servant-girl Mary Clifford (16).
Hangman: Thomas Turlis

Elizabeth Brownrigg was the wife of a prosperous plumber, James Brownrigg of Fleur-de-Lys Court, off Fleet Street, London, and they had 16 children. She was appointed by St Dunstan's Parish to be midwife to the poor women of the workhouse. She was to become the most hated woman of the century when the public heard about her savage cruelty to her girl-apprentices.

In 1765 two girls were apprenticed to her, for each of whom she received £5 towards their expenses as well as their unpaid labour. They were Mary Mitchell from Whitefriars and Mary Jones from the Foundling Hospital. The girls were kept half-starved, poorly clothed, and savagely beaten. Mary Jones was laid naked across two chairs and whipped for such a long time that Mrs Brownrigg had to stop a few times to give herself a rest. This form of punishment was repeated whenever Mrs Brownrigg felt the urge and was usually concluded by throwing a pail of cold water over the poor girl.

Early one morning Mary Jones escaped back to the Foundling Hospital where the governors were alarmed at her injuries. The hospital's solicitor wrote to Mr Brownrigg threatening prosecution unless a satisfactory explanation was given. The letter was not

308

answered and no further action was taken. Mary Mitchell was left with her fiendish mistress and suffered the same cruelties for another year, and then she also escaped. She did not get far: one of the younger Brownriggs chanced upon her in the street and marched her back to the house where she was given a severe whipping.

The overseers of Whitefriars sent the Brownriggs another girl, Mary Clifford, and this luckless 16-year-old was given even more brutal treatment. Stripped naked, with her wrists tied together, she would be drawn upwards to hang from a pipe running the length of the kitchen. Mrs Brownrigg would then thrash her with a cane, a whip, or a broomhandle, until the blood ran down her back. The beatings were so frequent that the pipe gave way and James Brownrigg had to install a hook into the beam from which the girls could be suspended.

The eldest son, John Brownrigg, would also whip Mary Clifford. Sometimes he took over and relieved his mother when she had exhausted herself from whipping, or initiate a beating on his own account. Often the girls had to remain naked for days at a time.

Mary Clifford suffered another form of torture from her evil mistress, having her cheeks grabbed and pulled downwards so that blood ran from the eyes. She slept in the freezing coal-hole on a sack of straw, with no coverings to give her warmth. The wretched girl complained of her treatment to a French lady lodger, who rebuked Mrs Brownrigg, and even more fury was unleashed upon poor Mary: Mrs Brownrigg attacked her and cut her tongue in two places with a pair of scissors, and on six occasions that day beat her about the head and shoulders with the butt-end of the whip.

Mary Clifford's stepmother called to see her and was refused access but, from neighbours, was told about the beatings and screaming coming from the house. The stepmother reported the matter to the parish authorities and Mary was found in the house with ulcerated injuries down her back, so weak that she could not speak. The two apprentice-girls were removed to St Bartholmew's Hospital where Mary Clifford died within a few days.

James Brownrigg was arrested. Elizabeth and her son John had absconded, but were later caught in Wandsworth. All three were tried at the Old Bailey for murder, with most of the public's hatred directed at Mrs Brownrigg. Father and son placed all the blame on her and she was convicted and sentenced to death. The father and son were acquitted but found guilty of a misdemeanour and each sentenced to six months' imprisonment and fined one shilling (5p). A huge crowd watched Mrs Brownrigg's procession to Tyburn and for once the criminal to be hanged received more abuse than the hangman. Afterwards her body was dissected and her skeleton was hung on display in Surgeon's Hall for many years.

Also hanged this day:

1793 at Gallows Hill, Lancaster Moor: Edward Miles (36) for the stabbing-murder and robbery of postboy James Hogworth (24) in 1791. Miles was afterwards hung in chains on the gibbet.

15 September

Hanged this day:

1741 at the Strand, London: James Hall for the murder of his master.

1811 at Ilchester: Arthur Baily.

1951 at Carlton Prison, Edinburgh: Robert Dobie Smith (30) for the shotgun-murder of police sergeant William Gibson on a Dumfries street on 22 May.

16 September

1830 '. . . AFTER A DESPERATE STRUGGLE'
William Griffith hanged at Beaumaris, Isle of Anglesey, Wales, for the attempted murder of his wife.
Hangman: S. Burrows

This was the first execution to have taken place on Anglesey for more than 40 years. The following report is quoted from the *North Wales Chronicle*:

'This unfortunate man, who was convicted at the last Anglesey Great Sessions of a most brutal and inhuman attempt to murder his wife, was yesterday executed upon a scaffold projected from the east side of the new jail, Beaumaris. From the time of condemnation, Griffith manifested a strong fear of death, attended by occasional bursts of despair, during which he made bodily efforts, as if to escape from confinement.

'On the morning of execution, having been for a few minutes left alone, he tore up the wooden bench on which his bed was placed, and fixed it against the door, which for some time prevented all access from without. The door being at length forced, he was secured, and every effort which humanity and Christian feeling could suggest having been in vain used to compose his mind, the requisite preparations were made for carrying the sentence of the law into execution, the criminal all the while uttering the most agonizing cries and groans.

'A little before ten o'clock, S. Burrows, the Chester executioner, was admitted into the cell, and after a desperate struggle, succeeded in pinioning the prisoner with a cord at the elbows. The reverend chaplain then commenced reading the funeral service, and the prisoner was led, or rather dragged between two officers to the scaffold, on which the javelin men and others whose duty required their presence were already placed.

'When arrived at the scaffold, and placed under the fatal beam, Griffith, who appears to have reserved his strength for a last struggle, made a desperate resistance to the executioner putting the halter round his neck; and even when this was accomplished, he made continual efforts to displace it till the drop was withdrawn, which was done within five minutes from the time he came upon the scaffold. His death was to all appearance instantaneous, and after hanging for about an hour, his body was cut down and placed in a coffin for interment, which took place in the evening.'

Also hanged this day:

1811   at Exeter: J. Cox.

17 September

1858 'DON'T YOU WANT TO SEE YOUR PA HUNG?'
Preston Turley, drunken Baptist minister, hanged at Charleston, Virginia, USA, for the strangling of his wife, Mary Susan.

Preston Turley had been dismissed from his job as Baptist minister earlier in the year because of his heavy drinking. His wife, Mary Susan Turley, joined him in his drunken revels. One night in August they had a drunken argument at home and Turley become enraged and lectured his wife, quoting the scriptures. He concluded by strangling her as their three children watched. His method of disposing of the body was to weigh it down and dump it in the river, allegedly watched by astonished neighbours. He was arrested and quickly convicted.

In front of the large crowd gathered for the execution he delivered a sermon lasting more than three hours, mainly on the evils of the demon drink, but other sins were thrown in. He was saddened that his children were not present and told the crowd about the letters he had sent the children, one of which included the enticement 'Don't you want to go and see your Pa hung?'

18 September

1953 BLACKPOOL POISONER
Mrs Louisa Merrifield (46) hanged at Strangeways Prison, Manchester, for poisoning her employer, Mrs Sarah Ann Ricketts (79).
Hangman: Albert Pierrepoint

Louisa Merrifield was a vulgar, nasty-minded and foul-mouthed middle-aged woman who lived mainly on her third husband's state pension, plus any odd domestic work she could get. Alfred Edward Merrifield (71) was a bewildered old man, with an erratic hearing aid, who rarely seemed aware of what was going on around him.

One day Louisa saw an advertisement in the local paper for a housekeeper-companion required by an old lady in the Northbreck area of Blackpool. Mrs Sarah Ann Ricketts was a cantankerous old widow (her two husbands had committed suicide in the kitchen gas-stove), partly paralysed, apparently as black-minded and evil-tongued as Mrs Merrifield. There were 50 applications for the job and, only two days after the advertisement appeared, the old woman had chosen Mr and Mrs Merrifield.

The Merrifields moved into 'Homestead' at 339 Devonshire Road on 12 March 1953. By 31 March Mrs Ricketts had changed her will in favour of her new employees. Louisa boasted to a drinking companion 'We are landed. We were living with an old lady and she has died leaving me a bungalow worth £4,000.' When she was asked who the old lady was who had died, her answer was 'She's not dead yet, but she soon will be.' On 14 April Mrs Ricketts died.

Mrs Merrifield contacted an undertaker, wanting to have the body cremated there and then, but this was refused. The postmortem revealed that Mrs Ricketts had died from consuming yellow phosphorus mixed with bran, a mixture found in a rat-poison under the brand name of Rodine. It may have been administered with a tot of rum. The Blackpool police called in Scotland Yard. Detectives searched the house and garden but could not find the Rodine tin, but they did find a spoon in Louisa's handbag that had a residue on it that was consistent with yellow phosphorus mixed in rum. A retail chemist from Manchester (50 miles away) came forward; he remembered a couple buying a tin of Rodine in mid-March and he positively identified Alfred Merrifield.

Mrs Merrifield was charged with murder and two weeks later Alfred Merrifield was also charged. Their trial at Manchester in July lasted 11 days. When asked about the premature news of her legacy, by the Attorney General at her trial, Mrs Merrifield adamantly replied 'I have never told anyone that Mrs Ricketts was dead before she died.'

312

Strictly speaking, this was true as she had never mentioned Mrs Ricketts by name. The jury returned after six hours; they could not agree about Alfred, but Louisa was guilty. She was sentenced to death. (The charge against Alfred Merrifield was dropped and, for a time, he went back to live at Homestead. His late employer's will was disputed by her daughters and the court ruled that Alfred should get only a one-sixth share and that he should move out of the bungalow. In newspaper articles he said that Louisa had shamed his good name and that he would have been her next victim. He also appeared in Blackpool sideshows before dying, aged 80, in 1962.)

Several hundred spectators assembled outside Strangeways at 9 a.m. on the morning of Mrs Merrifield's hanging, and waited for the notice of execution to be displayed on the gates. There was a silent sense of justice having been done for a cruel murder. There were no demonstrations from abolitionists, or from people concerned about hanging women. They would appear nearly two years later when Ruth Ellis was hanged (see 13 July).

Also hanged this day:

1787   at Burlington, New Jersey, USA: John Campbell, John Kease, and Patrick Kinnon for the knife-murder of an old woman during a burglary.

1849   at Liverpool: John Gleeson reportedly in front of a packed crowd of a hundred thousand. *Hangman: William Calcraft*

19 September

1714 MURDER DURING AN OLD BAILEY TRIAL!
William Johnson and Jane Housden hanged for the murder of Mr Spurling, principal turnkey, during Housden's trial, for coining, in the courtroom of the Old Bailey.

William Johnson, a butcher and highwayman, entered the courtroom during Jane Housden's trial on a charge of coining wishing to speak to her. Mr Spurling, the principal turnkey of Newgate Prison, told him that he could not speak to her until after her trial. Johnson immediately drew his pistol and, in front of all present, shot the turnkey who died instantly with Jane Housden shouting encouragement throughout.

The coining charge was dropped and, without any delay, Johnson and Housden were charged and tried there and then with Spurling's murder. Sentenced to death, this remarkable pair actually denied their

313

guilt all the way to execution and treated it all as an hilarious outing.

Also hanged this day:

1805 at York, Pennsylvania, USA: Charles Cunningham (18) for the murder of another boy, Joseph Rothrock, whom he accused of cheating at a dice game.

1851 at the Tombs Prison, New York, USA: Aaron B. Stookey for the stabbing-murder of Edward Moore during a fight on a Manhattan street.

1861 at Maidstone: Private Peter Masterson (22), Royal Artillery, for the murder of Sergeant Martin Murphy with an iron poker in the guardroom at Woolwich Garrison. *Hangman: William Calcraft*

1941 Eli Richards for the murder of Jane Turner.

1947 at Pentonville Prison: Charles Henry Jenkins (23) and Christopher James Geraghty (21) for the gangster-style shooting of Alec de Antiquis outside a jewellery shop in London's West End. *Hangman: Albert Pierrepoint* who had walked by the scene of the shooting while de Antiquis was still lying there. The hangings were followed by a fall in gun-related crimes.

20 September

1586 BABINGTON'S CATHOLIC PLOT
Anthony Babington (25), the Jesuit priest John Ballard, and five others, executed at Tyburn Tree for treasonously conspiring to assassinate Queen Elizabeth I.
Hangman: (probably) Bulle

Anthony Babington was the son of a rich Derbyshire family of Roman Catholics. He had served as a page to Mary, Queen of Scots, at Sheffield Castle where she was a prisoner. Catholics regarded Mary as the rightful Queen of England and she was, therefore, a constant threat to the throne of the Protestant Queen Elizabeth I.

Babington was a conspirator against Elizabeth from 1580, covertly carrying out work with the Jesuits. In 1586 he was persuaded by John Ballard to lead a rebellion to assassinate Queen Elizabeth, free Mary and install her on the throne of England. Mary would thereafter restore the country to the Roman Catholic faith.

Cipher messages, giving details of the plans and of Mary's warm approval, were intercepted by Elizabeth's spies headed by Sir Francis

Walsingham. Babington evaded immediate arrest by fleeing to Harrow, but was captured there in August. For this dangerous and undoubted treason there could be only one result at his and Ballard's trial.

Also hanged this day:

1756 at Tyburn Tree: William Conicutt for wife-murder.

1813 at Old Bailey: James Leary for the murder of Mrs Clifford.

1814 at Old Bailey: J. Mitchell and William Henry Hollings for murder.

1830 at Old Bailey: William Sapwell (a.k.a. John Smith) for the stabbing-murder of PC John Long in Grays Inn Lane.

1862 outside Kirkdale Prison, Liverpool: William Robert Taylor, killer of estate agent Mr Mellor; and John Ward, police killer. *Hangman: William Calcraft*

21 September

1829 THE CARELESS CARPENTER
David Evans hanged, twice, on the roof of Carmarthen County Gaol, Wales, for the murder of Hannah Davies on Pencarreg mountain.

One of the biggest crowds ever seen in Carmarthen gathered outside the County Gaol from dawn onwards. As well as almost the whole of the town's population, men on horseback, families in carts, and pedestrians arrived from different parts of Wales.

David Evans had shown great remorse for his crime while awaiting death and had confessed his guilt without reservation. After the iron shackles had been removed from him he was pinioned and prepared for execution, all this time attended by the chaplain and praying fervently. He was led out on to the roof of the gaol at 10 a.m., walking with a firm and steady gait. His arrival evinced a shock throughout the waiting crowd with many of the women sobbing and others shrieking hysterically.

Evans maintained his calm while the rope was adjusted and asked for the loan of a handkerchief to give the hangman the final signal. Without much of a pause he dropped the handkerchief and the stand beneath his feet was withdrawn. The chain on the gallows' beam, through which the rope was reeved, gave way and Evans dropped to the floor and landed on his feet. He fell down for an instant but

regained his feet without help, and then demanded to be set free: 'I
have been hanged once, and they have no more to do with me!' Like
many others, he seemed to believe that if the first attempt at execution
failed he was entitled to a reprieve or a pardon according to some
ancient custom: wrong. The sentence was 'to be hanged by the neck
until dead'. This was made clear to him and, with some difficulty, he
was again set upon the wooden stand with the noose around his neck
and the other end of the rope more firmly fitted to the beam. He
dropped the handkerchief for the second time, and died instantly.
After hanging for the usual time, the body was cut down and given to
the surgeons for dissection.

The Times, known in those days as the Thunderer, was scathing in its
comment and had no doubt to whom to allocate blame:

> '. . . we cannot too severely censure the carelessness of the county
> carpenter, whose neglect alone was the cause of it. The great
> wonder is, that the gallows frame did not sever and fall down
> altogether, as the carpenter had most unaccountably omitted to put
> in the pins that were to fasten the cross-beam to the perpendicular
> ones, so that when the pressure came upon the chain which had
> been passed round the cross-beam, that beam gave a turn round, by
> which means the hook of the chain that was fastened to the central
> hole became loosened from its hold, and occasioned the very
> reprehensible disorder described above.'

22 September

1776 NATHAN HALE'S DYING WORDS
**Captain Nathan Hale (21) hanged in New York City for spying behind
the British lines.**

Nathan Hale was a captain in George Washington's army in the
American War of Independence and was sent, some say by Washington himself, on a mission to spy behind the British lines. He was
caught and hanged. His fame derives from his supposed final words: 'I
only regret that I have but one life to lose for my country.'

There is considerable doubt that he actually spoke them. In recent
years the diary of Captain Frederick Mackenzie has come to light. He
was a British officer and was at the execution. He records Hale's last
words as 'It is the duty of every good officer to obey any orders given
him by his commander-in-chief.' The epigram originally attributed to
Hale in legend will probably survive regardless: it is a favourite
quotation in American folklore.

1714 at Tyburn Tree: Heny Plunkett for the murder of Thomas Brown.

1882 at Galway County Gaol, Ireland: Patrick Walsh for the murder of Martin Lynden.

23 September

Hanged this day:

1816 at Old Bailey: George A. Eglington for an 'abominable offence'.

24 September

1652 ATTACKED OLIVER CROMWELL
Captain James Hind (36), Royalist and highwayman, hanged, drawn, and quartered at Worcester 'for treason' according to Cromwell's Parliament.

Captain James Hind had fought for the young King Charles II against the Roundheads, notably at the Battle of Worcester in 1651. Many of his later enterprises as a highwayman were conducted against prominent members of Cromwell's hated Republican Party before, during, and after the Civil War. Hind led an attack in an attempt to rob Oliver Cromwell himself while travelling by carriage, but Cromwell's escort was too strong and the attempt failed. Hind escaped, but a number of his gang were captured. He was arrested in London for his part in a robbery in Berkshire and parliament had the charge altered to 'treason' because of his political activities. He was hanged, drawn, and quartered after a brief trial at Worcester; his head was placed on the Severn Bridge.

Also hanged this day:

1722 at Tyburn Tree: Robert Wilkinson, James Lincoln, and Thomas Milksop, for murder; John Brinsden for wife-murder.

25 September

1794 at Dresden, Maine, USA: Edmund Fortis for the rape-murder of Pamela Tilton. He was tearfully repentant on the gallows: 'All my life I have been taking things not my own, and lying with women.'

1821 at Old Bailey: George Lee for issuing forged notes; Thomas Patmore for cutting and maiming; William Thompson for highway robbery.

26 September

1803 THRICE HANGED THEN LOST AT SEA
Joseph Samuel (22) hanged three times at Brickfield Hill, near
Sydney, Australia, for the murder of Constable Joseph Luker.

Joseph Samuel first went on trial for his life as a 14-year-old lad in 1795. He was tried at the Old Bailey for taking part in a burglary at Moorfields, in the City of London.

Young Samuel claimed that he was at the home of his master when the crime was committed, but no one bothered to check to see if this was true. A witness had seen two men and a boy committing the crime and identified Samuel as the boy. He was found guilty of the non-capital offence of simple larceny, instead of burglary, and was sentenced to seven years' transportation to Australia. He served six years of his sentence on a Thames prison hulk before sailing to Australia in the summer of 1801 so that he had only a few months left to serve when he arrived in Sydney. In 1803 he was involved with others in a burglary which led to the murder of Constable Joseph Luker. Samuel was the only one convicted and was sentenced to death.

The following Monday there was plenty of drama at the scene of execution. A convicted thief who was also to be hanged was reprieved as he stood under the gallows. Samuel was asked about his crime and accused another man, present among the watchers, of having killed Luker. The watching crowd became uneasy, but the execution went ahead. Samuel was swung off the cart and left hanging, then the rope suddenly snapped and he fell to the ground. He was lifted up, another rope was fixed round his neck and he was hanged again. This time the noose came undone and his by now unconscious body slowly sank to the ground. A third rope was used and he was suspended from the gallows again, and this rope snapped as well!

The execution was stopped and the governor was hurriedly

informed of events. He ordered a reprieve, to the delight of the crowd who believed that divine intervention was at work that morning. Samuel was revived, but it was some days before he could get about. He later escaped from his commuted sentence and was lost at sea.

27 September

Hanged this day:

1825   at Old Bailey: James Goff for murder.

28 September

1850 THE KILLER UNCLE
Reuben Dunbar (21) hanged in New York, USA, for the murders of his nephews to obtain an inheritance.

This was a simple crime to obtain an inheritance. Dunbar's wealthy stepfather, a Mr Lester of Albany in New York, died leaving his fortune to Dunbar's two nephews, David (10) and Stephen Lester (8). Only if the boys failed to survive would the property go to Reuben Dunbar.
  Dunbar killed both boys to clear the way for him to inherit, hanging the elder David and clubbing Stephen to death. He could not get away with such blatant murders. His claim led to inquiries and the boys' bodies were discovered. Dunbar confessed before his execution.

29 September

Hanged this day:

1803   at Dublin, Ireland: Richard Hawley for high treason.

30 September

1952 MURDER OF WAR-TIME HEROINE
Dennis Muldowney (41) hanged at Pentonville Prison for the stabbing-murder of Countess Krystyna Skarbek.

Countess Skarbek, a Polish aristocrat, had operated as a British Intelligence agent in Occupied Europe during World War Two. Much decorated, her medals included Britain's George Medal and France's Croix de Guerre.

After the war the countess lived mainly in London and was generally known as Christine Granville. She had met Dennis Muldowney in 1951 on a ship and a friendship developed. Muldowney left the sea and obtained a job as night porter at the Reform Club. He became jealous because Christine saw other men; his jealousy consumed him when he learned that she had become engaged to a former war-time associate.

She had spent the evening of 15 June 1952 with a number of friends, dining at a cafe near her rooms at the Shelbourne Hotel in Earls Court. Muldowney had been hiding in the shadows near the Shelbourne. When he saw her return he followed her into the hotel. He caught up with her in the foyer and, in front of hotel staff, thrust a dagger into her chest and shouted 'You are not leaving me now!' He made no attempt to get away and waited until the police arrived to arrest him.

Countess Skarbek's funeral was attended by many of her World War Two colleagues from different countries, including Iron Curtain countries. Muldowney was put on trial at the Old Bailey. He pleaded guilty and was sentenced to death within three minutes, one of the shortest ever murder trials.

Also hanged this day:

1902   at Pentonville Prison: James MacDonald and another man, the first to be hanged at Pentonville. The scaffold had been transferred from Newgate and was equipped for triple hangings. MacDonald had stabbed Henry Greaves to death near Spitalfields Market, itself a former execution site. *Hangman: William Billington. Assistants: John Billington and Henry Pierrepoint*

1952   Cull for the murder of his wife Mrs R. J. Cull.

OCTOBER

1 October

1913 THE HOPETOUN QUARRY BODIES
Widower Patrick Higgins hanged over the staircase in Edinburgh Gaol for the murders of his sons, two years after he had thrown them into the quarry.

Patrick Higgins was a former soldier who had been medically discharged on account of epilepsy. He returned to Winchburgh in West Lothian, Scotland, and obtained work in the brickworks earning weekly wages of 24 shillings (£1.20). He married a local girl and they had two sons, William in 1904 and John in 1907.

His wife died in 1910 and Higgins spent more and more of his money on drink. He was jailed for two months in 1911 for neglecting the boys. He boarded the boys in a house in Broxburn for a time but, having failed to keep up the payments for them, took them away.

At some time, probably in November 1911, the boys were fed a last meal of Scotch broth after which Higgins took them on a walk to Hopetoun Quarry. William (7) and John (4) were tied together with sashcord and thrown into the watery quarry; whether they were alive or dead at the time is not clear. The bodies were not discovered until 1913, but they were in a remarkable state of preservation. Apart from the feet, almost all parts of the bodies were intact in an adipocerous condition. Adipocere can occur when the corpse is encased in damp earth or water: the body fats convert into a yellowy wax-like substance that sticks to the bones and helps to retain the natural body shape. The Edinburgh pathologist Sir Sydney Smith, studying the preserved bodies, was able to help with identifying the boys.

Patrick Higgins was still working at the local brickworks, and had given different explanations for the disappearance of the boys: he was arrested a few days later. His defence was based on insanity due to his epilepsy, but the jury rejected this and found him guilty of murder, although they did make a recommendation for mercy.

Higgins' last few years had been a miserably hard existence, sleeping rough or in a corner of the brickworks; he blamed his heavy drinking for all of his problems. After being condemned he seemed quietly resigned to being hanged, even admitting the justice of such an end for what he had done. He may have been weary of life. He was hanged on a specially erected scaffold over the staircase outside the condemned cell.

Also hanged this day:

1788 at Edinburgh: Deacon William Brodie (47) for burgling His Majesty's Excise Office. Brodie had a split-personality; a respectable burgher and tradesman by day and a criminal by night. Robert Louis Stevenson was fascinated by Brodie and used his story as the base for his classic novel *The Strange Case of Dr Jekyll and Mr Hyde*.

2 October

1780 BRITISH SPY
Major John Andre (29) hanged at Tappantown, New York, USA, as a British spy during the American War of Independence.

When the British army learned that the American Brigadier General Benedict Arnold, the commander of West Point, might be willing to help the British take the strategic fort, they realised that it could become the turning point of the war. An intelligence officer, Major John Andre, was sent to establish contact with Benedict Arnold and conclude a deal. He travelled deep into enemy territory in plain clothes, met the treasonous American, and successfully agreed terms.

Major Andre was stopped by three rebel militiamen on his way back to the British lines. Hidden in his boots they found documents that revealed the plan. He was tried by an American court martial for spying and sentenced to be hanged the next day. He appealed to George Washington to be permitted to die 'a soldier's death' in front of a firing squad rather than hanging, but Washington, still enraged at the treachery of one of his generals*, curtly refused.

At the gallows, Major Andre calmly saluted the American officers gathered to witness his execution and addressed them: 'The noose will cause me but a momentary pang. All I request of you gentlemen is that you bear witness to the world that I died like a brave man.' He was buried near the place of execution.

Major Andre's body was dug up and returned to Britain in 1820. He was re-interred in Westminster Abbey as a national hero where his impressive memorial, prominently positioned, can be seen on the wall of the south aisle leading to Poet's Corner.

* *Benedict Arnold fled to the British and was given the rank of Brigadier in their army. He remains the most hated man in the history of the United States: the name of Benedict Arnold is a byword for treachery.*

Also hanged this day:

1793 at White Plains, New York, USA: John Ryer for the murder of deputy sheriff Dr Isaac Smith, in a tavern while resisting arrest. He admitted at his trial that he was guilty of '. . . excess drinking, card playing, cock fighting, cursing, swearing, together with almost every kind of vice, wickedness and debauchery.' There was no reprieve.

1829   at Cumberland, Maryland, USA: George Swearingen for the murder of his rich, land-owning wife: he had claimed that she was killed in a fall from a horse. He was Sheriff of Washington County at the time and instead of 'running a beautiful whore out of town', he ran off with one as soon as his wife was dead. He was caught in New Orleans.

1930   at San Quentin Prison, California, USA: Gordon Stewart Northcott (22) for the sex abuse and murder of boys.

3 October

1750 THE 'GENTLEMAN HIGHWAYMAN'
James Maclane (26), the 'Gentleman Highwayman', hanged at Tyburn Tree.
Hangman: John Thrift

James Maclane came from a family of dissenting clergymen, inherited a fortune and wasted it away. He lived for a while as a grocer, having been set up in business by his wife's dowry; when she died he sold up and went looking for an heiress. To maintain his expensive style of living, he took to the road and became a highwayman and one of his first victims was Horace Walpole.

On 26 June 1750 he and a man named Plunkett robbed the Earl of Eglinton on Hounslow Heath and, later in the day, they plundered the Salisbury Stage. Maclane was caught when trying to dispose of items from the Salisbury Stage robbery. For some reason his notoriety captured the fancy of the public at his trial and he became a (temporary) popular hero. Horace Walpole wrote a description of the scene at Newgate on the Sunday after Maclane's trial: 'Three thousand people went to see him. He fainted away twice with the heat of his cell.' All this popular excitement ensured that a huge crowd assembled for his hanging at Tyburn Tree.

Also hanged this day:

1750   at Tyburn Tree: William Smith for forgery, George Lloyd and Will Wright for theft (hanged with Maclane).

1803   at Dublin, Ireland: John MacKintosh for high treason.

1873   at Fort Klamath, Oregon, USA: Madoc Indian leader Kintpuash (known as Captain Jack) and three other Madoc Indians, for the murder of Brigadier General Edward Canby at a peace conference in April 1873.

1878   at Cupar Prison, Fife, Scotland: William M'Donald for wife-murder.

4 October

1848 TOO BIG A FALL
Thomas Brennan publicly hanged, and decapitated, at Niagara Falls, on the Canadian/USA border.

Thomas Brennan was brought out to the front of the prison that morning and mounted the high scaffold. A normal hanging rope of the usual thickness was used, but an excessive amount of slack meant a ten-foot drop. The jerk tore his head from his body and both parts fell to the ground spouting blood.

Also hanged this day:

1570   at Edinburgh: Reverend John Kello for wife-murder.

1803   at Dublin, Ireland: Thomas Keenan for high treason.

1899   at Newgate Prison: Frederick Preston for the murder of a woman in Hackney. At Wandsworth Prison: Robert Ward for the murder of his two children.

5 October

Hanged this day:

1875   at Glasgow: Patrick Docherty for murder in Rutherglen.

1885   at Newgate Prison: Henry Norman for wife-murder.

6 October

1945 FIVE GERMAN PRISONERS OF WAR HANGED
Erich Koenig (20), Joachim Goltz and another three German POWs (soldiers) hanged at Pentonville Prison for the murder of fellow German POW, Sergeant Major Wolfgang Rosterg (35).

The murdered man was a patriotic German, but an anti-Nazi, held with other German soldiers as prisoners of war at Comrie Camp,

326

Perthshire, Scotland. When a large escape that was planned by Nazi POWs was discovered and prevented by the camp authorities, the Nazi plotters suspected that Rosterg had betrayed them. He was dragged from his bed in the middle of the night on 22 December 1944 and subjected to an unofficial trial by the Nazis. He was kicked and beaten to death by the five Nazis at this so-called trial and his nearly unrecognisable body was then taken to a latrine. Nazi NCO Joachim Goltz fixed a rope around the dead man's neck and hung the corpse from a waterpipe, where it was later found by guards.

The five Nazis were tried for murder by a British army court martial, which was conducted strictly in accordance with legal procedure, in sharp contrast to the savagery inflicted by the Germans upon Wolfgang Rosterg. All five were hanged wearing their uniforms, each walking firmly to the scaffold and showing no emotion.

Also hanged this day:

1815   at Mayfield, New York, USA: Barent Becker for the arsenic-murder of his wife.

1884   at Newgate Prison: Thomas Harris for wife-murder, and Thomas Henry Orrock (21) for the gun-murder of PC George Cole while under arrest and being taken to the police station. Bullets found in a tree trunk on Tottenham Marshes, into which it was known that Orrock had fired practice shots, matched the bullet taken from PC Cole's head.

1896   at Newgate Prison: James Jones for the murder of Edward White.

1942   P. W. Kingston for the murder of Sheila W. Wilson at Lewisham.

7 October

1847 'BY GOD, I AM INNOCENT!'
John Hutchings (43) hanged outside Maidstone Prison, Kent, for the poison-murder of his wife in Deptford.
Hangman: William Calcraft

Hutchings, a cooper by trade, had bought some arsenic for killing rats and it was kept in a locked drawer with the key to the drawer being kept by a son. Hutchings hit his wife during a quarrel on 26 August and she left the house, but returned at breakfast time the following morning. After dinner she became very ill and went to bed. While

Hutchings was boiling the kettle to make a pot of tea, he broke open the drawer and removed the bottle of arsenic. One of the children saw him tipping the powder on the fire and he told a son to throw the bottle away.

He sent a cup of tea up to his wife and, after drinking it, she was seized with pain. He called in another woman for help and told her that his wife had 'taken some stuff or other' which had made her ill, but the wife said she had only taken a little jalap (a strong purgative drug). Mrs Hutchings died during the night and 15 grains of arsenic was found in her stomach (a fatal dose is two to three grains).

Hutchings was suspected of having poisoned the cup of tea after breaking open the drawer to get the arsenic. He denied this and claimed that, fearing that his wife was suicidal, he had checked to see if she had taken any and then thrown it away to prevent her getting any more. He was found guilty and sentenced to death, whereupon he burst into tears and again protested his innocence.

Many people believed him and were convinced that Mrs Hutchings had committed suicide. Some gentlemen travelled to London to plead his case on the night before the execution and were received by the Prime Minister, Lord John Russell. A crowd gathered outside the prison, despite the heavy rain, and the prison bell began to toll at 11 a.m. A messenger arrived from London, respiting the execution for a few hours while the trial judge was consulted, and a notice was posted on the gate. Spectators saw another messenger arrive at 3 p.m. quickly followed by a notice of 'Immediate Execution' being placed outside the gate.

John Hutchings had suffered intensely during the extra hours of waiting and had to be assisted out to the scaffold. He refused to confess as he went to the gallows and said 'If I confess the crime to man I will go into another state of existence with a lie in my mouth.' When standing on the gallows he cried out to the crowd 'My God I am innocent, you are murdering an innocent man. By God, I am innocent!' He continued protesting until the drop fell; he struggled a short while and died. The prison chaplain believed in his innocence and he was not alone; Hangman Calcraft, convinced after sharing the condemned man's last painful hours, said he was never so put out in his life.

Also hanged this day:

1802 USA: hired hand Ebenezer Mason, for the murder of his farmer boss William Pitt Allen, whose head he battered with a shovel 'because I didn't like him ordering me about'.

8 October

Hanged this day:

1878 at Wandsworth Prison: Thomas Smithers for the murder of Amy Judge.

1900 at Chelmsford Gaol: William Barrett for wife-murder.

9 October

Hanged this day:

1866 at Old Bailey: J. R. Jefferies for the murder of his son (7).

1879 at Sunbury, Pennsylvania, USA: Peter McManus for the 'Molly Maguire' murder of Frederick Hesser, the twentieth and last of the Molly Maguires to be hanged (see 21 June).

1952 P. C. Johnson for the murder of C. Mead at Bethnal Green.

10 October

1923 FALSELY ACCUSED HUSBAND
Susan Newell (30) hanged at Duke Street Prison, Glasgow, for the strangling of newspaperboy John Johnston (13) and pushing his body through the streets of Glasgow in a handcart.
Hangman: John Ellis. Assistant: Robert Baxter

Susan Newell was a spiteful woman. In June 1923 she had assaulted her husband, John Newell, and twice dealt him blows to the head. He reported her to the police. On the following day there was another argument, this time because he was going to attend his brother's funeral, and John Newell walked out of their Coatbridge apartment. He spent the night at his father's house and most of the next day in Glasgow, about ten miles away. He went to his sister's house when he returned to Coatbridge at 10.30 p.m.

Earlier that evening, between 6 p.m. and 7 p.m., his wife had called 13-year-old newspaper seller John Johnston to the Newells' rented room. Susan Newell was unsuccessful in trying to get a paper without paying for it; she flew into a rage and strangled the boy, afterwards laying his dead body on the settee where it was seen by her eight-year-old

329

daughter Janet. Mrs Newell trussed the boy's body and enlisted Janet to help her stuff it into a rug-covered bundle.

Susan Newell now had to get rid of the body, and she had decided what to do by the next morning. Again with the help of little Janet, it was carried downstairs and put into a handcart. With Janet sitting on top of the bundle, they set off towards Glasgow.

A helpful lorry driver gave them a lift and set them down in Glasgow's Duke Street. As the cart was taken from the lorry the bundle was dislodged, a foot stuck out of one end and the boy's head from the other, but the driver didn't see it. However, a woman looking out of her window had seen everything before Mrs Newell was able to cover the bundle again; she and her sister left the house and followed.

Mrs Newell wheeled the cart through the streets of Glasgow until she unloaded the bundle into a courtyard. By now the police had been sent for and she was arrested as she climbed over a wall. Susan Newell had a story ready for the police: her husband had murdered the boy and she had got rid of the body to help him! This tale was corroborated by little Janet, who had been primed with what to say.

John and Susan Newell were both charged with murder and were brought to trial. John Newell was able conclusively to prove his movements on the day of the murder and the judge ordered his immediate release, adding that he should never have been brought to trial. Little Janet admitted she had lied on the orders of her mother. The jury brought in a majority verdict of guilty after little more than half an hour, adding a recommendation for mercy.

There was to be no reprieve and Susan Newell was the first woman to be hanged in Scotland for more than half a century. Hangman Ellis wrote to the Sheriff pointing out that there are special problems in hanging a woman and requested that the special body straps made for the hanging of Mrs Thompson at Pentonville* be made available. Ellis failed to pinion her correctly and she got her hands free and refused to allow him to put the white hood over her head. According to witnesses, she died bravely.

* *John Ellis and Robert Baxter had been the hangmen at the execution of Edith Thompson on 9 January 1923.*

11 October

1877 KILLING FOR 'THE OLD SOUTH'
'Wild Bill' Longley (26) hanged in Giddings, Texas, USA, for shooting 'about 30' blacks.

William P. Longley was born in Evergreen, Texas, in 1851. Too young to fight for the Southern cause in the Civil War (1861–65) he embarked on an 11-year career of killing 'for the old South' once the war was over.

His first killing happened a year after the Civil War, when he was 15: he shot a black lawyer because he thought the man had an 'arrogant manner'. The rest of his life was spent avenging the destruction of the old South, which he could barely have known. His 30 or more victims were mostly blacks, but he also hated (and killed) carpet-baggers and Northerners. For a year he rode with the outlaw vigilante gang led by Cullen Baker, the Confederate Irregulars, until the gang was wiped out at the end of 1868.

After 1868 he operated as a lone wolf throughout a number of southern states, killing blacks more or less at random. He returned to Evergreen in April 1875 to ambush and kill rancher Wilson Anderson, because he suspected Anderson of having killed a cousin in a local feud. After this he was a most wanted fugitive, but it was nearly two years before he was captured. Four thousand people, mostly blacks, watched his hanging, and cheered as he hung at the rope's end.

Also hanged this day:

1870   at Horsemonger Lane Gaol: Margaret Waters for the baby-farming murder of infants.

1892   at Wandsworth Prison: John J. Banbury for the murder of Emma Oakley.

12 October

1865 MURDER ON PARADE
Sapper John Currie (19), Royal Engineers, hanged outside Maidstone Prison, for the gun-murder of Major Horatio De Vere on the parade ground at Chatham Barracks.
Hangman: William Calcraft

Major De Vere was inspecting soldiers on the parade ground at Chatham Barracks on 11 August 1865 when Sapper John Currie, from a nearby window, took deliberate aim with his rifle and fired a single shot at the officer. Major De Vere was wounded in the chest and died on 22 August.

Sapper Currie, who had served for a year in the Royal Engineers, was quickly arrested. Rather than keeping Currie in custody for the Kent Winter Assizes he was sent for trial at the Central Criminal Court at the Old Bailey, 'in order that the law might the sooner take its course'. He was found guilty, sentenced to death, and returned to Maidstone Prison.

Currie had been a popular soldier with his comrades, had been well educated, and came from a decent Presbyterian family. It is not clear what his grievance was against Major De Vere, but he afterwards deeply regretted his crime and made this clear to visitors and prison officials. He wanted to write to Mrs De Vere, but was dissuaded; instead he wrote to the military chaplain and asked him to pass his regrets to Mrs De Vere and the family.

Currie was calmly resigned about what would happen to him. He slept well on his last night, ate a light breakfast, and walked to the scaffold without fuss, singing a hymn in a loud and firm voice. He was accompanied by a Presbyterian minister, whose lengthy prayers kept the young soldier standing for a long time beneath the gallows with the rope round his neck. Hangman Calcraft eventually pulled the bolt, but young John Currie's agonies were not over quickly: he struggled violently for a long time before lapsing into unconsciousness as a prelude to death by strangulation.

13 October

1660 DEATH FOR THE REGICIDES
The Regicides were 'the men who killed the king', Charles I: Hugh Peters (62), Major General Thomas Harrison (54), Cook and five others, hanged, drawn and quartered at Charing Cross.
Hangman: (probably) Edward Dun

The Regicides were the 67 judges and parliamentarians, headed by Oliver Cromwell, who conducted the trial of King Charles I and signed his death warrant. The king was sentenced to death and beheaded on a platform outside the Banqueting Hall in Whitehall on 30 January 1649.

After the Commonwealth failed and the monarchy was restored with Charles II on the throne, in May 1660, an Act of Pardon For Past Offences was signed, but this specifically excluded the Regicides and 20 others. Ten of the Regicides still living at the Restoration were tried and condemned to the traitors' death: hanging, drawing and quartering. Another 25 received life imprisonment and three more, captured abroad, were put to death later. Regicides who surrendered were promised their lives: Colonel Hutchinson and Henry Martin did so and were imprisoned for life.

The executions of the Regicides took place at Charing Cross*, although the original cross had been destroyed as 'a godless image' during the miserable Puritan regime. The former chaplain to Cromwell's army, Hugh Peters, arrived for execution on a sledge at the tail of a horse just as Cook was being cut down from the gallows to be drawn and quartered. The Sheriff ordered Peters to be brought closer to witness his friend's agony, and see what was soon to happen to him.

The executioner laid the still-living Cook on the table, stripped him of all his clothes, slit open his abdomen and drew out the intestines to burn them on the brazier in front of Cook's face. Then he cut off the head and quartered the body. The leering hangman rubbed his bloody hands together and asked 'Come, how do you like this work Mr Peters?' Major General Thomas Harrison is said to have jumped from the table and boxed the hangman's ears after being disembowelled, and was cheered by the mob for his pluck!

Even some dead Regicides were punished! The bodies of Oliver Cromwell, Henry Ireton, and John Bradshaw (who presided at the trial of Charles I) were disinterred from their graves in Westminster Abbey, dragged on a sledge to Tyburn, hanged on the gallows until sunset and then beheaded. The bodies were thrown into the common pit beside the Tyburn Tree. Cromwell's head was mounted on a 25-feet tall pole with an iron tip and left on display on top of Westminster Hall throughout the reign of Charles II.

* On the site of the executions is a statue of Charles I on a horse in sight of the spot where the Regicides had 'killed the king'.

Also hanged this day:

1874   at Horsemonger Lane Gaol: John Walter Coppen for wife-murder.

14 October

Hanged this day:

1861   at Old Bailey: William Cogan for wife-murder.

15 October

1867 MISTRESS-MURDERS
John Wiggins publicly hanged – after a struggle – at 8 a.m. at Old Bailey, outside Newgate Prison, for the murder of his mistress Agnes Oates in Limehouse. Louis Bordier hanged at 10 a.m. on the roof of Horsemonger Lane Gaol for the murder of his concubine, Mary Ann Snow.
Hangman at Newgate: William Calcraft

The execution of John Wiggins attracted the smallest crowd ever to witness a London hanging; there were fewer people at Old Bailey and on Ludgate Hill than on a normal working day.

While he was still in the Press Yard of Newgate Prison, being made ready to walk out to the scaffold in Old Bailey, he was told that he would not be able to address the crowd and that, if he had anything to say, he had better say it then in the presence of the press. He said:

'I am entirely innocent of the charge for which I am about to die. I can assure you on my dying oath I never did it. I can go with a clear conscience and a clear heart to my Almighty Maker. It was her that cut my throat and then cut her own. I never lifted a hand or a finger to her, with my dying breath.'

When they got on to the scaffold there was an awful struggle. Wiggins resisted Calcraft's efforts to get him under the gallows' beam and four warders were needed to manhandle him there. Even when the white hood was over his face he managed to work it loose and shouted 'I am innocent! Cut my head off, but don't hang me, I am innocent!'

Although his arms were pinioned at the elbows, in front of him, he somehow grabbed the rope and clung to it with a strong grip. Calcraft and the warders overcame his resistance using brute force and the trap doors were finally opened. Wiggins died swiftly once this was done.

There was a bigger crowd assembled at 10 a.m. to watch Bordier's hanging at Horsemonger Lane. It passed without incident.

Also hanged this day:

1737 at Tyburn Tree: Robert Barrow for theft.

1877 at Newgate Prison: John Lynch for wife-murder.

16 October

1946 NUREMBERG HANGINGS
Nazi leaders hanged in the gymnasium at Nuremberg Prison, for crimes against humanity.
Hangman: Master Sergeant John C. Woods (US army)

Twenty Nazi leaders were tried by the International Military Tribunal, which began on 18 October 1945, in the Palace of Justice at Nuremberg. On 30 September 1946, 11 of the Nazis were sentenced to death by hanging. They were not informed of the day or the place of execution, but some of them suspected that it was their last night when they went to bed at 10 p.m. on 15 October. They were to be woken at 11.45 p.m. to be informed that the executions were imminent, to have their sentences read to them again, and to choose their last meal from a limited menu.

A separate black cotton hood and a new rope, with the gruesome 'hangman's knot' which tends to strangle rather than bring instant death, was used on each of the condemned. Their deaths, with their final words, occurred in the following order:

Reichmarshal Hermann Wilhelm Goering (53), ex-Chief of the Luftwaffe and the most powerful Nazi after Hitler. He committed suicide by biting on a glass capsule of cyanide while in bed in his cell at about 10.50 p.m., the capsule's metal outer container lying open under his hand. How he obtained the poison and successfully hid it are still mysteries. It was probably smuggled to him while in prison at Nuremberg and secreted in a cavity under an old scar on his body.

Reichminister Joachim Von Ribbentrop (53), Hitler's last Foreign Minister. He was the first to be hanged and he entered the gymnasium handcuffed to two soldiers at two minutes after 1 a.m. looking pale and a physical wreck. Hangman Woods asked him for his full name and then led him up the 13 wooden steps to the wooden platform that had three gallows.

In accordance with the American custom, he was then asked if he had anything to say and a stenographer waited notebook in hand. His final words, standing on the trap door beneath the gallows, were: 'God guard Germany! God have mercy on my soul! My final wish is that Germany should recover her unity and that, for the sake of world peace, there should be understanding between East and West.'

Hangman Woods was in no hurry and a witness said that Ribbentrop 'had to wait an infinity of time for death'. Woods fitted the black hood over the head, tied it under the chin and then set about placing the rope. When Woods released the trap door Ribbentrop fell 'like a stone', but he took ten minutes to die at the end of the rope as the American and Russian doctors verified.

Field Marshal Wilhelm Von Keitel (64), ex-Chief of the High Command of the Armed Forces. He ordered the killing of the Allied air-force officers after the Great Escape (see 27 February). Wearing uniform trousers with the general's red stripes he spoke his final words: 'I call upon the Almighty to have mercy on the German people. Over two million soldiers have gone to their death for the Fatherland before me. I am following my sons. *Deutschland über alles!*' It was 24 minutes after the drop before he died.

General Ernst Kaltenbrunner (44), ex-Head of the Reich Central Security (SS and Gestapo), successor to Heydrich and deputy to Himmler. During the trial he had flatly denied that the concentration camp atrocities had taken place or that the SS had committed any of the crimes attributed to them.

'I have served my people and my Fatherland with all my heart. I

335

have done my duty according to the laws of my country. I regret that at this grave time my people are not being led exclusively by military men. I regret that crimes have been committed, I had no part in them. Good luck to Germany.'

Reichminister Alfred Rosenberg (53), ex-Minister for Occupied Eastern Territories.

Reichminister Hans Frank (46), ex-Governor General of Poland. His last, whispered, words were: 'I am grateful for the good treatment accorded me during imprisonment. I pray the Lord God to receive me with mercy.'

Reichminister Wilhelm Frick (69), ex-Minister of the Interior responsible for the anti-semitic and concentration camp laws. He almost collapsed while climbing the steps and had to be helped to the gallows, but gathered his wits enough to gasp 'Long live eternal Germany!' before dying. His nose was severed in the fall, either by his head hitting the edge of the trap or by the rope being loosely fitted.

Gauleiter Julius Streicher (61), Jew-baiter, pornographer, editor of the rabble-rousing *Die Stürmer*, perpetrator of atrocities against Jews. He had to be dragged into the gymnasium by his soldier escorts, screaming *'Heil Hitler!'* and wearing only his underclothes as he had refused to dress. Later he said 'Festival of Purim 1946, and now to God. The Bolshevists will hang you too! I am with God, Father.' And then, just before the trap was opened, 'Adele, my beloved Adele.' He swung on the rope, groaning, for a long time.

Reichminister Fritz Sauckel, ex-General Plenipotentiary for the Utilisation of Labour (the slave-labour programme). In a terrified voice he cried, 'I die in innocence! The judgement is wrong! God protect Germany and make Germany great once more. Long live Germany! God protect my family!' He, too, was heard to groan as he slowly strangled.

Colonel-General Alfred Jodl (56), ex-Chief of the General Staff and planner of the war. He maintained his pride to the last: 'I salute you my Germany.' He strangled slowly, taking 18 minutes to die.

Gauleiter Artur Von Seyss-Inquart (54), ex-Governor of Austria and later Commissioner for Occupied Holland. Calmly, solemnly, he stood awaiting death with these final words: 'I hope that this execution is the last act in the tragedy of the Second World War, that lessons will be learned from this World War and that peace and understanding between peoples will be the result. I have faith in Germany.'

The ten executions had taken exactly 1 hour and 43 minutes. The bodies were laid out on the gymnasium floor and Goering was brought and put there with them, as 'symbolically hanged': other reports claim that his corpse was hanged for real and that there was nothing symbolic about it. The men were photographed with the ropes still round their necks, both clothed and naked. Some of the faces were

336

bloodied, Frick's being particularly badly damaged.

Clearly, the hangings were brutally bungled and death had not been instantaneous. Some of the press witnesses claimed that the ropes had been too short, or wrongly positioned, which prolonged the process of dying. Others said that the trap door had been too small causing some to hit the sides as they fell.

Immediately after the executions the bodies were taken southwards down the *autobahn* to the former concentration camp at Dachau, on the northern outskirts of Munich, and cremated in the notorious ovens. The black hoods and the ropes were burned with them. The ashes were thrown into the River Isar.

Also hanged this day:

1771   at Tyburn Tree: Mary Jones for the theft of four pieces of muslin worth £5.10.0 (£5.50) from a shop on Ludgate Hill. *Hangman: Edward Dennis*

17 October

1941 THE *REAL* TONY MANCINI
Antonio 'Babe' Mancini (39) hanged at Pentonville Prison for the London gangland knife-murder of Harry 'Scarface' Distleman (36) in Wardour Street.
Hangman: Albert Pierrepoint (his first time in charge). Assistant: Steve Wade

The Brighton Trunk Murder of 1934 was a national sensation. The accused was an evil-looking brute whose greasy appearance sent thrills of horror through newspaper readers and he used the name Tony Mancini. He was on the run after the discovery of the body of prostitute Violette Kaye (Mancini had been her pimp), in a trunk at a Brighton lodging house.

Mancini was brilliantly defended by Norman Birkett and it was that advocate's greatest triumph to have Mancini acquitted. More than 40 years later, in 1976, Mancini admitted 'I've got away with murder' in a story in the *News Of The World*, confessing to a reporter that he had killed Violette Kaye after all. He was really Cecil Lois England, but he used a string of aliases including Jack Notyre, Hyman Gold and, most famously, Tony Mancini. The latter was the name of another London hoodlum who he knew slightly.

The *real* Tony Mancini, Antonio Babe Mancini, was to face his own murder trial in 1941, but he didn't have the luck to get away with it like the man who had used his name had. Babe Mancini was the manager of the Palm Beach Club in Soho's Wardour Street in May 1941. He got into a fight with two other gangsters in the Billiards Club in the same building and, in a mad rage, chased them around the billiard tables making stabbing thrusts with his knife. One of the pair, Harry Scarface Distleman, staggered outside, fell down and died in the street. He had been stabbed under the left armpit and the axillary artery had been severed; the work of an experienced knife-fighter.

Mancini tried to claim that the two men had attacked him and that he had fought in self-defence. He denied stabbing Distleman at all, but nearly 40 men had been in the Billiards Club at the time and had seen his violent rampage. He was found guilty and sentenced to death; the verdict was upheld at the Court of Criminal Appeal and at the House of Lords. Mancini walked calmly to the gallows and whispered 'Cheerio' as Pierrepoint pulled the white hood over his face.

Also hanged this day:

1911   at Pentonville Prison: Francisco Charles Godhino (40), a Lascar seaman, for the murder on the high seas of Miss Brewster, a stewardess on the P&O liner *China*. Also Edward Hill (41), a Kings Cross fireman, for wife-murder.

18 October

1837 FRENZY AFTER WORKMATES' TAUNTS
William Perrie (38) hanged in front of the County Hall in Paisley, Scotland, for wife-murder.

William Perrie, originally from Glasgow, had worked as a tobacco spinner in Paisley for ten years. He had been a decent and loving family man, with warm religious beliefs. His wife had died two years earlier and after more than a year he married his second wife, Mary Mitchell. Mary was a woman of loose habits who had been the paid mistress of a married man to whom she bore two children. In her company, William Perrie went downhill: he stopped attending church and took to heavy drinking.

About eight months after marrying Mary, the taunts of his fellow workers in the tobacco workshop about her unfaithful conduct inflamed him to a jealous rage. He went home for his midday dinner, put the children out of the house and bolted the door. He attacked his new wife in a wild frenzy and stabbed her eight times with a small three-edged file, so violently that any one of the wounds could have been the fatal one.

338

He was arrested and taken to the prison at once. He repented immediately and spent most of his time in prayer, admitting his guilt. He was visited by many Church of Scotland ministers as well as his relations. His two sons, aged 10 and 5, were with him for a tearful last meeting on the night before his execution when he hugged the eldest boy as close to him as possible through the iron grating that separated them. He slept soundly. After rising his final hours were spent in more prayers. He was taken out to the scaffold in front of the County Hall at 8 a.m., before a large crowd, attended by the sheriff, magistrates, and two church ministers. The last ten minutes of his life were spent with the noose around his neck, standing in silent personal prayer until, at 8.30 a.m., he gave the pre-arranged signal and the hangman released the drop. His death was immediate.

The *Times* correspondent reported 'The whole space in front of the County-buildings was completely filled, and Gilmour Street was likewise crowded from Dyer's Wynd to Sneddon Street. An involuntary shudder seemed to run through this immense crowd when the drop fell; all seemed shocked with the sight. . .'

19 October

1845 THE MURDER OF COLONEL DAVENPORT
John Long, his brother Aaron Long, and Granville Young, hanged at Rock Island, Iowa, USA, for the murder of the district's most prominent personality, Colonel George Davenport.

George Davenport had been born in England, but had moved to America when young and had become a US citizen. He rose to the rank of colonel in the US army and fought against the British in the war of 1812 and in the Indian wars. He built a fine mansion near Rock Island, prospered in the Indian fur trade, was well respected and was a fine looking man with a mane of white hair. He had entertained a guest in his home, John Baxter, who treacherously informed a gang of thieves that the mansion would be empty on 4 July 1845 when the whole household would be at independence celebrations at Rock Island.

The colonel was unwell and decided to stay on his own at the mansion. The gang arrived and broke in. At least one of them, Robert Birch, had been present at the murder of John Miller and Leicy two months earlier. The others were John and Aaron Long and William the 'Judge' Fox. Aaron Long stayed outside as lookout while John Long, Robert Birch and Judge Fox entered from the back of the house.

Colonel Davenport was sitting in the front room and heard a noise.

Going to investigate he was shot in the leg by John Long, the shell severing an artery. He was jumped upon by the three men, bound and blindfolded, and then dragged upstairs by his shirt collar. They forced him to open the safe, but were disappointed to find only about $700 there. They beat the old man to tell them where his other money was and he told them it was in the bank, which was true, but they would not believe him. They continued beating and choking him. When he lost consciousness they made off with the $700, his gold watch and chain, a double-barrelled shotgun and a pistol.

Davenport's cries for help were heard by a family out fishing who were passing by on the river. They raised the alarm and brought a doctor. The colonel was able to give a good description of his attackers, which led to their eventual capture by a man named Edward Bonney. Colonel Davenport died that night. The shocking murder horrified everyone in the area and there was intense pressure for the capture of his killers.

Edward Bonney, a private investigator, read the descriptions given by Davenport. He recognised them as fitting three of the men who had attempted to give a false alibi at the Hodges brothers' trial at West Point for the murders of Miller and Leicy (see 15 July): John and Aaron Long and Judge Fox. Bonney's investigations resulted in the capture of most of the gang that had been responsible for countless brutal robberies and cold-blooded murder.

Judge Fox and later Robert Birch, two of the worst gang members, escaped by bribing crooked lawmen. The treacherous guest, John Baxter, had his trial delayed until 1847 when he was sentenced to death, but this was commuted to life imprisonment. John and Aaron Long and Granville Young (accessory) were tried on 6 October and sentenced to hang ten days after the end of the trial.

When the trap door was released John Long and Young died at once, their necks broken by the drop, but Aaron Long's rope snapped and he fell to the ground. Still dazed by the fall, he was rushed up to the gallows again. While the new rope was fixed round his neck he saw his brother and Young hanging dead beside him. The chaplain cried 'They have gone and you must soon follow. You have no hope of escape. If you are guilty, confess your guilt to God!' Quaking, Aaron Long confessed his part in the murder with his brother John, Fox, and Birch.

Also hanged this day:

1685 at Tyburn Tree: John Fernley, William Ring and Henry Cornish hanged, drawn, beheaded and quartered for high treason. Elizabeth Gaunt was sentenced to be hanged and then burnt to death. Elizabeth Gaunt was convicted with the men but, it being considered unseemly to expose a woman's naked body in front of the mob for disembowelling and quartering, she was first hanged and then taken down before expiring and burned alive.

1825 at Old Bailey: William Austin for letter-stealing; Samuel Cook for burglary.

1829 at Old Bailey: Richard Chick and Jonah Nathan for burglary.

1875 at Dumbarton Prison, Scotland: David Wardlaw for wife-murder.

1883 at the Tombs Prison, New York, USA: Edward Hovey for the gun-murder of his sister-in-law at the dinner table, for criticising his table manners.

1928 at San Quentin Prison, California, USA: William Edward Hickman (20), known as the Fox, for the kidnapping-murder and dismemberment of Marian Parker (12).

20 October

Hanged this day:

1824 at Chester, Pennsylvania, USA: Michael Monroe, a.k.a. James Wellington, for the stabbing-murder of William Bonsall during a burglary.

1862 at Old Bailey: Catherine Wilson for the poisoning-murder of Mrs Soames and others.

1898 at Granite Falls, Minnesota, USA: Joseph Ott for beating his wife to death. A crowd of four hundred watched his hanging and, as he stood on the gallows, he greeted them 'I bid you all good evening!'

21 October

Hanged this day:

1803 at Dublin, Ireland: Thomas Russell for high treason.

1875 at Armley Gaol, Leeds: William Smedley for the murder of Elizabeth Firth.

22 October

Hanged this day:

1858 at Rochester, New York, USA: Marion Ira Stout for murder.

23 October

1834   at Cathcart Square, Greenock, Scotland: John Boyd for wife-murder.

1891   at Fergus Falls, Minnesota, USA: Adelbert Goheen for the gun-murder of his mistress Rosetta Bray after falling for another woman. He stood on the gallows and defiantly yelled 'Let her go, Jack! Goodbye!'

24 October

1707   at St James's Street, Piccadilly, London: John Brian for arson.

1748   at Tyburn Tree: Thomas Thompson for horse-stealing.

1820   at Old Bailey: Joseph Ellengor and George Edwards for highway robbery; James Marsden and Isaac Smith for issuing forged notes; Thomas Webb for sacrilege.

1831   at Inverness, Scotland: Hugh McLeod, schoolmaster of Assynt in Sutherland, for the hammer-murder and robbery of Murdock Grant (25), a pedlar.

25 October

1822 THE FRENZIED CUCKOLD
John Lechlar publicly hanged at Lancaster, Pennsylvania, USA, for the murder of his wife and her lover's wife.

When John Lechlar came home and discovered his wife in bed with a neighbour, John Haag, he flew into a murderous rage and was going to kill them both. Lechlar's fury was not an early Pennsylvanian version of the 'badger game' (see 19 February), it was for real. However, what followed was the badger game scenario: Haag, in a panic to save his life, offered Lechlar a sum of money as compensation for cuckolding him. Lechlar calmed down and the relieved Haag signed a promissory note.

342

Haag did not pay up and when Lechlar realised that he was never going to get the money his fury was regenerated. He went home and strangled his wife and hung her body from a rope thrown over a beam in the attic. He armed himself with two pistols and went looking for Haag. John Haag locked himself in his house and Lechlar stood outside raging at Haag and demanding that he come out, a request that was refused. Lechlar, in a frenzy, fired blindly through the door. Haag was unscathed, but his wife was killed.

Lechlar was tried and sentenced to hang. Lancaster newspapers organised what must have been one of the first opinion polls; the majority of those taking part voted in support of the execution going ahead.

Also hanged this day:

1706 at Turnham Green, Middlesex: Roger Lewin for murder.

26 October

1440 THE PERVERTED ARISTOCRAT
Marshal of France, the Baron Gilles de Rais (36) hanged with accomplices Poitou and Henriet outside the city of Nantes, France, for alchemy, Satanism, and the sexual torture and murder of between 140 and 800 boys.

Gilles de Rais was one of the richest aristocrats in France, owning five great estates. At 16 he was married to an heiress of almost equal wealth. He fought alongside Joan of Arc, financing her armies, and led his own personal retinue of two hundred knights into battle. At the age of only 25 he was created a Marshal of France and he personally placed the crown on the head of King Charles VII at his coronation. He saw Joan of Arc burned as a witch-heretic in 1431 and his character changed, for the worse.

He retired to his estates and had his servants kidnap or purchase orphans, or children of the poor, for his perverted pleasures in the cellar of the chateau. His 'pleasures' were devil-worship, sodomy, cruel torturings to death, mutilations, and throat-cuttings. At times, as he was about to orgasm inside a boy, either he or a servant would slit the child's jugular so that the blood spurted over him. Other times he would masturbate over the prostrate body of a child in its final agonised death-writhings.

He became obsessed with Satanism and alchemy and, it seems, anything debased and evil. His beating of a priest led to him being arraigned before an ecclesiastical court which, in turn, led to stories being told about his foul practices in the chateau cellar. His servants were put to torture and a damning case was prepared. He confessed when threatened with torture himself and admitted to the charge of killing 140 children, but agreed that there were more than that, 'at least 800'.

The Bishop of Nantes handed him and his accomplices over to a civil court accusing him of being a 'heretic, sorcerer, sodomite, invocator of evil spirits, diviner, alchemist, killer of innocents, apostate from the faith, and idolator'. A guilty verdict on these charges would ensure that his estates would be forfeited to the Church, which may have coloured some of the charges and the massed evidence.

About 20 of his servants were convicted: some were sentenced to burning at the stake, others to hanging or garrotting. De Rais was sentenced to be burned to death, but he was instead granted the 'mercy' of a hanging because of his contrition, his return to the faith and, no doubt, for not recanting his confession. Before going to his death he begged the Bishop for his forgiveness, which the Bishop granted. He was hanged outside the city of Nantes, along with his main accomplices Poitou and Henriet. Their bodies were then thrown into the raging fire and consumed.

Also hanged this day:

1855   at Colma, California, USA: J. V. Craine for the murder of his sweetheart Susan M. Newnham.

1946   at Pentonville Prison: Neville George Clevely Heath (28) for the sadistic sex-murder of Margery Gardner (32). He killed again while on the run. *Hangman: Albert Pierrepoint*

27 October

1666 THE GREAT FIRE OF LONDON
Robert Hubert (26), a French Huguenot, hanged at Tyburn Tree for starting the Great Fire of London.

The Great Fire had started in the shop of Thomas Farrynor, the king's baker, at 25 Pudding Lane. Farrynor's maid was the first fatal casualty, although he, his wife, daughter and another servant escaped from an attic window along a gutter. The fire began between 2 a.m. and 3 a.m. on 2 September 1666 and lasted four days. Some 84 parish churches and 13,200 houses were destroyed when 400 streets were engulfed in the Great Fire, leaving 100,000 homeless. Amazingly, it is believed that only six people were killed.

There was public fury at 'Papists and foreigners' who, in popular belief, must have been responsible for the disaster. A victim was needed and if a scapegoat became available the authorities would sacrifice him. Robert Hubert was a watchmaker from Rouen, France, who was seized at Romford in Essex as he apparently tried to flee the country. When questioned by Cary Harvie, the Justice at Romford, Hubert made the astonishing confession that he had thrown a fireball and started the Great Fire. He caused more excitement when he declared that he was a Catholic! (This was later found to be untrue; he had been a Protestant all his life.) Almost certainly a madman, he further declared that he belonged to a group of 320 Frenchmen led by a man named Stephen Peidloe and that they had conspired to destroy London by fire.

Hubert was sent to London and tried at the October Sessions at the Old Bailey. There was nothing against him except his own confession, and that was a mad, rambling story that was often contradictory. He now said that, at the suggestion of Peidloe, he had put a fireball on a pole and pushed it through the bakery window.

He was taken at night, blindfolded until arrival, to different parts of the city and asked if that was where he had committed the arson. He said 'no' each time until he got to Pudding Lane and then he accurately indicated the site where Farrynor's shop had been. He also described where the window had been through which he poked the fireball, but Thomas Farrynor, supported by his son and daughter, denied that any such window had existed at the bakery.

The judges seemed to doubt that Hubert was guilty, but could not ignore his confession, and the jury found him guilty. Hubert's identification of where Farrynor's bakery had been meant nothing, as the razed site where the fire began had been on public show. Too late it was discovered, on the sworn testimony of Captain Petersen, the Master of the ship that brought him to London, that Hubert did not leave the ship until two days after the fire had started. By the time this was known he had already been hanged.

Also hanged this day:

1714 at Tyburn Tree: Thomas Douglass for the murder of William Sparks; Nathaniel Parkhurst Esq. for the murder of Mr Plura, another gentleman.

1893 outside Fresno County Courthouse, California, USA: Dr Frederick Oscar Vincent for wife-murder. This was one of the last public executions in the state; it drew a large crowd.

28 October

1796 SHE NAGGED KNIFE-SHARPENING HUSBAND
Matthias Gotleib hanged at Newton, New Jersey, USA, for the knife-murder of his wife.

This would have been a commonplace case of wife-murder by a drunken husband, but the odd circumstances made it different. Gotleib returned home and his wife started nagging him about his drunken condition. Purposefully, he picked up a knife and started sharpening it while his wife looked on and continued attacking him with her sharp tongue. He responded with the sharp knife!

29 October

1792 THE MUTINY ON THE *BOUNTY*
Three of the *Bounty* mutineers, Birkitt, Millard, and Ellison, hanged on board HMS *Brunswick* at Portsmouth.

The *Bounty*, with Lieutenant William Bligh as captain, sailed for Tahiti in 1787 to collect breadfruit plants for transportation to the West Indies where they were intended to produce a cheap and plentiful source of food for the slaves. After six months of easy living on Tahiti the crew resented the hardship of life on board ship once they were under sail again, especially having to go short of drinking water while it was lavished on the plants. Morale and discipline degenerated and on 28 April 1789, under the leadership of First Mate Fletcher Christian, the crew mutinied and cast Bligh and 18 others adrift in a 23-foot open boat. Miraculously, Bligh and 12 of his men survived to reach Timor, near Java, on 14 June after an epic voyage of 3,600 miles.

The mutineers returned to Tahiti to take native wives and 15 of them, including Fletcher Christian, later departed and settled on Pitcairn Island. Their haven was not discovered until 1808. The ten mutineers who had remained on Tahiti were later captured and tried by court martial at Portsmouth, six of whom were convicted and sentenced to death. Two of the condemned, Mr Heywood and James Morrison, were told on 28 October that the king had pardoned them and that they were to be released. The sentence on William Musprat was respited for 14 days to allow the judges to consider new evidence admitted on his behalf.

Birkitt, Millard, and Ellison were brought on to the deck of the *Brunswick* at 11 a.m. the following morning. They embraced each other repeatedly, saying 'God bless you, God receive you in mercy.' At 11.30 a.m. the cannon signalling death was fired and they were hoisted to their deaths.

Captain Bligh's name became synonymous with the harsh and cruel disciplinarian in command of a ship at sea, mostly because of the three *Mutiny On The Bounty* films: with Charles Laughton (1935), Trevor Howard (1962), and Anthony Hopkins (1984), portraying Bligh. This is most unjust: he was one of the earliest captains to provide cirtrus fruits to prevent scurvy; in hot climates he had a part of the deck covered with a canvas awning to provide shade for off-watch crewmen, and even a fiddler to entertain them. Because he ordered fewer floggings than was the norm in those harsh days, his contemporary captains considered him to be too lenient.

Also hanged this day:

1900   at Newgate Prison: John Parr (19), a French-polisher, for the gun-murder of Sarah Willott (19) on 27 August.

30 October

1857 KILLED FOR THE WAGES
James Copeland (42) hanged at Mississippi, USA, for the $1,000 hired-gun killing of another assassin, James A. Harvey, in 1848. Copeland was hired by the Wages family to avenge the murder of their son.

Copeland was the leader of a gang of highwaymen and hired killers operating along the Mississippi during the 1840s. The Wages family owned extensive areas of land around Augusta. They were rich, powerful, and ruthlessly corrupt. One of them, Gale H. Wages, rode in Copeland's gang. Gale Wages and another gang member, Charles McGrath, were killed by James Harvey in 1848. The head of the Wages family wanted revenge for the death of his son and offered James Copeland $1,000 to kill Harvey.

Copeland took the job and shot Harvey in Augusta on 15 July 1848, but was soon arrested, tried and condemned to death. Copeland kept quiet about the involvement of the Wages family and they, in turn, used their power to delay execution for more than nine years.

31 October

1814 THE KENTISH TOWN MURDER
Thomas Sharpe publicly hanged at Old Bailey for the murder of washerwoman Elizabeth Dobbins in Kentish Town, London, and the theft of some clothes she had taken for washing. The 'Kentish Town Murder' gained some notoriety in 1814.

James Dobbins was a turncock for the Hampstead Water Company who lived with Elizabeth Buchanon, his common-law wife who was known as Mrs Dobbins, in a cottage at Millfield Lane, Kentish Town, north west of London. While Dobbins was out at his work on 4 October 1814, his wife was in the kitchen working on a pile of washing that she had taken in. A vagrant, Thomas Sharpe, entered the kitchen and battered Elizabeth to death with a poker, smashing her skull which was laid open from the right eye to the back of the head. Sharpe made off with a bundle of garments from the pile.

Dobbins came home and discovered the crime, with the bent poker laying nearby covered in blood and brain tissue. Going outside to get help he met neighbours, who had Sharpe in their custody! Sharpe had been seen acting suspiciously as he crossed Highgate Hill carrying the bundle of clothes and, unable to explain himself satisfactorily, had been detained. Dobbins was able to identify some of the stolen clothing, and Sharpe was taken to the magistrate and charged with murder.

His trial was held at the Old Bailey towards the end of the same month as the murder. Many witnesses gave evidence of having seen Sharpe in the vicinity of the cottage on the afternoon of the crime, and with the stolen clothes. Found guilty and condemned to death, the recorder added the customary 'And may the Lord have mercy on your soul', to which Sharpe replied by shouting 'May the curse of God be upon you night and day, both in this world and in the next!'

Thomas Sharpe refused all efforts to persuade him to confess while he waited, shackled in irons, in the condemned cell at Newgate. Taken out to be hanged on the following Monday morning he relented: 'I am the murderer, but there is a merciful God.'

Also hanged this day:

1793 at Worcester, Massachusetts, USA: Samuel Frost for murdering Captain Elisha Allen with a hoe. Ten years earlier he had killed his father by ramming a spike into his head, but was acquitted.

1940 S. E. Cole for the murder of Mrs D. E. Girl at Wimbledon.

NOVEMBER

1 November

1946 MURDER IN A KING'S HOUSE
Arthur Boyce hanged in the prison yard at Pentonville Prison, for the murder of housekeeper Miss Elizabeth McLindon (41) at the Belgravia home of King George II of Greece.

Arthur Boyce, convicted forger and bigamist, was employed as a painter on Brighton Pier, but made more money as an illegal bookmaker. He lived well and struck up a relationship with Elizabeth McLindon, a high-class prostitute. Miss McLindon wanted to obtain the position of housekeeper to the exiled King George II of Greece, who would soon be moving from a suite at Claridges to a house at 45 Chester Square in London's Belgravia. Boyce forged a number of glowing testimonials purporting to be from highly placed Greeks: Miss McLindon used them, and got the job. She was installed in the empty house in Chester Square to prepare it as the Greek king's London residence.

She continued to receive her gentlemen callers at her new address, which did not go unnoticed by the servants at other houses in Chester Square. Arthur Boyce was one of her callers and he wanted her to marry him. He had given her an expensive jewelled ring, just as her other lovers had given her high-priced jewellery, but her feelings for him had cooled. Having now obtained her new job with his forged letters and no longer needing him, she told him it was all over. The spurned and vengeful Boyce, equipped with a .32 pistol, was therefore the last man that she received into the king's house.

She let him into the house on the evening of Saturday 8 June 1946. Just as she did not know about the pistol, he did not know that earlier that day a jeweller had called and reclaimed the ring because his cheque for £135 had bounced. She took Boyce into the library and undoubtedly they had a row. The last action of her life was to sit at the table and lift the telephone. Was she calling the police to report his dud cheque? He shot her in the back of the neck, the .32 brass shell case falling to the floor. Boyce let himself out using her keys, had duplicates made, returned and put her keys back in her purse. He left her locked in the library inside the locked and empty house.

The king called at the house the following afternoon, but had no occasion to go to the library and, in any case, the only other key to the room was in his safe at Claridges. The body was not discovered until 14 June, when six days' deliveries of milk bottles on the back doorstep aroused suspicion and the police were called.

Pathologist Keith Simpson calculated that Miss McLindon had been dead for six days and this was confirmed by other evidence. Astonishingly, two opened letters were found in her bedroom which were postmarked 11 and 12 June – days after her death! Boyce had returned to the scene of his crime, possibly in an effort to confuse the police about the date of McLindon's death; all it did was draw attention to himself.

The pistol was never found, but its owner was. John Rowland had shared lodgings with Boyce when his Browning .32 automatic pistol had been stolen from his room, which he had reported to the police at the time. He still had a spent shell case and the firing-pin markings conclusively matched the one found on the library floor: it hanged Boyce.

Also hanged this day:

1819   at Old Bailey: Jane Holmsby for the murder of her illegitimate child.

1938   at Wandsworth Prison: George Brain (27) for the murder of prostitute 'Irish Rose' Atkins (30) at Wimbledon. He beat her with a starting handle, ran her over with his van, and robbed her of four shillings (20p).

2 November

1737 ESCAPED FROM CONDEMNED CELL – TWICE!
Daniel Malden hanged at Tyburn Tree for burglary and street robberies after two sensational escapes from the condemned hold at Newgate.

Daniel Malden was to be hanged on 22 October 1736. In the early hours of that very morning he was at work making a hole under a loose floorboard in the condemned cell at Newgate Prison. Soon he had made the hole big enough to squeeze through and he dropped down to the empty cell below. It was empty because another convict had escaped from it by cutting the window-bar.

Malden climbed out, with his leg-irons still attached, and made off across the roofs until he found an empty house and entered via a garret window. He wrapped his leg-irons in cloths which he bound around his legs and, walking 'as if I had been gouty or lame', he completed his escape, went into hiding and had his irons removed. He evaded recapture for a number of days, but when he sent a shoemaker with a message to his wife the messenger betrayed him. He was taken back to Newgate and stapled to the floor of the strongest condemned hold.

His next escape was made on 6 June 1737. A knife was smuggled to him and he was able to saw through the staple. Using only the knife and his fingernails, he dislodged a stone in the floor and wriggled through the hole, head first, to a tunnel below but got stuck. He hung there for half an hour before he was able to work himself free. He fell 30 feet and the heavy leg-irons (weighing about 100lb) increased the violence of his impact with the floor below.

When he had recovered he moved along the tunnel until he came to the main sewer, where he washed himself and his tattered clothes in the filthy water. Now he faced a new danger: his escape had been discovered and the gaolers were searching for him in the sewer. With incredible luck, he found a hollow in the side of the brickwork and twice the searchers passed him by. He remained hidden there for 48 hours*.

He rejoined his wife and they moved around the country taking what work they could find. His luck ran out at Canterbury after three months of freedom. He and his wife had worked the hop fields and he then became a jockey. Eventually, he was betrayed by a man he had helped.

He arrived back at Newgate on 26 September and was put back into the same condemned hold he had last escaped from, but this time he was handcuffed as well as having his new leg-irons chained to the floor. His original death sentence was confirmed at the Old Bailey in October and from this there was to be no escape, or reprieve.

* *Although the gaolers did not find Malden, they did find the bodies of two previous escapees who had smothered in the foul, gaseous passageways after an eight-man escape attempt in 1731.*

3 November

1925 PROHIBITION PIRATES
Owen B. Baker (39) and Harry Sowash (23) hanged at Okalla Prison, Vancouver, Canada, for the knife-murders of Captain Bill Gillis and his son, Bill junior (17).

Owen Baker spent a lifetime of crime including white-slaving, swindling, thieving, and bootlegging. Harry Sowash, with a clean complexion and crew-cut hair, looked like a college boy, but had a record of violent thievery. They teamed up with another criminal, Charlie Morris, to cash in on the opportunities presented by the American prohibition era. While freighters with their cargoes of liquor held off in international waters, fast launches would ferry the cases of booze across Canadian territorial waters to the coast of Vancouver Island, near the US border. This was a legal enterprise in Canada. Waiting bootleggers would load up their trucks to smuggle the contraband into the USA.

Baker, Sowash and Morris chartered a boat and roamed the sea off Vancouver Island. Posing as American excise officers they would board a liquor-running launch and 'confiscate' its cargo, then sell it to their own bootlegging contacts. They were prohibition pirates. On 15 September 1925 they behaved like the bloodthirsty pirates of old. They boarded the *Beryl G*. and Baker shot Captain Bill Gillis in the arm while Sowash hit the only other man on board, Bill Gillis junior, on the head and dropped him. Baker handcuffed the father and son together and produced a knife and slit open the fronts of their bodies, so that they would not float. Baker and Sowash threw them into the sea, weighed down with an anchor. Exhilarated by their bloodlust, Baker and Sowash stood in the pools of blood on the deck and clasped hands like two victorious warriors.

The horror of the bloody killings preyed on the mind of Paul Stromkins, whose boat the pirates had chartered, and he eventually broke down and told the police. A manhunt was mounted across Canada and America. Baker was picked up in New York harbour and Sowash in New Orleans. Sowash confessed and at the trial both men tried to put all the blame on the other. The pirates were sentenced to death, although that on Charlie Morris was commuted to life imprisonment. Paul Stromkins spent the rest of his life tortured by the memory of the bloody scene he had witnessed, even on his deathbed 50 years later.

4 November

1913 MURDER AT THE VILLAGE FEAST
Frederick Seekings (39) hanged at Cambridge Prison for the knife-murder of Martha Jane Beeby.

Seekings got himself hopelessly drunk at the village feast in Brampton, Huntingdonshire, on 28 July. Afterwards he attacked Martha Jane Beeby with his pocket-knife, cutting her throat and killing her.

Also hanged this day:

1789   at Old Bailey: George Dawson for coining; William Clarke and Alexander Thomas Gilderoy for burglary: Camel Delap Stewart and Mary Peters for assault with a knife.

1914   at Chelmsford Gaol: Charles Frembd (71), a German, for wife-murder.

5 November

1959 FROM BLACKMAILER TO POLICE KILLER
Gunther Fritz Erwin Podola (30) hanged at Wandsworth Prison for the gun-murder of Detective Sergeant Raymond Purdy.

Podola was a German-born criminal who had been deported from Canada after serving a prison sentence for burglary; he arrived in Britain in May 1959. After a few house-breakings in west London he tried to blackmail one of his victims, American model Mrs Verne Schiffman (30), during a telephone call. She agreed to speak to him again and, having nothing to fear from anything he might reveal, informed the police. When Podola phoned again, on 13 July, the police were listening in. While Mrs Schiffman kept him talking for 15 minutes, the call was traced and policemen surrounded a public phonebox in South Kensington. Podola was arrested, but broke away and ran to a house in Onslow Square.

Detective Sergeants Raymond Purdy and John Sandford caught him inside the entrance of the house. While Sandford was looking for the caretaker, Purdy had charge of Podola who was sitting at a window in the entrance hall. Purdy was momentarily distracted and Podola pulled out a black automatic weapon and shot the sergeant in the heart. The murderer made his getaway as Sandford tried to comfort his dying comrade.

Podola was found in a cheap hotel in Queen's Gate on 16 July. The party of policemen displayed great courage in making the arrest; their quarry was known to be a desperate and armed killer. After knocking and ordering him to open the door the only sound they heard was a metallic click, like that of a gun being cocked. Immediately they broke the door open and rushed into the room. Podola was hit by the inward-flying door, which had a 16-stone police sergeant behind it for added impact!

Podola was subdued after a fierce struggle, and came away bruised and with a black eye. He later used the injuries to support a claim of having totally lost his memory of all events in his life until the day after his final arrest. At his trial at the Old Bailey four doctors supported his claim of suffering from amnesia and two testified that he was malingering. The jury was not convinced by his claim of amnesia and returned a verdict that he was fit to plead. (The jury was right in deciding that his loss of memory was a sham. He gave himself away in a letter written while he was in custody.)

A new jury was sworn in and the actual trial for murder began; it lasted one-and-a-half days with the same judge. There was no doubt about him being the killer of Detective Sergeant Purdy and he was found guilty and sentenced to death.

6 November

1840 FAMILY PROBLEMS
Robert McConaghy (30) hanged at Huntingdon, Pennsylvania, USA, for murdering his wife, his mother-in-law and her four children.

Driven to despair by family problems, McConaghy had a furious argument with his wife's family on 30 May 1840. Something snapped and he raged through the house, beating everyone indoors. He strangled his mother-in-law, Mrs Brown, and then resumed beating his wife and Mrs Brown's four other children, aged between 10 and 21, before finishing them off with a gun.

McConaghy was arrested at once, but refused to admit that he had killed anyone. He maintained his impossible defiance throughout the trial and after. Still denying everything, even on the scaffold, he was hanged, but the rope broke. Taken back up on to the scaffold, a thicker rope was fitted round his neck and, at last, he admitted his guilt. He died at the second hanging.

Also hanged this day:

1805 at Ashford, Connecticut, USA: Samuel Freeman for beating to death his Indian mistress.

1818 at Albany, New York, USA: Private James Hamilton for the gun-murder of Major Benjamin Birdsall during a drunken rage.

1883 at Wandsworth Prison: Henry Powell for the murder of John D. Bruton, his employer's son. *Hangman: Bartholomew Binns*, who had experience as an assistant, but this was the first execution of which he was in charge after succeeding William Marwood. Bartholomew Binns was a failure as a hangman: he bungled three of his first four executions and turned up for the fifth too drunk to do anything. He was sacked and succeeded by James Berry.

7 November

1783 THE END OF TYBURN TREE
John Austin, the last man hanged at Tyburn Tree.
Hangman: Edward Dennis

Tyburn had been the scene of public hangings since the 1100s, long before the famous Triple Tree was built in 1571 (see British Hanging

Chronology). Tyburn itself had moved westward, with the expanding boundary of London, from the junction of Marylebone Lane and the present Oxford Street, to its final site, roughly where today's Marble Arch stands.

By 1783 it was considered to be no longer suitable. The vast and degenerate crowds of gawpers, drunks and pickpockets that gathered for Tyburn Fair on hanging days gave visitors a poor first impression of the capital, and hindered the western access to and from London.

John Austin was the last man to suffer the three-mile-long journey from Newgate Prison to Tyburn. For centuries the procession of Sheriff's officers and guards had accompanied the condemned, who were drawn in an open cart facing backwards, with the noose and rope around their necks. They carried their own wreath or posy, and travelled with their own coffin, if they could afford one. If the noisy crowds along the route were large enough it could take up to three hours to get to Tyburn and, throughout the long journey, the chaplain would be haranguing the condemned to repent their evil ways. After 1783 most of London's public hangings would take place at Old Bailey, outside Newgate Prison.

Tyburn evolved as the name for a place of public execution and was adopted in other cities such as York, Liverpool and Dublin.

Also hanged this day:

1750   at Ely, Cambridgeshire: Amy Hutchinson strangled and burned at the stake for petty treason (in this case, husband-murder) followed by the hanging of John Vicars for wife-murder. They were separate crimes.

1767   at Pensarn, Carmarthenshire, Wales: Edward Higgins (41), highwayman and burglar, for returning from transportation.

1905   at Pentonville Prison: George William Butler, a bootmaker, for the murder of his sweetheart, Mary Allen.

8 November

1752 DID ALLAN BRECK DO IT?
James Stewart (57) hanged at Ballachulish, Argyll, Scotland, 'for complicity in the murder of Colin Campbell'. Was Allan Breck the real killer?

This was the murder upon which Robert Louis Stevenson based his celebrated story *Kidnapped*. The Campbell clan had sided with

George II whereas the Stewarts were Jacobites who supported Bonnie Prince Charlie. After the slaughter of the Jacobite forces at the Battle of Culloden in 1745 their captured leaders were executed and those who escaped abroad had their estates forfeited to the Crown.

Colin Campbell was made the king's agent for the forfeited properties. Strongly rebuked by the king in 1751 for being too lenient, Campbell was forced to order a number of evictions. The day before the evictions were to be carried out, Campbell was shot from ambush while passing down a thickly wooded path.

Allan Breck Stewart was not the bold and romantic hero depicted in Stevenson's *Kidnapped*, but more the shifty sort. He was known to be in the vicinity and it was probably he who shot Campbell in the back.

Political necessity required that the killing of the king's agent in the troubled land could not go unpunished. Allan Breck Stewart had disappeared so the clan's patriarch, James Stewart, was charged as an accessory: probably as a scapegoat. The 15-man jury was packed with 11 of Colin Campbell's kinsmen and, on slender evidence, James Stewart was sentenced to death. He was hanged on a hillside at Ballachulish at midday and suffered a slow, strangling death. His body was hung in chains some hours later, and stayed on public display for another three years. Stevenson's hero Allan Breck Stewart, probably the real murderer, was never caught.

9 November

1942 STRANGLED TO GET THEIR VOICES
American GI, Private First Class Edward Joseph Leonski (24), hanged at Pentbridge Jail, Australia, for the murders of three women.

Eddie Leonski was a tall, muscular, blond-haired Texan with an amiable disposition whose hobby was weight training. All the other GIs at the tented Camp Pell in Melbourne liked him; at least, they liked him when he was sober: when drunk he was a troublemaker, going AWOL or returning to camp late and making a disturbance, sometimes waking up in the night screaming. On one occasion he had screamed to his tent-mates 'I'm a Dr Jekyll and Mr Hyde! I killed! I killed!' No one had complained about his disturbances because he was such 'a nice guy' when he was sober.

Melbourne was stunned when three women were strangled in frenzied attacks in the space of 16 days in 1942:
2 May: Mrs Ivy Violet McLeod (40). Her body was found in a doorway three miles from her home, strangled by someone with unusually strong hands and her neck had been grotesquely distorted. Although she had not been sexually assaulted, her clothes were torn into shreds.

9 May: Mrs Pauline Thompson was found in front of her lodgings, strangled by extra-strong hands, not sexually assaulted, but her clothes in tatters.

18 May: Miss Gladys Lillian Hosking (41) was found similarly strangled, laying face down in yellow mud by a slit-trench in Royal Park, her clothes torn into small strips and wildly scattered near the body along with her handbag, shoes and umbrella.

When detectives made inquiries at Camp Pell an Australian soldier, who had been on guard duty on the night of the last murder, reported that a GI had returned late at night, breathless and covered in yellow mud. When challenged by the guard about his appearance the GI said he had fallen in a ditch while taking a short cut across the park. Leonski was picked out from an identity parade and traces of the yellow mud were found in his tent. He was arrested.

He confessed straight away, telling the detectives that he had not wanted to kill the women, but that it was the only way he could possess their sweet voices. Pauline Thompson, in particular, had sung to him so softly as they walked together that he had felt himself going mad and had to have her voice.

He was tried by a US army court martial. The defence of insanity was rejected, although in addition to his strange obsessions about voices there was evidence of mental instability in his family. He was found guilty and sentenced to death by hanging.

Melbourne newspapers had first called the killer a Jack the Ripper type, which was inappropriate as far as the method of killing was concerned, but they may have been thinking about the atmosphere of terror that the murders induced. Later they dubbed him the 'Singing Strangler' because of his fixation with female voices. He did become a singer in the condemned cell, singing a song in a sweet female-like voice just before being taken to the gallows.

Also hanged this day:

1830 at Old Bailey: John Germaine for highway robbery.

10 November

1960 HANGING DIDN'T DETER FRIEND
Francis Robert George 'Flossie' Forsyth (18) hanged at Wandsworth Prison and Norman James Harris (23) hanged at Pentonville Prison, both for the mugging-murder of Alan Jee (23).

Alan Jee, a young engineer, was walking home after seeing his fiancée, to whom he had become engaged the day before. He walked through a lonely alley and was set upon by four local wasters: labourer Flossie Forsyth (18), unemployed driver Norman Harris (23), coalman Christopher Louis Darby (23), and labourer Terrence Lutt (17).

The powerful Lutt struck the first blow and Alan Jee fell to the ground, yelling 'What do you want me for?' Lutt, Darby and Harris held him down while Forsyth kicked him repeatedly around the head and neck with his sharply-pointed winkle-picker shoes. Harris searched their victim looking for money, while Flossie Forsyth stood above them kicking. Alan Jee was left on the ground and never recovered consciousness; he died in hospital two days later.

Harris had boasted about the attack and word got back to the police. When interviewed all four of them denied even being near the alley at the time of the assault, but there were still blood stains on Forsyth's shoes, and the young hoodlums started talking. Forsyth explained '. . . he was struggling so I kicked him in the head to shut him up.'

They were all charged with murder in the furtherance of theft, a capital crime, and tried at the Old Bailey in September. Forsyth, Harris and Lutt were found guilty of capital murder: Forsyth and Harris were sentenced to death while Lutt, because he was under 18, was ordered to be 'detained during Her Majesty's pleasure'. Darby was found guilty of non-capital murder and sentenced to life imprisonment. None of them ever expressed any remorse for their brutal and senseless killing.

Forsyth was hanged at Wandsworth at 9 a.m.; at the same time, Harris was hanged at Pentonville. A prisoner who was released from Wandsworth that morning said that Flossie Forsyth could be heard all over the prison, screaming 'I don't want to die! I don't want to die!'

Victor John Terry (20), a friend of Forsyth's who had his own record of criminal violence from the age of eight, listened to the news of the hangings on his car radio. Just 63 minutes later he shot and killed a bank guard in Worthing, for which he was later hanged on the same gallows as Flossie at Wandsworth (see 26 May).

With the news fresh in his mind of his friend's execution it is surprising that it did not make Terry more cautious. This could be cited as proof that hanging does not deter other murderers, just as 'life' imprisonment (in reality, it is often only seven to nine years) does not seem to deter. In the cases of brutal and remorseless killers like Forsyth, Harris and Terry one thing is definite: hanging stopped them from ever killing again.

Also hanged this day:

1914 at Northampton Prison: John Eayres for wife-murder. At Shepton Mallet Prison: Henry Quartley for the murder of Henry Pugsley.

11 November

1880 THE IRON-CLAD BUSHRANGER
Ned Kelly (25), Australia's most famous criminal, hanged at Melbourne for murder and robbery.

Ned Kelly's father had been a convict, transported from Belfast to Van Diemen's Land (now Tasmania) in 1841. The Kelly family were always in trouble with the constables, usually for thieving. Ned Kelly and his younger brother Dan teamed up with Joe Byrne and Steve Hart in the late 1870s for some bushranging: cattle and horse rustling, robbing prospectors, raiding banks. The gang survived shoot-outs and got away, becoming a legend among the poorer settlers. They killed three of the four lawmen sent to hunt them down in the bush, and the rewards offered for the capture of the Kelly gang rose to as much as £8,000, a colossal sum for those days.

In 1880 they stole some cast iron and forged an ungainly 97lb suit of armour for Ned. It had a high, cylindrical head and neck-piece with a narrow horizontal eye-slit, a waistcoat-like shoulder and bodypiece, and a hinged skirt.

As the most wanted criminals in Australia their final stand was at Glenrowan on 28 June 1880, and it was most likely intended as a last, flamboyant, fling. They had ripped up the main railway line from Melbourne with the aim of causing the train to crash so that they could slaughter those on board who survived, and plunder the wreckage. They captured the small town, locked up inhabitants, and waited for the crash in the Glenrowan Hotel, getting drunker and wilder as the time passed.

The town's schoolteacher got away and waved down the train to prevent the crash. The police soon arrived, surrounded the hotel and began firing. This was going to be a fight to the death and the battle lasted for most of the day.

Joe Byrne (23) was shot through the head as he drunkenly toasted 'the bold Kelly gang'. The hotel was set on fire, but Dan Kelly (19) and Steve Hart (21) kept firing until they died. Ned Kelly, in his suit of armour, was injured in the leg, but managed to crawl or stagger outside. He stood there shooting it out with the police until he collapsed from loss of blood.

Ned Kelly recovered from his wounds while in prison and was sentenced to death on 28 October. Such was the Ned Kelly legend that sixty thousand people signed a petition for his reprieve, but the authorities had had enough and a reprieve was out of the question. His legend persists; he is still Australia's most famous desperado and is lovingly remembered in the national folklore.

1724 at Tyburn Tree: Joseph Blake (a.k.a. 'Blueskin') for house-breaking. Sometime partner of Jack Sheppard (see 16 November).

1761 at Smithfield, London: John Perrott for fraudulent bankruptcy.

1831 at Jerusalem, Virginia, USA: Nat Turner (31), leader of a slaves' revolt, and 19 followers for the deaths of 57 whites.

1887 at Chicago, Illinois, USA: Adolph Fischer (28), George Engel (50), Albert Richard Parsons (40s) and August Spies (32) for inciting the Haymarket bombing – the first use of dynamite as a weapon – which killed seven policemen.

12 November

Hanged this day:

1817 at Old Bailey: John Varti and George Pearson for forgery.

1874 at Baltimore, Maryland, USA: William E. Udderzook for the murder of his brother-in-law Winfield Scott Goss (37). They were accomplices in a $25,000 life insurance swindle whereby the body of an unknown man was burnt beyond recognition in a fire at the workshop used by Goss, while Goss was hiding elsewhere. More than a year later Udderzook took Goss from the hiding place and murdered him.

1878 at Northampton Prison: Pat John Byrne for the murder of two fellow militiamen.

1908 at Knutsford Gaol: James Phipps (21) for the murder of Elizabeth Warburton (10). *Hangman: Henry Pierrepoint. Assistant: Tom Pierrepoint*

1941 at Pentonville Prison: Lionel Rupert Nathan Watson for the prussic-acid murder of the 'wife' he had bigamously married, Phyllis Elizabeth Crocker, and her daughter (18 months).

13 November

1849 THE FASHION KILLER
Frederick George Manning (30) and his wife Maria Manning (30) hanged in front of Horsemonger Lane Gaol for murdering Patrick O'Conner (52).
Hangman: William Calcraft

Maria De Roux, Swiss born lady's maid, met Patrick O'Conner in 1846 and they became lovers. The Irishman was a Customs Officer at

London Docks who had built up a fortune of about £8,000 in cash, shares, and bonds from his sparetime occupation as a moneylender.

Maria was also attracted to the repulsive Frederick Manning who was heavy-set, bull-necked and pale complexioned. He was a guard on the Great Western Railway, but was later sacked when he was implicated in a £4,000 bullion robbery. Maria married Manning in 1847, but continued to associate with O'Conner as his mistress. Manning seemed to accept the situation.

The preparations for the murder of O'Conner had lasted two to three weeks. The Mannings had dug a hole in the kitchen floor and bought an iron crowbar and a sack of quicklime. Patrick O'Conner was invited round for tea on 8 August 1849 and Maria enticed him down to the kitchen to wash his hands. She followed him down the stairs and, at the bottom, shot him in the back of the head. Manning joined her: as he later confessed, 'I found O'Conner moaning in the kitchen. I never liked him very much, and battered him in the head with a ripping chisel (crowbar).'

Between them they stripped the body, folded the legs back and tied them to the hips, then pushed the corpse face-down into the hole and covered it with the quicklime. Soil was shovelled back into the hole, covered with a layer of cement, and the flagstones were relaid. Next day Maria went to O'Conner's rooms and helped herself to anything of value, but especially foreign railway shares, cash and two gold watches.

Fellow workers at London Docks reported the disappearance of O'Conner to the police and pressed for an investigation. The Mannings were visited by the police three days after the murder, but feigned ignorance of where he could be. When the police returned after another two days they found the house empty, and immediately started to search. In the kitchen one of them noticed that two of the flagstones had fresh cement round them; he prised them up and the body was found.

Maria was quickly caught in Edinburgh when she tried to dispose of the foreign railway shares. Frederick Manning stayed free until his arrest in the Channel Islands on 21 August. They were held in Horsemonger Lane Gaol, where each accused the other of the crime.

They were moved to Newgate Prison for their trial at the Old Bailey on 25 October. By now the Mannings would not even speak to each other, and in the dock stood as far away from each other as possible. They were conclusively found guilty, of course. Frederick Manning received his sentence of death in silence. Not so Maria! She raged against her husband, the prosecutor, witnesses, the judge and the jury. When the judge donned the black cap she shouted 'No, no, I will not stand it! You ought to be ashamed of yourselves!' and tried to leave the dock and had to be restrained. She picked up a handful of rue* and threw it at the bench. She was even more violent when being removed from the court to Newgate Prison, struggling fiercely, rattling her handcuffs in officers' faces and screaming, time and again, 'Damnation seize you all!'

Away from the public, in the cab from Newgate back to Horsemonger Lane Gaol, she was quite different: relaxed and flippant, she asked the officers how they had liked her performance of 'resolution' in the courtroom!

The Mannings were hanged outside Horsemonger Lane Gaol at 8 a.m. The crowd is reported to have been fifty-thousand strong, including nearly a thousand policemen to maintain order. Charles Dickens was among the watchers and that same day wrote a famous letter to *The Times* denouncing public executions and 'the wickedness and levity of the immense crowd'.

In contrast with the crowd, the Mannings conducted themselves in a quiet and dignified manner. Maria Manning wore a new black satin dress for the occasion, wound tightly around her waist, with the immediate result of black satin disappearing from the fashion scene for the next 30 years.

As is usual with the bodies of those judicially hanged, the Mannings were buried in quicklime in an unmarked grave. It was particularly appropriate in view of their plan for the disposal of Patrick O'Conner's remains.

* *Rue, an evergreen shrub with strong scented leaves, was scattered around the dock at the Old Bailey, a custom that dated from the years of jail fever (typhus). It was discontinued after the Mannings' trial.*

Also hanged this day:

1768 at Edinburgh: Patrick Olgilvie (23) for the murder of his brother, Thomas Olgilvie.

1835 at Belle Vue Prison, New York, USA: Manuel Fernandez a.k.a. Richard C. Jackson, successful pirate, for the gun-murder of John Roberts, his wife's lover.

1882 at Bodmin Gaol: William Bartlett for the murder of his baby daughter.

1888 at Newgate Prison: Leir Richard Bartlett for wife-murder. After beating her brains out with a hammer and cutting her throat while in a drunken rage, he used the same razor to cut his own throat in an attempted suicide.

1970 at Pretoria, South Africa: Maria Groesbeek (formerly Buys) (34) for the arsenic-murder of her then husband Christiaan Buys (44). Her new husband, Gerhard Groesbeek (21), was tried separately and acquitted.

14 November

1864 FIRST RAILWAY MURDER

Franz Muller (25) publicly hanged at Old Bailey for the murder of Mr Thomas Briggs (70) on a train between Bow and Hackney Wick on the North London Line.
Hangman: William Calcraft

The first murder on a British train occurred on 9 July 1864, in a first-class compartment on the new North London Line running from Fenchurch Street to Hackney Wick. Thomas Briggs, chief clerk of a London bank, was attacked by German-born tailor Franz Muller, robbed of his gold watch and chain, and thrown out on to the line. Briggs was still alive when found, but died shortly afterwards.

By mistake, Muller left his own silk top hat behind and got off the train wearing the one belonging to Briggs: it was a mistake that cost him his life. The silk hat was recognised by the man who had bought two, one for himself and one for Franz Muller.

Scotland Yard's Chief Inspector William Tanner traced Muller's lodging and learned that he had suddenly departed for New York on the SS *Victoria*. The stolen gold watchchain was located at Mr John Death's jewellery shop in Cheapside and Mr Death remembered the man who had exchanged it for another chain: the description fitted Muller.

Chief Inspector Tanner and Detective Sergeant George Clarke sailed for New York on the SS *City of Manchester*, a faster ship which overtook the *Victoria*. Muller had shortened the height of his mistakenly acquired top hat, as a form of disguise, but it did not work: Tanner and Clarke arrested him on arrival in New York, searched him, and found the gold watch stolen from Mr Briggs.

The notoriety of the first train-murder and the trans-Atlantic chase ensured massive public interest in the trial at the Old Bailey on 27 October. Hatmakers and jewellers gave evidence that was accorded prominent attention. The jury returned a verdict of guilty after 15 minutes and Muller was sentenced to death. Appeals for a reprieve, including one from German royalty to Queen Victoria, all failed. Muller confessed to his crime at the last moment as he stood on the scaffold in front of a large crowd.

Also hanged this day:

1887 at Carlisle Prison: W. Hunter for the murder of Isabel Street, the daughter of his mistress.

1890 at Princeton, Ontario, Canada: Reginald (or Richard) Birchall for the gun-murder of his friend, Frederick Cornwallis Benwell, at Woodstock, Ontario. Strangled hanging.

1950   at Durham Gaol: Patrick Turnage (31) for strangling an elderly prostitute, Julia Beesley (78). Turnage lost his temper when she demanded £1 for sex. Turnage pleaded guilty during a seven-minute trial, because he wanted to die rather than face 15 years in prison for manslaughter. *Hangman: Steve Wade. Assistant: Syd Dernley*

15 November

1949 ASSASSINATION OF MAHATMA GANDHI
Nathuram Vinayak Godse (37) hanged and slowly strangled to death at New Delhi, India, for the assassination of Mahatma Gandhi (78).

Mohandas Karamchand Gandhi was the Hindu spiritual leader of India, known more affectionately as Mahatma meaning Great Soul. His campaign of civil disobedience and non-violence was the major factor in the end of British rule in India in 1949, but his agreement, the previous year, to the partition of India and Pakistan led to his murder by a band of Hindu extremists.

After a long fast, on 30 January 1948, Gandhi came out at 5.15 p.m. to greet hundreds of followers in the garden of Birla House, near New Delhi. Godse, a violently anti-Moslem newspaper editor, pushed himself to the front and shot Gandhi three times in the chest and stomach. Gandhi's dying words were '*Hai Rama! Hai Rama!*' ('Oh God! Oh God!').

The crowd set upon Godse in their rage, but he was rescued and removed to prison. The trial of the conspirators lasted over several months but resulted in the death sentence for Godse and another man, and life imprisonment for five others. His death by hanging was also a lengthy affair; instead of the instantaneous neck-breaking drop he slowly strangled on the end of the rope for 15 minutes.

Also hanged this day:

1822   at Cape Town, South Africa: J. V. L. Gebhard, son of the Reverend Mr Gebhard, for the murder of a slave by excessive beating.

1841   at Old Bailey: Robert Blakesley for the murder of his wife's brother-in-law, Mr James Burden, landlord of the King's Head pub in East Cheap, London.

1853   at the Tombs Prison, New York, USA: Patrick Fitzgerald for the gun-murder of his wife, Margaret, who had been nagging him about his drunkenness.

1869   at Maidstone Prison: Joseph Welch (42), a painter, for the knife-murder of John Abrahams in a Deptford pub during a dispute about payment for work. *Hangman: William Calcraft*

1887   at Oxford Castle: Joseph Walker for wife-murder.

1892   at Newgate Prison: Dr Thomas Neill Cream (42) for the poisoning-murder of four prostitutes. Cream was briefly suspected to be Jack the Ripper.

1898   at Newgate Prison: John Ryan for the murder of a policeman.

1899   at Newgate Prison: Thomas Skeffington for the murder of a woman.

1905   at Barlinnie Prison, Glasgow: Pasha Liffey (24), from Basutoland (later Lesotho), for the murder of a miner's wife.

1910   at Walton Gaol, Liverpool: Thomas Rawcliffe for wife-murder.

16 November

1724 END OF THE 'GREAT ESCAPER'
Famous highwayman, burglar and gaolbreaker, Jack Sheppard (22), hanged at Tyburn Tree. Followed by a riot.
Hangman: Richard Arnet

Jack Sheppard was a slenderly built lad standing only five feet four inches tall, but equipped with great strength. He was the son of a respectable Spitalfields carpenter and apprenticed to a joiner between the ages of 15 and 19, but he fell into dissolute company and left the honest life. Taught the art of picking pockets by whores, he graduated to burglary and highway robbery in the company of his partner Joseph Blake, or 'Blueskin' as he was known (see 11 November). It was to be a roaring, drunken life for Jack-the-lad . . . while it lasted.

Sheppard's fame rests not on his crimes but on his escapes, all of which were made in the last year of his young life:
(1) Locked in St Giles' Roundhouse after being betrayed by his brother, a file was smuggled to him from Blueskin. Sheppard did not stay in there long.
(2) New Prison. With a bent nail he loosened the concrete holding his shackles and squirmed out of them. He cut through a double grill of oak and iron bars and climbed down a 25-foot wall using a rope of blankets. After he had scaled another wall, 20 feet high, he was free again!

367

(3) 31 August. His first 'great escape', from the condemned cell at Newgate Prison, only four days before he was due to be executed. Using the escape gear bequeathed to him by Lumley Davis (see 28 August) and smuggled to him by two visiting whores, he loosened a spike holding the hatch to the cell. On the whores' next visit he prised the hatch open and they pulled him through. He probably left the prison in their company, still wearing his leg-irons concealed under a dress. He was caught soon after robbing a watchmaker's shop in Fleet Street little more than a week later.

(4) 15 October. Confined in Newgate's strongest condemned hold, known as the Castle, he was handcuffed, put in the prison's heaviest leg-irons, and chained to a staple in the concrete floor. At 2 p.m. the turnkeys checked that his irons were secure, and then left him unattended for the rest of the day.

Sheppard wriggled out of his handcuffs and got to work on his leg-shackles. Somehow he was able to break the centre link in the chain and slipped it from the ring in the floor. He tied the ankle chains to his legs with his stockings, and was able to move about more freely.

He climbed up the chimney from the Castle to the Red Room on the floor above. On the way he had to chip a heavy iron bar from the brickwork inside the chimney. By then it was night-time and he had to work in the dark.

From the 'Red Room' to the outside he had to force six heavily bolted doors (one of which had not been opened for seven years), using a nail and the three-foot long bar he had taken from the chimney, until he got to the roof. From there he climbed down to the roof of a private house and entered it via the garret and crept through the house unseen.

He had successfully escaped for the second time from Newgate's condemned cell, a feat never before accomplished by anyone in the prison's history!*

His freedom didn't last; he was captured within two weeks, incapably drunk in a tavern. When he was taken back to Newgate he was not only handcuffed and fettered to the floor in the heaviest chains, he was watched by shifts of two guards day and night.

He was hurriedly brought to trial again on the order of the Duke of Newcastle, Secretary of State, '. . . to the end that execution may without delay be awarded against him'. This was done on 10 November and he was hanged on 16 November – a month after his greatest triumph. Sheppard still had hopes of another escape. The plan was for him to cut himself free of his rope-bonds while in the cart on the way to Tyburn, jump into the crowd, and make off down an narrow alley near Little Turnstile. It failed when the turnkeys discovered a pocket-knife concealed in his clothes just before his departure from Newgate. There was a riot after his execution when the mob thought that his body was being taken away for the anatomists. Such was the ferocity of the riot that the police could not cope and the military had to be called.

Jack Sheppard was buried at St Martin-in-the-Fields. His coffin was rediscovered in 1866 by workmen digging on the site of what is now the National Gallery overlooking Trafalgar Square.

* Daniel Malden was to escape twice from Newgate's condemned cell: see 2 November.

Also hanged this day:

1750   at Tyburn Tree: James Carr for forgery.

1857   at Old Bailey: Thomas Davies for wife-murder.

1874   at Winchester Prison: Thomas Smith for the murder of Captain Bird. *Hangman: William Marwood (his first)*

1880   at Durham Gaol: William Brownlees for the murder of Elizabeth Holmes. Bungled hanging. *Hangman: William Marwood*

1886   at Newcastle Prison: Patrick Judge for the shooting-murder of his wife.

17 November

Hanged this day:

1903   at Devizes Prison: Edward Richard Palmer (24) for the murder in Swindon of barmaid Esther Swinford.

18 November

Hanged this day:

1784   at Long Island, New York, USA: seaman Alexander White for the murder of his captain to rob him.

1825   at New York, USA: barge worker James Reynolds for the murder of Captain W. M. West, his boss.

1878   at Usk Prison, Monmouthshire, Wales: Garcia for the multiple murders of William Watkins, his wife and three children.

19 November

1901 FIRST PIERREPOINT HANGING
Marcel Faugeron (or Fougeron), an anarchist, hanged at Newgate
Prison for the murder of Mr Jung, a Clerkenwell jeweller, to obtain
political funds.
Hangman: James Billington. Assistant: Henry Pierrepoint

Henry Pierrepoint's first execution and the first by any Pierrepoint.
He was 24 at the time. Billington spent the night before execution
in the Hangman's Room while Pierrepoint was put in the spare
condemned cell, which was only used when there was to be a double
hanging. This cell was next to the condemned cell occupied by
Faugeron.

Pierrepoint was unable to get to sleep and, at 2 a.m., discovered a
peephole through which he was able to observe Faugeron. The
Frenchman was pacing up and down, chain-smoking, when the bell of
St Sepulchre's struck the hour. He stopped and counted the echoing
gongs on his fingers, and then counted on his fingers again until he
reached eight – the hour at which he was to die.

Faugeron spoke no English but communicated with his warders by
indicating his six fingers and then thrusting his arm upwards and
pointing to the sky, meaning that that was how long it would be before
he went to Heaven. As the bell of St Sepulchre's struck each hour
Pierrepoint watched Faugeron, always smoking, meticulously counting the gongs on his fingers, and then again counting the remaining
hours and miming the same message to his warders.

A few minutes after the execution, having just pronounced
Faugeron dead, the prison doctor measured Pierrepoint's pulse.
'You will do' he smiled, turned about and left the room. A new
dynasty of hangmen had begun: from that day onwards, until 1956,
there would be one or two Pierrepoints continuously on the list of
hangmen.

Also hanged this day:

1858   at Jacinto, Mississippi, USA: local bully William H. Buse for
the gun-murder of Thomas M'Keever, who had accused him of
stealing his whisky.

1860   at Old Bailey: James Mullins, an ex-policeman, for the murder
of his employer, Mrs Elmsley. *Hangman: William Calcraft*

1877   at Exeter Prison: William Hassell for wife-murder.

1878   at Strangeways Prison, Manchester: M'Gowan for wife-murder.

370

1883 at Durham Gaol: Peter Bray for the murder of Thomas Pyle.

1895 at Newgate Prison: Richard Wingrove for the murder of Jane Eagle.

1948 at Walton Gaol, Liverpool: Guardsman Peter Griffiths (22) for the murder of June Anne Devaney (4) in the grounds of Queen's Park Hospital, Blackburn. After raping the child he swung her, head-first, against a wall. Fingerprints were taken of all males aged over 16 in Blackburn, resulting in more than 46,000 comparisons, before Griffiths was found. *Hangman: Albert Pierrepoint*

20 November

1903 CATTLE-BARONS' HIRED KILLER
Tom Horn (43), ex-lawman turned hired killer, hanged at Cheyenne, Wyoming, USA, for the murder of Willie Nickell (14) in error for the boy's father.

Tom Horn served with distinction as a US army scout during the Apache war and it was concluded when he negotiated Apache-leader Geronimo's final surrender. He was later employed as a deputy sheriff and then as an agent for the famous Pinkerton Detective Agency.

The rest of his career was quite different. He hired himself out to cattle-barons, for the right price, to kill small-time settlers who got in the way of the cattlemen. He considered himself a truly professional gunman, stalking his target for days if necessary and waiting for the perfect opportunity for a one-shot killing. It is not known just how many people he killed at this time, but killing was his full-time occupation. His mania for carrying out 'perfect killings' let him down in the case of the murder that resulted in his capture and execution. After waiting in ambush for his victim he shot and killed 14-year-old Willie Nickell in mistake for the boy's father.

Deputy US Marshal Joe Lefors set out to trap Horn. After winning the killer's confidence they got drunk together and Tom Horn regaled Lefors with the inside stories about his many hired killings, including that of Willie Nickell. He was arrested, put on trial, and then publicly hanged.

Also hanged this day:

1877 at Norwich Castle: Henry March for the double murder of his employer, Mr Mayes, and another workman, Henry Bidewell.

1885 at Richmond, Virginia, USA: Thomas J. Cluverius, son of a wealthy Virginia family, for the murder of Fannie Lilian Madison to prevent news of their secret marriage becoming known.

21 November

1827 SPECTATORS KILLED
Levi Kelley publicly hanged at Cooperstown, New York, USA, for the murder of his lodger, Abraham Spaford.

Kelley had been horrified when he had watched the hanging of Jesse Strang (see 24 August) and declared 'no one who has ever seen such a horrid spectacle as the hanging of Jesse Strang could ever commit murder'. However, just ten days later Kelley was at his boarding house when he was annoyed by a crippled delivery boy. He set about the boy and knocked him to the ground. He was about to club him as he lay there when one of his lodgers, Abraham Spaford, tried to intervene. Even more furious now, Kelley produced a pistol and shot Spaford to death.

A temporary wooden stand, holding hundreds of spectators, suddenly collapsed during Kelley's execution. Among the casualties were two deaths. Because of this, it was the last public execution in Otsego County.

Also hanged this day:

1720 in Jamaica: 'Calico Jack' Rackham for piracy.

1729 at Tyburn Tree: highwayman William Gordon hanged, and revived. Dr Chovot had experimented on dogs to prevent strangulation by making an opening in the windpipe. Chovot visited Gordon in the condemned cell at Newgate and secretly performed the operation. Those hanged with Gordon died quickly, but he survived, for a while. After being cut down he was rushed to a house in nearby Edgware Road and Chovot opened a vein and the blood ran freely. Gordon groaned, and died.

1816 at Execution Dock, Wapping: Robert Smith and Charles Feeney for murder on the high seas.

1821 at Old Bailey: Isaac Celebia and George Smith for highway robbery; William Gorton for private-stealing; William Harding for sheep-stealing; Thomas Tupley, Edward Sparrow, and Josiah Cadman for issuing forged notes.

1877 at Nottingham Prison: Thomas Grey for the murder of Ann Mellors.

1881 at Derby Prison: Alfred Gough for the murder of Eleanor Windle.

1887 at Chelmsford Gaol: Joseph Morley (17) for the murder of Mrs Bodger, his landlady at Chigwell Row, near Dagenham.

1899 at Ipswich Gaol: George Nunn for the murder of a woman.

22 November

1950 GURGLING IN THE PIT!
Norman Goldthorpe hanged at Norwich Gaol for the murder of Emma Howe (66) at Yarmouth.
Hangman: Harry Kirk. Assistant: Syd Dernley

Goldthorpe was a little man with a foul temper, especially at the time of a new moon according to his estranged wife. After a night of hard drinking and building up a hatred for his mistress, he was in one of his foulest moods. (Marguerite Myers had left him that week and gone back to visit her husband in Yorkshire.) He went to the one-room flat of an elderly prostitute, had sex and then strangled her in her bed. He had been seen arriving, and departing. The police arrested him within a few hours of the body being found.

This was the only occasion when Harry Kirk was chief hangman. He gave Goldthorpe a seven-foot-eight-inch drop. Everything appeared to be going normally, even for a moment or two after Kirk had operated the lever. Suddenly the official witnesses were struck with horror as loud gurgling noises came from Norman Goldthorpe as he hung in the execution pit below them!

The awful sounds lasted between 30 seconds and a minute. The doctor examined Goldthorpe and found no breathing or heartbeat so pronounced him dead. Death must have been instantaneous because his neck was broken and his head was hanging over to one side. The doctor attributed the gurgling noises to automatic muscular spasms.

When the body was taken down an hour later it was discovered that the noose had not tightened around Goldthorpe's neck and blocked off the air passage. The reason for this was that a part of the white cotton hood had caught in the eyelet of the noose. Goldthorpe had died the instant he had jerked to a halt at the end of his drop and knew nothing of the drama of the next few minutes, but it gave everyone else present a profound shock!

Also hanged this day:

1827 at Old Bailey: Edward Lowe for coining (he was the last coiner to be dragged to his execution on the traitors' sledge); Charles Smith for highway robbery; John Keats and John Powell for robbing their employers.

1880 at Horfield Gaol, Bristol: Joseph Distin for the murder of Mr Daniels.

1910 at Walton Gaol, Liverpool: Henry Thompson hanged at Liverpool for wife-murder. *Hangman: John Ellis.* Ellis described Thompson as the most callous murderer he had ever met. At his execution he had had a full night's sleep, claiming that he had slept better than at home. As he went to his execution he remarked, 'Well, I shall be senior to Crippen in the next shop.' (Crippen was hanged at Pentonville Prison the following morning, see below.)

23 November

1910 'THE MURDER OF THE CENTURY'
Dr Hawley Harvey Crippen (48) hanged at Pentonville Prison for the murder and dismemberment of his wife Cora Crippen a.k.a. Belle Elmore and formerly Kunigunde Mackamotzki a.k.a. Cora Motzki a.k.a. Cora Marsangar a.k.a. Cora Turner (37).
Hangman: John Ellis

This was Britain's 'murder of the century' and it sent thrills of horror throughout the world. Crippen was 'the little mouse of a man' who finally turned on his bullying wife, killed her and cut up her body and buried it in the cellar of their home at 39 Hilldrop Crescent in Holloway, North London. Then he ran off with a younger woman resulting in a police chase across the Atlantic, with the world breathlessly following the daily progress in the newspapers thanks to the trans-Atlantic wireless – the first time that wireless had been used in a murder hunt.

Crippen was an American doctor who had lived in Britain for ten years, with doubtful medical qualifications, making his living as a salesman of quack remedies. He was a mild, bespectacled little man who lived a miserable life as the chore-bound slave of his second wife, the shrill and overbearing Cora Crippen. (His first wife had died in Utah, USA, in 1891.)

Cora had started life in America with the name Kunigunde Mackamotzki, but used a stream of names to further her operatic and music hall ambitions, none of which came to much. For the English stage she used the name Belle Elmore. Crippen had to pay for her singing lessons, her costly costumes, and to entertain people who might be useful in furthering her career. Although never a success, she had a number of theatrical friends.

374

Crippen took comfort elsewhere and from 1902 his 19-year-old typist, Ethel Le Neve, became his mistress. Eight years later Mrs Crippen found out about Ethel and she gave her husband hell. Then she said she was going to leave him for another man and take their joint savings with her: it was the latter rather than the former that cost Cora her life.

Crippen bought five grains of the poison hyoscine hydrobromide from a West End chemist shop and, probably on 1 February 1910, used it to kill Cora. He dismembered her and buried the parts in the cellar, wrapped in bits of cloth that would later be identified as belonging to him. The head, internal organs and skeleton were never discovered.

He sent letters to her friends saying that she had returned to America suddenly to care for a seriously ill relative. Within a month Ethel Le Neve had moved into 39 Hilldrop Crescent and was seen wearing Cora's clothes and jewellery. These events caused gossip, but it was when Crippen published his wife's obituary notice, saying that she had died in California, that inquiries were made by Cora's friends. Scotland Yard was informed and Chief Inspector Walter Dew was ordered to question Crippen.

Crippen admitted to Dew that he had invented the obituary to avoid a scandal after Mrs Crippen ran off with another man, not known to Crippen. He showed the policemen all over the Hilldrop Crescent house, after which the Chief Inspector and his men departed. Dew was satisfied and considered the case closed, but Crippen was unaware of this and panicked. He fled with Ethel to the Continent.

Chief Inspector Dew called at Crippen's office quite by chance. On being told that Crippen had gone abroad he decided to have another look at 39 Hilldrop Crescent and, on the third day, he noticed a loose brick in the floor of the cellar – and the murder chase of the century began. The gruesome discoveries in Crippen's cellar led to the issue of warrants for the arrest of Crippen and Le Neve. Newspaper headlines screamed the ghastly details of what had been found in the cellar at horrified readers. 39 Hilldrop Crescent became the most famous house in England*.

The runaways departed from Antwerp on the SS *Montrose* bound for Quebec, Canada. Crippen had shaved off his moustache and had stopped wearing his spectacles outside their cabin. He was calling himself Mr Robinson with Ethel disguised as his 16-year-old son. After two days Captain Henry Kendall suspected that the girlish Master Robinson and father were the London cellar-murder fugitives, and sent a wireless message to the Canadian Pacific office in Liverpool – making history by using radiotelegraphy for the first time in a murder hunt.

Scotland Yard was notified and Chief Inspector Dew left Liverpool on the SS *Laurentic*, which would arrive in Quebec in seven days' time. The *Montrose* would take 11 days on the trip from Antwerp to Quebec. The chase was on!

Captain Kendall kept newspapers on both sides of the Atlantic informed of the daily activities of the fugitives, while Crippen and Ethel enjoyed the voyage, not knowing that their every move was avidly being followed by millions. No titbit was too small for the hungry presses, and newspapers brought out special editions with the latest news and maps showing the positions of the two liners in the chase. Bookmakers enjoyed a boom-trade from punters betting on which ship would arrive at Quebec first.

The *Laurentic* met the *Montrose* in Canadian waters and Chief Inspector Dew boarded the *Montrose* and greeted his unsuspecting quarry with the polite phrase 'Good morning, Dr Crippen. I am Chief Inspector Dew of Scotland Yard, I think that you know me?' Crippen meekly replied, 'Good morning, Mr Dew.' Crippen and Le Neve were extradited and tried separately at the Old Bailey.

The world's newspapers reported every facet of Crippen's five-day trial and brought fame to a young pathologist making his first court appearance in a major case, Bernard Spilsbury. The prosecution's evidence, especially Spilsbury's, was damning and the jury took only 27 minutes to find Crippen guilty. He was sentenced to death. Ethel Le Neve was tried as an accessory four days later, and acquitted.

Crippen made an attempt at suicide in the condemned cell on his last night on earth. He had concealed a part of the metal from his glasses in the seam of his trousers hoping to puncture an artery and quietly bleed to death in his bed: a loser to the end, this failed too.

The mild-mannered little man walked to the scaffold bravely and without fuss. His love for Ethel endured to the end; she had given him the only spell of joy that he had known during a sad life. His last request was granted: to have the photograph and letters of Ethel Le Neve buried with him.

Ethel Le Neve (previously plain Ethel Neave) sailed for New York on the morning that Crippen was executed, as 'Miss Allen'. By the time she arrived in Toronto, Canada, she was calling herself Ethel Harvey. (There is a story that she had promised Crippen to change her name to his when she started a new life, but Crippen would not have given her the anonymity she was seeking.) She returned to London during World War One and married a clerk named Stanley Smith. They lived in Croydon and had children, and later grandchildren. She died in a hospital at the age of 84, in 1967. In 1985 a Sunday newspaper traced her children and they were astonished to learn that their mother had been the notorious Ethel Le Neve – the 'other woman' in the twentieth century's most celebrated murder case.

---

* *39 Hilldrop Crescent and the houses close by were destroyed by bombing during an air raid in World War Two.*

Also hanged this day:

1867 at Salford Prison, Manchester: William O'Meara Allen, Michael Larkin, and William Gould (a.k.a. O'Brien). They were Fenians who killed PC Brett. *Hangman: William Calcraft*

1877 at Dolgellau Prison, Merionethshire, Wales: Cadwallader Jones for the murder of Sabar Hughes. Jones bludgeoned her to death with a rock and then dismembered her and threw the pieces into the river.

1885 at Hereford Prison: John Hill and John Williams for the murder of Ann Dickson.

1932 at Oxford Castle: Edward Hutchinson for murder.

24 November

1740 NAKED REVIVAL
William Duell (16), hanged at Tyburn Tree for the rape and murder of Sarah Griffin, and then revived at Surgeons' Hall.
Hangman: John Thrift

Condemned for the rape and murder of Sarah Griffin in a barn, this 16-year-old youth was hanged with four others on Tyburn Tree. Duell's body was taken to Surgeons' Hall to be anatomised but, while a servant was washing his naked corpse as it lay on the dissecting table, he was seen to move slightly. As his breathing improved, a surgeon took some ounces of blood from him and he regained consciousness, telling the surgeon that he had had a bad dream. Duell was able to sit in a chair two hours later and was committed to Newgate again that evening. He was later transported.

Also hanged this day:

1740 at Tyburn Tree: (hanged with William Duell, above) Thomas Clock, William Meers, Henry Stanton, and Eleanor Munoman for burglary and robbery.

1884 at Strangeways Prison, Manchester: Kay Howarth for the murder of Richard Dugdale with the intention of robbery; Harry Hammond Swindells for the murder of James Wild.

25 November

1824 WHERE TO HANG THEM?
Joseph Moseley and William Garside hanged at Horsemonger Lane
Gaol for shooting the son of their employer.
Hangman: Thomas Cheshire

This was a case that excited the public at the time. Moseley and
Garside were cotton spinners at Hyde in Cheshire and they shot the
son of their employer during a dispute about their wages. Local
opinion was outraged at the crime and compared it to the horrors of
the Luddites (see 12 and 14 January) of 12 years before.

Moseley and Garside fled to the South and evaded capture for three
years. There followed a dispute between the sheriffs of Lancashire and
Cheshire about which county should hang them and, unable to resolve
the problem it was referred to the Court of King's Bench for a
decision. The latter ruled that the pair should be hanged in Surrey as
that was where they had been apprehended. Even so, they were
hanged by Thomas Cheshire!

Also hanged this day:

1822   at Old Bailey: John Holland and William King for an unnatural
offence.

1824   at Old Bailey: Joseph Hayward for highway robbery.

1878   at Great Stukeley Prison: Henry Gilbert for the murder of his
illegitimate child.

26 November

Hanged this day:

1746   at Tyburn Tree: Henry Sims, a runaway convict, for robbery.

1819   at Old Bailey: James Cassidy, John Henley, and Henry Lovell
for robbery and other crimes.

1823   at Old Bailey: Henry Crisp for burglary.

1883   at Strangeways Prison, Manchester: Thomas Riley for the
murder of Elizabeth Alston.

1940   W. H. Cooper for the murder of John J. Harrison.

27 November

1750 at Tyburn Tree: Thomas Reynolds for treason, having enlisted men to serve in the army of the king of France.

1821 at Old Bailey: Andrew Ferris for robbery; Joseph Smith for issuing forged notes.

1877 at Leicester Prison: James Satchell, John William Swift, and John Upton for the murder by kicking of Joseph Tugby, a poor pedlar.

1894 at Strangeways Prison, Manchester: James Wilshaw Whitehead for wife-murder.

1906 at Knutsford Gaol: Edward Hartigan (58) for wife-murder while both were drunk. *Hangman: Henry Pierrepoint*

28 November

1962 'I'LL BET YOU £5 I NEVER HANG'
James Smith (26) hanged at Strangeways Prison, Manchester, for the capital murder of shopkeeper Mrs Isabella Cross.

Mrs Cross took delivery of some cases of cigarettes at her corner shop at 4.25 p.m. on Friday 4 May 1962; by 4.30 p.m. she had been battered to death. It was at 4.30 p.m. that a customer, a nine-year-old girl, saw Mrs Cross lying behind the counter amidst a mass of broken glass. Her killer had attacked her with bottles full of mineral water taken from the shelf, five in all, and the body was soaked with the liquid. The murderer had taken the money from the till and then rifled the private rooms behind the shop and left by the back door.

The forensic investigation was thorough and dedicated. On the door from the living room to the kitchen, which had been painted only two days before, were three fingerprints that did not belong to Mr or Mrs Cross. It was three weeks before a match was found.

Meanwhile, Detective Chief Inspector Louis Allen at the Forensic Science Laboratory in Preston carefully rebuilt the five bottles from the fragments found on and around Mrs Cross's body. 'Carefully' is the right word: as well as gluing the bits together to make a physical fit, as in a jigsaw puzzle, he also checked the pieces under his microscope to ensure that the stress marks within the glass corresponded.

Scotland Yard produced the identity of the man who had left his fingerprints on the newly painted door. He was James Smith, whose home was only a brisk 16-minute walk away from the corner shop. Detective Chief Superintendent Eric Cunningham and Detective Inspector Tom Butcher arrested Smith at his home on Sunday 27 May. He denied ever having been in the shop.

During the search of his house they found a glass fragment down the side of the settee: it was proved to belong to one of the murder bottles rebuilt by Louis Allen, the physical fit and the stress marks proving this beyond any doubt. The fingerprints proved that Smith had been in the private rooms of the shop within 48 hours of the murder; the glass fragment proved that he had been there at the time of the murder.

After being formally charged with murder, James Smith turned to Detective Inspector Butcher and said, 'I'll bet you £5 I never hang.' Tom Butcher answered 'You're on!' James Smith was hanged at 8 a.m. on 28 November at Strangeways. Tom Butcher had to make the formal identification when the body was taken down an hour later, but he was never paid the £5 he had won.

Also hanged this day:

1881   at Strangeways Prison, Manchester: John Aspinal Simpson (21) for the murder of Anne Ratcliffe (16). *Hangman: William Marwood*

1882   at York Castle: Edward Wheatfill for the murder of Peter Hughes.

1887   at Gloucester Prison: Enoch Wadley for the murder of Elizabeth Hannah Earls at Kempley. He was a discharged soldier who had served in India and who may have been deranged.

1893   at Strangeways Prison, Manchester: Emanuel Hamar for the murder of Catherine Tyrer, an old woman.

1899   at Reading Gaol: Charles Scott for the murder of a woman.

1950   at Strangeways Prison, Manchester: James Henry Corbett (37) for the murder of a friend, Mrs E. Wood. *Hangman: Albert Pierrepoint.* Corbett was a regular customer at Pierrepoint's pub and Pierrepoint knew him as 'Tish'. He called Pierrepoint 'Tosh', using a popular catchphrase of the time. He sometimes sang at the piano, sometimes with Pierrepoint. After leaving the pub one Saturday night he strangled his girlfriend at a boarding house in Ashton-Under-Lyne.

29 November

1881 THE CHINLESS KILLER
Percy Lefroy Mapleton a.k.a. Percy Lefroy (22) hanged at Lewes Prison for the murder of Isaac Frederick Gold (64) after robbing him on a train on the Brighton line.
Hangman: William Marwood

Percy Lefroy Mapleton was a slightly built youth with a prominent nose and a receding chin. His profile was to become famous after a drawing of it was published in the *Daily Telegraph* and later used on a Scotland Yard poster offering £200 for his capture. The cause of the excitement was another train murder, the only one since the sensational Muller case 17 years earlier (see 14 November).

This one had occurred on the London Bridge-Brighton line on 27 June 1881. Isaac Frederick Gold, a retired businessman who still dealt in foreign coins, was stabbed and shot by Mapleton as the train entered the mile-long Merstham Tunnel, near Crawley. Four shots were fired, one of the bullets hitting Mr Gold in the neck. Mapleton took what valuables he could find and, seven miles further along the line, he pushed Mr Gold out on to the track as the train was entering the Balcombe Tunnel.

Mapleton got out at Preston Park, on the edge of Brighton. His clothing was blood stained and attracted attention. He said his name was Percy Lefroy and claimed that he had been attacked by two men during the journey. He was searched and found to have German coins in his pockets, and a watch with the chain inside his shoe. He was taken to Brighton Town Hall to make a full statement, which was apparently not believed because he was kept in police custody.

Mapleton was being taken back to London by police when they were told, at one of the stops, that a body had been found on the track at the Balcombe Tunnel. The obliging police allowed Mapleton to stop off at Croydon to collect some things from his lodgings and, while they waited at the front door, he made a getaway from the back door!

His disappearance caused a sensation and everyone was looking for him. He shut himself up in a room in Stepney, which he had taken in a false name, and kept out of sight. He was too easily recognisable thanks to the poster of his strange profile! His next action was stupid. He sent a telegram to his employer asking him to send his wages to his Stepney lodgings; it was the police who knocked on his door.

The pocket-watch and chain taken from Mapleton's shoe had belonged to Mr Gold and the German coins were of the type that the old man bought and sold. The circumstantial evidence at his trial at Maidstone was enough to convince the jury that he was guilty, but he left the dock still protesting his innocence. However, he made a full confession on the day before his execution. Hangman Marwood must have had problems ensuring that the rope was properly fitted so that it wouldn't slip upwards over Mapleton's almost chinless face, especially as it was reported that the young man was in a state of collapse at the time.

Also hanged this day:

1803 at Windham, Connecticut, USA: Caleb Adams (18) for the axe- and throat-cutting murder of Oliver Woodworth (5) because the boy annoyed him.

1826 at Old Bailey: the infamous Spitalfields Gang – James Boyce, James Goulby, Robert King, George Nicholls, and John Robinson for highway robbery.

1880 at St Alban's Prison: Thomas Wheeler for the murder of a farm labourer named Anstree. He was the father of Mary Eleanor Wheeler, better known as Mary Eleanor Pearcey, hanged ten years later for the murder of a mother and baby (see 23 December). *Hangman: William Marwood*

1894 at Carmarthen Prison, Wales: Thomas Richards, a sailor, for the murder of Mary Davies in Borth, Cardiganshire.

30 November

1774 '16-STRING' JACK
Highwayman '16-string' Jack Rann hanged at Tyburn Tree for a robbery on the Uxbridge Road.
Hangman: Edward Dennis

Jack Rann was a former pedlar from Bath, then a stable lad and eventually a coachman to a gentleman of quality. It was the latter occupation that gave him his first, and joyous, taste for flamboyant clothes. He embarked on a short but highly publicised career as a highwayman, always turned out in the height of fashion. His nickname of 16-string Jack derived from his practice of wearing eight strings of brightly coloured beads, or silk ribbons, hanging from each knee.

During the summer of 1774 he appeared before the magistrates almost every month, but had to be released time and again, usually for lack of sufficient evidence to convict him. He thereby became a popular hero of the common people. On one occasion he came into court with his leg-irons festooned with ribbons and carrying a nosegay!

He was arrested in September and this time there was evidence enough to hang him. Charged with robbing Dr William Bell, the king's chaplain, on the Uxbridge Road he arrived in court wearing a new pea-green suit, a ruffled shirt, a hat trimmed with silver, and his trademark of 16 strings flapping from his knees. His bold flamboyance was not dulled when he was found guilty and sentenced to death.

On his final Sunday night in Newgate Prison he held a riotous party for seven girls and himself, and they wined and dined in style. He maintained his bravado on the trip to Tyburn, to the noisy admiration of the gathered mob.

Also hanged this day:

1824   at Old Bailey: Henry Fauntleroy Esq. (43) for forgery. *Hangman: James Foxon*

1885   at Norwich Castle: Robert Goodale for wife-murder. The execution became known as the 'Goodale Mess' after the 15-stone prisoner was decapitated by the rope. *Hangman: James Berry*

1962   in the prison yard at Leavenworth, Kansas, USA: Lowell Lee Andrews (18), a student weighing 22 stone, for the gun-murders of his parents and sister as they watched television in the living room of their home. He gorged a last meal of two fried chickens, extra helpings of mashed potatoes, green beans, pie and ice-cream.

DECEMBER

1 December

Hanged this day:

1828 at Old Bailey: James Higgins for cutting and maiming.

1903 at Chelmsford Gaol: Bernard White for the murder of Maud Garrett.

2 December

1859 JOHN BROWN'S BODY
John Brown (59) hanged with four others at Charleston, West
Virginia, USA, for treason, murder and conspiring with slaves.

Brown's name is immortalised in the hymn:

> 'John Brown's body lies a-mouldering in the grave,
> John Brown's body lies a-mouldering in the grave,
> John Brown's body lies a-mouldering in the grave,
> But his soul goes marching on!'

He was a famous fighter for the abolition of slavery who first became famous in May 1856 when, with his four sons and three others, he attacked pro-slavery settlers at Pottawatomie Creek in Kansas in retaliation for their attack on his anti-slavery headquarters in Lawrence, Virginia. The raid left five pro-slavery settlers dead.

Brown was now a hero of the abolitionists and triumphantly toured New England. He told his supporters that God had ordered him to free the slaves in Virginia. In October 1859, with 22 others including his sons, he attacked and occupied the Federal Armory at Harper's Ferry to start the uprising. No slaves joined them.

The Armory was recaptured after two days of fighting by a force of marines under the command of Colonel Robert E. Lee (later to become famous as the leader of the Southern forces in the American Civil War).

Tried for treason, John Brown refused to answer any questions at his trial, claiming that he had received orders from God to free the slaves. On the scaffold he was asked if he was tired and replied 'No, but don't keep me waiting for longer than necessary.' He now became an emancipationist martyr and *John Brown's Body* was used as a marching song by the Union soldiers in the Civil War.

Also hanged this day:

1816   at Old Bailey: John Rawlinson and Thomas Pegg for robbery on the River Thames (more of the Rawlinson family were hanged for the same crime on 25 February 1818).

1902   at Strangeways Prison, Manchester: Henry Mack (29) for the murder of Esther Elizabeth Bedford at Oldham.

1948   at Oxford Castle: George Russell for the murder of recluse Mrs Freeman Lee (94) during a burglary.

1977   on Bermuda: Erskine Durrant Burrows and Larry Winfield Tacklyn for the murders of Police Commissioner George Duckett (41) on 9 September 1972; of Governor Sir Richard Sharples and his ADC Captain Hugh Sayers on 10 March 1973, and of two shopkeepers on 6 April 1973.

3 December

1901 HANGING A FRIEND
Patrick M'Kenna hanged at Strangeways Prison, Manchester, for murdering his wife while drunk.
Hangman: James Billington. Assistant: Henry Pierrepoint

M'Kenna was horrified when he realised what he had done, and blamed his drunkenness. He demonstrated great remorse, from the time of the murder right up to his final, tearful, moment on the fatal trap doors of the gallows. Henry Pierrepoint said that he had never seen a more penitent convict.

M'Kenna was a friend of Billington and the hangman was greatly distressed by the hanging, which must have added to the misery of his own fatal illness. This was James Billington's 147th and last hanging. He died ten days later and the story went around that his death was from grief, but it was from a severe attack of bronchitis. His three sons were also hangmen: Thomas, William and John. Thomas died of pneumonia and dropsy the following month, having assisted William at executions before and after his father's death.

Also hanged this day:

1879   at Ipswich Gaol: Henry Bedingford for the murder of Eliza Rudd.

1883   at Kirkdale Prison, Liverpool: Henry Dutton for the murder of Hannah Hamshaw.

1895 at Bedford Gaol: Arthur Covington (27) for the murder of Effie Burgin (20).

4 December

1723 'WALTHAM BLACKS'
Seven 'Waltham Blacks': Richard Parvin, Edward Elliot (17), Robert Kingshell, Henry Marshall, Edward Pink, John Pink, and James Ansell, hanged at Tyburn Tree for murder and deer-stealing.

The Waltham Blacks Act (see British Hanging Chronology) or more simply the Black Act was a special Bill that was hurried through Parliament in May 1723 as a counter to the increasing amount of poaching and damage being done to forests and parks owned by the nobility. It made a number of offences capital crimes and had such a wide scope that, by subsequent interpretation, it increased the number of capital crimes from about 30 to 150 and, within a few years, to 250. If the criminals blacked their faces or disguised themselves they were punishable by hanging. The Black Act was also known as the Bloody Code and was to gather more severity over the next hundred years.

The first to become victims of the new Act were the seven Waltham Blacks who had indeed blackened their faces while poaching the king's deer in Waltham Chase in Hampshire. They had also killed the Bishop of Winchester's gamekeeper. Because of the importance of the case, they were taken to London in irons and tried at the Old Bailey and afterwards hanged at Tyburn Tree.

Also hanged this day:

1882 at Kirkdale Prison, Liverpool: Bernard Mullarkey for the murder of Thomas Cruise.

1894 at Chelmsford Gaol: James Canham Read for the murder of one of his mistresses, Florence Dennis (18), at Southend.

1900 at Strangeways Prison, Manchester: Joseph Holden for the murder of his grandson in Bury, Lancashire.

1902 at Bedford Gaol: William Chambers for wife-murder.

1941 J. E. Smith for the murder of Miss C. Dicksee.

1957 Dennis Howard (24) for the murder of a 21-year-old shop-keeper during a robbery.

5 December

1831 THE BODY SNATCHERS
John Bishop and his brother-in-law Thomas Head a.k.a. Williams hanged at Old Bailey for the murder of an Italian boy and a woman (to sell the bodies to the anatomists).
Hangman: William Calcraft

Bishop had been a body snatcher for 12 years and boasted that he had 'resurrected' a thousand bodies. He had been joined for the last five years by his brother-in-law Thomas Head (usually known as Williams). They had been impressed by the famous Edinburgh body snatchers Burke and Hare. The pair's trial, three years earlier, revealed that they had murdered to sell fresh bodies to the surgeons, at a better price, rather than bothering to dig up dead ones. No one will ever know how many murders Bishop and Head committed, but the final three were of Fanny Pigburn, a boy named Cunningham, and Carlo Ferrari (14).

Carlo Ferrari, an Italian boy, was in show business: he exhibited his performing white mice in the street and made a precarious living. Bishop and Head lured him to their home and gave him a drink of rum laced with laudanum. When he was insensible they tied a rope round his ankles and lowered him into the well in their backyard until he drowned. They extracted his teeth and sold them separately to a dentist. They were joined by another body snatcher, John May, to help them sell the body. They tried three private anatomy schools and Guy's Hospital without success before making a deal at King's College for nine guineas (£9.45p). This was their undoing: the staff at King's were suspicious at receiving such a fresh young body that did not appear to have died naturally. They delayed Bishop and Head until the arrival of the police. Clothes found buried in a corner of their backyard were identified as those that Carlo Ferrari had last been seen wearing. Male and female clothing (probably Fanny Pigburn's and Cunningham's) was found buried a few yards away.

After they had all three been condemned first Bishop, and then Head, confessed to the killings. Oddly, they claimed that Ferrari was not Italian at all but a Lincolnshire lad even though there was plenty of corroboration that he was Italian. Not that it mattered. As a result of the confessions John May was reprieved, but died a few months later.

The case had attracted a lot of attention in the newspapers of the day and a reported thirty thousand turned up to see them hanged at Old Bailey. Bishop died at once, Head struggled for some minutes. The crowd was excited by Thomas Head's death-struggles and pushed towards the gallows for a better look; many of them were injured in the crush. The hanged remains of the body snatchers were, appropriately, delivered to the anatomists, Bishop's to King's College and Head's to St Bartholomew's.

Also hanged this day:

1820　at Old Bailey: T. F. Arnett for forgery; John Madden and Samuel Brill for issuing forged notes.

1893　at Reading Gaol: John Carter for wife-murder.

1899　at Chelmsford Gaol: Samuel Crozier for wife-murder.

1905　at Worcester Prison: William Yarnold for wife-murder.

6 December

1928 LAKE DISTRICT HONEYMOON
Chung Yi Miao (28) hanged at Strangeways Prison for murdering his wife, Wai Sheung Sui (29), on their honeymoon in the Lake District.

Chung Yi Miao was a moneyed Chinese barrister who had met and married Wai Sheung Sui, an heiress, in America. Their prolonged honeymoon took them touring America and then England and Scotland. They booked into an hotel on the edge of Derwentwater in the Lake District on 18 June 1928.

The following afternoon they went for a walk. Detective Constable Pendlebury, on holiday, happened to see Chung walking alone near Cumma Catta Woods. Chung returned to the hotel at 4 p.m. and told a maid that Mrs Chung had gone shopping in Keswick. He dined alone and went to bed.

Detective Constable Pendlebury was having a drink in a pub that evening when he overheard a farmer saying that a Chinese woman was lying on the ground near a pool in Cumma Catta Woods. Suspicious, Pendlebury asked the farmer to show him the spot. They found Mrs Chung at 7.30 p.m. She had been strangled with pieces of white cord, her dress had been pulled up over her chest and her underclothes had been torn away as though there had been a sexual assault. She was still wearing her jewel-studded watch, but two expensive rings were missing.

Chung was woken and told of his wife's death with the white cords around her neck, to which he responded 'Had she knickers on?' (Although he spoke fluent and unaccented English, he later claimed he had said 'Has she necklace on?' but had been misunderstood because of his accent.) In the morning Chung exclaimed 'Its terrible! My wife assaulted, robbed and murdered!' He had not been told about the assault and robbery.

The white cord was the same as that used in the hotel. Blood was found on the overcoat that Pendlebury had seen Chung wearing at Cumma Catta Woods. Mrs Chung's two missing diamond rings were found hidden in a roll of camera film in the hotel room. Chung was charged with murder. His defence, at the trial at Carlisle Assizes in November, was that he and his wife had been followed by two oriental strangers and that they must be the murderers. Chung had no need to rob his wife as under Chinese law the husband owns all of his wife's property, as Lawyer Chung was well aware. No satisfactory motive was established at the trial. Chung was found guilty and sentenced to death. He conducted his own case at the Appeal Court, unsuccessfully.

In 1929 the *Sunday Express* ran an article, apparently quoting Chung himself, explaining that his wife was sterile as a result of an operation and, without a son to revere his memory, his soul would be accursed. As the headline said, Mrs Chung was 'Killed To Save Her Husband's Soul'.

Also hanged this day:

1815   at Canterbury, Kent: Nicholas Nolam for robbery.

1893   at Winchester Prison: George Mason for the murder of Sergeant James Robertson.

1899   at Strangeways Prison, Manchester: Michael Dowdle for wife-murder.

1905   at Newcastle Prison: Henry Perkins (40) for the murder of Patrick Durkin.

1948   at Cardiff Gaol: Clifford Godfrey Wills (30s) for the murder of Sillvinea May Parry.

7 December

1724 ACQUITTED THEN FOUND GUILTY
John (or Louis) Houssart hanged at the scene of his crime in Swan Alley, Shoreditch, for wife-murder.

Louis Houssart and Ann Rondeau, both of French extraction, were married in a French church in Spitalfields. After three years he had had enough and left her. He posed as a single man and was soon married again, to a Mrs Hern. When his new wife mentioned that there were rumours about him being already married he decided to get rid of the first Mrs Houssart.

Ann was living with her mother, Mrs Rondeau, in Swan Alley in Shoreditch. His first attempt at murder was to poison her, but she recovered. Then he appeared in Swan Alley one night and gave a 13-year-old boy a penny to tell Mrs Rondeau that a gentleman wanted to see her in a nearby pub. When he saw his mother-in-law leave, he went indoors and slit Ann's throat with his razor. He was suspected and charged, but without any real evidence, as the boy could not be found. Houssart was acquitted, but detained to face a charge of bigamy.

The boy knew about the murder but feared that if it were known that he had carried the message he would be hanged himself. Eventually the lad was taken to Newgate where he immediately picked out Houssart from a group of prisoners. He also recognised Mrs Rondeau as the woman to whom he had given the message. Solomon Rondeau, Ann's brother, initiated an appeal and Houssart was brought to trial again. The most conclusive evidence at the second trial was that Houssart had called a friend to visit him in Newgate and tried to bribe him to swear a false alibi, admitting to this friend that he had given Ann 'a touch with the razor'. He was sentenced to be hanged at the end of Swan Alley.

Also hanged this day:

1716   at Tyburn Tree: seven Jacobites for treason. *Hangman: William Marvel*

1885   at Newgate Prison: Daniel Minahan for wife-murder.

8 December

1828 WILLIAM CALCRAFT'S NEW CAREER
Joseph Hunton, a Quaker, hanged at Old Bailey for forgery.
Hangman: James Foxon

Hunton was a prosperous businessman from Bury St Edmunds who had succeeded as a sugar baker in London. He married and his wife brought a large fortune with her that Hunton used, with his own fortune, to speculate on the stock exchange. He lost heavily and forged a number of bills of exchange to meet his debts. When the forgeries were discovered he tried to flee abroad, but was caught at Plymouth as his ship, bound for New York, was about to depart. He was tried at the Old Bailey and sentenced to death.

The regular Newgate hangman was Tom Cheshire, but he was 'temporarily incapacitated by illness' (actually drunk and suffering from delirium tremens) and Foxon had been called in at short notice. Foxon was about to retire, and the occasion of Hunton's execution had a bearing on the appointment of his successor. A certain William Calcraft was engaged in selling pies to the assembled mob. Standing near the scaffold, he stopped yelling to sell his wares while the execution procedure was taking place but started again as soon as Hunton's death-struggles had stopped. Just then he saw Foxon emerge from beneath the gallows, looking faint, and trying to call the nearby beer seller for refreshment. Calcraft offered to get the ale for Foxon, and did so.

They started talking and Foxon revealed his intention to retire shortly. Learning that Calcraft was eager to become a hangman, he offered to recommend him to his City masters. Before long Calcraft was called to Newgate for his first task as an executioner: the flogging of four boys. When Foxon dropped dead a few months later, on 14 February, Calcraft was given his job and was the public hangman for the next 45 years.

Also hanged this day:

1811 at Sheerness: Thomas O'Hara.

1828 at Old Bailey: John James for burglary; Dan Mahoney for cutting and maiming.

1884 at Kirkdale Prison, Liverpool: Arthur Shaw (31) for wife-murder; Ernest Ewerstadt for the murder of Elizabeth Hamblin. *Hangman: James Berry*

1901 at Newcastle Prison: John Miller and his nephew John Miller for the murder of itinerant showman John Ferguson. *Hangman: William Billington. Assistant: John Billington.* Their father, James Billington, had collapsed the previous morning having risen from his sickbed after a bout of bronchitis and pneumonia. The brothers, both experienced hangmen, appointed themselves as substitutes and none of the Newcastle officials seemed to mind. James died on 13 December aged 54.

1903 at Durham Gaol: James Duffy (46) for the murder of Ellen Newman.

1909 at Durham Gaol: Abel Atherton (30) for the murder of his former landlady. *Hangman: Henry Pierrepoint*

1944 at Seattle, Washington, USA: Edward Heberling for the rape-murder of Harriet Lindstrom (19) and two others.

9 December

1783 FIRST HANGINGS AT OLD BAILEY
Ten persons, the first to be hanged at Old Bailey, outside the gate of Newgate Prison, since the end of the Tyburn era.
Hangman: Edward Dennis. Assistant: William Brunskill

Executions had ended at Tyburn the previous month (see 7 November). Since then there had been a few London hangings at specific locations, but the intention was for the regular place of execution to be outside the gate of Newgate Prison, in the street known as Old Bailey. As reported in a contemporary broadsheet, the neighbours were not keen on the idea:

'Ten were executed; the scaffold hung with black; and the inhabitants of the neighbourhood, having petitioned the sheriffs to remove the scene of execution to the old place, were told that the plan had been well considered, and would be persevered in.'

The 'perseverance' continued for as long as there were public executions, indeed Britain's last public hanging was on that very spot in 1868 (see 26 May).

Also hanged this day:

1872 at Old Bailey: A. Elliott for the murder of his mistress.

1885 at Kirkdale Prison, Liverpool: George Thomas for the jealousy-inspired murder of Margaret Askins.

1889 at Devizes Prison: Benjamin Pursell for wife-murder.

1894 at Leicester Prison: John William Newell for wife-murder.

1902 at Pentonville Prison: Thomas Fairclough Barrow (42) for the stabbing-murder of Emily Coates, his stepdaughter.

10 December

1827 'AWFUL BLOODY HANGING'
John Williams (23) publicly hanged at Old Bailey for theft from a dwelling house.

On the morning of his execution young Williams, in a desperate attempt at escaping the gallows, climbed up a pipe towards a water cistern in the corner of the Press Yard*. Before reaching the cistern he fell backwards and suffered severe leg injuries. He was treated and bandaged by a surgeon and had to be carried out to the scaffold in Old Bailey, barely conscious and almost dead.

He was hanged with four others (see below), but it was the sight of the pitiful and half-dead Williams that incensed the crowd. Even worse, the bandages could not contain the wounds to his legs and his blood poured down on to the platform below. As one report said, it was an 'awful bloody hanging'.

* *Henry Williams, a chimney sweep also under sentence of death for burglary, succeeded in escaping by the same route via the water cistern nine years later.*

Also hanged this day:

1827   at Old Bailey: John French, William Chapman, and William Johnson for horse-stealing; John Smith for robbery.

1901   at Durham Gaol: John George Thompson for the murder of a young woman.

1931   at Oxford Castle: Henry Daniel Seymour (52) for the murder of Mrs Anne Louisa Kempson (54).

11 December

1951 HEART BEATS 20 MINUTES AFTER HANGING
Herbert Leonard Mills (19) hanged at Lincoln Prison, for the strangling-murder of Mrs Mabel Tattershaw (48).
Hangman: Albert Pierrepoint

Herbert Mills, an out-of-work clerk, went to the Roxy Cinema in Nottingham one Thursday afternoon, 2 August 1951, and sat next to Mabel Tattershaw. They talked to each other and agreed to meet the next day. As Mills later confessed, 'I had always considered the possibility of a perfect murder' and he decided to conduct 'an experiment'.

He met Mabel on that Friday evening and took her to a secluded orchard in Sherwood Vale, a rural area on the outskirts of Notting-ham. Mabel lay down, but complained that she was cold. Mills used the cold as an excuse to cover her with her overcoat and his own, as a means of containing her should she struggle. Wearing gloves, he hit her a few times with a blunt instrument and then strangled her. There was no sexual or robbery motive, this was his experiment in murder. Once Tattershaw was dead he bludgeoned her again before leaving.

Whatever joy he may have experienced, a sense of disappointment replaced it after the weekend because Mabel's body had not been discovered. He wanted to gloat over the bewilderment of the police in their futile efforts to solve his 'perfect murder'. By Thursday 9 August he ran out of patience and telephoned the *News Of The World* in London and spoke to the Chief Crime Reporter, Norman Rae: 'I've just found a woman's body. It looks like murder.'

Norman Rae kept Mills talking while the Nottingham police were informed, and persuaded the youth to reveal the telephone number of the call box saying that he could ring back when the money ran out. Police arrived at the call box while Mills was still talking to Rae. He took them to the body and then they let him go after he had made a statement. The police had doubts about Mills. He had said that the woman had been strangled, yet she appeared to have been bludgeoned to death and strangulation was not apparent until the autopsy. How did Herbert Mills know she had been strangled?

The police confided their doubts to Norman Rae and encouraged the reporter to discuss it with Mills. There was no difficulty in doing that: Mills was keen to tell his story to the *News Of The World* for £250. His story was printed under the headline 'How I Met Murder'. Rae met Mills at a Nottingham hotel on 24 August and heard more and more about the crime. Mills eventually confessed to Rae, and sat down and wrote all about it on the hotel's headed paper. The next morning they went to the police. The confession was corroborated by forensic evidence; there were hairs from Mills' head on Mabel's body and fibres from his blue suit under her fingernails. He was found guilty at Nottingham Assizes in November and sentenced to death.

Mills still thought he had committed a perfect murder because there had been no motive or link between him and the victim: '. . . if I had not reported finding the body I should not have been connected with the crime in any manner whatsoever. I am quite proud of my achievement.' He had been too impatient.

Herbert Leonard Mills was hanged at Lincoln Prison. The drop ensured that his spinal column was instantly dislocated, which would normally bring about an equally instant death, but in this case there is some doubt when his life actually became extinct. The medical officer reported at the inquest that the heart had continued to beat for 20 minutes after the drop.

Also hanged this day:

1757 at Nottingham: John Horn Esq. for murder.

1857 at St John, New Brunswick, Canada: Patrick Slavin for the murders of Robert McKenzie, his wife and four children at Mispeck.

1876 at Newgate Prison: Charles O'Donnell for wife-murder.

1888   at Worcester Prison: Samuel Crowther for the murder of John Willis.

1894   at Newcastle Prison: Samuel George Emery (20) for the murder of Mary Ann Marshall.

1895   at Minneapolis, Minnesota, USA: Harry T. Hayward for procuring the murder of his fiancée Kitty Ging for $10,000 insurance money. His brother Adry Hayward informed on him and his partner, Claus Blixt (who shot Kitty), turned state's evidence. At Hayward's request, the scaffold was painted his favourite colour of fire-engine red. He stood calmly on the trap and smoked a cigarette before adjusting the rope round his neck, then he told the hangman, 'Pull her tight, I'll stand pat.' He died slowly, strangling for several minutes.

12 December

Hanged this day:

1816   at Old Bailey: William Anderson for murder.

1820   at Old Bailey: Daniel Gentle and William Read for robbing their employers.

1882   at Wandsworth Prison: Charles Taylor for wife-murder.

1894   at Winchester Prison: Cyrus Knight (45) for wife-murder; William Rogers for the murder of a woman.

1900   at Durham Gaol: John Bowes for wife-murder.

1902   at Usk Prison, Monmouthshire, Wales: Jeremiah Callaghan (42) for the murder of Hannah Shee at Tredegar.

13 December

1945 VENGEANCE AT BELSEN
Belsen concentration camp killers hanged at Hameln Gaol, Westfalia, Germany.
Hangman: Albert Pierrepoint. Assistant: Regimental Sergeant Major O'Neil

British troops liberated Belsen and it was one of the first of the Nazi concentration camps to be entered by the Allies. The British troops found thirteen thousand corpses lying unburied among appalling filth.

Death had come to them from starvation, thirst, beating, shooting – and from attacks by dogs. Forty thousand living skeletons were mixed with the scattered dead and thirteen thousand of them died within the next six weeks, too weak to recover. The well-fed staff of sadists responsible for this incredible mass murder were put on trial and 13 of them were sentenced to death. The women were hanged first, singly at 30-minute intervals, in the following order:

Irma Grese (21) had whipped prisoners to death and was responsible for about 30 killings a day.

Elizabeth Volkenrath also made 'selections' and survivors called her 'the most-hated woman in the camp'.

Juanna Bormann (42), 'the woman with the dogs' who set her wolfhounds to tear prisoners apart.

Double executions followed for the ten males, also at 30-minute intervals. The first pair were:

Josef Kramer (39), former commandant dubbed the 'Beast of Belsen'.

Dr Fritz Klein (55), camp doctor, made daily 'selections' of naked prisoners for the gas chambers and killed others by hypodermic injections in the stomach.

Thirteen killers were hanged on Friday 13 December before 13 official witnesses.

Albert Pierrepoint revealed in his book *Executioner Pierrepoint* that he received a plain envelope at Christmas enclosing a piece of paper with the single word 'Belsen' and a £5 note. Many Christmases thereafter he was sent a £5 note with no message.

Also hanged this day:

1713   at Clerkenwell Green, London: William Lowther and Richard Keele for the murder of a turnkey at the Clerkenwell Bridewell.

1869   at Newgate Prison: Frederick Hinson for the murder of his mistress, Maria Death, and her other lover, W. Boyd, at Wood Green, London.

1880   at Newgate Prison: William Herbert for the murder of his sister-in-law; George Pavey for the murder of a little girl.

1886   at Norwich Castle: George Harmer for the murder of Henry Last.

1901   at Northampton Prison: Alick Claydon for wife-murder.

1904   at Pentonville Prison: Joseph Potten (a.k.a. Conrad Donovan) and his half-brother Charles Wade (22) for the murder of newsagent

Miss Matilda Emily Farmer at Stepney, London.

1907 at Cardiff Gaol, Wales: George 'Notty' Stills (30) for the murder of his mother Mrs Rachel Stills (70).

1954 at Holloway Prison: Mrs Styllou Christofi (53) for the crude murder of her daughter-in-law Hella Christofi (36). She had probably murdered before, in Cyprus. Being of the Greek Orthodox religion she requested that a Maltese cross be in sight when she was hanged. The request was granted and the cross was nailed to the wall in front of where she would stand when she arrived at the chalk marks on the trap door. However, as the white hood was placed over her head immediately, it is doubtful whether she saw it. It was still nailed to the wall when the execution chamber was dismantled in 1967. *Hangman: Albert Pierrepoint*

14 December

1650 ANN GREEN LIVES AGAIN!
Ann Green hanged at Oxford for the murder of her newly born child – and raised from the dead.

Ann Green was an unmarried servant-girl who killed her new born baby. Charged with murder and found guilty, she was publicly hanged at Oxford Gaol. Strangling on the rope, her friends hung on to her legs to put her out of her misery. She was cut down after half an hour and her friends laid her out on the ground where she was seen to twitch again. One of them jumped on her stomach to finish her, and a soldier struck her on the head with his musket.

She was then pronounced dead by three university physicians and removed to the Surgeons' Hall for dissection. As the Professor of Anatomy, Sir William Petty, and other doctors prepared to cut her open a rattling was heard from her throat. She was put into a warm bed and given cordials and her breathing restarted. Next day she was almost fully recovered. A Royal pardon followed and she later married and had three more children. She died in 1659, nine years after her ghastly execution and being declared dead.

Also hanged this day:

1876 at Cambridge Prison: Robert Browning for the murder of Emma Rolf.

1898 at Maidstone Prison: Thomas Daley for the murder of a woman.

400

15 December

1950 FAKED ROAD ACCIDENT
Police Constable James Ronald Robertson (33) hanged at Barlinnie Prison, Glasgow, for the murder of his mistress, Catherine McCluskey (40).

PC Robertson was married with two children and was probably also the father of one of Catherine McCluskey's two illegitimate children. She had told a friend that a policeman was the father, and PC Robertson was one of her current boyfriends.

Robertson left his beat at 11.15 p.m. on the night of 28 July 1950 and told his colleague that he was going to drive a woman home. He returned to his beat at 1.10 a.m. looking strained with his uniform untidy and explained that the exhaust had fallen off his car.

Catherine McCluskey's body was found on a road on the southern outskirts of Glasgow and, at first, she appeared to be the victim of a road accident. The pathologist became suspicious when he realised that she had been run over twice by the same car. There were no injuries to the lower part of her body consistent with impact to a person in an upright posture. Nor were there the other usual indications, such as broken glass or paint fragments. The woman had been run over, but she had not been knocked down. This had been murder!

Robertson's house was searched and a number of stolen goods were found. His car had been stolen from a solicitor some months before and was now fitted with numberplates taken from a tractor. The underside of the car had traces of blood, skin and hair, but there were no signs of an impact on the body of the car. In addition to his regulation truncheon, Robertson was found to be in possession of a cosh that bore a small blood stain: a blow from this weapon would be consistent with the bruise found on the victim's right temple.

The prosecution's case was that Robertson had knocked McCluskey unconscious with a blow from the cosh and then twice deliberately driven over her prostrate body. Robertson's story was that he had accidentally knocked her down and run over her while reversing. He claimed he had been unable to extricate her from under the car and had moved the car backwards and forwards until she was free and then driven away. The jury did not believe him.

Also hanged this day:

1761 at Strabane, County Tyrone, Ireland: John M'Naughton (38) and his accomplice Dunlap for the murder of Miss Knox.

1815 at Old Bailey: John Bansted for forgery; John Holliday for burglary.

1818 at Old Bailey: William Burton, John Driscoll, William Weller, and George Cashman for issuing forged notes.

1856 at Old Bailey: Joseph Jenkins (a.k.a. Robert Marley) for the murder of a shopkeeper named Cope in Westminster.

1882 at Galway County Gaol, Ireland: Myles Joyce, Pat Joyce, and Pat Casey, for the slaughter and mutilation of five members of the Joyce family in their cottage at Maamtrasna on 18 August 1882. The 'Maamtrasna murders' caused a shock-wave of horror throughout the British Isles and ten local men were arrested, of whom two were induced to give Queen's Evidence. The remaining eight were convicted and condemned to death, five being reprieved. Two years later one of the informers publicly confessed in church that he had given perjured evidence under threat of being hanged himself. *Hangman: William Marwood*

1891 at Shepton Mallet Prison: Harry Dainton for wife-murder.

1903 at Hereford Prison: William Haywood (61) for wife-murder.

16 December

1831 'KILL NOT CURE!'
John William Holloway (25) publicly hanged at Lewes, Sussex, for the murder and dismemberment of his wife, a midget.
Hangman: William Calcraft

Holloway enjoyed a successful love-life among the local girls in Brighton. It was surprising, therefore, that he took an interest in a plain-looking midget with an over-sized head, the four-foot tall Celia Bashford. She became pregnant and he succumbed to pressure to marry her. She had two children by him. He abandoned her in 1830.

He met and fell in love with the pretty Ann Kennett and bigamously married her. He worked at various jobs, legal and illegal, until they settled in Brighton as Mr and Mrs Goldsmith. Celia found him and he was forced to pay her maintenance of two shillings (10p) a week for herself and the children. Ann knew all about this.

Holloway murdered Celia in a dingy alleyway on 14 July while Ann watched. He cut up the body and buried parts of it under a tree and threw the rest into a cesspit near to where he and Ann lived. Both lots were soon found and identified. The 'Goldsmiths' were both charged with murder and the case against Holloway was so complete that he admitted his part, but testified that Ann was innocent. She was acquitted and he was sentenced to hang.

When Holloway appeared on the scaffold the crowd greeted him with groans and yells. Calcraft had been accompanied throughout the proceedings by a man with a large and unsightly wen on his neck. Ancient books claimed that the only certain cure for those afflicted with an ugly wen (a benign tumour usually found on the scalp, but which can occur elsewhere on the body) was to rub it with the hand of a freshly hanged man. The afflicted man had paid Calcraft handsomely to apply that cure to him!

When Calcraft was satisfied that Holloway was dead, he untied the arms and, grabbing one of the limp hands, started stroking it on the wen on the man's neck. The crowd, thinking the pair were indulging themselves in callous larking, started to hiss and yell. The sheriff demanded an explanation and, after hearing Calcraft's reply, indignantly ordered him to stop and told the hangman that it was his duty to kill and not to cure!

Also hanged this day:

1830 at Execution Dock, Wapping: George John Davis and William Watts for piracy.

1839 at Old Bailey: William Lees for wife-murder.

1897 at Maidstone Prison: William Betts (47) for the murder of his father.

1902 at Durham Gaol: Thomas Walton (31) for the murder of his wife, his child and his mother-in-law at Spennymoor; Thomas Nicholson (24) for the murder of a little girl near Newcastle. At Wandsworth Prison: William Brown for the murder of his wife by kicking her to death.

1903 at Winchester Prison: William Brown, a soldier, and Thomas Cowdrey, a labourer, for the murder of Esther Atkins.

17 December

1963 THEY KILLED FOR £4 AND MISSED £3,000
Russell Pascoe (23), hanged at Horfield Gaol, Bristol and Dennis John Whitty (22), hanged at Winchester Prison, for the brutal and cowardly murder of World War One deserter, and rich Cornish recluse, William Garfield Rowe (64).

William Garfield Rowe was an amazing man, and far more interesting than the pair of thugs who so brutally murdered him. Rowe was conscripted into the army in 1917, but ran away one week later. He was caught by the military police and fled from them as well. He returned to the family farm and stayed hidden in an upstairs bedroom until they moved to Nanjarrow Farm at Constantine, about six miles from Falmouth. On the journey to their new home he lay hidden under a pile of clothes in the back of a cart.

At Nanjarrow Farm he stayed inside the house during daylight hours, but ventured out at night to work on the farm. When Queen Elizabeth II, early in her reign, announced an amnesty for all deserters from both World Wars William Rowe was able to emerge and resume his official identity. For 39 years the family had publicly pretended that he had died in World War One.

When Rowe's mother died he was left on his own at the farm. His nocturnal habits continued, however, and he never went out by day. The house was never cleaned or dusted and it was rumoured that he never cleaned himself either, or changed his clothes. He amused himself learning foreign languages from teach-yourself books, even studying Esperanto.

Russell Pascoe may have been employed by Rowe to do some odd jobs and it was almost certainly Pascoe who burgled the house in 1960 and got away with £200. It was inevitable that rumours should begin about an eccentric recluse sitting on a miser's hoard in his littered and filthy farmhouse. Russell Pascoe believed the stories. By 14 August 1963, he had teamed up with another hard case and petty criminal, Dennis John Whitty. They lived with three teenage girls in a caravan at nearby Truro. That night they told the girls that they were 'going out on a job': they left on Pascoe's motorcycle equipped with a starting pistol, an iron bar, and a knife.

They attacked the old recluse with the iron bar and the knife; according to the pathologist the attacks were simultaneous, but the killers blamed each other. Russell Pascoe claimed:

'We went on my motorbike and knocked on his door at 11 o'clock. Old man Rowe answered the door. Dennis was standing in front of the door and said he was a helicopter pilot and had crashed and wanted to use the phone. I then hit Rowe on the back of the head with a small iron bar. I only meant to knock him out, that's all. He (Whitty) took the iron bar and went for him. I had to walk away, honest I did . . .' And later: 'I didn't kill him – that was my mate. He went mad he did. I didn't stop him in fear he would stick me. I had to walk away. I couldn't stop him. He said he finished him when he stuck the knife in his throat. I only knocked him on the head with a bar. I just knocked him out.'

Whitty said: 'Pascoe made me stick him. I stabbed him in the chest. Pascoe was going to hit me, so I stuck him in the neck.'

The attack lasted only a few seconds, but William Rowe sustained seven cuts on the scalp, a fractured skull, a fractured jaw, five stab wounds in the chest (including one in the heart), and his throat was gashed. When they returned to the caravan, about 18 miles from Nanjarrow Farm, Pascoe was looking scared and withdrawn, Whitty was grinning.

Like a storybook murderer, Russell Pascoe returned to the scene of his crime; he was stopped at a police roadblock as he rode through Constantine on 16 August. The local police knew him and their questioning of his movements soon produced results and he was charged the next day. Whitty was brought in and also charged.

Like a storybook recluse, William Rowe really did have a fortune hidden on the farm. His killers found only £4 under a piano, but detectives found £3,000 in banknotes hidden in different parts of the house. In a diary were directions, written in Esperanto, that led to the discovery of a large glass jar stuffed with more money buried on the farm, and a packed safe buried in the cowshed.

The murderers paid in full for their foul crime: Pascoe at the gallows at Horfield Gaol, Whitty at Winchester, both at 9 a.m. precisely.

Also hanged this day:

1708 at Tyburn Tree: Deborah Churchill for murder.

1771 at Tyburn Tree: Dr Levi Weil, his brother Asher Weil, Lazarus Jacobs, and Solomon Porteous for murder and burglary. They belonged to one of the ruthless Jewish gangs then active in London. Also Francis Phoenix, Charles Barton, and Henry Jones for burgling the premises of Alderman Ladbrooke.

1804 at Old Bailey: John Kennedy and Malton Moody for highway robbery.

1815 at Old Bailey: John Bradford for forgery.

1895 at Walton Gaol, Liverpool: Elijah Winstanley (31) for the murder in Wigan of Detective Sergeant Robert Kidd (37). *Hangman: James Billington*

1913 at Strangeways Prison, Manchester: Ernest Kelly for the murder of Oldham newsagent Mrs Bardsley.

1958 Brian Chandler (20) for the hammering-murder and theft of £4 from an 83-year-old widow, a capital crime under the 1957 Homicide Act.

18 December

Hanged this day:

1773 at Lancaster, Pennsylvania, USA: Samuel Brand for the slaughter of his brother and parents.

1812 at Execution Dock, Wapping: Charles Frederick Palm and Sam Tilling, two sailors, for mutiny and the murder on the high seas of their captain, James Keith.

1840 at Schenectady, New York, USA: Charles Cook for the rape-murder of Mrs Catherine Merry.

1883 at Dublin, Ireland: Joseph Poole for murder in Sevile Place, Dublin.

1888 at Durham Gaol: William Waddell for the murder of Jane Beardsley.

19 December

1946 CABINET MINISTER'S TRAITOR SON
John Amery (33) hanged at Wandsworth Prison for treason.
Hangman: Albert Pierrepoint

John Amery was the son of Cabinet Minister L. S. (Leo) Amery and elder brother of Julian Amery who later became a minister in Harold Macmillan's government.

Leo Amery was a highly respected statesman who helped bring about the resignation of Prime Minister Chamberlain during the debate that followed the failure of the Norway campaign in 1940. Leo Amery's younger son Julian was a war hero who was parachuted behind enemy lines. By contrast, his weak-minded eldest son, John, must have brought continual grief to his father. The problem child became a silly young man, bankrupt by the age of 24, without any charm or other redeeming qualities. He amassed a total of 74 motoring convictions because he apparently considered that normal laws did not apply to him. Once, having caused an accident, he produced a pistol and threatened the other driver, adding that it would be no use calling the police because he was too important for them.

He was a gun-runner for Franco during the Spanish Civil War in the 1930s. He became a traitor in 1942 and went to Berlin. The Germans used him for massive propaganda schemes, including extensively publicised broadcasts. Flattered and accorded pomp, he agreed to form the Legion of St George, later called the British Free Corps. He toured internment and prisoner-of-war camps trying to recruit captured Britons to fight for the Germans, converting only a few dissolute misfits.

After the war he was charged with treason and pleaded guilty at his Old Bailey trial, which lasted a mere eight minutes. Inevitably he was sentenced to death. In his muddle-headed way he may have thought that he would be treated leniently, as he always had been, or reprieved because of his father's position in the government. That was not the way Britain treated traitors at that period in her history.

Also hanged this day:

1748 at Edinburgh: John Young for robbery. He had previously been a brave soldier with a good record.

1876 at Horsemonger Lane Gaol: Silas Barlow for the murder of Ellen Sloper. At Carlisle Prison: James Dalgleish for the murder of Sarah Wright.

1893 at Lincoln Prison: Henry Rumbold for the murder of a woman named Rushby.

1934 at Hull Prison: Ethel Lillie Major (44) for the murder of her husband Arthur with corned beef laced with strychnine. *Hangman: Tom Pierrepoint*

1950 at Strangeways Prison, Manchester: Nicholas Persoulious Crosby (22), a gypsy, for the throat-cutting murder of Ruth Massey (19). *Hangman: Albert Pierrepoint. Assistant: Syd Dernley*

20 December

1689 THE 'GOLDEN FARMER'
William Davis (64) hanged in Fleet Street, London, for highway robbery.

William Davis was a successful farmer in Sudbury, Gloucestershire, and was known as the Golden Farmer because of his habit of paying bills with gold. He was married and fathered 18 children. What was not known by his neighbours was that he was a successful highwayman from the age of 22 until his execution. A highwayman's career was usually short, but Davis enjoyed more than four decades of highway robbery. He survived for so long by performing his hold-ups well away from his home territory. He worked across southern England, as far away as the outskirts of London itself. He worked alone and carried out his robberies at lonely spots, taking no chances. He was finally caught in London and publicly hanged in Fleet Street, afterwards being hung in chains outside a house he used in Bagshot, Surrey.

Also hanged this day:

1701   at Tyburn Tree: John Cowland for the murder of Sir Andrew Stanning, Baronet.

1738   at Execution Dock, Wapping: James Buchanan (31) hanged for murder. Friends charged the scaffold, cut him down while still alive and escaped. Buchanan was never recaptured.

1786   at New London, Connecticut, USA: a half-witted Paquot Indian girl, Hannah Ocuish (12), for the murder of Eunice Bolles (6) who had stolen her strawberries.

1856   at Chester: W. Jackson for the murder of two childen.

1876   at Leicester Prison: John Thomas Green for wife-murder.

1892   at Strangeways Prison, Manchester: Joseph Mellor (33) for the murder of his wife, Mary Jane Mellor (36), during Oldham Wakes Week. *Hangman: James Billington*

1904   at York Castle: Edward Hall for the murder of John Dalby, his father-in-law. At Cardiff Gaol, Wales: Russian seaman Eric Lange for the murder of publican John Jones. At Armagh County Gaol, Ireland: Joseph Fee hanged for murder after facing trial three times. The jury twice disagreed, but Fee was found guilty and sentenced to death the third time.

1905   at Maidstone Prison: Samuel Curtis for the murder of his sweetheart, Alice Clover.

21 December

1875 WAINWRIGHT'S FATAL ERROR
Henry Wainwright hanged in the Execution Shed at Newgate for murdering his mistress Harriet Louisa Lane (23) (a.k.a. Mrs Percy King).
Hangman: William Marwood

The adage that 'murder will out' is based on the theory that every murderer, no matter how clever, will always make the one fatal error that will lead to his discovery and his downfall. For Henry Wainwright the moment of carelessness was when he went to get a cab. It led to the discovery of his awful crime and, literally, to his final downfall – through the trap door in the Execution Shed at Newgate.

Henry Wainwright was a respected Victorian businessman in the East End of London, living with his wife and children at 40 Tredegar Square. He had shared in an inheritance of £11,000 from his father and had a shop at 84 Whitechapel Road and opposite, at 215, a brush-making workshop and warehouse.

An educated, church-going man, he often gave public readings of the scriptures and passages from Dickens. His most popular lecture was 'The Wit of Sydney Smith', but his favourite recitation was of Thomas Hood's poem, 'The Dream of Eugene Aram' (about the eighteenth century Yorkshire murderer – see 6 August).

Like many 'respectable' Victorians, Wainwright led a double life. He had a mistress, Harriet Lane, living in a house in St Peter's Street, Mile End. He paid the rent and gave Lane a generous allowance of £5 a week. Two daughters were born and, for decency's sake, Wainwright assumed the name of Percy King and a newspaper notice was published of Mr King's 'marriage' to Harriet.

Wainwright's business suffered as he drained its funds to maintain his expensive life style. He was keeping two homes and lavishing furs and jewellery on Harriet. His brother William ended their partnership and Wainwright never recovered from the blow. He made further business errors and became burdened with crippling debts.

Severe economies had to be made, and Harriet was to be the first! It is unlikely that he originally intended to murder her, but she didn't take kindly to the cutting of her weekly £5. Also her recently acquired noisy drinking habits must have driven him to seek another way of avoiding adding a sex-scandal to his many problems.

With another brother, Thomas, posing as Mr Edward Frieake (the name of an auctioneer friend of Wainwright) the plan was to entice Harriet into living abroad with Teddy Frieake. She liked the idea and left the children with friends in June 1874, telling them that she and Teddy were going away on holiday. She was never seen again. She had been taken to the workshop at 215 Whitechapel Road where Henry Wainwright fired two bullets into her head, afterwards burying her under the floor. The awful stench of her decaying body could not be disguised by the workshop smells of fresh paint, but despite complaints no investigation was made to discover its cause.

The business continued to crumble, even with the 'economic removal' of Harriet, and Wainwright could not keep his creditors at bay. In June 1875, a year after the murder of Harriet, he was made bankrupt and his business premises changed hands.

He dug up Harriet's remains, cut them down to manageable chunks, and wrapped them in American cloth. He put them with his few remaining personal belongings ready for removal to brother Thomas's house at London Bridge. He hired a former employee, a youth named Stokes, to assist him with the removal. They carried the parcels outside and he left Stokes to guard the packages while he went in search of a cab, thereby committing his fatal blunder.

Had he sent Stokes for the cab his crime would probably have gone undiscovered. Instead, while he was looking for the cab Stokes looked into one of the foul-smelling parcels, and out fell a decaying human hand. Stokes covered it again, and gave no outward sign of his discovery.

When the cab departed with Wainwright and the parcels, Stokes ran along behind and tried to alert policemen of his grisly find, but was laughed at. Stokes eventually found two policemen who believed him, and they arrived at London Bridge as Wainwright was shifting the parcels from the cab. Wainwright offered the constables £50 each to go away, but was immediately arrested.

Henry and Thomas Wainwright were tried at the Old Bailey at the end of November 1875, and Henry bull-headedly denied everything throughout the trial. Thomas was found guilty as an accessory and sentenced to seven years; Henry was sentenced to death. Wainwright spent his last evening strolling with the Newgate Governor in the prison yard, smoking a cigar. He took great care with his grooming and dressing before the execution, and went on to the scaffold with great dignity. But, when he entered the Execution Shed he turned to the hundred or so official witnesses and shouted, 'You curs! Come to see a man die, have you?' Then he resumed his stoic pose and uttered not another word.

Also hanged this day:

1721 at Tyburn Tree: Nathaniel Hawes for highway robbery on Finchley Common. He refused to plead at his Old Bailey trial and was ordered to suffer *peine forte et dure* (pressing to death). After enduring 250lb for seven minutes he gave in and pleaded not guilty, but was convicted and condemned.

1739 at Tyburn Tree: Edward Joiner for wife-murder; Thomas Beckwith for robbery (his first offence).

1820 at Old Bailey: Charles Goodwin, Martin Feeley and Richard Scott for issuing forged notes.

1876 at Strangeways Prison, Manchester: William Flanagan for the murder of Margaret Dockerty.

1893 at Gloucester Prison: James Wyndham for murdering his father.

1896 at Derby Gaol: John Cotton for wife-murder.

410

1945 James McNichol for the murder of Sergeant D.A.R. Kirkaldie; J. R. Young for the murder of F. B. Lucas.

22 December

1953 'YOU KNOW BLOODY WELL I DONE IT'
Alfred Charles Whiteway (22) hanged at Wandsworth Prison for the Thames towpath murder of Barbara Songhurst (16). Christine Reed (18) was murdered at the same time.

Alfred Whiteway, a muscular building-site labourer, committed a series of rapes in the country areas of outer London. Dressed in a white polo vest and leather jacket, he cycled around a wide area and committed more than a dozen rape-attacks on victims ranging from a 12-year-old schoolgirl to a woman in her late 50s. The victims were overpowered by his strength and violence; he brandished an axe or knife. They also remembered his pale, acne-marked face and the permanently narrowed eyelids caused by his defective eyesight. The police realised that the attacks were all committed by the same young man, but they could not catch him.

The body of Barbara Songhurst (16) was taken from the River Thames at Ham Fields, Richmond, Surrey, on the morning of 1 June 1953. She had been raped before being brutally killed; her head had been battered and there were three stab wounds in her back. Five days later the body of her missing companion, Christine Reed (18), was recovered from the Thames, also at Richmond. Christine's skull had been fractured in two places and she had been stabbed ten times in the chest and back, four deep knife-thrusts going into one of the wounds. She had also been raped, possibly after death. Both girls had been virgins before the assault.

The police investigation revealed that the girls had been cycling along the towpath the previous night. They spent some time enjoying innocent fun and 'skylarking' with three youths who were camping by the river. The girls left to cycle home along the towpath. Campers further along the river heard screams from Teddington Lock at 11 p.m., and a man was seen riding a woman's bicycle on the towpath at 11.20 p.m.

The investigation showed that the serial-rapist and the murderer had identical modus operandi and the police feared that now he had resorted to murder he might continue to do so. A dangerous sex-maniac was at large. Scotland Yard issued an appeal to the public to help them find the killer and a massive investigation followed in which more than seven thousand people were interviewed. At the end of the month a man was arrested after two women had been attacked with an

411

axe and raped at Oxshott Woods: Alfred Whiteway had been caught and the series of violent attacks ended that afternoon.

Whiteway's shoes were discovered to be heavily stained with human blood. When the shoes, along with his axe and kukri-knife, were laid on the table in front of him, he confessed:

'Its all up. You know bloody well I done it. That shoe's buggered me. What a bloody mess. I am mental. Me head must be wrong. I cannot stop meself. I am not a bloody murderer. I only see one girl. She came round the tree where I stood and I bashed her and she went down like log. Then the other screamed out down by the lock. Never saw her until then I didn't. I nipped over and shut her up. Two of them. Then I tumbled the other one knew me. If it had not been for that it would not have happened. Put that bloody chopper away. It haunts me. What more do they want to know? Why don't the doctors do something? It will be mental, won't it? It must be. I can't stop it. Give us it, I will sign it.'

His sanity, and his responsibility for murdering Barbara Songhurst, were not in doubt. The jury took less than an hour to find him guilty.

Also hanged this day:

1690 at Newgate: Ann Hereford for robbery and arson.

1822 at Cambridge, Massachusetts, USA: Michael Martin (47) better known as 'Captain Lightfoot', for highway robbery.

1831 at Maidstone: Richard Dixon (35) for setting fire to a barn at Eastry. *Hangman: William Calcraft*

1854 at Old Bailey: Emile Barthelemy for the murder of George Moore in Warren Street, Marylebone. He may also have killed a man named Collard.

1875 at Newcastle Prison: John William Anderson for wife-murder while they were both drunk.

1891 at Durham Gaol: John William Johnson for the murder of Margaret Addison.

1892 at Usk Prison, Monmouthshire, Wales: Thomas Edwards for the murder of Mary Conolly.

1896 at York Castle: Swedish seaman Carlsen for killing Julia Wood.

1902 William Bolton (43) for the murder of Jane Allen.

1903 at Hull Prison: Charles W. Ashton (19) for the murder of Annie Marshall.

23 December

1948 JAPANESE WAR CRIMINALS
Former Prime Minister General Hideki Tojo (63) and six other
Japanese war leaders were hanged at Sugamo Prison, Tokyo, for
'crimes against peace and responsibility for atrocities'.

Tojo graduated from the army to War Minister in 1940. The following
year he became Prime Minister and dictator of Japan. He launched the
attack on Pearl Harbour without war having been declared, an action
described by President Roosevelt as 'a day of infamy'. The Japanese
fought the war with savagery, and the horrific atrocities committed
upon civilian populations and prisoners of war disgusted the civilised
world.

Tojo was arrested after the defeat of Japan and failed in an
attempted suicide by disembowelling. He and 27 other war criminals
were tried by the International Military Tribunal and, in November
1948, seven were sentenced to death and 16 received sentences of life
imprisonment. Tojo and the other six condemned war criminals
recited Buddhist prayers on the way to the gallows. Their bodies were
cremated in Yokohama.

Also hanged this day:

1715   at Tyburn Tree: Henry Powell for highway robbery.

1799   at Execution Dock, Wapping: Jean-Baptiste Prevot for mutiny
on the *Lady Shore*.

1819   at Old Bailey: John Micklin for an unnatural offence.

1822   at Penenden Heath, Kent: John Smith (80), a pensioner of
Greenwich Hospital, for the murder of Catherine Smith with whom he
cohabited.

1856   at Winchester: Lagava, Bartelano, and Pettrick for the murder
of two ship's officers and piracy.

1875   at Morpeth Prison: Richard Charlton for wife-murder with a
gun.

1888   at the Tombs Prison, New York, USA: Harry Carlton for the
murder of a policeman.

1890   at Newgate Prison: Mary Eleanor Wheeler (24), a.k.a. Eleanor
Pearcey, for the murders of Mrs Phoebe Hogg and daughter Phoebe
Hanalope Hogg. (Her father, Thomas Wheeler, had been hanged for
murder on 30 November 1880.) *Hangman: James Berry*

1896 at Nottingham Prison: Joseph Allcock for wife-murder.

1925 at Cape Town, South Africa: Petrus Hauptfleisch for murdering his mother (67) during a drunken rage.

1952 at Winsom Green Prison, Birmingham: Leslie Green (29) for the murder of Mrs Alice Wiltshaw (62). *Hangman: Albert Pierrepoint. Assistant: Syd Dernley*

24 December

1867 THE MURDER AND MUTILATION OF SWEET FANNY ADAMS
Frederick Baker (29) publicly hanged at Winchester Prison for the ghastly murder of Fanny Adams (8).
Hangman: William Calcraft

Fanny Adams was playing with her sister Lizzie (7) and a friend, Minnie Warner (8), in Flood Meadow only four hundred yards from their home in Tanhouse Lane, at Alton in Hampshire. It was early afternoon on Saturday 24 August 1867.

Frederick Baker (29), a solicitor's clerk for Messrs Clements in Alton, joined the girls in picking blackberries. He later gave Minnie and Lizzie three halfpennies to go and buy sweets. Giving Fanny a halfpenny for herself, he took her by the hand. Fanny began to cry but Baker calmed her, 'Don't cry, my dear, keep quiet, and if you will come up into the hop garden I will give you some more money' and led her away.

Between 7 p.m. and 8 p.m. a labourer named Thomas Gates was crossing the hop garden when he discovered the severed head of a child in a pool of blood; the eyes had been gouged out and the right ear had been sliced off. The blood-covered head had been carefully placed on two hop poles laid on the ground under a hedge. He picked up the head and ran to the nearest cottages.

When Fanny had not returned home for tea her parents tried without success to find out where she could be. They were standing with neighbours outside the cottages when Thomas Gates came running up to them with Fanny's bloody head in his hands. Fanny's mother collapsed in hysterics.

The police were called and a search was begun. That evening, and the next morning, the searchers found the scattered remains of poor Fanny Adams: a leg, a thigh, an arm; her torso had been cut open and almost all the organs and intestines had been removed. The eyes were found floating in the River Wey.

Baker had been seen in the vicinity by a woman and the police

414

arrested him at his desk in the office of Messrs Clements at 9 p.m. His trousers, boots and socks were still wet from recent attempts at washing. His waistcoat was splashed with blood and his shirt cuffs saturated with it. His diary was found in the desk during a search on Monday morning, and in his own firm handwriting the entry for Saturday 24 read 'Killed a young girl; it was fine and hot.'

The ghastly details of the murder of an innocent little girl were sensationally reported in newspapers. The tragic fate of 'Sweet Fanny Adams'* touched the hearts of readers in homes across the country.

Baker was tried at Winchester Town Hall in December, found guilty and sentenced to death. While being conveyed back to Winchester Prison he had to be heavily protected by the police from a still angry crowd. No attempt was made to have him reprieved. On Christmas Eve, five thousand gathered outside the prison and cheered as he was hanged.

* *'Sweet Fanny Adams' came into common usage as meaning 'nothing at all', i.e. all that was left of the child after her murder.*

Also hanged this day:

1705   at Tyburn Tree: John 'Half-hanged' Smith (43) for burglary. After hanging for 15 minutes a reprieve arrived and he was cut down. He was revived and later gave a vivid account of his agony on the end of the rope. *Hangman: Richard Pearse*

1723   at Tyburn Tree: John Stanley for murder.

1750   at Tyburn Tree: George Anderson for thieving.

1889   at Strangeways Prison, Manchester: William Dukes for the murder of his employer, furniture dealer Mr Jordan.

1895   at Nottingham Prison: Henry Wright (35) for the murders of Mary K. Reynolds, her two sons and a grandson.

1901   at Walton Gaol, Liverpool: John Harrison for the murder of a young woman.

25 December

(Hangman's holiday, apparently. It has proved impossible to trace any judicial hangings on this day, even in non-Christian countries where hanging was or still is the method of execution.)

26 December

1833 SEX OFFENDERS HANGED
Private George Cropper (27) hanged at 10 a.m. outside Maidstone
Prison, Kent, for an 'unnatural offence' with Charles Pike. William
Allen hanged at midday outside Maidstone Prison for the rape of Mrs
Ruth Roffe Austen at Lydd.
Hangman: (both times) William Calcraft

Cropper was described as having led 'a licentious life', but became
penitent after his conviction, at the Kent Winter Assizes, for an
'unnatural offence' at Deptford (probably sodomy which was still a
capital crime*). Charles Pike was tried with him, but was acquitted.
Cropper mounted the scaffold with a firm step and showed no fear as
Calcraft took his time with his preparations. He died immediately with
the drop.
   Allen was hanged two hours after Cropper 'in consequence of the
difference in their crimes', whatever that meant. Allen suffered mental
agonies in anticipation of his execution, right from the time of being
sentenced. On his last morning he paced his cell 'writhing with agony
of spirit' and once Cropper had departed to his death Allen's extra
two-hour wait must have been dreadful. Yet, when his time came, he
walked with tolerable firmness to the scaffold and did not last long
after the drop.

* *In March 1835 John Smith and James Pratt, both from Surrey, were hanged
at Old Bailey for a similar offence.*

27 December

1905 MAD REVENGE ON A BABY
Frederick William Edge hanged at Stafford Gaol for the murder of an
infant, Frank Evans.
Hangman: Henry Pierrepoint. Assistant: John Ellis

Frederick Edge had an unstable personality and scraped a living as a
billiard marker, earning tips for keeping the score, chalking cues and,
probably, fetching drinks. He lodged with a miner's family and his
landlady decided to get rid of him and ordered him out of the house. In
a fit of revenge he murdered the infant son of the house. It was a
mindless and pathetic tragedy for all concerned, and Edge may have
been insane.

Also hanged this day:

1822 at Old Bailey: William Corbett and Samuel Greenwood for highway robbery. An innocent youth of similar appearance to Greenwood was almost convicted of the offence, but was saved by the gallant confession of Greenwood.

1825 at Old Bailey: Henry William Jaspar for forgery; John Samuel Edmunds for horse-stealing.

1833 at Providence, Rhode Island, USA: Amos Miner, a travelling pedlar, for the axe-murder of Deputy Sheriff John Smith.

1867 at Rutledge, Tennessee, USA: Union soldier John Nance for the drunken murder of Confederate soldier William M'Bee during the Civil War.

1900 at Walton Gaol, Liverpool: James Bargin for the murder of his sweetheart.

28 December

1911 THE CHANGED PERSONALITY OF GEORGE LOAKE
Pathetic case of George Loake (64) hanged at Stafford Gaol for killing his wife Elizabeth (46) at Walsall on August Bank Holiday Monday.

George Loake had been a happy, popular, and skilled engine driver with more than 50 years' service with the London and North Western Railway Company. He had started as a lad and had worked his way up to the peak of pride and railwayman's prestige as a driver of express passenger trains.

He was a widower with nine children in 1903 when he married Elizabeth Newitt, a divorcee 18 years younger than him, who had two children of her own. He was a fit and robust man, looking many years younger than his true age. They lived happily for their first six years together in a rented house at 110 Portland Street, Walsall. Their circumstances changed dramatically in the summer of 1909.

While engaged in shunting at Bescot sidings, just outside Walsall, his engine drove into a buffer-block. There was little damage done to the engine, but Loake was severely injured, suffering internal damage and a fearful blow to the head that resulted in an immediate and massive swelling. Company medical care was almost non-existent in those days. Although a doctor was called he carelessly, or callously, decided that treatment was unnecessary and sent Loake home. Two hours later, the pains in Loake's head were driving him wild, and he threw himself into the canal, but was rescued by two passing workmen.

417

George Loake was a different man from that day, and one changed for the worse. He complained of splitting headaches and became a bad tempered and violent man, often seen wandering about with wild staring eyes, raging obscene comments at anyone about him. And he took to drinking heavily, and became nasty with it. He was suspended from work after the inquiry into the accident, which was entirely blamed on him. He was later allowed back to work, but he was a changed man. His heavy drinking continued and, after an incident in March 1911 when he left his engine unattended while he went to buy more drink, he was sacked.

Without employment, or the prospect of any, the family's life went rapidly downhill. Having been sacked he was also deprived of the pension prospects he had accumulated in the 50 or more years he had worked faithfully and well for the LNWR Company. The weekly rent went unpaid and the arrears built up. Loake frequently threatened suicide, and became so fascinated with knives that they had to be locked away out of his sight.

Elizabeth became the victim of his raging outbursts of violence and was often seen bruised about the face. In June 1911 the family was evicted from their home in Portland Street. Elizabeth could stand no more and she left her bullying husband. Taking her two children she went to stay with her friends George and Jane Dolloway at 8A The Butts, off Warwick Street, Walsall.

The violent climax of this sad tragedy occurred in the Dolloways' front living room on August Bank Holiday Monday. George Loake had gone to speak to Elizabeth to try once more, after several failed appeals before, to persuade her to take him back. She refused and angry words followed.

Unknown to them both, they were being watched by 11-year-old Tommy Dolloway who was hiding on the staircase outside the living room. As Elizabeth walked out of the room her husband launched himself upon her in a furious attack. He threw his left arm around her neck and, using a blunt pocket knife, his right hand repeatedly stabbed her in the face and neck. Tommy Dolloway ran upstairs and hid in his room.

Loake walked outside with the knife, now covered with blood, and stood there in a daze. Elizabeth staggered out and fell against a wall. A crowd gathered and PC Woolley arrived. As George Loake was trying to cut his own throat with the blunt knife PC Woolley, using his truncheon, hit him on the back of the hand causing him to drop the knife. Woolley handcuffed him and then attended to Elizabeth. She died soon after a doctor arrived.

Young Tommy Dolloway was the main prosecution witness at the trial, with more than a dozen others testifying to Loake's wild and violent drunkenness. The jury were not impressed with the defence counsel's account of Loake's tragic change of personality after the accident. They quickly dismissed the plea of insanity, and of manslaughter, and took ten minutes to decide upon a verdict of guilty of murder.

About a dozen onlookers waited outside Stafford Gaol at 8 a.m. as George Loake was hanged in the final part of the tragedy that began two and a half years before, when an industrial accident occurred at Bescot sidings. Perhaps the directors of the London and North West Railway Company should also have been condemned, for their callous and uncaring attitude to a loyal employee injured in their service? But that was the way things were in the railway companies in 1911.

Also hanged this day:

1712   at Tyburn Tree: Richard Town for fraudulent bankruptcy.

1863   at Chester: Alice Holt for the murder of her mother.

1874   at Durham Gaol: Hugh Daly for the cruel murder of Philip Burdy by beating him with a poker for two hours.

1883   at Nevada, Missouri, USA: William Fox for the gun-murder of J. W. Hayward in revenge for an insult.

1891   at Hereford Prison: Charles Saunders for murdering his child.

1905   at Armley Gaol, Leeds: George Smith (48) for the frenzied murder of his wife, Martha, during which he stabbed her 40 times. *Hangman: Henry Pierrepoint. Assistant: John Ellis*

29 December

1901 FOND FAREWELLS
John Gallagher (30) and Mrs Emily Swan (42) hanged at Armley
Gaol, Leeds, for the murder of Emily's husband, William Swan.
Hangman: William Billington. Assistant: John Ellis

Mrs Swan had to be revived with brandy before being taken to the scaffold. The brandy calmed her enough to greet her lover as they stood together, hooded and noosed, beneath the gallows beam: 'Good morning, John.'

'Good morning, love,' replied Gallagher.

'Goodbye, God bless you' said Mrs Swan, having the final word.

Also hanged this day:

1750   at Tyburn Tree: John Jones for robbery.

1874   at Stafford Gaol: Robert Taylor (21) for the murder of a woman.

1903 at Walton Gaol, Liverpool: Henry Starr for the murder of his wife, Mary. *Hangman: John Billington*

1904 at Armley Gaol, Leeds: Arthur Jeffries (44) for the stabbing-murder of his life-long friend Sam Barker in a Rotherham alley following a dispute about poaching. *Hangman: John Billington. Assistant: Henry Pierrepoint*

1905 at Derby Gaol: John Silk (31) for the murder of his crippled mother. *Hangman: Henry Pierrepoint. Assistant John Ellis (their third hanging in three days)*

1933 at Winsom Green Prison, Birmingham: Stanley Eric Hobday for the multiple stabbing-murder of Charles William Fox (24) during a burglary. *Hangman: Tom Pierrepoint*

30 December

1937 FILTHY 'UNCLE FRED'
Frederick Nodder (44) (a.k.a. Frederick Hudson) hanged at Lincoln Prison, for the sex-murder of Mona Lilian Tinsley (10).

In 1937 Frederick Nodder became a rarity in the British legal system when he was convicted on separate charges, at two trials, in different towns, for the same crime.

He was a filthy and repulsive creature. He had separated from his wife, was on the run from a bastardy warrant, and was sacked from job after job for being drunk and dishonest. His lack of personal hygiene, and his foul living habits, caused him to be ordered out of a succession of lodgings.

Back in 1934 he been living at the home of a Mr and Mrs Grimes at 9 Neil Road, Sheffield. He was then using the name of Frederick Hudson. The Grimeses knew his real name, but did not seem bothered about the alias and he stayed with them until the following summer.

When he left he moved to the home of Mr and Mrs Tinsley at 11 Thoresby Avenue, Newark, Nottinghamshire. Mr Tinsley was a local coal-carter and his wife was the sister of Mrs Grimes, and 'Hudson' arrived with a letter of introduction from Mrs Grimes. Surprisingly, the Tinsley children liked him and called him Uncle Fred, but he left after only three weeks without paying his rent.

He moved on to East Retford, on the Nottinghamshire and Lincolnshire border. In June 1936, using his real name of Frederick Nodder again, he moved into 'Peacehaven', a small semi-detached house in Hayton, a village three-and-a-half miles from East Retford and 20 miles from the Tinsley home in Newark. He lived there in filthy

420

squalor – the police later described it as 'in a revolting condition' – and was shunned by his neighbours. He had not seen any of the Tinsley family since leaving Newark but Mrs Grimes, his former landlady in Sheffield, visited him regularly at Peacehaven.

At 4 p.m. on 5 January 1937 he was seen loitering by the gate of the Wesleyan School in Guildhall Street, Newark. Mona Tinsley (10) came out of school about that time and she and Nodder were later seen waiting together at Newark bus station. Other witnesses saw them on the Newark to Retford bus and in Retford. Mona was last seen the following morning, by a neighbour's cleaner, standing in the doorway of Peacehaven.

The police were informed that Mona was missing on the evening of 5 January and a search was started. Nodder was interviewed the following evening at Peacehaven and denied having seen her. After being identified by witnesses as the man seen with Mona he changed his story, saying he had brought her to Peacehaven to see her aunt, Mrs Grimes, and her new-born baby. When he received a letter from Mrs Grimes postponing the visit he took Mona to Worksop to put her on a bus to Sheffield. No one had seen her in Worksop, or on the bus, or in Sheffield.

The massive search continued over a wide area, but there was no trace of Mona except for a scribbled note in her writing which was found inside Peacehaven. Nodder was arrested. He was tried and convicted at the Warwick Winter Assizes in Birmingham in March 1937, but only for abducting Mona Tinsley by fraud, although everyone in the courtroom knew that a more serious crime had been committed.

Sentencing him to seven years Mr Justice Swift said, 'Frederick Nodder you have been, most properly in my opinion, convicted by the jury of a dreadful crime. What you did with that little girl, what became of her, only you know. It may be that time will reveal the dreadful secret which you carry in your breast.'

Time did reveal the truth. On 6 June her body was found in the River Idle, a tributary of which passes near Hayton. She had been strangled from behind with a ligature and put in the water at the time of death, the cold water delaying the decomposition of the body and allowing the cause of death to be established beyond doubt.

Nodder was brought from prison to Retford Police Station and charged with murder. Upon this second charge he was tried at Nottinghamshire Assizes on 29 July. He was found guilty and sentenced to death the following day. He appealed, but this was dismissed, although it did delay his execution by a few months. He was hanged at Lincoln Prison 51 weeks after the crime for which he had been tried and convicted twice. His first judge had told him that time would reveal his secret and his second judge, while sentencing him to death, told him 'Justice has slowly but surely overtaken you.'

Also hanged this day:

1825   at New Philadelphia, USA: John Funston (25) for the murder of postboy William Cartmell during a mailbags' robbery.

1874   at Ohio, USA: John Goodman for the gun-murders of John and Susan Hayward after a business argument at Sugar Creek.

1890   at York Castle: Robert Kitching for the murder of Police Sergeant Weedy at Leeming.

1902   at Warwick Gaol: George Place (28), a miner, for the murder of his landlady, her daughter, and the daughter's baby. At Sligo County Gaol, Ireland: James Doherty, an aged farmer, for the murder of Patrick Doherty, his son.

1908   at Cardiff Gaol, Wales: Patrick (or Percy) Collins for the murder of his girlfriend.

1945   Robert Blaine for the murder of Captain J. A. Ritchie.

1948   at Armley Gaol, Leeds: Arthur Osborne (27) for the murder of Ernest Westwood (70), stabbing him with a screwdriver during a burglary.

31 December

1829 THE LAST HANGING FOR FORGERY
Thomas Maynard hanged at Old Bailey, the last man to be hanged for forgery.
Hangman: William Calcraft

Maynard conspired with two others to defraud the Customs House; one of his accomplices was a clerk there who had access to the official records. He forged a Customs House Warrant to the value of £1,973 and collected payment on it. One of the accomplices was reprieved and the other acquitted. On the last day of the year, Maynard was the last man to be hanged for forgery.

Other forgers continued to be sentenced to death until 1832, but they were all reprieved. Between 1830 and 1832 the House of Commons voted to abolish capital punishment for all forgery offences, but this was resisted by the House of Lords. After 1832 some acts of forgery still carried the death sentence, but no more hangings were enforced for them.

Also hanged this day:

1750   at Tyburn Tree: Benjamin Beckonfield for the theft of a hat.

1819   at Old Bailey: Thomas Wildish and John Booth for letter-stealing.

1829   at Old Bailey: Stephen Stanford and William Leslie for burglary; William Newett for sheep-stealing.

1841   at Mason, Kentucky, USA: Moses W. Keen for wife-murder. He was unconcerned at his execution, joking and laughing noisily.

1889   at Armley Gaol, Leeds: travelling showman Robert West for wife-murder; railway labourer Frederick Brett for wife-murder. At Maidstone Prison: William Thomas Hook for wife-murder.

1890   at Kirkdale Prison, Liverpool: Thomas MacDonald (34) for the murder of Miss Alice Holt (21), a teacher at the Belmont village school, near Bolton. *Hangman: James Berry*

1895   at Armley Gaol, Leeds: Patrick Morley (38) for the drunken pistol-murder of his wife Elizabeth in front of a witness; he then turned the gun on himself, but missed. *Hangman: James Billington.*

British Hanging Chronology

c400s AD	Hanging generally believed to have been introduced as the main method of execution during the Anglo-Saxon period, after the departure of the Romans from Britain.
c1100s	First hangings at Tyburn, at the western entrance to London.
c1500	Eight capital crimes: treason, petit (or petty) treason, murder, larceny, robbery, burglary, rape, arson. Petit treason, or petty treason, was a crime in which a person killed someone to whom they owed a special obedience such as a servant to a master, a cleric to a superior, or a wife to her husband. It remained a crime until 1793.
1 June 1571	First hangings on Tyburn's new Triple Tree where three beams were arranged in a triangle, each beam able to suspend eight persons. The 18-feet high gallows was positioned at the 'three-went-way' of three main roads: now Marble Arch where Bayswater Road, Oxford Street and Edgware Road meet.
1671	The Coventry Act introduced by Parliament whereby it was a capital offence to lie in wait with intent to disfigure by putting out an eye, disabling the tongue or slitting the nose. It was named after Sir John Coventry MP who was attacked in Covent Garden that year and severely disfigured. The attackers slit his nose.
7 September 1685	First executions resulting from the 'Bloody Assizes' following the Monmouth Rebellion in the West Country. Five hundred were sentenced to death of whom 320 were actually executed; they were hanged, drawn and quartered in groups of varying sizes at different towns in Dorset, Devon and Somerset.
1699	The Shoplifting Act made it a capital crime to steal goods from a shop valued at more than five shillings (25p).
May 1723	The Waltham Blacks Act passed as a counter to the increasing amount of poaching and damage to forests and parks owned by the nobility, especially in Waltham Forest. It made a number of offences capital crimes and had such a wide scope that it increased the number of capital crimes from about 30 to 150 and within a few years, by interpretation, to

over two hundred. If the criminals blacked their faces or disguised themselves it was punishable by hanging. It made almost any form of poaching or causing damage a capital crime, even sending a letter without a name or with a false name.

22 June 1752	Thomas Wilford (17) hanged and anatomised, the first to suffer under the new Act of Parliament which required that following execution murderers should be either hung in chains or anatomised.
1759	Tyburn's Triple-Tree was replaced by a portable gallows that included a short drop.
7 November 1783	Last hanging at Tyburn: John Austin.
9 December 1783	First hangings at Old Bailey, outside Newgate Prison.
18 March 1789	Last hanging and burning: Mrs Christian Murphy at Old Bailey, for high treason (coining).
1793	Petty treason abolished.
1810	222 capital crimes which included: treason, piracy, mutiny, murder, attempted murder, rape, sodomy, robbery, burglary, theft from a dwelling house, shoplifting, theft from the mail, horse-stealing, cattle or sheep-stealing, forgery, coining, passing forged notes, adopting a disguise, prisoners returning from transportation before completing their sentence, and sacrilege.
1 May 1820	Last hanging and beheading: the Cato Street conspirators, at Old Bailey, for treason.
31 December 1829	Last hanging for forgery: Thomas Maynard, at Old Bailey.
1818–33	Offences contained in about 30 statutes removed from the list of capital crimes, including: horse-stealing, cattle-stealing, sheep-stealing, shoplifting, house-breaking.
1834	Hanging in chains on a gibbet abolished.
1835	Sacrilege, letter-stealing and returning from transportation removed from capital crimes.
1836	Forgery and coining removed from capital crimes.
1837	Burglary and theft from a dwelling house removed from capital crimes.
1841	Rape removed from capital crimes.
27 August 1861	Last hanging for attempted murder: Martin Doyle, at Chester.
1861	Criminal Law Consolidation Act reduced the number of capital crimes to four: treason (including malicious damage by setting fire to arsenals and dockyards), piracy, mutiny and murder.
22 May 1866	Last fully public hanging in Scotland: Joseph Bell at Perth, for murder.
2 April 1868	Last public hanging of a woman: Frances Kidder, at Maidstone, Kent.
12 May 1868	Last public hanging in Scotland: Robert Smith outside Dumfries Prison, for murder. Public onlookers saw little

	because they were held back by barricades at some distance.
26 May 1868	Last public hanging in Britain: Michael Barrett at Old Bailey, for the Fenian bomb outrage at Clerkenwell.
29 May 1868	Parliament passed the Capital Punishment Within Prisons Bill by 181 votes to 25, ending public executions.
13 August 1868	First 'private hanging' within a prison: Thomas Wells at Maidstone, Kent, for murder.
1874–83	During William Marwood's period as principal hangman he introduced the following to bring about a speedier and more humane end: (1) The long-drop of up to ten feet, depending on the weight of the person being hanged, to bring about instant death by dislocation of the cervical vertebrae, instead of strangling. (2) Fastening the knot under the left ear or left jawbone to hasten dislocation by jerking the head backwards. (3) A metal slip-ring instead of the traditional hangman's knot on the noose.
1908	Persons under 16 no longer subject to hanging.
1922	Infanticide Act: women who killed their new-born babies no longer subject to hanging.
1931	Pregnant women no longer subject to hanging.
1933	Children and Young Persons Act: those under 18 when the crime was committed no longer subject to hanging, instead the sentence was 'to be detained during His Majesty's Pleasure'.
April 1948	House of Commons approve the suspending of capital punishment for an experimental period of five years, but it was reversed by the House of Lords.
13 July 1955	Last woman to be hanged: Ruth Ellis at Holloway Prison, for murder.
March 1956	Death Penalty (Abolition) Bill passed on second reading in House of Commons by 286 votes to 262, but this was also rejected by the House of Lords.
March 1957	Parliament passed the 1957 Homicide Act limiting capital murder to five categories: 1. Murder in the course or furtherance of theft. 2. Murder by shooting or causing an explosion. 3. Murder while resisting arrest or during an escape. 4. Murder of a policeman or prison officer. 5. Two murders committed on different occasions.
23 July 1957	First hanging under 1957 Homicide Act: John Vickers at Durham Gaol, for murder during a burglary.
13 August 1964	Last British hangings: Peter Anthony Allen at Walton Gaol, Liverpool, and Gwynne Owen Evans at Strangeways Prison, Manchester, for murder in the course of theft.
9 November 1965	Murder (Abolition of Death Penalty) Bill suspending capital punishment for murder for an experimental period of five years passed by Parliament. Hanging was retained for treason, piracy with violence, and arson to Her Majesty's ships.
December 1969	Parliament confirmed the abolition of capital punishment for murder.

Notable English Hangmen

c1360s	Thomas de Warblynton
1534–38	Cratwell (hanged 1538)
1553–56	Stump-leg (hanged 1556)
c1583–1608	Bulle
c1600–15	Derrick
c1615–40	Gregory Brandon
1640–49	Richard Brandon
1649	William Lowen
c1650s–63	Edward Dun
1663–86	Jack Ketch
1686	Pascha Rose (hanged by Jack Ketch)
1686–1714	Richard Pearse and others who were commonly called 'Jack Ketch'.
1714–15	John Price (hanged 31 May 1718)
1715–17	William Marvel
1717–19(?)	Bailiff Banks
1719–28	Richard Arnet
1728–35	John 'Laughing Jack' Hooper
1735–52	John Thrift
1752–71	Thomas Turlis
1771–86	Edward Dennis
1782–1806	Edward Barlow (at Lancaster)
1786–1814	William Brunskill
1802–35	John 'Mutton' Curry (at York)
1814–17	John Langley
1817–20	James Botting
1820–29	James Foxon
1829–74	William Calcraft
1874–83	William Marwood
1883–4	Bartholomew Binns
1884–92	James Berry
1884–1901	James Billington
1902–5	William, Thomas and John Billington
1903–14	Henry Pierrepoint
1907–23	John Ellis
1908–45	Tom Pierrepoint

1928–30s	Robert Baxter
1941–56	Albert Pierrepoint
1940s–50s	Steve Wade
1956–64	Harry Allen
1956–64	Leslie Stewart

Select Bibliography

An Almanack of Murder Fenton Bresler (Seven House, 1987)

The Bedside Book of Murder Richard and Molly Whittington-Egan (David and Charles, 1988)

Bernard Spilsbury, His Life and Cases Douglas C. Browne and E. V. Tullett (Harrap, 1954)

The Black Plaque Guide to London Felix Barker and Denise Silvester-Carr (Constable, 1987)

The Bloody Assizes, Notable British Trials (William Hodge, 1929)

Bothersome Bodies Max Haines (Futura, 1990)

The Chronicles of Newgate Arthur Griffiths (Bracken Books, 1987)

Classics In Murder edited by Robert Meadley (Xanadu, 1984)

Compendium of World Crime Jay Robert Nash (Harrap, 1983)

Crime Chronology Jay Robert Nash (Facts On File Publications, 1984)

Crime Strange But True James Bland (Futura, 1991)

Crimes and Criminals (Black Cat, 1990)

Crimes and Criminals in Victorian Kent Adrian Gray (Meresborough Book, 1985)

Criminal Justice Rene Weis (Hamish Hamilton, 1988)

A Date With the Hangman T. J. Leech (True Crime Library, 1992)

Detection Stranger than Fiction Leo Grex (Hale, 1977)

Dictionary of Culprits and Criminals George C. Kohn (Scarecrow Press, 1986)

Directory of Infamy Jonathan Green (Mills and Boon, 1980)

Dorset Murders Roger Guttridge (Ensign, 1990)

Encyclopedia of Modern Murder Colin Wilson and Donald Seaman (Barker, 1983)

Encyclopedia of Murder Colin Wilson and Pat Pitman (Barker, 1964)

Executioner Pierrepoint Albert Pierrepoint (Harrap, 1974)

Forty Years of Murder Keith Simpson (Panther, 1980)

Hampshire Murders Roger Guttridge (Ensign, 1990)

The Hangman's Record (Sungolf Publications, 1926)

The Hangman's Tale Syd Dernley (Hale, 1989)

Hangmen of England Brian Bailey (Allen, 1989)

The Illustrated Story of Crime Edgar Lustgarten (Weidenfeld and Nicolson, 1975)

Infamous Address Roger Wilkes (Grafton, 1989)

431

Infamous Crimes (Black Cat, 1989)

Infamous Murders (Treasure Press, 1985)

Lament For the Molly Maguires Arthur H. Lewis (Harcourt, Brace and World, 1964)

The Life of Sir Edward Marshall Hall Edward Marjoriebanks (Gollancz, 1929)

The London Hanged Peter Linebaugh (Allen Lane, 1991)

Lords of the Scaffold Geoffrey Abbott (Headline, 1992)

Madame Tussaud's Chamber of Horrors Pauline Chapman (Grafton, 1986)

The Mammoth Book of True Crime Colin Wilson (Robinson, 1988)

The Mammoth Book of True Crime 2 Colin Wilson and Damon Wilson (Robinson, 1990)

Memories of Murder Tony Fletcher (Grafton, 1987)

Most of My Murders John Parris (Muller, 1962)

Murder America Jay Robert Nash (Harrap, 1981)

The Murder Club Guide to Eastern and Home Counties Brian Lane (Harrap, 1989)

The Murder Club Guide to London Brian Lane (Harrap, 1988)

The Murder Club Guide to the Midlands Brian Lane (Harrap, 1988)

The Murder Club Guide to North-West England Brian Lane (Harrap, 1988)

The Murder Club Guide to South-Eastern England Brian Lane (Harrap, 1988)

The Murder Club Guide to South-West England and Wales Brian Lane (Harrap, 1989)

Murder Guide to London Martin Fido (Grafton, 1987)

Murder In Kent Philip MacDougal (Hale, 1989)

Murder In Lancashire Alan Stewart (Hale, 1988)

Murder Squad Tom Tullett (Triad Granada, 1981)

Murder Whatdunit J. H. H. Gaute and Robin Odell (Pan, 1984)

Murder Whereabouts J. H. H. Gaute and Robin Odell (Harrap, 1986)

Murderer's England Ivan Butler (Hale, 1973)

Murderers' Who's Who J. H. H. Gaute and Robin Odell (Harrap, 1981)

The Murderous Kind Max Haines (Futura, 1991)

Murders of the Black Museum Gordon Honeycombe (Hutchinson, 1982)

My Experiences As an Executioner James Berry, editied by H. Snowden Ward (Percy Lund & Co, 1892)

My Experiences As an Executioner James Berry, edited by H. Snowden Ward, with additional material by Jonathan Goodman (David and Charles Reprints, 1972)

The New Handbook of Hanging Charles Duff (Anchor Press, 1954)

The Newgate Calendar Volume 2 G. T. Wilkinson (Panther, 1962)

The Newgate Calendar Volume 3 G. T. Wilkinson (Panther, 1963)

The Newgate Noose Howard Culpin (Muller, 1957)

Norman Birkitt H. Montgomery Hyde (Reprint Society, 1965)

'Orrible Murder Leonard De Vries (Book Club Associates, 1974)

Outrages Fatal and Others (Cheshire) Derek Yarwood (Didsbury Press, 1991)

Oxford Book of Legal Anecdotes (Oxford University Publications, 1989)

Prisons and Punishments of London Richard Byrne (Harrap)

Public and Private Executions at Maidstone 1831–81

Ready to Hang Robert Tallant (Harper Bros, 1952)

The Rise and Fall of the Third Reich William L. Shirer (Pan, 1964)

Sir Richard Muir S. T. Felstead and Lady Muir (Bodley Head, 1927)
Tales From The Newgate Calendar Rayner Heppenstall (Futura, 1983)
The Times Index (and files) 1785–1964
Tower Of London Walter G. Bell (Duckworth, 1935)
Trail of Blood Frank Jones (McGraw Hill, 1981)
The Triple Tree Donald Rumbelow (Harrap, 1982)
True Crime Diary James Bland (Futura, 1987)
True Crime Diary 2 James Bland (Futura, 1989)
True Crime Magazine (various issues)
True Detective Magazine (various issues)
William Roughead's Chronicles of Murder Richard Whittington-Egan (Lochar, 1991)
Written In Blood Colin Wilson (Grafton, 1990)

Index of the Hanged

Baker, Frederick 24 December
Baker, James 8 February
Baker, James 5 March
Baker, James 3 September
Baker, John 13 May
Baker, Joseph 9 May
Baker, Owen B. 3 November
Baker, Philip 22 April
Baker, William 5 September
Balaban, John 24 August
Ball, George 26 February
Ball, William 20 August
Ballard, Father John 20 September
Ballington, Fred 28 July
Banbury, John J. 11 October
Banks, Elizabeth 6 July
Banks, John 11 July
Bannister, James 2 April
Bansted, John 15 December
Barber, Ann 25 August
Barber, Elizabeth a.k.a. Mrs Dalby 25 March
Barbour, James 15 January
Bardie, Frederick 13 September
Bargin, James 27 December
Barkstead, John 19 April
Barlow, Kevin 7 July see 21 July
Barlow, Silas 19 December
Barnes, Peter 7 February
Barr, Thomas 31 May
Barratt, John 13 February
Barrett, James 23 January
Barrett, Michael 26 May
Barrett, Percy 8 January
Barrett, Peter and Timothy 22 March
Barrett, Thomas 3 January
Barrett, William 8 October
Barrow, Robert 15 October
Barrow, Thomas Fairclough 9 December
Barry, Ann 12 January
Bartelano 23 December
Barthelemy, Emile 22 December
Bartholomew, William 22 May
Bartlett, Leir Richard 13 November
Bartlett, William 13 November
Barton, Andrew 14 March
Barton, Charles 17 December
Bateman, Mary 20 March
Bates, Thomas 30 January
Bave, Jesse George 4 June
Bayly, William Alfred 20 July
Bazoft, Farzad 16 March

Beale, John William 12 January
Beauchamp, Jereboam O. 7 July
Beavers 15 February
Becker, Barent 6 October
Beckett, Henry see Perry, Henry
Beckonfield, Benjamin 31 December
Beckwith, Thomas 21 December
Bedford, John 30 July
Bedingford, Henry 3 December
Beitzel, Russell St Clair a.k.a. Burholme 2 August
Bell, Edward 25 July
Bell, John Any Bird 1 August
Bell, Joseph 22 May
Bellamy, Edward 27 May
Bellingham, John 18 May
Benali, Ferat Mohamed 1 August
Bennet a.k.a. Dickson 23 July
Bennett, Herbert John 21 March
Benson, Ben 7 January
Bentley, Derek 28 January
Bergen, Martin 16 January
Bernardis, Lieutenant General 8 August
Berrouse 9 May
Berry, Elizabeth 14 March
Berry, Henry 21 February
Berry, Thomas 24 May
Berry, Thomas 27 July
Betts, William 16 December
Beury, G. 30 March
Bevan, Thomas Henry 16 August
Bhutto, Ali Zulfikar 4 April
Bicknell, John B. 24 August
Bilansky, Ann 23 March
Billee, John 16 January
Billings, Thomas 9 May
Birchall, Reginald 14 November
Bird, Lieutenant Edward 23 February
Bird, John and George 20 March
Birger, Charlie 21 April
Birkett, Arthur 9 July
Birkitt 29 October
Birmingham, Thomas 24 March
Bishop, Bridget 10 June
Bishop, John 5 December
Bishop, Richard 30 April
Black, Ernest Edward 24 March
Black Jack 25 January
Blaine, Robert 30 December
Blake, Joseph a.k.a. 'Blueskin' 11 November
Blakesley, Robert 15 November

Blanchard, Peter 9 August
Blanco 22 February
Blandy, Mary 6 April
Blastock, Henry 26 May
Blewitt, Charles 28 August
Blewitt, William 24 May
Blood, Andrew 30 July
Bloxham, Thomas 11 February
'Blueskin' *see* Blake, Joseph
Bollard, James 18 March
Bolton, William 22 December
Bombas, Emmanuel Christos 26 August
Bond, Thomas 20 August
Bonfield, James 15 May
Bonhoeffer, Pastor Dietrich 9 April
Booher, Vernon 26 April
Booth, John 31 December
Booth, William 20 August
Bordier, Louis 15 October
Bormann, Juanna 13 December
Bostock, Alfred 3 September
Boston, Patience 24 July
Boswell, Joseph and Samuel 11 March
Boulton, Thomas 17 August
Bousfield, William 31 March
Bowen, William 12 August
Bowes, John 12 December
Bowler, Thomas 10 August
Bowser, Joseph 27 July
Bowsey, Benjamin 20 June
Boyce, Arthur 1 November
Boyce, James 29 November
Boyce, Joseph 27 July
Boyd, John 23 October
Boyle, James 21 June
Bradford, John 17 December
Bradford, Private Francis 13 August
Bradshaw, John 13 October
Bradshaw, Robert 19 August
Brady, Joe 14 May
Bragg, Matthew 7 September
Brain, George 1 November
Branch, Elizabeth and Mary 3 May
Brand, Osmond Otto 26 May
Brand, Samuel 18 December
Bray, Peter 19 November
Breeze, George 2 August
Brennan, Thomas 4 October
Bressington, William Francis A. 31 March
Brett, Frederick 31 December
Brian, John 24 October

Bridgeman, Alfred 26 April
Brill, Samuel 5 December
Brinkley, Richard 13 August
Brinsden, John 24 September
Britland, Mary Ann 9 August
Brittain, John 20 August
Broach, John 25 May
Brodie, Deacon William 1 October
Brooke, Thomas 12 January
Brooker, Hugh 1 February
Brookman, John 31 January
Brooks, J. 27 April
Brooks, John 13 February
Brooks, Private William 2 July
Broughton, James 21 February
Broughton, Spence 14 April
Brown, Albert Edward 31 May
Brown, Elizabeth Martha 9 August
Brown, Ernest 6 February
Brown, Henry 5 January
Brown, Henry 7 July
Brown, James 30 April
Brown, James 24 August
Brown, John 13 May
Brown, John 2 December
Brown, Joseph 20 April
Brown, Joseph 25 April
Brown, Nichol 16 June
Brown, Patrick 14 March
Brown, Russell 13 May
Brown, Thomas 30 April
Brown, Thomas 15 August
Brown, William 11 June
Brown, William 10 August
Brown, William 16 December 1902
Brown, William 16 December 1903
Browne, Frederick Guy 31 May
Browning, Robert 14 December
Brownlees, William 16 November
Brownrigg, Elizabeth 14 September
Bruce, David 7 January
Brunt, John Thomas 1 May
Bryant, Charlotte 15 July
Buchanan, James 20 December
Buchanan, Sergeant John 2 July
Buck, Rufus 1 July
Buckhouse, Charles 16 August
Bullock, Henry 13 February
Bullock, Thomas 10 July
Bulmer, Charles 3 January
Buranelli, Luigi 30 April
Burbage, James 7 April

Burden, Frederick 21 July
Burdet, Thomas 10 May
Burdock, Mary Ann 15 April
Burgess, W. 4 January
Burholme, Russell *see* Beitzel.
Burke, William 28 January
Burke, William 8 April
Burnham, Joseph 17 February
Burns, Alfred 25 April
Burns, Hugh 2 March
Burns, James 21 June
Burns, Private Thomas 4 June
Burnworth, Edward 24 May
Burridge, William 22 March
Burridge, William 2 May
Burroughs, Reverend George 19 August
Burrows, Albert Edward 8 August
Burrows, Erskine Durrant 2 December
Burrows, Police Constable Herbert 17 February
Burrows, James 25 August
Burton, James 6 August
Burton, Robert Alexander 11 April
Burton, William 15 December
Burton, William Walter 21 June
Bury, William Henry 24 April
Buse, William H. 19 November
Bush, Edwin Albert 6 July
Butcher, Charles 8 August
Butler, George William 7 November
Butler, James 9 February
Butler, James 10 August
Butler, James 14 August
Butler, James 24 August
Butler, Richard 10 February
Butler, Thomas, Esq. 10 March
Butler, William 29 March
Butt, Edward 12 January
Buttledore, Thomas 2 February
Byrne, James 5 September
Byrne, Pat John 12 November
Bywaters, Frederick Edward Francis 9 January

Cacaris, Gioranni 23 May
Caddell, George 21 July
Cadman, Josiah 21 November
Cadogan, Timothy 11 January
Caffyn, James 11 February
Caladis, Pascaler 23 May
Calaghan, Charles 2 April
Calcraft, Thomas 3 August

Caldough, William 2 July
Caler, Tom 14 April
Callaghan, Jeremiah 12 December
Calvert, Louie a.k.a Gomersal and Louise Jackson 26 June
Cameron, Dr Archibald 7 June
Campbell 8 July
Campbell, Alex 21 June
Campbell, Archibald, Esq. 24 August
Campbell, John 18 September
Campion, James 14 April
Canaris, Admiral Wilhelm 9 April
Cann, Thomas 5 March
Cannaday, John Eli a.k.a. Sneedom 24 May
Canning, Joseph 18 June
Caplan, David 6 January
'Captain Jack' *see* Kintpuash
Cardoza, Antonio 14 January
Cardwell, George 8 January
Carey, May and Howard 6 June
Carlsen 22 December
Carlton, Harry 23 December
Carr, Andrew 28 July
Carr, James 16 November
Carr, William Henry 19 May
Carraher, Patrick 6 April
Carrol, Patrick 18 May
Carroll, James 21 June
Carter, Horace 1 January
Carter, John 5 December
Carter, William 18 January
Casement, Roger David 3 August
Casey, Pat 15 December
Casey, Patrick 8 May
Cashiere, Catharine 7 May
Cashman, George 15 December
Cashman, John 12 March
Casler, Abraham 29 May
Cassidy, James 26 November
Cassidy, Peter 19 August
Cassidy, William 16 February
Castillano, Jose 1 June
Castle, J. 31 March
Cato 22 April
Celebia, Isaac 21 November
Chacon, Miguel 9 July
Chadwick, T. Esq. 30 July
Chadwick, Matthew William 15 April
Chamberlain, Thomas 31 March
Chambers, Brian 7 July *see* 21 July
Chambers, William 4 December

Chandler, Brian 17 December
Channing, Mary 12 March
Chantrelle, Eugene Marie 31 May
Chapman, Ann 30 June
Chapman, George real name Severin
  Klosovski 7 April
Chapman, Gerald 5 April
Chapman, William 10 December
Chappell, Martha 20 July
Charlton, Richard 23 December
Charlton, William 15 March
Chennell, John, Junior 3 August
Chick, Richard 19 October
Chipperfield, Alfred 25 February
Chivers, Elizabeth 1 August
Cholerton, Thomas 12 August
Chrimes, Joseph 28 April
Christie, John Reginald Halliday 15 July
Christofi, Styllou 13 December
Chung Yi Miao 6 December
Churcher, William 22 July
Churchill, Catherine 26 May
Churchill, Deborah 17 December
Churchill, Nicholas 23 May
Clark, Guy C. 3 February
Clark, Dr Henry Lovell William 26
  March
Clark, Joseph 11 February
Clark, Matthew 28 July
Clark, Thomas 22 July
Clarke, George 27 March
Clarke, Mary 10 March
Clarke, William 26 March
Clarke, William 4 November
Claxton, George 2 June
Claydon, Alick 13 December
Clayton, Robert David 19 February
Clemmons, Abel 30 June
Clench, Martin 5 June
Clewes, Thomas 3 January
Clock, Thomas 24 November
Close, John 22 May
Clough, Joel 26 July
Cloytan 19 February
Clutter, William 8 June
Cluverius, Thomas J. 20 November
Coates, Richard 29 March
Cobby, John 18 January
Coci, Jerry 8 August
Cock, George 13 June
Cock, Henry 22 January
Cockerill, Edward 21 February

Cockin, Edward 23 February
Coffin, John 5 September
Coffin, Wilbert 10 February
Cogan, William 14 October
Coke, Arundel, Esq. a.k.a. Cook 5
  April
Cole, Mary 28 June
Cole, S. E. 31 October
Cole, Thomas see Collett, Thomas
Coleman, Edward 28 July
Coleman, Richard 12 April
Coleman, William 26 March
Collett, Thomas a.k.a. Cole 5 July
Collington, Thomas 7 April
Collins, John Baptist 30 July
Collins, Patrick (or Percy) 30 December
Colson, Sylvester 1 February
Comyn, Mr 18 March
Coney, George 23 April
Conicutt, William 20 September
Connelly, James see O'Sullivan, Joseph
Conner, J. 2 June
Conner, Terence 28 February
Connolly, John 25 May
Conway, Catherine 6 July
Conway, John 20 August
Conway, Peter 14 May
Cook 13 October
Cook, Arundel, Esq. see Coke, Arundel
Cook, Charles 18 December
Cook, Eliza see Ross, Eliza
Cook, James 10 August
Cook, Samuel 19 October
Cook, Thomas 11 August
Cooke, Police Constable George S. 25
  July
Coomey 9 April
Cooper, Edward 6 September
Cooper, James 21 August
Cooper, Ronald Frank 16 January
Cooper, Thomas 17 April
Cooper, W. H. 26 November
Cooper, William 20 May
Copeland, James 30 October
Coppen, John Walter 13 October
Corbet, Miles 19 April
Corbett, James Henry 28 November
Corbett, William 27 December
Corder, William 11 August
Corderoy, John 15 February
Corgalis, Matteo 23 May
Corkery, Jeremiah 27 July

Cornish, Henry 19 October
Cornwell, William 9 August
Corrie, Daniel Stewart 10 June
Corrigan, Thomas 5 January
Cotton, John 13 March
Cotton, John 21 December
Cotton, Mary Ann 24 March
Coulson, John Raper 9 August
Courvoisier, Francis Benjamin 6 July
Cove, J. 27 February
Covington, Arthur 3 December
Cowdrey, Thomas 16 December
Cowell, W. C. 24 April
Cowland, John 20 December
Cowle, Charles James 18 May
Cowle, W. A. 8 August
Cox, Chastine 16 July
Cox, J. 16 September
Cox, Robert 1 September
Cox, Tom 3 June
Coyle, Richard 25 January
Craig, John H. 6 June
Craig, Thomas 10 July
Craine, J. V. 26 October
Crane, Mary 16 January
Cranwell, James 4 January
Cratwell 1 September
Crawley, Robert 26 May
Cream, Dr Thomas Neill 15 November
Crippen, Dr Hawley Harvey 23
    November
Crisp, Andrew 12 January
Crisp, Henry 26 November
Cromwell, Oliver 13 October
Cronin, John 12 January
Cropper, George 26 December
Crosby, Nicholas Persoulious 19
    December
Cross, Dr Philip Henry Eustace 10
    January
Crossley, William 31 July
Crouch, W. 27 May
Crowe, Thomas 25 August
Crowther, Joseph 12 January
Crowther, Samuel 11 December
Crowther, Thomas 19 May
Crozier, Samuel 5 December
Crummins, John 30 March
Cull 30 September
Cumber, Thomas 7 July
Cummins, Leading Aircraftman Gordon
    Frederick 25 June

Cunceen, Thomas 10 January
Cundell, William 16 March
Cundell, William 7 July
Cunningham, Charles 19 September
Currell, Thomas William 18 April
Currie, Sapper John 12 October
Curtis, Samuel 20 December
Curtis, Winslow see Colson, Sylvester

Dagoe, Hannah 4 March
Dainton, Harry 15 December
Dalby, Mrs see Barber, Elizabeth
Daley, Neal 15 January
Daley, Thomas 14 December
Dalgleish, James 19 December
Dallas, John 11 March
Daly, Mrs 7 January
Daly, Hugh 28 December
Daly, Mary 9 January
Daniels, George Nathaniel 28 August
Darcy, John 27 May
Dashwood, Sammy 12 September
Davidson, William 1 May
Davies, Thomas 16 November
Davis, Edward 'Jewboy' 16 March
Davis, Frederick 28 August
Davis, George 5 July
Davis, George John 16 December
Davis, John 1 January
Davis, John 31 January
Davis, John 28 May
Davis, John 16 August
Davis, John see Joyce, John
Davis, Lewis and Lucky 1 July
Davis, Lumley 28 August
Davis, 'Mail robber' 3 April
Davis, Richard 8 April
Davis, Vincent 30 April
Davis, William 2 January
Davis, William 20 December
Dawson, Daniel 18 July
Dawson, George 4 November
Dawson, Hugh 21 August
Dawson, John, Esq. 30 July
De Balsham, Inetta 16 August
De Freitas, Michael a.k.a. Michael X see
    Malik, Abdul
De Paleotti, The Marquis 17 March
De Rais, Baron Gilles 26 October
Deacon, Edward 24 April
Deacon, Thomas 30 July
Deamore 9 May

440

Dean, Cyrus B. 23 August
Dean, John 12 January
Dean, Minnie 12 August
Deeming, Frederick Bailey 23 May
Delahunt, J. 5 February
Delane, Dennis 13 April
Delaney, Arthur T. 10 August
Demaree, Daniel 15 June
Denham, Henry 22 February
Dent, Edward 24 March
Deschamps, Dr Etienne 12 May
Despard, Colonel Edward Marcus 21
  February
Devereux, Arthur 15 August
Devlin, Edward 25 April
Dews, Alfred 21 August
Dhingra, Madar Lal 31 August
Dickman, John Alexander 10 August
Dickson see Bennet
Dickson, Margaret 2 September
Digby, Sir Everard 30 January
Dilley, James 25 August
Distin, Joseph 22 November
Dixon, Emanuel 24 May
Dixon, Richard 22 December
Dobell, Charles Joseph 1 January
Dobkin, Harry 27 January
Docherty, Patrick 5 October
Dodd, Reverend Dr William 27 June
Dodds, Matthew James 4 August
Doherty, James 30 December
Dolan, 'Dandy Johnny' 21 April
Donaghue, John 'Yellow Jack' 21 June
Done, Thomas 2 May
Donelan, J., Esq. 2 April
Donnelly, Dennis 'Buckey' 11 June
Donnelly, Edward 8 February
Donnelly, Dr James P. 5 January
Donovan, Conrad see Potten, Joseph
Dorsey, John 17 July
Dougal, Samuel Herbert 14 July
Dougherty, Caleb and Daniel 14 March
Douglass, Robert 29 April
Douglass, Thomas 27 October
Dove, W. 9 August
Dowdell, Joseph 17 June
Dowdle, Michael 6 December
Downey, Michael 16 January
Doyle, Martin 27 August
Doyle, Michael J. 21 June
Dramatti, John Peter 7 July
Dreher, Dr Tom 1 February

Drenth, Herman 18 March
Drewitt, John 9 July
Driscoll, Daniel 27 January
Driscoll, John 15 December
Dromelius, Gerard 10 July
Dronkers, Johannes Maximum see 4
  January
Du Plessis, Andries Stephanus 17 June
Dubois, J. 30 March
Duckworth, Cross 3 January
Duell, William 24 November
Duffy, Thomas 21 June
Duffy, James 8 December
Duggan, James 11 July
Dukes, William 24 December
Dumdleton, William 10 May
Dunbar, Reuben 28 September
Dunlop, Thomas 17 February
Dunn, Edward Davis 27 June
Dunn, James 2 February
Dunn, Thomas 9 July
Dunne, Reginald a.k.a. John O'Brien 10
  August
Dunphy, Patrick 10 April
Duranno 22 February
Durling, George 23 August
Durrant, William Henry Theodore 7
  January
Dutton, Henry 3 December
Duvall, Claude 21 January
Dyer, Amelia Elizabeth 10 June
Dyer, Charles Samuel 5 April

Eades, Richard 31 July
Eagles, John 29 May
Earl, Charles Robert 29 April
Easterly, John 23 March
Eayres, John 10 November
Eblethrift, John 29 August
Edge, Frederick William 27 December
Edmondson, D. 24 June
Edmund, Robert 17 March
Edmunds, John Samuel 27 December
Edmundson, D. 24 June
Edwards, Edgar see Owen, Edgar
Edwards, George 24 October
Edwards, George Kebble 20 August
Edwards, Thomas 22 December
Edwards, William 16 April
Eggleton, Frederick 17 March
Eglington, George A. 23 September
Eichmann, Karl Adolf 31 May

Eldridge, Alfred 20 August
Elkins, Samuel 18 July
Ellengor, Joseph 24 October
Elliott, A. 9 December
Elliott, Charles *see* Foreword
Elliott, Edward 4 December
Elliott, Thomas 13 February
Ellis, Joseph Robert 25 August
Ellis, Ruth 13 July
Ellison, 29 October
Emery, Samuel George 11 December
Emlay, Cyrus 12 June
Emmett, Robert, Esq. 3 September
Engel, George 11 November
Erpenstein, John 30 March
Evans, David 23 February
Evans, David 21 September
Evans, Gwynne Owen real name John
    Robson Welby 13 August
Evans, Hadyn Evan 3 February
Evans, John 2 February
Evans, Timothy John 9 March
Everett, John 20 July
Ewerstadt, Ernest 8 December

Fadon, James 9 April
Fairbanks, Jason 10 September
Farmer, Daniel Davis 3 January
Farrell, James 29 March
Farrell, John 26 April
Faugeron, Marcel a.k.a. Fougeron 19
    November
Faulkner, Richard 13 July
Fauntleroy, Henry, Esq. 30
    November
Fawkes, Guy 31 January
Fee, Joseph 20 December
Feeley, Martin 21 December
Feeney, Charles 21 November
Fellows, John 15 February
Fenning, Eliza 26 July
Fenton, Frederick W. 4 April
Fenwick, John 20 June
Ferguson, John 30 March
Ferguson, Richard 'Galloping Dick' 17
    March
Fernandez, Manuel a.k.a. Richard C.
    Jackson 13 November
Fernley, John 19 October
Ferrers, The Earl 5 May
Ferris, Andrew 27 November
Fiddler, Mark 16 August

Field, Frederick Herbert Charles 30
    June
Field, Jack Alfred 4 February
Finden, Charles Edward 11 August
Finder, William 2 February
Fischer, Adolph 11 November
Fish, William 14 August
Fisher, Bishop John 22 June
Fisher, Tom 28 March
Fitzgerald, Patrick 15 November
Fitzwilliam, James 20 August
Flaherty, Timothy 4 April
Flanagan, 31 August
Flanagan, Thomas 15 January
Flanagan, William 21 December
Flannigan, Catherine 16 February
Fleming, Jim 6 September
Fleming, John 5 January
Fletcher, George 30 July
Fletcher, James 10 January
Fletcher, Joseph 14 January
Flood, Matthew 23 February
Fly, Captain William 12 July
Flying Highwayman, *see* Hawke,
    William
Flynn, Michael 17 January
Foane, John 7 September
Foote, Henry L. 19 June
Ford, Henry 7 September
Fordred, Thomas 4 April
Foreman, Frederick 14 July
Forsyth, Francis Robert George 'Flossie'
    10 November
Fortis, Edmund 25 September
Forward, Stephen a.k.a. Ernest Walter
    Southey 11 January
Foster, Catherine 17 April
Foster, George 18 January
Foster, Police Constable 25 April
Foster, William 21 March
Fougeron *see* Faugeron, Marcel
Fowler, Henry 9 June
Fowler, Lawrence 4 September
Fowler, Wilfred 3 September
Fox, Sidney Harry 8 April
Fox, Stephen 20 August
Fox, William 28 December
Foy, William Joseph 10 May
Franchett, John 17 April
Francis, George 12 March
Francis, John 21 February
Frank, Reichminister Hans 16 October

442

Frampton, John 14 March
Frazier, J. 29 January
Freedman, Maurice 4 May
Freeman, Samuel 6 November
Frembd, Charles 4 November
French, John 10 December
Frick, Reichminister Wilhelm 16 October
Fricker, Eliza 5 March
Friery, Bernard 17 August
Frith, William 20 March
Frost, Samuel 31 October
Fruin, J. 27 February
Fuller, Robert 30 April
Funston, John 30 December
Furtado, Emanuel 30 July
Fury, Thomas 16 May

Gahagan, Usher 28 February
Galbraith, James 26 July
Gallagher, John 29 December
Gamble, John 20 June
Gambrill, Stephen 4 February
Game, John 7 September
Garcia 18 November
Garcia, Manuel Philip 1 June
Gardelle, Theodore 4 April
Gardiner, Benjamin 29 July
Gardiner, Charlotte 11 June
Gardner, James 7 July
Gardner, Stephen 3 February
Garner, Philip 3 April
Garnet, Father Henry 3 May
Garry, Thomas 7 May
Garside, William 25 November
Gartside, John Edward 22 August
Gates, George 5 March
Gaunt, Elizabeth 19 October
Gavan, John 20 June
Gebbia, Leonardo 16 July
Gebhard, J. V. L. 15 November
Geith, Eduard 27 February
Gell, John Alfred 15 May
Gentle, Daniel 12 December
Geraghty, Christopher James 19 September
Germaine, John 9 November
Gerrish, Charles 31 January
Gibbons, Patrick 17 August
Gibbs, Charles 22 April
Gibbs, James Henry 24 August
Giffard, Miles William 24 February

Giglio 9 May
Gilbert, George Jacob 4 August
Gilbert, Henry 25 November
Gilderoy, Alexander Thomas 4 November
Gillingham Michael 2 August
Gillman, John 31 January
Giovanni, Valeri 9 July
Gleeson, John 18 September
Glover, George 28 July
Glover, John 20 June
Gmeiner, Josef 27 February
Godfrey, Captain Arthur see Goslett, Arthur
Godfrey, Samuel E. 13 February
Godhino, Francisco Charles 17 October
Godse, Nathuram Vinayak 15 November
Godwin, James 25 May
Goering, Reichmarshal Hermann 16 October
Goff, James 27 June
Goff, James 27 September
Goheen, Adelbert 23 October
Goldenberg, Lance Corporal Abraham (Jack) 30 July
Golding, John 21 August
Goldsby, Crawford 17 March
Goldsmith, George 2 February
Goldthorpe, Norman 22 November
Goltz, Joachim 6 October
Gomersal, Louie a.k.a Louise Jackson see Calvert, Louie
Good, Daniel 23 May
Good, Sarah see 19 August
Goodale, Robert 30 November
Gooden, Captain Samuel 20 April
Goodlad, Charles 24 March
Goodman, John 12 August
Goodman, John 30 December
Goodwin, Charles 21 December
Gordon, Horace Beresford 9 January
Gordon, John 14 February
Gordon, John True 25 June
Gordon, Captain Nathaniel 21 February
Gordon, Thomas 17 August
Gordon, William 21 November
Gorton, William 21 November
Goslett, Arthur a.k.a. Captain Arthur Godfrey, 27 July
Gotleib, Matthias 28 October
Gough, Alfred 21 November
Goulby, James 29 November

Gould, John 9 April
Gould, Captain John 11 August
Gould, William 23 November
Goulding, Robert 4 July
Gower, William 1 January
Gower, Zbigniew 7 July
Grammer, G. Edward 11 June
Grant 30 January
Grant 9 April
Gray, Ben 7 September
Gray, John 22 June
Gray, William Thomas 4 February
Green, Ann 14 December
Green, Edward W. 27 January
Green, Henry G. 10 September
Green, John Thomas 20 December
Green, Leslie 23 December
Green, Robert 21 February
Green, Samuel 25 April
Green, William 7 April
Greenacre, James 2 May
Greenwood, Samuel 27 December
Gregory, Derrick 21 July
Gregory, William 27 July
Greig, William 28 April
Grese, Irma 13 December
Grey, Thomas 21 November
Griffith, William 16 September
Griffiths, George 1 May
Griffiths, George Warner 7 July
Griffiths, Jack 27 February
Griffiths, Peter 19 November
Grindler, Martha 19 January
Groesbeek, Maria 13 November
Grondkowski, Marion 2 April
Grove, Henry 22 May
Grunsig, Otto 27 February
Guay, Joseph Albert 12 January
Guiteau, Charles 30 June
Gummel, John 21 August
Gunning, Thomas 26 July
Gurd, John a.k.a Louis Hamilton 26 July
Gusiane, Richard 25 June

Haberfield, W. 29 January
Hackman, Reverend James 19 April
Hagger, Harold 'Basher' a.k.a. Sydney
    Sinclair 18 March
Haggerty, Owen 23 February
Haigh, James 12 January
Haigh, John George 10 August
Hale, Captain Nathan 22 September

Hale, William 26 April
Hall, E. 29 January
Hall, Edward 20 December
Hall, George Albert 22 April
Hall, James 15 September
Hall, John, Esq. 18 July
Hall, Lawrence 2 February
Hallam, Isaac and Thomas 20 February
Hallam, Robert 14 February
Hamar, Emanuel 28 November
Hamilton, James 2 February
Hamilton, Private James 6 November
Hamilton, Louis see Gurd, John
Hammerton, Ernest E. 27 March
Hammond, John 18 January
Hammond, Thomas 7 August
Hancocks, William Alfred 9 August
Hanratty, James 4 April
Harcourt, William 20 June
Harden, Reverend Jacob S. 6 July
Harding, Ernest Charles 8 August
Harding, William 21 November
Hare, Joseph Thompson 10 September
Harmer, George 13 December
Harpe, Wiley 'Little' 8 February
Harper, James 30 June
Harpham, James 4 July
Harpham, Robert 24 May
Harries, Thomas Ronald Lewis 28 April
Harris, Charles 12 April
Harris, Edward 'Kiddy' 22 February
Harris, George 2 February
Harris, John 24 February
Harris, Joseph 27 June
Harris, Norman James 10 November
Harris, Thomas 6 October
Harris, William a.k.a Haynes 1 January
Harrison, James 28 August
Harrison, John 24 December
Harrison, Major General Thomas 13
    October
Harrow, William 28 March
Harry, James 13 August
Hart, George 3 January
Hart, Henry 28 May
Hartigan, Edward 27 November
Hartley, John 4 May
Hartley, William 12 January
Harvey, George see Lake, Charles
Harvey, Margaret 6 July
Harwood, Levi 7 April
Haslam, Max Mayer 4 February

Hassell, William 19 November
Hastings, William 7 January
Hatchman, William 18 February
Hatfield, John 3 September
Hauer, John 14 July
Hauptfleish, Petrus 23 December
'Haw-Haw', Lord *see* Joyce, William
Hawes, Nathaniel 21 December
Hawke, William the 'Flying
Highwayman' 1 July
Hawkins, Henry 5 May
Hawkins, John 19 May
Hawkins, John 21 May
Hawley, Richard 29 September
Hay, James and Joseph 12 January
Haycock, George 27 July
Hayed, Daniel 28 May
Hayes, John 8 August
Hayman, Robert 9 February
Haynes *see* Harris, William
Haynes, Philip 10 March
Haynes, Thomas 22 August
Hayward, Harry T. 11 December
Hayward, Joseph 25 November
Haywood, William 15 December
Head, Thomas a.k.a. Williams 5
December
Heap, Alfred Thomas 19 April
Heath, Neville George Clevely 26
October
Heberling, Edward 8 December
Hellier, Thomas 5 August
Hemmings, Edward 4 April
Henderson, Matthew 25 February
Hendrickson, John 6 March
Henley, John 26 November
Henriet 26 October
Henry, James 12 June
Henry, Private Philip 30 July
Hepburn 7 March
Hepper, William Sanchez de Pina 11
August
Herberg, Walter 27 February
Herbert, William 13 December
Herdman, John 14 March
Hereford, Ann 22 December
Herold, David 7 July
Hester, Pat 25 March
Hewitt, Edward 13 June
Hewitt, John T. 15 August
Heys, Leading Aircraftman Arthur 13
March

Hibbs, George William 13 August
Hibner, Esther 13 April
Hickock, Richard Eugene 14 April
Hickman, Isaac 3 September
Hickman, William Edward 19 October
Hicks, Albert E. 13 July
Higginbottom, Charles Lister 7 January
Higgins, Edward 7 November
Higgins, James 1 December
Higgins, Margaret 15 February
Higgins, Patrick 15 January
Higgins, Patrick 1 October
Higgins, Thomas 17 January
Higgins, W. 29 January
Higgs, John 24 May
Highfield, Alfred 17 July
Hill, Edward 17 October
Hill, George 10 April
Hill, Private Harold 1 May
Hill, John 12 January
Hill, John 23 November
Hill, Lawrence 21 February
Hill, William 23 March
Hill, William 21 April
Hilliard, Samuel 7 September
Hind *see* Massey, Louis
Hind, Captain James 24 September
Hinks, Reginald Ivor 3 May
Hinson, Frederick 13 December
Hirst, Joseph 4 August
Hoare, James L. 27 January
Hobday, Stanley Eric 29 December
Hobson, Henry 22 August
Hobson, Richard 2 February
Hoch, Johann Otto 23 February
Hocker, Thomas Henry 28 April
Hodge, The Hon. Arthur William 8 May
Hodges, Stephen and William 15 July *see
also* 19 October
Hoeppner, Colonel General Erich 8
August
Hoess, Rudolf Franz 16 April
Hogan, Martin 24 January
Holden, Private Alfred 20 August
Holden, George 30 May
Holden, Joseph 4 December
Holden, Martha 31 July
Holden, Samuel 17 August
Holden, William 8 September
Holland, John 25 November
Holland, Latitia 22 June
Holland, Nan 11 August

Holliday, John 15 December
Hollings, William Henry 20 September
Holloway, John 23 February
Holloway, John William 16 December
Holong, Nels Olson 13 April
Holt, Alice 28 December
Holt, Lieutenant Frederick 13 April
Holmes, Clifford 11 February
Holmes H. H. real name Hermann
    Webster Mudgett 7 May
Holmes, Patrick 8 January
Holmsby, Jane 1 November
Hooe, William F. 30 June
Hook, William Thomas 31 December
Hoolhouse, Robert 26 May
Hope, William 15 April
Hopkins, William Seeley 20 February
Horler, H. 15 January
Horn, John, Esq. 11 December
Horn, Tom 20 November
Horsford, Walter 28 June
Horton, George 1 February
Horton, John 1 February
Housden, Jane 19 September
Houssart, John (or Louis) 7 December
Hovey, Edward 19 October
How, David D. 19 March
How, Elizabeth 'Goody' see 19 August
Howard, Dennis 4 December
Howard, Isaac 16 March
Howarth, Kay 24 November
Howe, George W. 22 February
Howe, James 23 May
Howell, Charles 7 July
Hoyle, Nathaniel 12 January
Hubert, Robert 27 October
Hudson, Frederick see Nodder,
    Frederick
Hudson, William George 12 May
Hudson, Robert 13 August
Hughes, Thomas Alvarez 11 September
Hughes, William 17 February
Hulten, Karl Gustav 8 March
Hunter, George 28 March
Hunter, Reverend Thomas 1 August
Hunter, W. 14 November
Huntingford, Sarah 8 March
Hunton, Joseph 8 December
Hurd, William 30 April
Hussey, Charles 3 August
Hutchings, John 7 October
Hutchinson, Amy 7 November

Hutchinson, Edward 23 November
Hutchinson, John 29 March
Hynes, Francis 11 August

Inglis, James 8 May
Ings, James 1 May
Innes, William 31 March
Insole, Richard 21 February
Ireton, Henry 13 October
Irwin, William James 14 August
Istrick, Thomas 10 May
Ives, Esther 11 March

Jacoby, Henry Julius 5 June
Jackson, James 20 June
Jackson, John 7 August
Jackson, Louise a.k.a. Gomersal see
    Calvert, Louie
Jackson, Nathaniel 10 July
Jackson, Richard C. see Fernandez,
    Manuel
Jackson, W. 20 December
Jackson, William 18 August
Jacobs, Lazarus 17 December
Jacobs, Walter 27 February
Jago, Richard 23 January
James, John 8 December
James, Robert 'Rattlesnake' a.k.a.
    Raymond Lisemga 1 May
Jaspar, Henry William 27 December
Jay, Horace Robert 13 January
Jeffcott, Thomas 23 June
Jefferies, Eliza 28 March
Jefferies, J. R. 9 October
Jeffreys, Edward 13 September
Jeffries, Arthur 29 December
Jenkins 19 February
Jenkins, Albert Edward 19 April
Jenkins, Charles Henry 19 September
Jenkins, Ebenezer Samuel 6 March
Jenkins, Joseph a.k.a. Robert Marley 15
    December
Jennings, D. M. 25 July
Jessops, Thomas W. 25 May
Jodl, Colonel General Alfred 16
    October
Johnson, C. 15 April
Johnson, Charles 23 January
Johnson, Christian 3 July
Johnson, Courtland C. 25 August
Johnson, Edward 2 February
Johnson, George 31 January

Johnson, Henry 14 March
Johnson, James 7 March
Johnson, James 7 June
Johnson, John 2 April
Johnson, John 19 June
Johnson, John 6 July
Johnson, John Henry 3 April
Johnson, John William 22 December
Johnson, P. C. 9 October
Johnson, Richard 7 May
Johnson, Robert 5 January
Johnson, Robert 28 June
Johnson, Thomas 28 May
Johnson, William 27 January
Johnson, William 19 September
Johnson, William 10 December
Johnstone, Abraham 8 July
Joiner, Edward 21 December
Jones, Cadwallader 23 November
Jones, Charles 22 July
Jones, Ernest R. 10 February
Jones, Harry Benjamin 28 August
Jones, Henry 17 December
Jones, James 20 March
Jones, James 6 October
Jones, John 2 February
Jones, John 24 May
Jones, John 28 May
Jones, John 29 December
Jones, Johnny 16 March
Jones, Joseph Edwin 13 April
Jones, Mary 16 October
Jones, Mary Ann 18 February
Jones, Thomas 12 April
Jones, Thomas 3 August
Joy, James 31 March
Joyce, John a.k.a. Davis 14 March
Joyce, John 20 August
Joyce, Myles and Pat 15 December
Joyce, William a.k.a. 'Lord Haw-Haw' 3
   January
Juanita 4 July
Judge, Patrick 16 November
July, Maomi 1 July

Kadi, George 23 May
Kahler, Hans 27 February
Kaltenbrunner, Obergruppenfuhrer
   Ernst 16 October
Kampf, Felix 7 March
Karditzi 10 May
Kavanagh, Matthew 12 August

Kay, John Thomas 17 August
Kearney, Edward 3 September
Kearns, Patrick 2 March
Kease, John 18 September
Keats, John 22 November
Keats, Royal 20 May
Keele, Richard 13 December
Keen, Moses W. 31 December
Keenan, Thomas 4 October
Kehoe, 'Black Jack' 18 January
Kelley, Daniel 8 March
Kelley, Levi 21 November
Kelley, William 5 March
Kello, Reverend John 4 October
Kelly, Edward 21 June
Kelly, Ernest 17 December
Kelly, George 28 March
Kelly, John 15 April
Kelly, Ned 11 November
Kelly, Thomas 10 January
Kelly, William 24 March
Kelsey, John 2 February
Kemp, Ernest James Harmon 6 June
Kendall, Richard 7 July
Kennedy, John 17 December
Kennedy, Patrick Michael *see* Kennedy,
   William Henry
Kennedy, William Henry a.k.a. Patrick
   Michael 31 May
Kennett, William 20 March
Kenny, Private 5 April
Kent, Charles 22 June
Kesteven, Edmund 26 March
Keston, Daniel 20 March
Ketchum, Black Jack 25 April
Keyes, Robert 31 January
Kidd, Captain William 23 May
Kidder, Frances 2 April
Kimberley, Henry 17 March
King, Jessie 11 March
King, Joseph 28 August
King, Philip 13 January
King, Robert 29 November
King, William 27 July
King, William 25 November
Kingshell, Robert 4 December
Kingsmill, Thomas 26 April
Kingston, P. W. 6 October
Kinnon, Patrick 18 September
Kintpuash 3 October
Kirwan, Owen 8 September
Kirwan, William 31 May

Kitching, Robert 30 December
Kite, Charles 25 February
Kitsell, James 27 March
Klausing, Captain Karl 8 August
Klein, Dr Fritz 13 December
Klosovski, Severin see Chapman, George
Knatchbull, John 13 February
Knight, Cyrus 12 December
Koczula, Paul 14 August
Koenig, Erich 6 October
Kramer, Josef 13 December
Kriegler, Henry 1 March
Kyriakos 10 May

LaCroix 9 May
Lacy, William 21 August
Lagava 23 December
Lake, Charles a.k.a. George Harvey 13 March
Lamb, John 14 January
Lamson, Dr George 28 April
Lanahan, Private Michael 6 January
Lane, William 12 August
Laney, John 7 January
Lange, Eric 20 December
Langford, John 22 May
Lani, G. 26 April
Larkin, Michael 23 November
Larocque, William J. 15 March
Lavictoire, Emmanuel 15 March
Lawler, Catherine see Webster, Kate
Lawrence, Ann 10 January
Lawson, Joseph 28 May
Laycock, Joseph 26 August
Le Blanc, Antoine 6 September
Le Brun, Joseph Philip 11 August
Leach, William 15 May
Leary, James 20 September
Leatherbarrow, Thomas 15 February
Lechlar, John 25 October
Lee, George 25 September
Lee, James 18 May
Lee, Jean 19 February
Lee, John 5 February
Lee, John 23 February
Lees, William 16 December
Lefley, Mary 26 May
Lefroy, Percy see Mapleton, Percy
Legge, John 24 May
Legrose, Robert 18 March
Leigh, Henry 13 August

Leighton, Augustus D. 19 May
Leon see Lyons, John
Leona 9 May
Leonski, Private Edward Joseph 9 November
Leslie, William 31 December
Levermore, Philip 7 September
Levy, John 23 February
Lewin, Roger 25 October
Lewis, Harry 21 April
Lewis, John 4 May
Lewis, Joseph 30 August
Liffey, Pasha 15 November
'Lightfoot', 'Captain' see Martin, Michael
Lightfoot, James and William 1 June
Lincoln, Bombardier John 2 March
Lincoln, James 24 September
Lintott, James 30 March
Lipski, Israel 22 August
Lisemga, Raymond see James, Robert 'Rattlesnake'
Lloyd, George 3 October
Lloyd, Thomas 18 August
Loake, George 28 December
Lock Ah Tam 23 March
Loff, Gabriel 23 May
Loish, William 29 July
Lomas, Jane 23 July
Lomas, Thomas 26 May
Long, Aaron and John 19 October
Longley, William P. 11 October
Lopez 22 February
Lovell, Henry 26 November
Lovering, John E. 3 January
Lowe, Edward 22 November
Lownds, William 21 April
Lowry, Captain James 25 March
Lowther, William 13 December
Lynch, J. 23 April
Lynch, John 15 October
Lyon, John 9 February
Lyons, Danny 21 August
Lyons, John a.k.a. Leon 22 February
Lyons, Lewis W. 24 March

McCall, 'Black Jack' 1 March
Macartney, Terence 7 April
McCloud, Peter see Foreword
McConaghy, Robert 6 November
M'Crave, John 4 January
McCue, J. Samuel 20 January

M'Cullogh, William 16 August
M'Daid 24 March
M'Donald, Hugh 27 April
MacDonald 10 August
McDonald *see* Murphy, John Esmond
M'Donald, Donald 22 April
MacDonald, James 30 September
MacDonald, Thomas 31 December
McDonald, William 11 June
M'Donald, William 3 October
McDonnell, James 15 January
M'Entee, Joseph Patrick 31 May
McGehen, Hugh 21 June
McGhee, Ernest 16 March
M'Gill, Owen 22 February
M'Govern 21 August
M'Gowan 19 November
M'Guiness, William 11 February
McHugh, Pete 25 March
M'Hugh, William 2 August
M'Hugo, Martin 16 January
McIntosh, H. 27 April
Mack, Henry 2 December
Mackay, Alexander 8 September
Mackay, George a.k.a. John Williams 29 January
M'Kean, James 25 January
M'Kenna, John 27 March
M'Kenna, Patrick 3 December
McKeown, Arthur 14 January
Mackeson, Stephen 22 August
MacKintosh, John 3 October
MacLane, James 3 October
McLaughlin, Samuel 25 July
McLean, Michael 10 March
McLeod, Hugh 24 October
Mackley, James 5 June
M'Manus, Charles 14 July
McManus, Peter 9 October
MacNamara, John 21 February
M'Naughton, John 15 December
McNichol, James 21 December
McPhail, Duncan 26 April
M'Rae, Andrew 10 January
M'Vey, Robert 7 April
Madden, John 5 December
Mahon, Patrick Herbert 9 September
Mahoney, Dan 8 December
Mahoney, Matthew 20 April
Maidment, Charles 12 July
Majone, Pasquale 9 March
Major, Ethel Lillie 19 December

Maksimowski, Piotr 29 March
Malcolm, Sarah 7 March
Malden, Daniel 2 November
Malik, Abdul a.k.a. Michael de Freitas and Michael X 16 May
Malinowski, Henryk 2 April
Mancini, Antonio 'Babe' 17 October
Manley, George 14 August
Mann, Thomas 28 August
Manning, Albert 16 March
Manning, Frederick George and Maria 13 November
Mansell, Thomas 6 July
Manteau, Francois 27 August
Manuel, Peter Thomas Anthony 11 July
Mapleton, Percy Lefroy 29 November
March, Henry 20 November
Marchant, John W. 8 July
Marjeram, Albert Edward 13 June
Marks, Isaac 2 January
Markus, Edward 14 April
Marley, Robert *see* Jenkins, Joseph
Marsden, James 24 October
Marshall, Henry 4 December
Martelly, John 19 May
Martin, Joseph 31 January
Martin, John 8 February
Martin, Michael 22 December
Martin, Susanna *see* 19 August
Marwood, Ronald Henry 8 May
Marx, Gustave 22 April
Mason, Ebenezer 7 October
Mason, Elizabeth 18 June
Mason, George 6 December
Masset, Louisa Josephine 9 January
Massey, Louis a.k.a. Hind 6 January
Massy, Captain John 25 July
Masterson, Private Peter 19 September
Mathews, Peter *see* Matthias, Peter
Mathias, Peter a.k.a. Mathews 14 March
Matthews, Phillip 21 July
Maynard, Thomas 31 December
Maynard, William John 27 July
Mays, Sam 8 February
Meacham, Jeremiah 12 April
Means, Wade 14 August
Meers, William 24 November
Meff, John 11 September
Meffen, W. F. G. 8 August
Meier, Carl *see* 4 January

Melford, Charles and William 12 May
Mellor 16 August
Mellor, George 16 January
Mellor, Joseph 20 December
Merrifield, Louisa 18 September
Merry, H. O. 13 September
Meunier, Amie 19 July
Micklin, John 23 December
Miles, Edward 14 September
Milksop, Thomas 24 September
Millain, John 24 April
Millar, Walter 1 August
Millard 29 October
Millen, George 29 March
Miller, John and John 8 December
Miller, Peter 7 July
Miller, William 4 June
Mills, Herbert Leonard 11 December
Mills, John 15 July
Mills, Richard senior and junior 18
    January
Mills, William Samuel 21 July
Milsom, Albert 9 June
Mina, Lino Amalia Espos y 21 June
Minahan, Daniel 7 December
Miner, Amos 27 December
Mirza Riza 12 August
Misters, J. 3 April
Miszka, Stanislaw 6 February
Mitchell, J. 20 September
Mitchell, S. Wild 7 January
Moders, Mary 2 January
Mommers, Johannes Josephus Cornelius
    27 July
Monroe, Michael a.k.a. James
    Wellington 20 October
Montgomery, Sub-Inspector Thomas
    Hartley 26 August
Moody, John 2 February
Moody, Malton 17 December
Mooney, Richard 24 May
Moore, Albert 17 May
Moore, Alfred 6 February
Moore, Dennis A. R. 19 July
Moore, Thomas 13 August
Morgan, David 30 July
Morgan, Davy 12 April
Morgan, Bandsman John 30 March
Morgan, John 25 May
Morgan, Mary 18 April
Morgan, Samuel 9 April
Morgan, William James 4 February

Moriarty, Daniel 28 May
Morley, Joseph 21 November
Morley, Patrick 31 December
Morris, Stephen 12 January
Morris, William 14 March
Mortimer, Charles 15 May
Morton, Robert Victor 27 February
Moseley, Joseph 25 November
Moshik, John 18 March
Mudgett, Hermann Webster *see* Holmes
    H. H.
Muggridge, John 28 April
Muir, James 1 March
Muldowney, Dennis 30 September
Mullarkey, Bernard 4 December
Mullen, Michael 4 January
Muller, Franz 14 November
Mullins, Darby 23 May
Mullins, James 19 November
Munch, Franz Joseph 21 July
Munks, James 23 January
Munley, Thomas 21 June
Munoman, Eleanor 24 November
Murphy, Christian and husband 18
    March
Murphy, James 11 July
Murphy, John Esmond a.k.a. McDonald
    6 January
Murphy, William 15 February
Murray, Edith 11 March
Muschet, Nicol 6 January
Musquito 25 January
Myers 10 September

Nairns, George 24 July
Nance, John 27 December
Nathan, Jonah 19 October
Neader, Peter 15 May
Neal, Thomas 26 March
Neale, Benjamin 14 August
Neale, Thomas 12 August
Neidermeier, Peter 22 April
Nelson, 'Gorilla' Earle Leonard a.k.a.
    Wilson, Roger and Wilson, Virgil 13
    January
Neu, Kenneth 1 February
Nevison, John 15 March
Newell, John William 9 December
Newell, Susan 10 October
Newell, William 12 February
Newett, William 31 December
Newington, William 26 August

Newman, Charlotte 18 February
Newman, Oliver 'Tiggy' 5 August
Nicholls, George 29 November
Nicholls, John 7 May
Nichols, John and Nathan 26 March
Nicholson, George 8 January
Nicholson, James 22 April
Nicholson, Philip 23 August
Nicholson, Thomas 16 December
Nicholson, William Lawrence Warren 12 August
Niemasz, Henryk 8 September
Nixon, Michael 16 May
Noble, Benjamin 28 July
Noble, John 29 March
Noble, Joseph William 24 March
Noble, Richard 21 January
Nodder, Frederick a.k.a. Hudson 30 December
Nolam, Nicholas 6 December
Nolan, 'Dandy Johnny' 21 April
Nopoty, Jonus 8 August
Norbury, John 7 January
Norman, Henry 5 October
Northcott, Gordon Stewart 2 October
Norton, Thomas 27 August
Noyse, John 11 March
Nunbria, John 26 May
Nunn, George 21 November
Nurse, Rebecca see 19 August
Nutt, William 24 February
Nuttall, John 4 September

O'Brien 11 September
O'Brien, Jeremiah 9 August
O'Brien, John see Dunne, Reginald
O'Brien, William see Gould, William
O'Coigley, John James 7 June
O'Donnell, Charles 11 December
O'Farrell 21 April
O'Hara, Thomas 8 December
O'Keefe, Timothy 30 April
O'Sullivan, Joseph a.k.a. James Connelly 10 August
Oakey, Robert 23 February
Ocuish, Hannah 20 December
Ogden, John 12 January
Ogilvie, Patrick 13 November
Okey, John 19 April
Oldfield, William 26 July
Olgive, Walter 22 April
Orrock, Thomas Henry 6 October

Orton, Joseph see Strang, Jesse
Osborne, Arthur 30 December
Oster, Colonel Hans 9 April
Ostler, V. 11 July
Ott, Joseph 20 October
Oudworth, Moses 18 August
Owen, Edgar a.k.a. Edwards 3 March
Owen, John 8 August
Owens, Abel 23 May
Oxburgh, Colonel Henry 14 June

Pachett, Leonard 28 July
Paine, Lewis 7 July
Palacha, Augustus 30 July
Palm, Charles Frederick 18 December
Palmer, Edward Richard 17 November
Palmer, Dr William 14 June
Palmer, William Henry 19 July
Panzram, Carl 5 September
Parker, Frederick William 4 May
Parker, George Henry 19 March
Parker, Joseph Cornelius 11 July
Parker, Richard 30 June
Parker, Thomas 1 February
Parkhurst, Nathaniel, Esq. 27 October
Parr, Elias 9 August
Parr, John 29 October
Parris, James 1 August
Parrot, Hugh 23 May
Parry, James 7 January
Parry, Martha 24 February
Parry, Thomas 20 January
Parsons, Albert Richard 11 November
Parsons, William 11 February
Parvin, Richard 4 December
Pascoe, Russell 17 December
Patch, Richard 8 April
Pate, Andrew J. 27 May
Pateman, William 11 June
Pater, John 1 February
Paterson, Charles 7 August
Paterson, George 7 June
Patmore, Thomas 25 September
Paul, Reverend William 18 July
Pavey, George 13 December
Peace, Charles 25 February
Peach, A. 30 January
Pearcey, Eleanor see Wheeler, Mary Eleanor
Pearson, Elizabeth 2 August
Pearson, George 12 November
Pegg, Thomas 2 December

Pegsworth, John 7 March
Perdovitch, Hyman 6 January
Perkins, Henry 6 December
Perovskaya, Sophia 15 April
Perreau, Robert and Daniel 17 January
Perrie, William 18 October
Perrin, Captain Richard 26 April
Perrott, John 11 November
Perry, George Henry 1 March
Perry, Private Henry a.k.a. Beckett 10 July
Peters, Hugh 13 October
Peters, Mary 4 November
Pettrick 23 December
Phillips, F. 29 January
Phillips, Henry 13 March
Phillips, James Jeter 22 July
Phillips, Thomas 8 February
Phipoe, Maria Theresa 25 January
Phipps, James 12 November
Phoenix, Francis 17 December
Picken, Joshua 1 February
Pickering, Harry 14 June
Piggott, George 4 February
Pilcher, James 27 March
Pink, Edward and John 4 December
Pinney, Robert 7 September
Pistoria, Guiseppe 25 August
Pitre, Marguerite 9 January
Place, George 30 December
Platts, John 1 April
Plummer, Sheriff Henry 10 January
Plunkett, Heny 22 September
Podmore, William Henry a.k.a. William F. Thomas 22 April
Podola, Gunther Fritz Erwin 5 November
Pof, Sylvester 23 January
Pohl, Obergruppenfuehrer Oswald 8 June
Poitou 26 October
Pomp 6 August
Pong Lun 31 May
Poole, Joseph 18 December
Poole, Peter Harold 8 August
Pople, Private G. T. 10 March
Porteous, Captain John 7 July
Porteous, Solomon 17 December
Porter 21 July
Post, Johannes 27 February
Potten, Joseph a.k.a. Conrad Donovan 13 December

Potter, Private Bruce 10 January
Powell, Henry 6 November
Powell, Henry 23 December
Powell, John 22 November
Powers, Michael 11 April
Pratt, James see 26 December
Preiss, Otto 27 February
Prentice, Frederick 7 April
Prescott, Matthew 4 July
Preston 21 July
Preston, Frederick 4 October
Prevot, Jean-Baptiste 23 December
Price, Hanby 13 May
Price, James 30 April
Price, John 31 May
Price, Thomas 21 June
Pritchard, Edward 17 February
Pritchard, Dr Edward William 28 July
Probert, Albert 4 May
Probert, William 30 June
Probst, Anton 8 June
Proudlove, William 28 July
Pryor, Thomas 31 March
Pugh, William 5 August
Pursell, Benjamin 9 December
Purvis, Will 7 February

Quartley, Henry 10 November
Quayle, William 3 August
Quin, Thomas 17 June
Quinn 9 April
Quinn, John 8 March

Raber, Samuel 2 January
Rackham, 'Calico Jack' 21 November
Rae, John 4 May
Ralph, John 26 August
Rann, '16-string' Jack 30 November
Rau, Gustave 2 June
Raven, Daniel 6 January
Rawcliffe, Thomas 15 November
Rawlinson, John 2 December
Rawlinson, William and John 25 February
Rayner, Charles 17 March
Rea, William 4 July
Read, James Canham 4 December
Read, William 12 December
Reading, John 1 June
Real, John 5 August
Reardon, Eliza see Ross, Eliza
Redanies, Dedea 1 January

Redel, Roman 7 July
Redguard, Joseph 24 March
Redmond, Patrick 24 January
Reeves, John 31 January
Reeves, Thomas 4 May
Reeves, William 23 January
Reid, Patrick 8 January
Reilly, Thomas 11 July
Reuben, Morris and Marks 20 May
Reynolds, Alfred G. 19 July
Reynolds, Jack 8 April
Reynolds, James 18 November
Reynolds, Thomas 26 July
Reynolds, Thomas 27 November
Richards, Eli 19 September
Richards, James 7 February
Richards, Stephen Lee 26 April
Richards, Thomas 29 November
Richardson, James William 23 May
Richardson, John 25 January
Richardson, Thomas 7 September
Richter, Karel Richard see 4 January
Riley, George 9 February
Riley, Thomas 26 November
Ring, William 19 October
Rini 9 May
Rivett, J. F. 8 March
Roarity, James 21 June
Roarke, Felix 6 September
Roberts, Amelia 2 January
Roberts, David 2 March
Roberts, G. E. 8 August
Roberts, James 3 April
Roberts, John 13 May
Roberts, Mary 11 June
Roberts, Richard 12 June
Roberts, Ronald 10 February
Robertson, George 28 March
Robertson, Police Constable James
    Ronald 15 December
Robinson, John 12 August
Robinson, John 8 September
Robinson, John 29 November
Robinson, Joseph 17 August
Robinson, Peter 16 April
Robinson, Walter 17 August
Robinson, William 14 March
Roche, Philip 5 August
Roche, T. Maxwell 8 September
Roesch, Andreas 6 March
Rogers, Captain H. 11 September
Rogers, William 12 December

Rookwood, Ambrose 31 January
Rose, John 11 August
Rose, Pascha 28 May
Rosenberg, Reichminister Alfred 16
    October
Ross, Charles William 11 January
Ross, Colin Campbell 24 April
Ross, Eliza a.k.a Cook and Reardon 9
    January
Ross, Private Ezra 2 July
Ross, Norman 8 January
Rottman, Arthur 8 March
Rouse, Alfred Arthur 10 March
Roussouw, Marthinius 19 June
Rowe, Robert 21 July
Rowland, Walter Graham 27 February
Rowlands, Edward 27 January
Rowledge, Sam 13 July
Rowles, Henry 1 April
Rowles, Stanley 'Snowy' see Smith, John
    Thomas
Rudge, Antony Benjamin 8 February
Ruest, Genereux 25 July
Rulloff, Edward 17 May
Rumbold, Henry 19 December
Rush, James Blomfield 21 April
Russell, George 2 December
Russell, Thomas 21 October
Ruxton, Dr Buck 12 May
Ryan, John 15 November
Ryer, John 2 October
Ryland, William Wynne 29 August
Rysakov, Nikolai 15 April

Sabey, Richard 18 July
Sach, Amelia 3 February
Sadler, Thomas 18 August
Salem witches see 19 August
Sales, James 9 April
Salisbury, Bert 11 May
Salmon, Sampson Silas 19 February
Sampson, Sam 1 July
Samuel, Joseph 26 September
Samuels, William 27 July
Sanders, Benjamin 29 May
Sangret, Private August 29 April
Sankey, Thomas 20 February
Sapwell, William a.k.a. John Smith 20
    September
Sargisons 10 September
Satchell, James 27 November
Sattler, Christian 8 February

Sauckel, Reichminister Fritz 16 October
Saunders, Charles 28 December
Saunders, George 16 February
Saunders, William 5 May
Savage, Benjamin and Andrew 5 March
Savage, Robert 15 May
Sawyer, William 15 May
Sayer, George, Esq. 15 March
Scandrett, Alfred 20 March
Scanlan, Squire John 10 March
Schild, John 20 January
Schimmel, Dr Alfred 27 February
Schmidt, Oskar 27 February
Schneider, Johan 27 February
Schneider, Johann 3 January
Schofield, Henry 6 September
Schulz, Emil 27 February
Schurch, Herr 4 January
Scott, Charles 28 November
Scott, Richard 21 December
Seager, Samuel 28 March
Seaman, William 9 June
Seaton, Henry 30 April
Seaward, George 7 September
Sedden, Frederick Henry 18 April
Sedgewick, James 21 February
Seekings, Frederick 4 November
Sergeant, William 30 June
Seymour, Henry Daniel 10 December
Sharpe, Charles 15 January
Sharpe, Thomas 31 October
Sharpe, Walter 30 March
Shaw, Arthur 8 December
Shaw, John 2 February
Shaw, John 19 May
Shaw, William 16 August
Sheehan, William 20 January
Shelley, William 'Moosh' 5 August
Shelton, William 24 May
Sheppard, Jack 16 November
Sheppard, James 27 March
Sheward, William 20 April
Shrimpton, Moses 25 May
Shufflebotham, Joseph 2 April
Silk, John 29 December
Silverosa, George 12 September
Simmonds, Melvyn 2 February
Simmons, Thomas 'Man of Blood' 7
    March
Simms, 'Gentleman Harry' 16 June
Simms, James 24 March
Simpson, James 21 May

Simpson, John Aspinal 28 November
Sims, Henry 26 November
Sinclair, Christian 4 January
Sinclair, Sydney see Hagger
Sindram, William 21 April
Singh, Udham 31 July
Skeffington, Thomas 15 November
Skelton, Hart 24 April
Skene, George 18 March
Skinner, Cy 26 January
Slack, Martin 26 March
Slater, Ephraim 26 May
Slater, Private see Woolfe, George
Slaughterford, Christopher 9 July
Slavin, Patrick 11 December
Small, Frederick 15 January
Smedley, William 21 October
Smith, Caleb 14 August
Smith, Charles 22 March
Smith, Charles 22 November
Smith, Edward Charles 25 April
Smith, Elizabeth 26 March
Smith, Private G. E. 13 May
Smith, George 15 January
Smith, George 21 November
Smith, George 28 December
Smith, George Joseph 13 August
Smith, Isaac 24 October
Smith, J. E. 4 December
Smith, James 10 August
Smith, James 28 November
Smith, John see Sapwell, William
Smith, John 7 March
Smith, John 16 March
Smith, John 23 March
Smith, John 26 March
Smith, John 12 April
Smith, John 10 May
Smith, John 21 July
Smith, John 10 August
Smith, John 4 September
Smith, John 10 December
Smith, John 23 December
Smith, John 'Half-hanged' 24 December
Smith, John see 26 December
Smith, John Thomas a.k.a. Stanley
    'Snowy' Rowles 13 June
Smith, Joseph 17 February
Smith, Joseph 27 November
Smith, Perry 14 April
Smith, Lieutenant Richard 4 February
Smith, Robert 12 May

Smith, Robert 21 November
Smith, Robert Dobie 15 September
Smith, Private Samuel Edward 21 July
Smith, Samuel H. 10 March
Smith, Sidney George 9 March
Smith, Thomas 16 January
Smith, Thomas 7 September
Smith, Thomas 16 November
Smith, Walter 27 March
Smith, Willem 2 June
Smith, William 1 April
Smith, William 13 April
Smith, William 3 October
Smithers, Thomas 8 October
Smyth, Captain J. 12 April
Sneedom, John *see* Cannaday, John Eli
Snipe, John 4 July
Snow, William 26 March
Sodeman, Arnold 2 June
Solomons, Samuel 20 June
Southey, Ernest Walter *see* Forward,
    Stephen
Sowash, Harry 3 November
Sowrey, Alfred 1 August
Sparrow, Edward 21 November
Speed, Joseph 7 September
Spencer, Arthur 28 July
Spicer, Felix 22 August
Spies, August 11 November
Spiggot, William 8 February
Spooner, Bathsheba 2 July
Springett, John 17 January
Sproull, William 20 May
Squires, Charles 10 August
Stacey, John 10 May
Stacy, Jonathan 21 June
Stafford, Peter 8 April
Stanfield, Philip 24 February
Stanford, Stephen 31 December
Stanley, John 24 December
Stanton, Henry 24 November
Stanton, John 30 March
Stanway, William 21 February
Staples, George 21 June
Starr, Henry 29 December
Steer, Peter 24 April
Stephens, James 3 February
Stewart, Camel Delap 4 November
Stewart, Francis 29 June
Stewart, Frederick 6 June
Stewart, James 8 November
Stewart, Mr and Mrs 24 July

Stewart, William 2 February
Stieff, Major General Hemuth 8 August
Still, Joseph 17 March
Stills, George 'Notty' 13 December
Stilwell, Stephen 26 March
Stockdale, John 3 July
Stockwell, James 5 January
Stokes, Frank 3 September
Stone, John 7 April
Stone, John 10 July
Stone, Leslie George 13 August
Stookey, Aaron B. 19 September
Storey, John 1 June
Stout, Marion Ira 22 October
Stout, Peter 13 May
Strang, Jesse a.k.a. Joseph Orton 24
    August
Stratton, Alfred and Albert 23 May
Street, Philip 14 June
Streicher, Gauleiter Julius 16 October
Strodman, Herman 18 July
Stroud, Henry 8 July
Stuart, John and Catherine 19 August
Sturman, William 2 April
Suleiman Daoud Sami 9 June
Sullivan, Dennis 12 May
Sullivan, John 12 July
Sullivan, Stephen 27 July
Summers, William 25 March
Surety, Charles 5 January
Surratt, Mary 7 July
Sutherland, Captain John 29 June
Sutherland, Neil 27 April
Swallow, John 12 January
Swallow, John 14 January
Swan, Emily 29 December
Swan, John 28 March
Swearingen, George 2 October
Sweeting, Whiting 26 August
Swift, John William 27 November
Swindell, Harry Hammond 24
    November
Sykes, William 23 April
Sympson, Thomas 'Old Mobb' 30
    May

Tabbs, Thomas 2 February
Tacklyn, Larry Winfield 2 December
Talbot, Thomas 17 June
Taplin, Thomas 12 June
Tapner, Benjamin 18 January
Tapping, J. 14 March

Tarraf, Ibrahim Tarraf 7 April
Tattersall, Thomas George 15 August
Tatum, Michael 14 May
Tawell, John 28 March
Taylor, Charles 12 December
Taylor, James 16 August
Taylor, John 3 September
Taylor, Joseph 7 January
Taylor, Louisa Jane 2 January
Taylor, M. 22 June
Taylor, Robert 29 December
Taylor, William Robert 20 September
Teed, Vivian 6 May
Teller, William 6 September
Templeton, Robert 13 February
Terry, Benjamin 22 February
Terry, Victor John 26 May
Tetzner, Kurt Erich 2 May
Thayer, Isaac, Israel, and Nelson 17 June
Thistlewood, Arthur 1 May
Thomas, Charles 24 June
Thomas, George 13 February
Thomas, George 9 December
Thomas, Sarah 20 April
Thomas, William F. *see* Podmore
Thompson, Edith Jessie 9 January
Thompson, Harry 9 March
Thompson, Henry 23 January
Thompson, Henry 22 November
Thompson, John a.k.a. Walker, P. 14 January
Thompson, John 1 April
Thompson, John George 10 December
Thompson, Richard 14 August
Thompson, Thomas 24 October
Thompson, William 25 September
Thorley, Samuel 10 April
Thorne, John Norman Holmes 22 April
Thorp, William 16 January
Thurston, John 10 February
Thurtell, John 9 January *see also* 30 June
Tickner, Henry 2 July
Tidbury, Henry 12 March
Tidd, Richard 1 May
Tilling, Sam 18 December
Tipping 25 March
Toal, Gerard 29 August
Tobin, James 26 August
Tobin, William 19 April
Tojo, General Hideki 23 December
Tombs, John 21 February

Tooke, Annie 11 August
Toole, John 7 March
Toon, Joan 26 May
Tooth, Royal Marine James 13 August
Torbin, Henry 31 January
Town, Richard 28 December
Townley, Francis, Esq. 30 July
Townley, William 28 March
Tracy, Martha 10 April
Trenoweth, G. H. 6 April
Trevor, Harold Dorian 11 March
Trickett, James 12 February
Tripp, Grace 27 March
Trower, E. 26 March
Trueman, W. 27 February
Tucker, Charles Louis 12 June
Tucker, Joseph 3 August
Tucker, Samuel 6 August
Tuffen, William Joseph 11 August
Tuite 2 March
Tully, Pat 25 March
Tupley, Thomas 21 November
Turley, Preston 17 September
Turnage, Patrick 14 November
Turner, Alfred 19 May
Turner, Antony 20 June
Turner, George Thomas 17 April
Turner, John 19 May
Turner, Nat 11 November
Turner, Walter Lewis 18 August
Turner, William 21 August
Turner, William 3 September
Turpin, Dick 10 April
Tye, John 23 January

Uddal, John 14 March
Udderzook, William E. 12 November
Underwood, Thomas *see* Foreword
Upton, John 27 November

Valentine, T. R. 3 September
Van Aan, Solomon 25 June
Van Alstine, John 19 March
Van Den Kieboom, Charles Albert *see* 4 January
Van Dine, Harvey 22 April
Van Niekerk, Andries 14 April
Van Valkenburgh, Elizabeth 24 January
Van Wyk, Stephanus Louis 12 June
Vanberger, Matthew and Cuthbert 10 July
Vanhollen, George Speth 26 July

Vaquier, Jean-Pierre 12 August
Varti, John 12 November
Vartos the Turk 22 February
Vasquez, Tiburcio 19 March
Vest, Robert 30 July
Vicars, John 7 November
Vickers, John 23 July
Vickers, Robert Flockart 31 March
Videto, Stephen 25 August
Vincent, Dr Frederick Oscar 27 October
Virrels, James 26 April
Voisin, Louis 2 March
Volkenrath, Elizabeth 13 December
Von Hagen, Lieutenant Colonel Dr
  Hans 8 August
Von Hase, Lieutenant General Paul 8
  August
Von Keitel, Field Marshal Wilhelm 16
  October
Von Ribbentrop, Reichminister Joachim
  16 October
Von Seyss-Inquart, Gauleiter Artur 16
  October
Von Wartenburg, Lieutenant Count
  Peter Yorck 8 August
Von Witzleben, Field Marshal Erwin 8
  August
Voss, Edward 20 March

Waddell, William 18 December
Wadden, Samuel 26 May
Waddingham, Nurse Dorothea 16 April
Waddington, William 11 May
Wade, Charles 13 December
Wade, Peter 16 January
Wadge, Selina 15 August
Wadley, Enoch 28 November
Wagner, George 1 March
Wagner, Louis 25 June
Wagstaff, John 23 March
Wainwright, Henry 21 December
Waisenen, John 28 August
Waite, Charles 4 July
Waite, John 24 February
Wakefield, John 16 August
Walber, Margaret 2 April
Waldberg, Jose see 4 January
Walden, Bernard 14 August
Walker, John 12 January
Walker, John 30 April
Walker, Joseph 15 November
Walker, P. see Thompson, John

Walker, Vincent Knowles 15 April
Wall, Governor Joseph 28 January
Wallace, William 23 August
Waller, Ralph 17 June
Walmsley, Amasa 1 June
Walsh, Patrick 22 September
Walters, Annie 3 February
Walton, Thomas 16 December
Wanderer, Carl Otto 19 March
Ward, Edward 22 May
Ward, John 20 March
Ward, John 24 April
Ward, John 20 September
Ward, Robert 4 October
Wardell, William Horsley 18 June
Wardlaw, David 19 October
Warmer, Julius 10 August
Waters, Benjamin 21 June
Waters, Margaret 11 October
Watkins, Charles 30 July
Watkins, Oliver 2 August
Watson, Lionel Rupert Nathan 12
  November
Watts, Edward H. F. 26 August
Watts, William 30 April
Watts, William 16 December
Waylor, John 23 February
Webb, George 29 June
Webb, Thomas 24 October
Webber, Joseph N. 25 April
Webster, Professor John White 30
  August
Webster, Kate a.k.a. Catherine Lawler
  29 July
Wedlake, Joseph 21 May
Weeks, Mathew 12 August
Weil, Emil 27 February
Weil, Dr Levi and Asher 9 December
Welby, John Robson see Evans, Gwynne
  Owen
Welch, Catherine 14 April
Welch, Joseph 15 November
Welch, Thomas 12 April
Welch, Thomas 7 September
Weller, William 15 December
Wellington, James see Monroe, Michael
Wells, Thomas 13 August
Wenzel, John G. 16 August
West, Robert 31 December
Weston, George and Joseph 3
  September
Wetherill, Miles 4 April

Weyburn, William 26 March
Wheatfill, Edward 28 November
Wheed, 'Ammunition Eddie' 15 February
Wheeler, Mary Eleanor a.k.a. Pearcey 23 December
Wheeler, Thomas 21 January
Wheeler, Thomas 29 November
Whelan, James 11 February
Whelan, James 31 May
Whelpton, George 7 January
Whiston, Enoch 10 February
Whitbread, Thomas 20 June
White 7 March
White, Alexander 18 November
White, Benjamin D. 26 April
White, Bernard 1 December
White, Charles 20 April
White, Charles Thomas 2 January
White, George 21 May
White, Henry L. 7 March
White, Huffey 7 July
Whitehead, James Wilshaw 27 November
Whitehead, P. 29 January
Whitehouse, Abraham 3 September
Whiteway, Alfred Charles 22 December
Withey, John 11 April
Whitney, James 1 February
Whitty, Dennis 17 December
Wickham, Ernest 18 August
Wiggins, John 15 October
Wigley, Richard 18 March
Wild, Jonathan 24 May
Wild, Sarah see 19 August
Wildish, Thomas 31 December
Wilford, John 21 July
Wilford, Thomas 22 June
Wilkins, John 20 August
Wilkinson, Alec 12 August
Wilkinson, Robert 24 September
Wilkinson, Samuel 11 August
Wilks, Henry 12 April
Willard, John see 19 August
Willett, John 24 March
Williams, 5 July
Williams, Ada Chard 8 March
Williams, Allen 2 February
Williams, Daniel 14 August
Williams, George 29 May
Williams, James 22 February
Williams, Jane and John 22 August

Williams, John see Mackay, George
Williams, John 19 March
Williams, John 26 July
Williams, John 23 November
Williams, John 10 December
Williams, Mary 31 August
Williams, Thomas see Head, Thomas
Williams, William A. 13 February
Willis, Private George 4 July
Willis, Rhoda 14 August
Wills, Clifford Godfrey 6 December
Wills, John 7 September
Wilson, Catherine 20 October
Wilson, Elizabeth 3 January
Wilson, Joseph 22 March
Wilson, Roger see Nelson, 'Gorilla'
Wilson, Virgil see Nelson, 'Gorilla'
Wilton, W. 26 August
Wingfield, James 20 May
Wingfield, John 22 March
Wingrove, Richard 19 November
Winstanley, Elijah 17 December
Winter, Franciscus Johannes 26 January
Winter, Robert 30 January
Winter, Thomas 31 January
Withers, Jack 16 April
Withey, John 11 April
Wood, Cornelius 22 February
Wood, George H. 26 April
Wood, Isaac 9 July
Wood, John 21 February
Wood, John Henry 11 May
Wood, Joseph see Foreword
Wood, Walter 30 June
Woodbourne, John a.k.a. Woodman 5 April
Woodman, John see Woodbourne, John
Woods, George 26 April
Woods, William 11 January
Wooldridge, Trooper Charles Thomas 7 July
Woolfe, George 6 May
Wootton, James 13 February
Worms, Pamela Lee 30 January
Worrall, Ashton and William 16 March
Worthington, William 4 January
Wright, Charles 28 July
Wright, Dr David 11 July
Wright, Henry 24 December
Wright, J. W. 10 September